THE WORLD NATURALIST

The Natural History of Fossils

THE WORLD NATURALIST
Editor: L. Harrison Matthews

Other titles in the series

The Age of Mammals
Björn Kurtén

The Carnivores
R. F. Ewer

Insects and History
J. L. Cloudsley-Thompson

The Natural History of Trees
Herbert L. Edlin

The Natural History of the Whale
L. Harrison Matthews

The Natural History of Fossils

Chris Paul
Lecturer in Geology, University of Liverpool

Weidenfeld and Nicolson
London

Copyright © C. R. C. Paul 1980

All rights reserved. No part of this publication may be reproduced, stored in a retrieval system, or transmitted, in any form or by any means, electronic, mechanical, photocopying, recording or otherwise, without the prior permission of the copyright owner.

First published in Great Britain by
Weidenfeld and Nicolson
91 Clapham High Street
London SW4

ISBN 0 297 77579 0 hardback
ISBN 0 297 77584 7 paperback

Filmset by Willmer Brothers Ltd,
Birkenhead, Merseyside
Printed by Camelot Press Ltd.,
Southampton

Contents

	List of plates	vii
	List of figures	ix
	Acknowledgements	xii
	INTRODUCTION	1
1	PRESERVATION HISTORY – HOW LIVING THINGS BECOME FOSSIL	10
2	EVIDENCE FROM SEDIMENTS	46
3	FOSSIL COMMUNITIES AND ASSOCIATIONS	80
4	FAUNAL PROVINCES AND CONTINENTAL DRIFT	107
5	GROWTH STUDIES	136
6	TIME IN GEOLOGY	162
7	FAUNAL SUCCESSION AND EVOLUTION	190
8	THE ORIGIN OF LIFE AND EARLY EVOLUTION	220
9	LIFE ON LAND	248
	EPILOGUE	271
	References and further reading	274
	Index	283

Plates

Between pages 116 and 117

1A	Baby mammoth dima from Siberia (by courtesy of the Society of Economic Paleontologists and Mineralogists and Robert F. Lundin)
1B	Eocene fish from Italy
2	Small ichthyosaur from the Lower Jurassic of Dorset
3A	Fossil cuttlefish from the Upper Jurassic of Germany
3B	Middle Jurassic belemnite, *Cylindroteuthis*
3C	Guard of another species of *Cylindroteuthis* from the Middle Jurassic
4	*Parkinsonia*, a large Middle Jurassic ammonite
5	*Phylloceras*, a large Lower Jurassic ammonite
6A	Lower Jurassic ammonite *Dactylioceras*
6B	*Kosmoceras*, a Middle Jurassic ammonite
6C	Section through Middle Jurassic ammonite showing chambers filled with sediment or only partly filled with calcite crystals
7A	Jurassic bivalve, *Trigonia*
7B	Example of *Trigonia* in which the shell has been dissolved away entirely to reveal internal structures
7C	*Arctostrea*, an Upper Cretaceous oyster
7D	Eocene bivalve, *Panopea*
8A	Several examples of *Neritina*, an Eocene gastropod
8B	Shell of the snail *Xenophora*
8C	Piece of Upper Jurassic Portland Stone with remains of many high-spired snails
9A	Piece of rock bored into by the bivalve *Lithophaga*
9B	Piece of Middle Carboniferous sandstone full of trace-fossil burrows
10A	Middle Jurassic terebratulid brachiopod on which a small epifaunal oyster had begun to grow
10B	'Nest' of terebratulid brachiopods with one rhynchonellid
10C	Cambrian trilobite, *Paradoxides*
10D	Silurian trilobite, *Calymene*
11A	Assemblage of Lower Ordovician graptolites
11B	*Chasmatopora*, a Middle Ordovician bryozoan colony from Estonia

PLATES

11C   'Crystal apple', Lower Ordovician cystoid *Sphaeronites* from Sweden
12A   Large slab of Upper Silurian rock from North Wales on which are preserved the remains of several crinoids
12B   Slab of Lower Jurassic limestone covered with the crinoid *Pentacrinus*
13A   Regular Jurassic sea urchin, *Cidaris*
13B   Irregular sea urchin, *Clypeaster*
13C   Sand-dollar, *Mellita*
14A   Slab of Lower Jurassic rock with the remains of several brittlestars preserved on it
14B   Large slab of Middle Jurassic coral reef with remains of several small colonies with other reef-dwelling organisms
15A   Silurian tabulate coral, *Halysites*
15B   Polished surface of a Carboniferous rugose coral which reveals the detailed structure of the individual corallites
15C   Polished section of a Tertiary hexacoral
16A   Frond of the Middle Jurassic gymnosperm *Williamsonia*
16B   Section through a piece of fossil wood showing the tree rings
16C   Impression of the trunk of a birch tree, *Betula*, from the Caerwys Tufa, North Wales

Figures

		page
1	The geological column	8
2	Two brachiopods	11
3	The enigmatic Tully Monster	14
4	An ichthyosaur	15
5	*Lingula*	16
6	A cross-section through a bioherm and the flank beds to show geopetal structures and *Stromatactis*	21
7	A fossil belemnite guard	23
8	A cross-section through a cystoid which has suffered pressure solution	24
9	Distortion of trilobite tails due to compression of rocks	25
10	*Nereites*, a systematic searching pattern which was caused by an animal feeding in sediments	25
11	Stages in the formation of some fossil footprints	28
12	The difference between a surface trace and an internal trace which happens to follow a bedding surface	32
13	The burrow system formed by the modern worm *Paraonis*	32
14	Part of the trace-fossil burrow system, *Palaeodictyon*	32
15	The trace-fossil burrow system, *Squamodictyon*	33
16	The feeding trace, *Chondrites*	34
17	'T' and 'V' orientations of cylindrical fossils which indicate current directions	44
18	A histogram for loess	51
19	Wentworth's scale of sediment-particle size with mm. and phi scales	52
20	Mechanical analysis histogram of dune sand	53
21	Mechanical analysis histogram of river sand	53
22	Graded bedding	59
23	Cross bedding	60
24	Sections to illustrate the Folk–Dunham classification of limestones	66
25	An idealized coal cyclothem	73
26	Isostatic uplift of the shoreline of glacial Lake Bonneville in the Great Basin of the western United States	76
27	Reconstructions of the life orientations of the brachiopod *Productus* and the bivalve mollusc *Gryphaea*	84
28	The inferred life orientation of cylindrical species of the Silurian cystoid *Holocystites*	85

FIGURES

		page
29	The shell of an ascoceratid nautiloid	88
30	Moults revealed by the size clustering of the carapaces of the ostracod, *Theriosynoecum fittoni*	89
31	A spiriferid brachiopod covered with small worm tubes	92
32	The inferred life orientation of the Ordovician brachiopod *Rafinesquina*	92
33	An edrioasteroid	93
34	The distribution of Ziegler's Lower Silurian (Llandovery) brachiopod 'communities' in Wales	99
35	Possible depth-controlled confederations of graptolites and the resulting fossil associations	105
36	The earth's dipole magnetic field and the resulting magnetic inclination	109
37	The pattern of linear magnetic anomalies on either side of the Reykjanes Ridge in the Atlantic south of Iceland	109
38	The magnetic reversal time scale for the last three and a half million years	110
39	The distribution of earthquakes and inferred plate margins over the earth	112
40	The drifting of continents around the globe	113
41	A borehole through interglacial lake sediments between two tills and the resulting pollen diagram	129
42	Section through a belemnite guard to show growth rings, and palaeotemperature curve for a belemnite	135
43	A crushed example of the Jurassic ammonite *Kosmoceras*	138
44	Growth stages of trilobites	139
45	Section of head of the human femur to show trabecular bone; stress lines of Culmann's crane; and the femur	143
46	Growth of a crinoid columnal	143
47	Contrasting styles of growth in snails	146
48	The modified T-shaped aperture of the brevicone nautiloid *Gomphoceras*	148
49	The Cretaceous heteromorph ammonite *Scaphites*	148
50	Gnomons to a triangle	149
51	A section through an Upper Silurian *Favosites* colony from New Creek, W. Virginia	151
52	Colony increase in *Tetradium* as seen in cross-section	151
53	Graph of deviations in the radiocarbon time scale	160
54	Superposition	163
55	The diachronous boundary between the Gualt Clay and Upper Greensand in southern Britain	170
56	The sequence of graptolite faunas in the Ordovician and Silurian	172
57	A section in a quarry with a fault offsetting the beds	174
58	A section to illustrate folding	174
59	A section to illustrate an igneous intrusion	175
60	A section to illustrate an unconformity	175
61	A complex section	177
62	Block diagrams to illustrate the use of mudcracks to determine way up	178

FIGURES

		page
63	Cross beds and graded beds	179
64	The use of bedding/cleavage relationships to determine way up	180
65	The known stratigraphic occurrences of cystoid families in the Palaeozoic	200
66	Survivorship curves for cystoid families	202
67	Graph of the increase in knowledge of cystoid families, genera and species since 1772	207
68	The inferred evolutionary relationship between two species with the stratigraphic ranges illustrated	210
69	Speciation in stratigraphic lineages	211
70	An agnostid trilobite	236
71	The estimated increase in the diversity of life through the Phanerozoic	243
72	Increasingly efficient protection of the divaricator muscles in early orthids and later brachiopods	245
73	The increased efficiency of filter-feeding in Cambrian and Ordovician echinoderms	246
74	Osmosis	253
75	The gait of a spider in front view	259
76	The gait of a newt or lizard	261
77	The positions of chloroplasts in cells of the leaves of duckweed in weak and in strong light	261
78	A pelycosaur	263
79	*Rhynia*, from the Lower Devonian, Rhynie Chert of Scotland	263
80	*Ichthyostega*, from the Upper Devonian of Greenland	267
81	*Anthracopupa*, from the Upper Carboniferous of Ohio	267

Acknowledgements

In a general book such as this inevitably one draws a great deal of information from other people's research. I have tried to indicate the origin of the more important ideas and discoveries I mention and sincerely hope that I have not omitted anyone. I should like to take the opportunity to acknowledge the work of my colleagues all over the world without whose efforts a book such as this would be impossible. At the same time may I thank Mr D. H. Birch and Mr D. Smart of Liverpool University for their help with the photographs, and especially Mr J. Lynch, not only for producing many of the text figures, but for much invaluable advice and help on all matters of illustration over the last several years.

Introduction

Fossils are evidence of the former existence of life. The term is usually attributed to Georgius Agricola who published a book, *De natura fossilium lib.* (On the nature of fossils), in 1546.[1] The word comes from the Latin and means approximately 'something dug up'. This was quite literally what most of Agricola's fossil objects were. He included minerals, stones and artifacts as well as what we would now consider to be fossils. Gradually the objects Agricola included within his all-embracing term 'fossil' have been recognized for what they are and the definition of a fossil is now restricted to evidence of former life. There are clear-cut categories of organic fossils and inorganic non-fossils, but even so enigmatic objects do come to light the original organic nature of which is open to question. In the same way, some objects once thought to have been inorganic in origin are reappraised and accepted as being true fossils. We have not yet adequately classified *all* the things we dig up. Nevertheless, by modern definition fossils are evidence of the former existence of life, not only direct evidence like skeletons and shells, but traces of activity such as footprints, burrows and borings, teeth marks, attachment structures and so forth.

One basic attribute of any fossil is that it is dead. It may seem strange, then, to write a book on the natural history of something which is not only dead, but in many cases died millions and millions of years ago. However, the whole point about fossils is that they were once alive – they are evidence of life. When they were alive they had a natural history just as all modern living things do. Those of us who study or use them need to understand this natural history as much as any modern naturalist needs to understand the world about him. One of three points I shall emphasize throughout this book is that fossils were once alive and we can only know them for what they are if we view them in this light. This is not just a desirable attitude on the part of a few professional scientists who, like myself, study fossils for their own sake. As I hope to show, fossils contribute to the understanding of a variety of geological and evolutionary problems, both practical and esoteric, but they can only be used to their fullest extent if we understand their natural history. Indeed in some cases failure to understand fully the mode of life of a fossil may lead to quite erroneous conclusions.

Stony fossils, especially those covered with dust in some museum drawer, seem about as far removed from the vitality of living things, such as a tiger or an orchid, as it is possible to get. Living things do not become fossils overnight just by dying. They may become fossilized in a variety of ways, which I shall discuss in the next chapter. During the process of preservation all sorts of misfortunes may befall a potential fossil so that most living things are totally destroyed and not preserved at all. Everything that occurs between the death of the original organism and the discovery of a fossil constitutes the preservation history of that particular fossil. A sound interpretation of a fossil depends on an understanding of its mode of life and preservation history.

During preservation, information about the original living organisms is lost or distorted. We must understand what sorts of information have been lost and what sorts preserved. Moreover, we may not be able to determine the natural history of a fossil until we have retraced its preservation history as, for example, in the case of a freshwater snail swept down to sea and buried in a marine sediment. So my second argument is that the preservation history of a fossil, which may have been very long and complicated, must be understood before we can use fossils to the best advantage. Indeed it is so important that we ought to determine the preservation history before we do anything else.

Once we understand something about the process of preservation we soon realize that the chances against any individual being preserved at all are astronomical, particularly in groups of soft-bodied organisms like worms. Millions and millions of shells may be cast up on a beach after a winter storm and yet not one remain a month or so later, all the shells having been destroyed by the pounding of the waves. Inevitably the fossil record is incomplete and, more importantly, incompletely known. Not all the organisms that have ever lived have been preserved as fossils and we certainly have not yet discovered all those that have been preserved. New species of fossils are being described every year and in no group is there any sign of the pace of discovery slowing down. In most it is increasing rapidly. Furthermore, if new fossils can still be found in a well-explored country like Britain, there must be enormous reserves of

INTRODUCTION

undiscovered fossils in the more unexplored parts of the globe. It is so universally accepted that the fossil record, as we know it, is incomplete, that virtually no one has even tried to estimate how much remains unrecorded. My attention was forcibly drawn to this fact as recently as January 1978, since when I have come to realize that there are many ways in which the fossil record can be tested for its incompleteness. Some of these ways are outlined in chapter 7 in an evolutionary context. Rather surprisingly, I have concluded that the fossil record, although incomplete, is *adequate* for most purposes and, as more information is added, the situation can only improve. This is indeed comforting because it means that the sorts of interpretations of past environments, climates, geographies, faunal provinces and so on described in chapters 3, 4 and 5, are quite likely to be valid rather than artifacts of preservation. It also means that in tracing the actual course of evolution we *must* accept the evidence in the fossil record. We can no longer be selective, as we have been so often in the past, accepting only that evidence which agrees with our theories and hiding behind the incompleteness of the record every time an awkward fact comes to light. This is the third major point I wish to stress. However incomplete it may be, the fossil record is generally reliable and documents the actual course of evolution. So the three points which it is important to emphasize are first, that we must understand the natural history of fossils to make best use of them; secondly, that this can only be done if we unravel, indeed reverse, their preservation history to get back to the original living organism; and thirdly, that, notwithstanding the incompleteness of the fossil record and our knowledge of it, if we achieve the first two things we can make sound interpretations of other aspects of the history of life on earth and of the earth itself.

The aim of this book then is to discuss the uses of fossils, their shortcomings and strengths and their application to wider aspects of the history of the earth. The book is not a systematic treatment of the various groups of fossils, although I have chosen examples from as wide a range of organisms as possible. Some familiarity with different types of fossils (and recent forms of life) is desirable. The book will undoubtedly be more comprehensible to those with such a background, which is generally acquired by collecting, or at least handling, fossils. The illustrations have been chosen to exemplify the main groups of fossils discussed in the text. A quick glance through these will help you to familiarize yourself with them. Wherever possible, reference to the appropriate illustration is made in the text when a new fossil type is mentioned for the first time.

Every scientific discipline and even every hobby has its own language. The border between terminology and jargon is not always easy to recognize and to a certain extent the specialized vocabulary of any subject serves as a barrier to the novice, however useful it may be in communication between officianados. I have tried to avoid unnecessary terminology, preferring simple English words where they are adequate. Nevertheless, names are very useful. My criterion for introducing technical terms has been that if they will save repeating a phrase several times they should be used. I have tried to define them where they are first introduced. For example, hermatypic corals are reef-building corals confined to warm shallow seas. The term 'hermatypic' is indispensible in discussing both fossil reefs and past climates. Similarly, rhipidistean fish are believed to be the ancestral group from which amphibians evolved. They had lungs, internal openings to the nostrils and fleshy lobes at the bases of their fins which, in the case of the paired fins, were the antecedents of our limbs. However unfamiliar (and unpronounceable) rhipidistean may seem, it conveys a great deal of information about these particular fossil fish very briefly. Even if we abbreviate the phrase to 'the fish that were ancestral to amphibians', rhipidistean is still more economical.

Scientists give all living and fossil organisms an official name which is either Latin or Greek in origin, or else a latinized modern name. There are two principal codes of nomenclature, one for plants and one for animals. The great Swedish naturalist Carl Linnaeus initiated the formal naming of organisms in 1758.[2] He gave every known living thing two names: a generic name, e.g. *Felis* or *Viola* (for cats and violets, respectively) and a trivial name which distinguishes the species within each genus, as in *Viola odorata*, the common sweet smelling violet, *Viola palustris*, the marsh violet, or *Felis domesticus*, the domestic cat and *Felis sylvestris*, the common European wild cat. Under this system all species of living things, including fossils, have two names, which constitute their scientific description. The generic name starts with an initial capital, the trivial does not and both are written in italics as a convention. The codes maintain that the first valid specific name given after 1758 is to be used in preference to all others. This rule of priority is designed to ensure that all scientists all over the world use the same specific name for the same species, no matter what their native language. While this obviously facilitates international communication between scientists, it may seem

INTRODUCTION

unnecessary to the layman. Most readers would probably rather refer to the chaffinch or meadowsweet, than to *Fringilla coelebs* or *Filipendula ulmaria*, their scientific names, but with fossils and some exotic living things, this is not so easy. There is no accepted English name for any but the very commonest of fossils, so there is usually no alternative to using the official scientific name. If this seems unfortunate, take comfort in the fact that most eight-year-olds have not only mastered the pronunciation of common dinosaur names, but can recognize the appropriate animals. With a little interest one soon becomes familiar with the names of the more common fossils.

Not only are fossils and living things given formal names, but they are classified into a systematic biological framework, within which the highest categories are the kingdoms; the lowest, species or varieties. Traditionally, two kingdoms have been recognized, the plant and animal kingdoms. Sometimes minute single-celled organisms, the Protista, are separated as a third kingdom since some have attributes of both plants and animals, and arguments have been put forward for recognizing the fungi and bacteria as yet other kingdoms. As you will realize, there is no finalized biological classification accepted universally. We need not get involved in debates about classification, but it is useful to know the hierarchy of terms used. Kingdoms are divided into major groupings called phyla, for example all jellyfish, corals, sea anemones and so on are grouped in the phylum Coelenterata (or Cnidaria – regrettably there is no priority on names above the genus). All starfish, sea urchins, sand dollars, sea lillies and sea cucumbers belong in the phylum Echinodermata. Within each phylum there are major subdivisions called classes. Starfish and sea urchins are two of the classes of echinoderms. The classes are themselves divided into orders and the orders into families. Families contain related genera, as for example, *Felis*, *Lynx* and *Panthera* all belong in the Felidae, the cat family. Genera, as we have already seen, may contain several species. In very large groups further subdivisions may be required and subfamilies or superfamilies, suborders and superorders are created as needed. We have not yet discovered all the living animals and plants in the world, let alone all the fossil species. Inevitably as new organisms are discovered they have to be fitted into existing classifications which are consequently in a state of continuous change. Perhaps when we have named all forms of life we may be able to decide on one finalized classification, but that time is still a long way off.

A few basic ideas on fossils and their uses must be introduced here before embarking on more detailed discussions. First of all, how do living things become fossils? Soft tissue decays very rapidly after death, usually in a few days, weeks at most. Hard durable parts of an organism, like the skeleton or shell, survive better and are more likely to be preserved, but even so bones and shells last only a few years if exposed to the weather. They may also be consumed entirely by scavengers like dogs. So to be preserved, even the more durable parts of an organism must be buried in sediment and, because most sediment accumulates in the sea, most fossils are of marine animals. We know a great deal about the processes of death, decay and burial in fossils because of the efforts of a research team at Wilhelmshaven on the North Sea Coast.[3] Their work is an excellent example of a general method in geology and palaeontology – the actualistic, or uniformitarian, method. Actualistic, which derives more from the French 'actuel' meaning 'recent' than from the English 'actual', describes a method whereby observations or experiments on present-day processes are extrapolated back through geological time. Thus the German team have tried to find out how the skeleton of a fish disarticulates after death in the hope that this will enable them to interpret the burial attitudes of fossil fish; recognizing for example those skeletons that have been disturbed by scavengers from those disarticulated by current action. Another common example of actualistic arguments about fossils is used in interpreting past environments. All known living echinoderms (plates 12 and 13) or brachiopods (figure 2, plates 10A and B) are marine, and we almost automatically assume that all fossil examples were as well. Thus sediments containing abundant remains of echinoderms and brachiopods are also likely to be marine. If they are ancient sediments containing extinct fossils like trilobites (plates 10C and D) as well as echinoderms and brachiopods, we may use this to interpret the living environment of the extinct fossils. Indeed, as far as we know, all trilobites were marine. Actualistic methods and arguments are very widespread in geology and palaeontology.

Understanding the preservation history of fossils allows us to distinguish those preserved *in situ*, i.e. where they lived, from those which were transported after death and before burial. If a fossil is *in situ*, the surrounding sediments may reveal a lot about the environment in which it lived. More importantly we may use the presence of the fossil to reconstruct past geography. For example, if the fossil is marine and *in situ*, we know that that part of the world was under the sea when the fossil was alive. The positions of land and sea

INTRODUCTION

have changed so much in the past that there is no part of the world which has always been either dry land or under water. Indeed the discovery of marine fossils high up on mountains was one of the lines of evidence which called into question the idea that all fossils were traces of organisms that perished in the Biblical Flood. A plethora of 'palaeo-sciences', palaeogeography, palaeoclimatology, palaeoecology, palaeothermometry, and more, has developed. These are discussed in chapters 2–4 and in all of them the prefix 'palaeo-' means ancient. Palaeogeography is the study of ancient geographies, tracing the various positions of land and sea through geological time. Palaeontology, the oldest of these terms, means literally the study of ancient life, i.e. fossils. The opposite is neontology, the study of present-day life. Palaeontology is sometimes split into palaeobotany and palaozoology. Interestingly, whereas palaeobotany is usually only taught in botany schools and vertebrate palaeozoology in zoology schools, invertebrate palaeozoology is usually left to geology departments. The reason is largely that fossils are very useful for purposes of correlation. Geologists can determine the relative ages of rocks using fossils and, since most fossils are invertebrates, geologists teach invertebrate palaeozoology. Indeed this is so common that the word 'palaeontology' has frequently been used as a synonym for invertebrate palaeozoology. One deplorable result has been that fossils were used as mere indicators of age, often to be memorized in their correct chronological context, with no thought to their biological meaning. However useful fossils may be for correlation, palaeontology is, or should be, a *life science*. Even in the most common and fundamental use of fossils, knowledge of their life style and their preservation history can only improve correlation. Happily, this narrow use of fossils by geologists is largely a thing of the past.

Fossils can be used for correlation because life on earth has evolved. The faunas and floras of any particular past period are unique because that mixture of life forms only existed at that particular time. At some later time the less successful forms would have become extinct and some new forms would have evolved, producing a new distinctive suite of fossils. This was not known, however, when the basic principles which enable us to correlate using fossils were discovered. Steno, in the mid-seventeenth century, realized the first principle.[4] He argued that layers of rocks were originally deposited horizontally and that the oldest must be at the bottom of the pile (see figure 54, and chapter 6 for a fuller explanation). Nearly 150 years later the second idea was added,

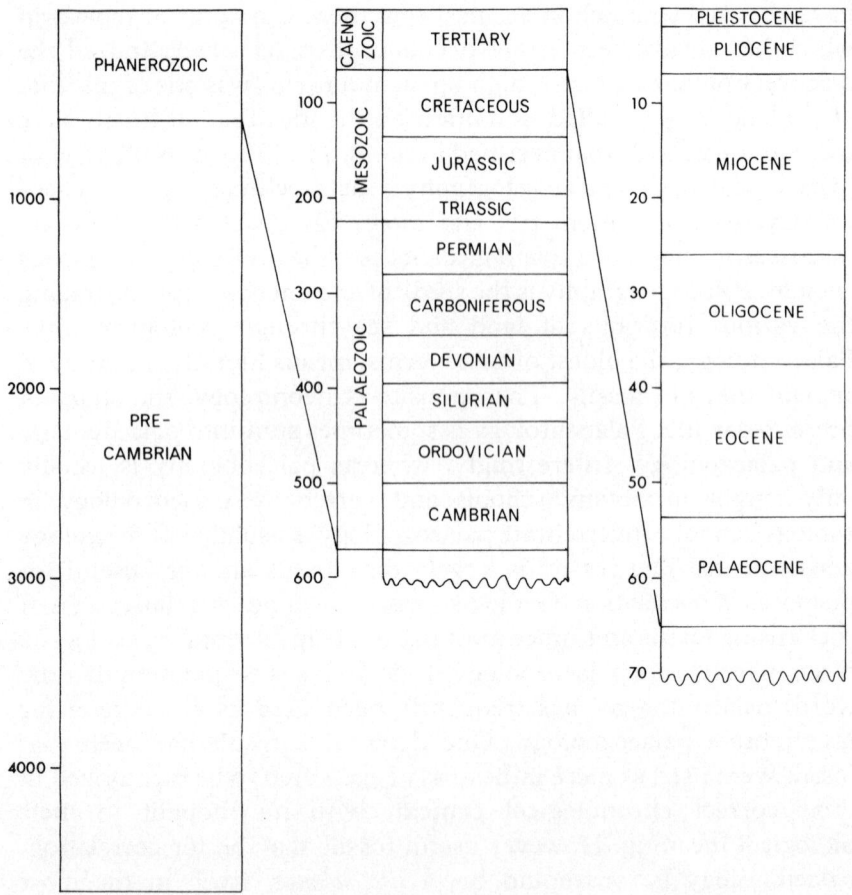

1. The geological column. Figures at the side of the columns indicate ages in millions of years.

principally by William Smith in England.[5] Smith noticed that rocks were characterized by their enclosed fossils and that the different suites of fossils always occurred in the same sequence. Using Steno's idea, which is now called superposition, rocks in any one place can be dated relatively because those below are older than those above, and using Smith's idea of faunal succession, rocks can be correlated between separate outcrops. Smith published his geological map of most of Britain in 1815, forty-four years before Darwin converted us to evolution, and within the next twenty years or so the geological column (figure 1) was developed. The geological column is one of the few things worth memorizing in geology. It is so basic and will be referred to so often in this book, that it is essential to know the

INTRODUCTION

sequence of geological periods. The methods by which the column was built up, and by which the ages of the geological periods in millions of years were deduced, are discussed in chapter 6. Once the column was established, it soon became apparent that unknown animals and plants had lived on earth in former times and that the most unfamiliar had lived in the oldest geological periods while the youngest fossils were similar to, or even identical with, living forms. A succession of life through time was established, but did not lead to a theory of evolution as one might have expected. The gradual recognition of the succession of life through time and its influence, or lack of it, on evolutionary theory are discussed in chapter 7, while the actual course of evolution as revealed by the fossil record is the subject of chapters 8 and 9.

Chapter 1

Preservation history—how living things become fossil

The possession of hard parts, a skeleton or shell, and rapid burial after death are usually cited as prerequisites of fossilization. While this is certainly true, there is very much more to the process of fossilization and all fossils have a preservation history of their own. It is vital to understand this preservation history, which may be complex, before using fossils for any geological or biological purpose. To cite obvious examples: in Cretaceous times pyritized Jurassic ammonites (extinct molluscs related to the modern *Nautilus*, plates 4–6) were eroded from the Oxford Clay and deposited in the Lower Greensand of the Weald district of southern England. Clearly these derived fossils are useless to date the rocks in which they now occur since they are themselves much older. They can be recognized as derived fossils because the pyrite, originally a bright brassy yellow mineral sometimes called fool's gold, has weathered to a rusty brown, they are worn and they often occur as pebbles in the Greensand. Similarly, derived Jurassic oysters (*Gryphaea*) occur in the glacial drift of East Anglia. The oysters lived in warm shallow seas, but are now preserved in sediments deposited on land by the great ice sheets which covered northern Europe several times during the last million years or so. Again the climatic and environmental conditions under which the oysters lived are drastically different from the conditions under which the deposits, in which they are now found, were formed. To use the fossils to determine the conditions of deposition of the sediments (or vice versa) would be entirely misleading. The oysters can be recognized as derived because they often bear scratch marks and fresh breakages caused by transport under ice sheets. Both of these examples are simple and obvious, but they serve to emphasize the need to understand all the events that have befallen a fossil since its death if we are to make the best use of what is admittedly an incomplete fossil record. In short, before we can make good use of

PRESERVATION HISTORY – HOW LIVING THINGS BECOME FOSSIL

fossils we need to reverse the processes of preservation to get back to the original living organisms.

This chapter is concerned with the preservation history of fossils and the preservation potential of organisms in an attempt to answer the questions 'How do living things become fossils?' and 'Why are some organisms fossilized more often than others?' During the process of fossilization information about the original living organisms is lost. With any fossil we need to know what sorts of information have been lost and what kinds preserved, because different modes of preservation retain different types of information. Since the fossil record is incomplete, we owe it to ourselves to extract all the information that we can from what remains. Clearly we need to understand what sort of information is required to solve our own particular problem and which kinds of fossils are most likely to preserve this information. For example, brachiopods (marine shellfish with two shells, superficially similar to bivalve molluscs like cockles, figure 2) are classified by the internal structures of their shells. Students of fossil brachiopods look for individual valves (as the shells are called) or natural moulds which reveal the internal surfaces, rather than complete pairs of shells preserved 'in the round', even though conventionally the latter are better preserved. Similarly, trace fossils (plate 7), which preserve the least information about the original living organism, tell us more about fossil behaviour than all body fossils put together. In reviewing different modes of preservation I shall point out which sorts of information have been lost and which preserved for each type, starting with the famous frozen mammoths of Siberia and progressing to trace fossils.

Complete carcasses of mammoths (extinct hairy elephants adapted

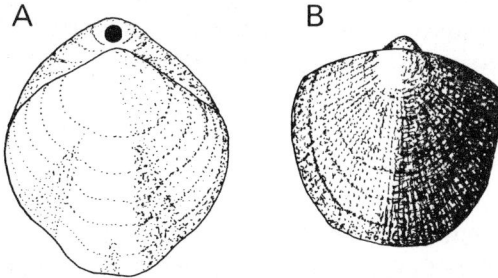

2. Two brachiopods. A. The Jurassic *Epithyris* with a pronounced pedicle foramen (the hole for the attachment stalk). B. The Silurian *Atrypa* which lacked a pedicle and was unattached in life. (After Rhona H. Black, *The elements of palaeontology*, figs 93 c and e, p. 152, Cambridge University Press, 1972.)

to cold climates) have been discovered in permanently frozen ground, not ice as is frequently stated, in Siberia.[1] Reports of Russian scientists dining on mammoth steaks are also incorrect, but certainly some of the carcasses were discovered when dogs gnawed at the meat; it was sufficiently fresh to be edible, if not palatable. Remains of mammoths and the extinct woolly rhinoceros were not uncommon in Siberia and became exposed when spring floods eroded frozen river banks. Mammoth tusks were a significant, perhaps the major, source of ivory in Tsarist Russia. A flourishing trade existed last century with 30–70,000 lbs of ivory sold in Tungusk market each year. By far the greater majority of specimens consisted of loose isolated tusks or at best tusks still attached to skulls. The inhabitants of Siberia regularly collected tusks, but were superstitious of complete carcasses and avoided them like the plague. On several occasions two years or more elapsed between the discovery of a carcass; the news reaching Moscow; and the subsequent arrival of the scientists at the site. During this time more of the carcass would become exposed and decay. Often when an expedition eventually reached the site, little remained to examine. Nevertheless one or two extremely well preserved carcasses were collected, together with some information on how they were preserved. They seem to have become trapped in viscous mud caused by summer melting on permanently frozen ground. The carcass was then either engulfed in the mud, or preserved from decay by ice-cold stream water and subsequently incorporated in sediments which remained frozen to the present–a sort of natural deep-freeze. The Beresovca mammoth had undigested buttercups and other herbs in its stomach indicating that it died in the short summer season, not in winter. The most recent discovery in 1977 of a baby mammoth (plate 1A) should add greatly to our understanding of these animals and their preservation.[2] So far only a preliminary report has been published which indicates that the mammoth was just a few months old when it died 44,000 years ago. Similar, but less complete, remains are known from Alaska.

Amber is the fossilized resin (gum) of pine trees. Considerable quantities have been eroded from Tertiary (Miocene) deposits exposed in the Baltic Sea and amber was formerly quite common along the east coast of Denmark. Occasionally the amber contains so-called 'perfectly' preserved insects and spiders. Minute anatomical details, like hairs, are preserved and available for study if the amber is polished or sectioned. These specimens are often cited as another example of the preservation of complete carcasses, although the soft tissue is dehydrated in them and not so well preserved as in frozen mammoths.

Both of these examples represent the best preservation that a palaeontologist could hope for. Soft and hard parts remain together and their inter-relationships can be studied directly. Blood cells, evidence of food, parasites, diseases, the external appearance, etc. can all be examined and recorded. Usually such features are totally unknown in fossils and have to be reconstructed, often by little more than guesswork. Nevertheless, frozen mammoths do not preserve all the information that we can gather about living elephants. Most notably, behaviour cannot be observed in these 'perfectly' preserved fossils. Thus even in these, the best preserved and most complete fossils known, some loss of information about the original living animal has already occurred. As we shall see later, direct evidence of behaviour can be preserved in fossils, but no fossil preserves *all* the information that we can gather directly from living animals and plants. All palaeontology involves a certain amount of detective work.

Other examples of traces of soft tissue are known in the fossil record. Usually on death bacterial decay and the activities of scavengers destroy soft tissue completely within a few days or weeks at most. The most durable unmineralized parts like skin, cartilage and hair rarely survive for more than a month or two in the presence of water and oxygen. If somehow either are absent from the site of burial, traces of soft tissue may be preserved. This can happen in two ways: either the carcass reaches a part of the sea floor or a swamp which lacks oxygen; or it may be dried out completely (mummified) on land. The latter is essentially the same process as hanging up strips of meat to dry. Mummified remains of dinosaurs are known from the American west and elsewhere. Here the carcasses were buried by dry drifting sand in a near-desert environment. The sands desiccated the carcasses and traces of skin have been preserved to the present.

The Middle Cambrian Burgess Shale of British Columbia has long been famous for its exceptional fauna which includes soft-bodied organisms as well as those with skeletons. Most are excellently preserved with minute details of anatomy. They seem to have been overwhelmed by a submarine avalanche and carried over a cliff into deeper water where rapid burial and the lack of oxygen allowed preservation of the impressions of even soft-bodied organisms.[3] Indeed the richness of this fauna, combined with its antiquity, is almost a source of embarassment to palaeontologists, since it is very difficult to decide where to place many of the more unusual forms in a

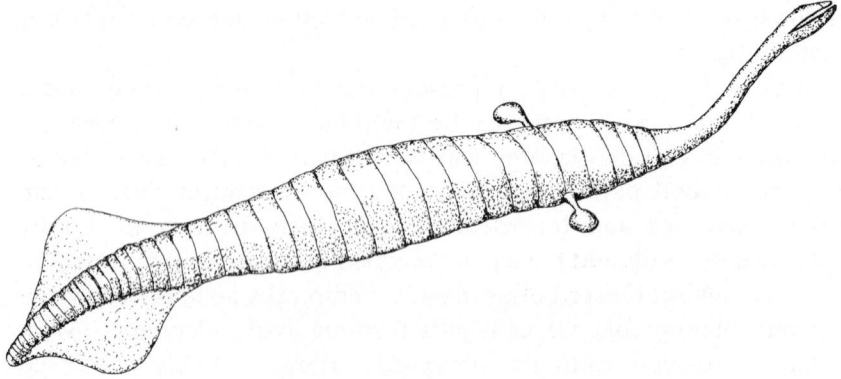

3. The enigmatic Tully Monster (*Tullimonstrum gregarium*) from the Upper Carboniferous of Illinois, USA. (After Eugene S. Richardson Jr, *Bull. Field Mus. nat. Hist.*, 37, fig. 1, pp. 4–5, 1966.)

scheme of classification. At Mazon Creek, Illinois a second almost as complete glimpse of life in the Pennsylvanian (Upper Carboniferous) coal measures' seas has recently been discovered.[4] This fauna, like that of the Burgess Shale, contains abundant remains of soft-bodied organisms preserved in concretions, nodular masses of hard cemented mudstone. Splitting open these concretions often reveals detailed impressions of creatures just as bizarre as those of the Burgess Shale. The most famous is the Tully Monster (figure 3), a peculiar worm-like animal with a head bearing jaws and eyes set on a crossbar a third of the way down the body.[5] In this case the bodies of the animals seem to have been preserved in stagnant conditions for long enough for the concretions to form and preserve their impressions. The sea was relatively shallow, however, and near land. An adjacent site has long been famous for the quantity of plant remains preserved from the coal forests.

All these examples are obviously fossils with exceptional preservation. Most palaeontologists can never hope to find anything like them. Much more commonly we find complete, or almost complete, skeletons of animals. In these cases an obvious further loss of information has occurred – the soft tissue is no longer preserved, nor any impression of it. Under this heading are included all fossils whose hard parts are more or less completely preserved. Thus a fossil sea urchin with the spines attached, a complete ichthyosaur (an extinct marine fish-like reptile, figure 4 and plate 2) skeleton, both shells of a bivalved mollusc or brachiopod, complete crabs with legs and pincers

PRESERVATION HISTORY – HOW LIVING THINGS BECOME FOSSIL

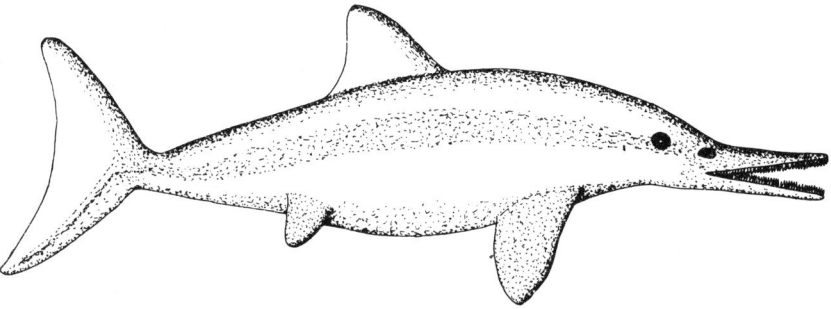

4. An ichthyosaur (the name means fish-lizard). Ichthyosaurs were major predators in the Jurassic seas just as dolphins are today.

still preserved, all belong in this category. Clearly it is much more likely that a skeleton or shell will be preserved entire if it consists of one piece, as is the case with snails. Soft tissue normally decays very rapidly, in a few days up to about two months at most, so skeletons with many parts disintegrate very rapidly if disturbed after death. Spines of sea urchins fall off within seven days in the North Sea. This period would be shorter in warmer seas where decay takes place more quickly. Clearly to be preserved complete, skeletons of more than one part must be buried rapidly after death and not disturbed subsequently. These conditions are exceedingly rare on land which is continually undergoing erosion and are still relatively rare in the seas where eroded sediment is eventually deposited. On death many marine vertebrates sink to the sea floor, but are refloated later by decomposition gases. They drift for up to two months in the case of whales and dolphins, gradually falling apart and scattering bones over enormous areas. If they should become stranded on a shore and left undisturbed by scavengers, fairly complete skeletons may remain together, but shorelines are very unstable environments and the bones are likely to be reworked by the tides. A few fish like the plaice have a sufficiently high ratio of bone to flesh that they are never refloated and their skeletons remain more or less intact. Nevertheless, they live (and die) in seas with abundant scavengers and strong currents which usually rework and scatter the bones.

One might expect that infaunal sea urchins (those that live *within* sediments) or hermit crabs which live inside a shell would tend to be preserved complete more often than surface-dwelling animals. Unfortunately when these animals are near death they often emerge from their protection and are then as much subject to the vagaries of preservation as any other marine organisms. Even so the fossil record of infaunal sea urchins is more complete than that of surface-dwelling echinoids. This limitation does not apply to infaunal bivalves which quite frequently die in life position within sediments. Complete bivalve shells are not at all uncommon in the fossil record. In bivalves an elastic ligament opens the shell while muscles close it. On death the muscles rot long before the ligament and the shells gape open. In life, under water, the ligament causes the valves to gape only a few mm. at most, except in a few, rare, specialized species. When exposed to the atmosphere the ligament dries and the shells gape much further, 30–45° or more. Shells with the valves completely open at 180° only occur when the ligament has almost rotted through. Thus even when preserved complete, bivalves may have had different preservation histories before burial. With the exception of *Lingula* (figure 5), all brachiopods, which also have two parts to their shells, are epifaunal (that is they live on the surface of sediments, rocks, or other organisms). Brachiopod shells are both opened and closed by

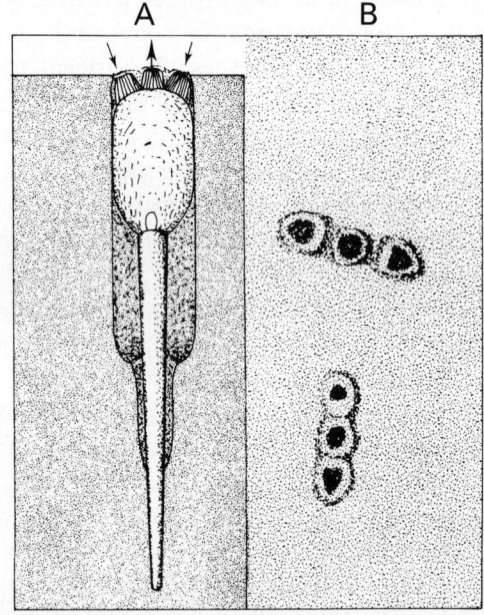

5. *Lingula*, the only infaunal brachiopod. A shows the brachiopod in its burrow with the long pedicle stalk. B shows the appearance of the feeding brachiopod at the surface of the sand. The hair-like setae maintain three openings, two entrances and one exit, for respiratory and feeding currents. (After M. J. S. Rudwick, *Living and fossil brachiopods*, fig. 48, p. 94, Hutchinson University Library, 1970.)

muscles. There is no ligament and therefore no preferential tendency to open or to remain closed after death and decay of the muscles. In quiet conditions the shells remain together; in agitated seas they separate, and more rapidly than those of bivalves.

Complete shells of snails or cephalopods with only a single part are common. Abrasion marks and other damage may indicate some post-mortem movement before burial, but at least in the case of snails, abrasion and boring may occur in life.

Preservation of complete skeletons of complex organisms like echinoderms, arthropods or vertebrates requires that the animals be buried very soon after death *and not subsequently disturbed*. This can occur when the carcass settles in stagnant water without oxygen, which inhibits bacterial decay and excludes scavengers. Since the water is stagnant, there will be no bottom currents to disturb the skeleton or rework the sediments. A second method of preservation of complete skeletons occurs when storms or volcanic eruptions deposit a thick layer of sediment over living organisms, burying them alive. If there is no subsequent disturbance, these conditions can lead to the preservation of exceptionally complete records of past environments in addition to well-preserved fossils. Pompei and Herculaneum are the most famous archaeological examples of such volcanic events, but note that even in these the record is biased, at least as far as human fossils are concerned. Vesuvius provided adequate warning of its eruption in AD 79. Preliminary tremors occurred for three days before the catastrophic eruption and the more circumspect citizens had long since left the towns. Those whose bodies were preserved in the ruins were either poor people with nowhere to go, or looters. The Middle Cambrian Burgess Shale is a more strictly palaeontological example of this type of preservation.

Preservation of complete complex skeletons requires rather special conditions. More usually the skeleton is at least disarticulated, if not completely destroyed, before any net accumulation of sediment occurs. The most resistant parts of the skeleton will outlast the rest, as for example the teeth of sharks which are very resistant compared with their cartilaginous (gristly) 'bones'. Isolated teeth, bones or echinoderm plates, dispersed valves (shells) of bivalves or brachiopods, broken shells and so on are much more common as fossils than complete skeletons. Sometimes the impression is given that it is possible to reconstruct the entire animal from a single tooth or bone. Usually this is possible only if an entire skeleton is already known, with which the isolated part may be compared. Occasionally, if enough scattered parts are available, it is possible to reconstruct what the entire skeleton would have looked like and even restore a few missing bones. This is certainly true of the most dramatic dinosaur skeletons on view in major museums, very few of which represent a single complete individual. This process of reconstruction and restoration is full of pitfalls for palaeontologists, as some of the earlier reconstructions of fossil dinosaurs attest.

Up to now we have considered merely the disintegration of organisms – the loss of soft tissue and then the separation of skeletal parts which mostly takes place before final burial. We have not considered any alteration of the original material of which the skeleton was made, either by the addition of new minerals or by the solution or replacement of the original constituents. Many fossils, whether preserved whole or in part, are completely altered in their chemical composition, or even dissolved away entirely leaving only natural moulds to indicate their original form. In these cases information is lost concerning the detailed structure and composition of the skeleton. These changes usually occur after burial, although they may begin while the hard parts are still exposed and are covered by the collective term diagenesis. This includes all the changes that affect fossils and other sedimentary particles between deposition and the present. The term is appropriate to describe the changes from loose sediment to solid rock as well as those from a skeleton to a stony fossil.

Most animal skeletons are composed of calcium phosphate (bone), calcium carbonate ($CaCO_3$) in the form of aragonite or calcite, or silica (SiO_2). The most resistant parts of plants (leaf and spore cuticle) are composed of the organic compounds cutin and sporopollenin, which are very resistant to all chemical changes except oxidation. Bone is nearly always porous; carbonate or siliceous skeletons may or may not be, while many plant tissues, like wood, are also porous. Porous skeletons like bone and wood are commonly preserved with the pore spaces filled with secondary minerals (see plate 16B). The new minerals are sometimes the same as those of the original skeleton, but occasionally other minerals such as pyrite may be involved. It is this impregnation with minerals, or per-mineralization, which makes fossil bone or wood so much heavier than their living counterparts and which gives fossils their stony appearance. They are often said to have been petrified – literally turned to stone. Such preservation is easy to recognize and does little to alter the nature of the durable tissues. Indeed impregnation prevents the wood or bone from being crushed by the weight of overlying sediments and often prevents further bacterial decay. Examples of wood preserved in concretions are known from Indiana, USA, where the central part preserved within the concretion is impregnated and has the detailed structure of the original tissue very well preserved, but the ends where the wood protruded from the concretion continued to rot away and nothing is left of the woody structure but a few fine organic particles. Polished surfaces or thin sections reveal the fine structure of the fossils and also make very ornamental objects. Polished fossil wood is often used in tables, paper weights, pen holders and other things. The striking appearance of these objects is partly due to the preserved fossil structure and partly to the particular mineral filling. Those impregnated with opal, a semi-precious form of silica with a characteristic 'fire', are the most impressive.

The skeletons of echinoderms – sea urchins, starfish, sea lilies, (plates 12, 13, 14A) – are composed of numerous plates of calcite, each with a porous structure and each acting as a single crystal. After death the most common form of diagenesis is for the original spaces to be filled up with secondary calcite which grows in the same crystal orientation as the original organic calcite. This results in most fossil echinoderm plates becoming solid single crystals. One characteristic property of calcite is that it splits readily (cleaves) in three directions to produce rhombic chips, so-called 'calcite rhombs'. Fossil echinoderm remains also cleave, and since the cleavage planes are absolutely flat and parallel, they reflect light like a mirror and will flash when held in the correct orientation to a light source, such as the sun. This makes echinoderm remains very easy to identify in rocks. In sedimentary rocks, particularly limestones, particles which reveal cleavage planes may well be echinoderm remains. Indeed many so-called 'crystalline limestones' are simply made of echinoderm plates; the crystals being in fact broken plates showing the cleavage.

This addition of secondary calcite to echinoderm plates can start very early in diagenesis. I have seen sea urchin tests (the internal skeletons of echinoderms) with minute crystals beginning to form on the inside surface only. This implies that the inside of the test formed a different chemical environment from that outside and hence that the membranes covering the mouth and anus were intact. Since these membranes rupture within five days of death, the crystals must have begun to grow within that period. These observations help to explain some unusually preserved fossil echinoderms. The plates of some sea urchins and extinct cystoids (plate 11C), for example, have a sheet-like meshwork in the inner part and a fibrous meshwork in the outer part. In the late Ordovician of South Wales some cystoids are preserved with the inner, but not the outer, meshwork impregnated with pyrite. Other cystoids from the Middle Silurian of the Midwest USA have the inner part replaced by dolomite (a calcium magnesium carbonate mineral), while the outer meshwork has been dissolved away. In all examples from both localities the tests were complete which implies that early diagenesis took a different form within and without the test. It is also likely that these animals were buried entire immediately following death.

When sea urchins are buried alive they tend to be preserved with very little sediment inside the test and the spines still attached to the outside. If the tests are rolled about or remain on the sediment surface, the covering membranes of the mouth and anus rupture and sediment penetrates the test cavity, often filling it completely. Spines also disarticulate and are carried away. When the test is not completely filled with sediment, the remaining cavity may eventually fill with calcite crystals which grow in from each of the plates that make up the test. If these crystals fill the test completely it becomes a solid ball of radiating calcite crystals. Cystoids preserved in this way are abundant in the Middle Ordovician of Öland, Sweden, where they have been known for centuries as 'crystal apples' (plate 11C). Linnaeus, founder of our modern system of naming animals and plants, described these 'crystal apples', but included them in his mineral kingdom.

The filling of cavities in fossils may be a complex process and the mineral present may depend on the size of the cavities being filled. Glauconite, a complex iron silicate which forms *in situ* only in marine sediments, rarely fills cavities larger than 1 mm. across. It occurs quite commonly in the chambers of fossil Foraminifera (protozoans). Similarly, pyrite lines cavities only in the chambers of early whorls of ammonites in the Jurassic Oxford Clay of Buckinghamshire. In the latter case the ammonite shells were lined initially with pyrite only up to about 25 mm. diameter. This was then followed by a complete filling of calcite and the original aragonitic shell has been entirely dissolved away. Small gastropods (snails) and brachiopods are also pyritized in the Oxford Clay. Ammonites from the Lower Liass at Lyme Regis and Charmouth in Dorset (plate 5) frequently show at least a three-stage process of filling. The earliest stage is often a very thin lining of pyrite which is not confined to the early whorls in this case, followed by three or more stages of calcite filling. The calcite is light or dark brown, green or colourless depending on the presence of small traces of impurities. Special staining techniques exist to detect the different stages of calcite cement and slight traces of impurities produce characteristic colours under cathode ray bombardment. Both techniques can be used to unravel the detailed diagenesis of carbonate fills and cements in fossils and sediments.

Finally, in considering diagenetic additions to fossils, when a fossil cavity is only partly filled with sediment, the sediment usually settles to the bottom of the cavity with its upper surface exactly horizontal. If this sediment is then cemented and the rest of the cavity filled with a mineral such as calcite, we have, in effect, a fossil spirit-level. Such structures are called 'geopetal structures' and are very useful in determining the correct 'way up' of rocks which have been overturned or otherwise deformed by earth movements. They are also useful in determining and measuring the original orientation of sediments which were not laid down horizontally, as happens, for example, around the flanks of organic reefs (figure 6). Occasionally one comes across fossils with geopetal fills which are randomly orientated within a single sediment layer. The most obvious explanation of these is that they were initially deposited and partly filled, cemented to preserve the geopetal surface and then reworked, rolled around and redeposited. Geopetal structures can be used to demonstrate reworking in sediments. Whatever use is made of them, it is essential to examine a number of examples to check whether they are parallel or randomly orientated.

Diagenesis may not add new minerals; it may replace or simply remove the original organic skeletal material. The net chemical

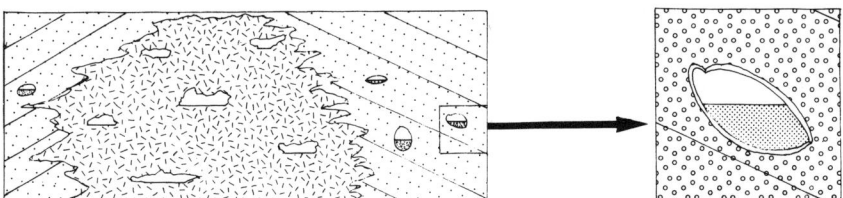

6. A cross-section through a bioherm (a type of fossil reef) and the flank beds to show geopetal structures and *Stromatactis* (the irregular holes in the bioherm). The enlargement shows a brachiopod partly filled with sediment, the top surface of which was originally horizontal. We can infer that that the flank beds were originally deposited at an angle because all the geopetal surfaces are still horizontal, but at an angle to the bedding of the flank deposits.

composition may not change much, as happens, for example, when aragonite, which is unstable at normal temperatures and pressures, recrystallizes to its stable form, calcite. Alternatively there may be a complete change in the chemical composition, as, for example, when silica (SiO_2) replaces calcite ($CaCO_3$). Even when there is no chemical change, considerable information may be lost. Aragonitic skeletons often dissolve completely away in percolating waters leaving a cavity which may be filled in at a much later date by calcite. Here there is no change in the gross chemical composition, but all trace of the original fine structure of the aragonitic skeleton will have been lost. The calcite crystals will have the same configuration as in any other cavity fill. Using thin slices of rock one can study the detailed structure of the preserved skeleton. When recrystallization occurs directly from aragonite to calcite without any intervening cavity, 'ghosts' of the fine structure of the original shell may be preserved.

Replacement by pyrite (FeS_2) is much less common than cavity filling, or, more correctly, cavity lining. Most pyritized fossils are usually lined with pyrite and filled with calcite, rather than having the original shell material replaced by pyrite. Pyrite replacements often take the form of pyrite cubes which penetrate the shell and sediment indifferently, or clusters of crystals which may not only replace but also coat the entire fossil, leaving only the vaguest trace of its original form. In such cases not only is the original chemical composition changed, but the detailed morphology is destroyed as well. Similarly, dolomite [$(Ca,Mg)CO_3$] is more dense than calcite, and so early and late dolomitization can often be distinguished. In early dolomitization the chances of preservation of detailed structures are quite high because the volume changes can be accommodated by the individual sediment grains. Once the sediment has been lithified (cemented into solid rock) late dolomitization causes volume changes which cannot easily be accommodated. Irregular voids form in the rock and fossils are usually completely destroyed. Since these chemical changes are surface reactions, large solid fossils like calcite-impregnated echinoderm plates, or belemnite guards, pencil-like fossils of extinct animals related to the modern squids (figure 7, plate 3B and C), may withstand them and remain as the only evidence that the rock was once fossiliferous. Both types of dolomitization may occur together, and dedolomitization, the reversal back to calcite, is also known. In the Middle Silurian dolomites of the midwest USA some of the cystoids have been partially dolomitized by early

PRESERVATION HISTORY – HOW LIVING THINGS BECOME FOSSIL

7. A fossil belemnite guard.

diagenesis, the remaining calcite of the test has been dissolved away and the resulting cavities are lined with small rhombic dolomite crystals formed during a later stage of dolomitization.

Solution of the original skeletal material, leaving natural moulds of the shell in the rock, is a very common form of preservation. Clearly we have lost any evidence of the original composition and structure in such cases. However, internal moulds often reveal details of the inner surface of the shell which would not be visible if the shell were still preserved. Compare, for example, two *Trigonias* (plates 7A and B). In many cases, particularly in brachiopods, knowledge of the internal structures is essential to identify the fossils. Natural moulds are very useful and are best studied by preparing artificial casts from them using latex or silicone rubbers. These materials distort readily to allow their removal from irregular cavities, but regain their original shape once removed.

If solution occurs early while the sediment is still soft and plastic, all trace of the original shell may be lost. This is common in animals with aragonitic shells and traces of them may be preserved fortuitously as, for example, when oysters attach themselves to a shell before it becomes buried and dissolved. Several species of fossil snail are known only from such preservation in Tertiary clays of the Paris Basin. Similarly, traces of Jurassic ammonites are preserved in this way in the Kimmeridge Clay of Cambridgeshire. Attachment surfaces of epizoans (animals which live directly attached to other animals or plants) are a useful source of information about other fauna in such sediments.

Related to natural moulds are fossil impressions, a term with a precise meaning in this context. Many plant tissues, but also soft-bodied animals, leave slight imprints in the sediment before the tissue decays away or is destroyed by diagenesis. These impressions may survive to form fossils. Most fossil leaves are preserved in this way with the only trace of the original tissue being at most a thin carbonaceous film on the surface (see plate 16A). Some of the fossil ichthyosaurs of the Liass retain a similar film of carbonaceous material indicating the outline of the body. The bodies of belemnites, worms, etc. are also known from impressions. Most of the soft-bodied organisms in the Burgess Shale and Mazon Creek faunas already mentioned are fossil impressions. The best-known Precambrian fauna, the Ediacara fauna of Australia, is entirely composed of fossil impressions of soft-bodied animals and plants. Here, as with natural moulds, the original material cannot be examined directly and its chemical composition can only be inferred. Sometimes details of soft tissue structures can be revealed or enhanced by ultra-violet (UV) light.

So far we have treated loss of information involving disintegration of organisms and diagenetic chemical changes, but the basic shapes of the skeletal parts have remained more or less unaltered. In plant compressions and distorted fossils, even the original shape may have been modified. When fossil wood or other plant tissues are not impregnated with minerals, the weight of the overlying sediments gradually compresses the porous tissue until all the spaces are completely flattened. Commonly tree trunks occur with flattened oval sections which can be used to estimate the amount of compression if it is known that they were originally circular. Similarly ammonites filled with clay may be crushed flat as the clay compacts (see plate 6B). Examples are common in the Kimmeridge Clay of Chapman's Pool, Dorset, and almost any other Mesozoic clay. The rib cages of vertebrates usually become distorted by compaction

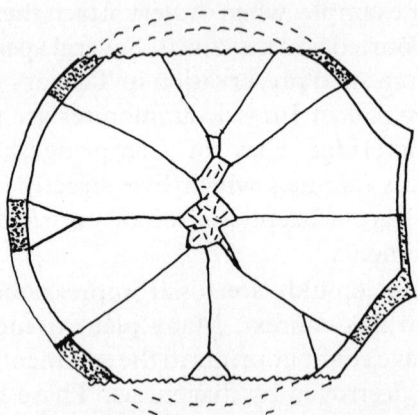

8. A cross-section through a cystoid which has suffered pressure solution. The cystoid was buried lying on its side and subsequently filled with secondary calcite growing in from the skeletal plates. Later the weight of overlying sediments caused the top and bottom parts to dissolve away. Since we know that the cystoid was approximately circular in section originally, we can estimate how much has been dissolved.

of sediments with the ribs on one side bending forwards while those on the other are bent backwards (see plate 2). Spherical plant spores collapse in characteristic patterns under compression.

Several minerals, particularly calcite, tend to dissolve under immense pressures, a process known as pressure solution. In the Ordovician of Sweden many spherical cystoids have been changed to discus-shaped objects by pressure solution of the upper and lower surfaces due to the weight of the overlying sediments. The original test is only preserved in a band around the middle where there was least pressure (figure 8).

These examples arise because of the action of gravity. They involve only vertical compression or solution and restoration of the original shape is not very difficult. More confusing are the distortions induced by earth movements when the rocks themselves change shape and volume. Symmetrical objects like trilobites become asymmetrical (figure 9) and the precise shape of a fossil depends on its orientation to the distortion. If one imagines a sphere within the undisturbed rock, after distortion its shape becomes ellipsoidal. The longest axis marks the direction of maximum extension and the shortest that of maximum compression. Fossils will be stretched in the direction of maximum extension and shortened in the direction of maximum compression.

Restoring asymmetrical fossils to their original symmetry is a useful technique in structural geology since it gives an indication of the orientation and the amount of distortion. Until recently it was a tedious business, but now, with a combination of computer and

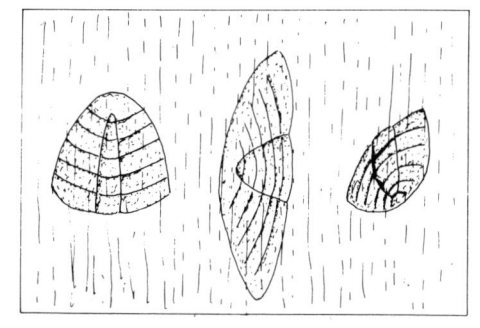

9. Distortion of trilobite tails due to compression of rocks. The different shapes result solely from the distortion of the rock; all were originally the same shape.

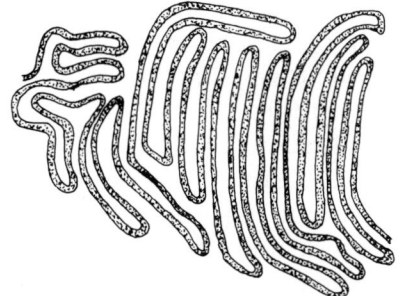

10. *Nereites*, a systematic searching pattern which was caused by an animal feeding in sediments. (After A. Seilacher, 'Fossil behaviour', *Scientific American*, **217**, no. 2, 1967.)

closed-circuit TV, a facility exists at Swansea in south Wales which can perform such operations very quickly and measure the transformations very accurately.

Carried to the extreme, deformation of rocks involves metamorphism and will destroy all traces of fossils as the rock recrystallizes. Few fossils can survive metamorphism, although microfossils have been described from within felspar crystals in Alpine schists. The presence in some Alpine schists of belemnite guards, which resist metamorphic recrystallization in the same way that they resist diagenetic replacement, convinced geologists last century that not all highly metamorphosed rocks were Precambrian in age. Previously it had been thought that the degree of metamorphism and geological age were broadly correlated, i.e. the most highly deformed rocks were also the oldest and vice versa.

The entire previous discussion, from frozen mammoths to fragmentary remains, dealt with 'body fossils', that is those which preserve direct evidence of the actual body or skeleton of the original organisms. 'Trace fossils', on the other hand, rarely preserve any evidence of the organism itself, but are evidence of its activities. Trace fossils include tracks and trails, burrows (plate 9B), borings (plate 9A), footprints, teeth marks, indeed any trace of organic activity. Unlike body fossils, where we usually know exactly which animal we have found but little about its behaviour, trace fossils may tell us a great deal about the activity involved, but we may have no idea at all what sort of animal produced the trace. As a result palaeontologists who study trace fossils use a classification based on the type of activity rather than on the systematic zoological classification of body fossils.[6] Trace fossils may be subdivided into dwelling traces, resting traces, feeding traces and so on. Ichnologists, people who study traces, also name the trace itself not the animal that caused it.

Trace fossils may seem to exemplify the type of preservation which yields least information of all, since we usually have no idea what the original organism was. It is more true to say that the type of information preserved is different, but equally useful. Information from trace fossils complements that from body fossils. Trace fossils preserve the best evidence of fossil behaviour and are often excellent environmental indicators. Tracks, trails and burrows in soft sediments can never be preserved out of place. They are always *in situ* and can therefore be used to interpret environmental conditions of deposition; this is only rarely the case with body fossils. For the purposes of this discussion I shall divide trace fossils into those which are *in situ* and those which may not be. The first category can be further subdivided into traces which are formed on the surface of sediments (tracks and trails) and internal traces within the sediment (burrows) or rock (borings).

Surface traces are made when an animal moves over the surface of a soft sediment and leaves an impression of its movement behind. Footprints on a sandy beach are the most familiar example. Normally, of course, the incoming tide destroys the footprints and leaves a fresh unsullied beach twice every day. For a surface trace to be preserved the sediment must either harden before anything disturbs the trace or be buried by a new influx of sediment and remain undisturbed thereafter. To judge from the abundant surface traces in many shallow marine sedimentary rocks, these circumstances are not as rare as one might expect. Some surface trails show a systematic pattern in which an area of sediment surface is densely and evenly covered and no part is crossed more than once (figure 10, page 25). Such patterns indicate systematic searching behaviour and are usually interpreted as feeding traces. The pattern may take the form of radiating grooves, as in the feeding traces of tellinacean bivalves. These bivalves lie on one side within the sediment. The long siphons protrude from the shell at an angle which often makes the posterior end of the shell asymmetrical. The slender inhalant siphon 'hoovers' food particles from the sediment surface, which produces a star-shaped pattern. Similar patterns have been described from rocks dating back to the Carboniferous. After a time these bivalves usually move slightly and any one individual will produce many traces in its lifetime. Alternatively, the related bivalve *Scrobicularia*, which lives in muddy salt flats, relies on the tides regularly bringing in a fresh supply of nutritious material and may remain static for long periods. The bivalve shells are frequently not preserved with the traces, the shells being dissolved away by ground waters. Other regular patterns include straight and curved zig-zag paths (figure 10). All these patterns have in common the systematic coverage of an area, leaving no portion unsearched but without recrossing any part. Computers have been used to simulate these patterns. The instructions which are needed to get the computer to produce patterns similar to the real traces are an indication of the complexity of the animal's behaviour. Apparently complex patterns can be simulated with only a few simple instructions, indicating that a comparatively complex trace may be produced by an animal with relatively simple behaviour. For example, the pattern shown in figure 10 could be produced by a worm which first proceeded until its body was straight, and then turned through 180°; proceeded again until its body was straight and again turned through 180° away from its previous trace. Repetition of these simple instructions can produce a remarkably regular zig-zag pattern with the amplitude of the zig-zags controlled by the length of the worm's body. Often the complexity of

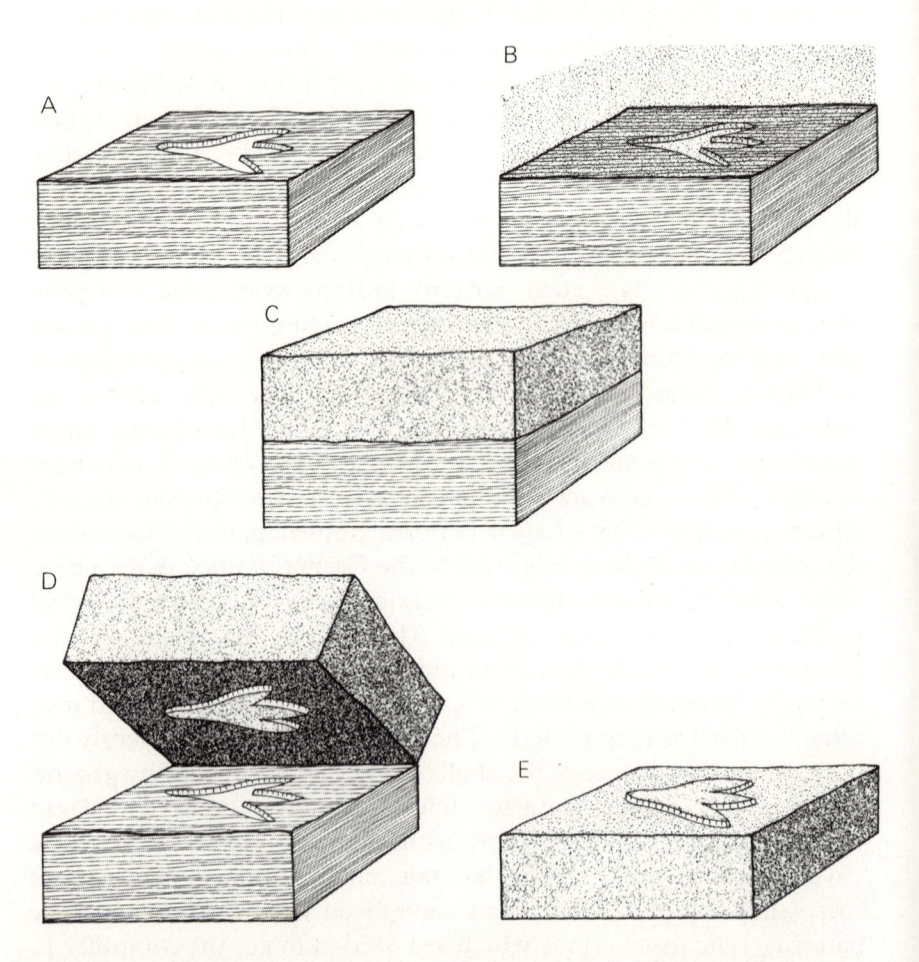

11. Stages in the formation of some fossil footprints. A. A footprint is formed in soft mud. B. The footprint is covered with loose sand. C. The sand is consolidated into sandstone. D. The rock is split open along the bedding surface to reveal the original footprint in the shale and the cast of it in the sandstone. E. The sandstone cast showing reversed relief.

PRESERVATION HISTORY – HOW LIVING THINGS BECOME FOSSIL

the behaviour can be used to infer how the trace was produced, as we shall see below.

More difficult to recognize as feeding traces are the random trails made, for example, by some snails. Many browsing snails feed as they move, but rarely produce systematic searching patterns. Other snails, like the scavenging common whelk *Buccinum*, plough through the surface sediment in search of food leaving random trails behind. Birds feeding in soft sediment along the tide line produce random prod marks in the sediment with their beaks. Since they feed at the tide line, like our own footprints their traces are usually destroyed by the advancing tide and I know of no fossilized examples of such beak marks.

Many tracks and trails are random, as for example most fossil footprint tracks, and are best regarded as evidence of locomotion without any implied purpose. Dinosaur footprints are some of the most spectacular of such tracks and they impress us with the size of the original animals almost as well as the mounted skeletons in museums. Certainly where a series of footprints is preserved the enormous stride of a large dinosaur is revealed in a way that no static museum skeleton can show. Footprints are often the only fossils preserved in Triassic sandstones in Britain. Good examples have been found near Elgin in Scotland (where it is rumoured that all the tracks were heading south!) and near Liverpool. The latter series are preserved in ripple-marked sandstones with a few other associated traces. The mounted display series is in fact the underside of the bed above the one containing the footprints. The sequence of formation (figure 11) was as follows. First some silty sediment was deposited, probably in a shallow temporary pool. A dinosaur walked over the sediment leaving its characteristic three-toed footprints. Then the sediment hardened and was buried by a fresh layer of sand which filled the footprints and other depressions in the silt. The whole series of rocks was lithified and eventually uncovered in a quarry. Since the sandstone holds together well while the silty layer tends to flake off and is lost, such traces are more easily studied as a natural cast of the original.

Trilobites left behind them very distinctive trails. Their jointed legs produced characteristic grooves on either side of a central ridge. Some snails which have the foot divided by a groove which runs from front to back, produce similar double trails, but trilobite trails also have the characteristic scratch marks formed by the legs and are usually much larger. These trails have long been known as *Cruziana*.

We know for certain that some examples of *Cruziana* are trilobite trails as occasionally the unfortunate trilobites have been found at the end of the trail – literally dead in their tracks.

Trilobites also formed another sort of trace – a resting trace, called *Rusophycus*. It seems that trilobites, like modern crabs, occasionally dug themselves into the sand and sat with perhaps just their eyes protruding above the sediment. In doing so they produced double-grooved traces with scratch marks, similar to *Cruziana*, but oval and just about the size and shape of a trilobite. Again occasional specimens are known with a trilobite body fossil on top and a *Rusophycus* trace fossil underneath. Most examples of *Cruziana* and *Rusophycus* are preserved, like the dinosaur footprints, as natural casts of the actual original trace. Resting traces of other animals are also known and even free-swimming animals, like fish, may occasionally rest on the sediment surface to form the only trace of their activities we are ever likely to find.

All these numerous traces formed because the sediment was soft and unconsolidated when the animal moved over it or rested on it. There is not the slightest chance that such traces could be moved and buried elsewhere as the sediment particles would separate and all evidence of the trace would disappear like footprints before the tide. The same sort of thing happens within sediments where many animals live permanently. Here we can not only recognize all the activities discussed under surface traces, but in addition the actual dwellings of infaunal organisms.

The simplest form of a dwelling trace is a single, vertical burrow which is usually circular in section. Many worms dwell in such burrows, plastering the sides with mucus or otherwise lining their tubes to prevent the walls collapsing. Millions of these tubes, formed by the modern worm *Lanice*, may be exposed at low tide, sticking up out of the sand. Further erosion may exhume the more robust, better cemented tubes and they accumulate in untold numbers along the strand line after winter storms. Life is fraught with such dangers for any infaunal animal; erosion may remove the supporting sediment or deposition may bury the dwelling to a greater or lesser degree. When sediment is deposited evidence of another type of behaviour, escape, may be preserved in the fossil record. Thus internal traces reveal even more evidence about the behaviour of living animals than tracks and trails. Again, to be preserved such traces must first be formed in soft, plastic sediment and then not subsequently disturbed. If there are no infaunal animals at all, sediment usually accumulates in

PRESERVATION HISTORY – HOW LIVING THINGS BECOME FOSSIL

horizontal beds and the resulting rock will exhibit good stratification or layering. If there are abundant infaunal organisms they churn up the sediment mixing it completely (just as earthworms do in soil), destroying all trace of bedding and eventually producing a homogeneous sediment. This process is known as bioturbation and, carried to its extreme, the animals destroy their own traces because burrows can only be distinguished if they disturb bedding or are filled with material which is slightly different from the surrounding sediment. In a completely homogeneous sediment there are no bedding surfaces and the burrow fill will be identical to its surroundings. Thus from a palaeontological point of view, the best internal traces form in sediments which start with good bedding surfaces, are partly disturbed by organisms, but are then buried by a new layer of sediment, which either kills the infauna or forces it to migrate up into the new layer before the initial layer is completely homogenized. Again, infaunal traces are so abundant that these conditions must have occurred repeatedly in the past. Finally, before considering some examples of infaunal traces in more detail, many internal burrows, particularly feeding traces, follow bedding surfaces. If a past buried bedding surface was rich in food, an infaunal organism will tend to feed preferentially along that surface. Thus the mere fact that a trace occurs on a bedding surface is no guarantee that it is a surface trace. Surface and internal traces which follow bedding can be distinguished because an internal trace (burrow) should have the entire tubular cross-section preserved while a surface trace will only reveal the impression on the original surface (figure 12).

As with surface traces, we find internal traces which indicate systematic searching behaviour. The patterns may be more complex and varied as they now occur in three dimensions, not just two. At least two new patterns occur along with the radiating and zig-zag patterns of surface traces. The modern worm *Paraonis* produces horizontal spiral patterns (figure 13), working outwards from the centre and then ascending or descending to a new level and commencing a new spiral. Similar spiral patterns are known as trace fossils and, even if we did not know the behaviour of *Paraonis*, we could predict which way the fossil went along the trace by considering the complexity of the behaviour necessary for the animal to have gone in either direction. Generally, the more simple behaviour is likely to provide the correct interpretation. Regular spiral patterns are a good example which you may test yourself by trying to draw one from the centre outwards and then from the

THE NATURAL HISTORY OF FOSSILS

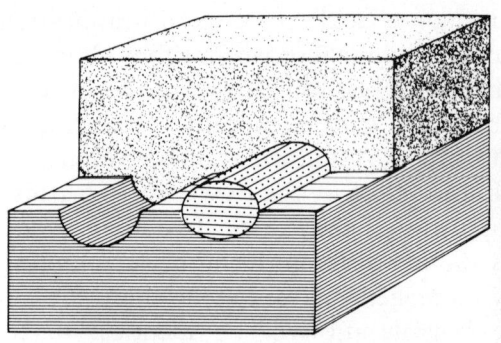

12. The difference between a surface trace (trail) and an internal trace (burrow) which happens to follow a bedding surface. In the surface trail (left) the overlying sediment fills the trace as happened in the footprint in figure 11. The burrow passes through both layers and is often filled with a third type of sediment (right).

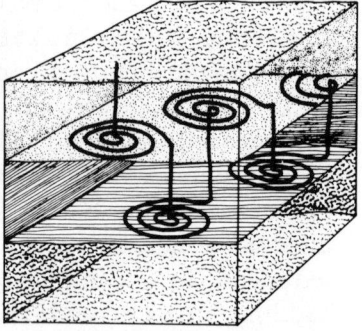

13. The burrow system formed by the modern worm *Paraonis*. This is a dwelling trace which probably represents 'farming' activity.

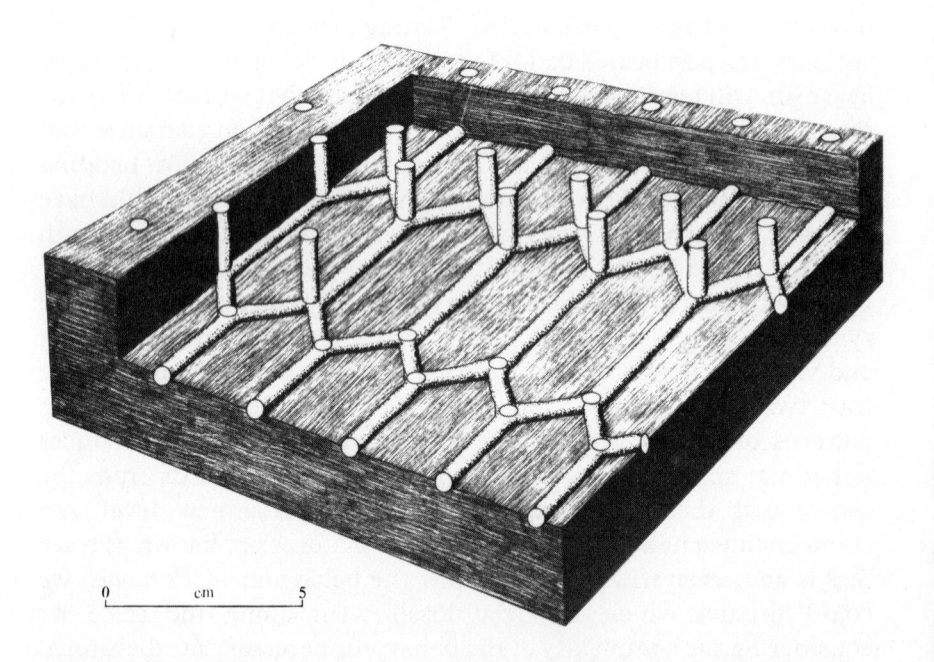

14. Part of the trace-fossil burrow system, *Palaeodictyon*. A system of horizontal hexagonal burrows is connected to the surface at each corner by short vertical tubes. This is a dwelling trace and probably represents 'farming' activity. (Diagram reproduced by courtesy of Dr T. P. Crimes.)

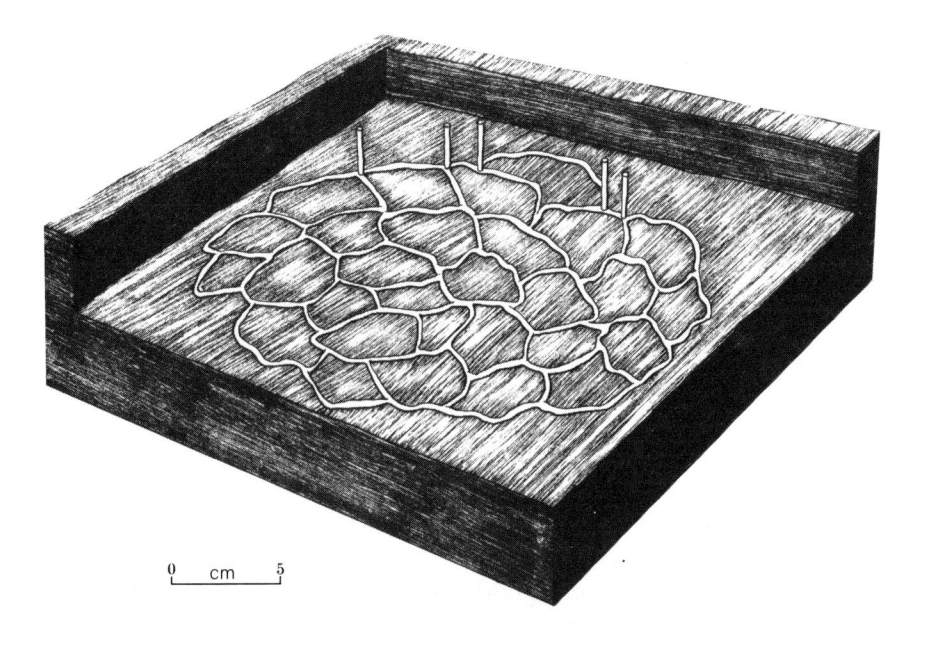

PRESERVATION HISTORY – HOW LIVING THINGS BECOME FOSSIL

15. The trace-fossil burrow system, *Squamodictyon*. This is very like *Palaeodictyon*, but has a more irregular horizontal network of burrows. For clarity most of the vertical tubes have been omitted, but there is one at each corner as in *Palaeodictyon*. (Reproduced by courtesy of Dr T. P. Crimes.)

outside inwards. To produce the trace, *Paraonis* changes level within the sediment until it finds a suitable buried bedding surface. It then spirals outwards at that level, keeping a set distance away from the previous track, until it changes level again. If one assumes that *Paraonis* spiralled in towards the centre, it would have to decide how large to make the initial whorl and fix its radius of curvature exactly in order to make a regular spiral. In other words there is nothing to guide the worm in making its spiral if it starts from the outside, whereas there is if it starts at the centre. Clearly it is much easier to produce a regular spiral from the inside outwards.

Although the trace made by *Paraonis* resembles a systematic searching pattern, the worm actually retraces its steps and lives permanently within the burrow. It is believed to 'farm' bacteria and other interstitial organisms by attracting them from the surrounding sediment to the mucus lining its burrow. When a considerable amount of bacteria has accumulated, the worm returns, eats the food and relines the burrow with fresh mucus. This behaviour may well explain otherwise very puzzling traces such as *Palaeodictyon* and *Squamodictyon* (figures 14 and 15), which can never be produced without retracing one's steps over some part of the pattern.

Chondrites, a dendritic (tree-like) branching internal trace (figure 16) is another feeding trace. The animal responsible for producing *Chondrites* is unknown and may perhaps be extinct since *Chondrites* has yet to be found within recent sediments. The behaviour differs from that of other feeding traces and, as with spiral traces, the evidence for this statement comes from the pattern itself. In other feeding traces, the animal went one way through the trace; in *Chondrites* it must have back-tracked over the entire pattern, first going forward and then returning to the beginning. Furthermore, we can deduce that all side branches were produced on the way back, because no side branch ever crosses another, and side branches nearer the stem (by analogy with a tree) terminate adjacent to more distal branches. The reverse does not occur. Assuming that the animal which produced *Chondrites* could detect its own burrow, it could stop short of a pre-existing branch. This explains why branches do not cross each other and it enables us to determine which was the earlier of two branches. The alternative implies that the animal knew the entire pattern of branching before it started to burrow so that it could stop one burrow at the point where a future branch was going to be: a very improbable explanation. Again you may test this by trying to draw an exact copy of a *Chondrites* pattern starting at either end. Using the above argument we can deduce that in forming *Chondrites*, the animal pushed right to the end of the trace first and then back-

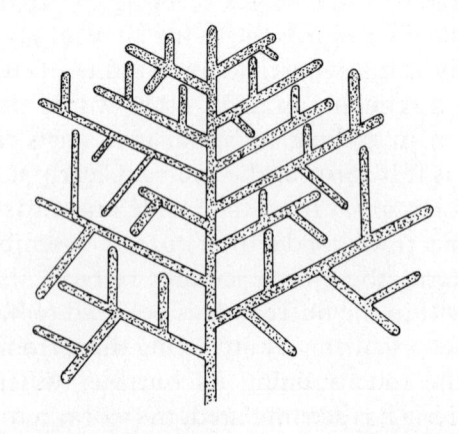

16. The feeding trace, *Chondrites*.

tracked, branching from side to side periodically as it did so. With each side branch it repeated the pattern of pushing to the end first and then back-tracking and branching. Where the density of branches is high, food was probably abundant and, conversely, where branches are entirely missing there was probably little or no food. The behaviour pattern exhibited by *Chondrites* is so distinctive that I suspect it was produced by a particular type of organism–probably a worm with a proboscis–the length of the main trunks reflecting the maximum extension of the worm and its proboscis. *Chondrites* descends from a surface and extends out horizontally within the sediment at a lower level. It seems quite likely that the worm, or whatever, that produced *Chondrites* may have kept its rear end out of the sediment and had posterior gills. Such an arrangement would enable the animal to breathe while most of its body was buried within the sediment.

As with surface traces, we find internal traces which show no characteristic pattern and which may be just locomotory traces. However, many deposit-feeding organisms eat their way through the sediment in a random fashion. Earthworms and the common heart-shaped sea urchin, *Echinocardium*, are examples. Both leave traces behind which would be difficult to characterize as feeding traces if we did not know the animals that formed them.

Dwelling traces vary from simple, usually vertical, tubes to complex underground systems that branch repeatedly, have several entrances, passing places and nurseries and in every way rival the complexity of rabbit warrens. Whenever the complete burrow system can be seen, and some are very extensive, characteristic patterns have been named. Modern examples are studied by pouring dense plastic emulsions down the entrances which displace sea water and, if all goes well, penetrate to the bottom of the system. When the plastic has set solid the system can be excavated. Direct observation reveals which animals inhabit recent burrows and with some of the most distinctive we may infer the makers of fossil burrows. Occasionally remains of the makers are found within fossil burrow systems, but there is always the possibility that the remains represent animals which merely took shelter in the burrows, or skeletal material that fell into the burrow after it had been vacated.

The simplest dwelling traces are vertical blind-ending tubes. The sea anemone, *Ceriantharia*, produces such a burrow by forcing sediment aside and then plastering the walls with mucus. The anemone spreads its tentacles on the surface to feed, but withdraws completely into the burrow at times of danger. A constant opening is maintained at the surface to allow sea water to penetrate for respiration. When fresh sediment accumulates, *Ceriantharia* climbs up through it and then plasters mucus around the wall of a new tube connecting to the surface. In this way, what was originally a simple blind-ending vertical tube may become quite complex in its morphology. Many polychaete worms (segmented worms like the common lugworm, *Arenicola*) produce burrows, usually of somewhat more complex morphology than a simple vertical tube; however only the top part near the surface may be supported by mucus and hence give rise to a recognizable trace fossil. Simple vertical burrows are known in the fossil record since the lower Cambrian and are called *Skolithos*, or *Monocraterion* if they have a funnel-shaped expansion at the surface. The modern worm *Sabellaria* cements sand grains around its dwelling tube and may form small 'reefs' when the worm tubes are closely packed together and grow up from the sediment surface.

The polychaete *Lanice* produces a complex dwelling burrow. The upper part is plastered and lined with mucus and is strong enough to hold together if exhumed by erosion. On top of this, protruding from the sediment surface is an agglutinated trunk with sand grains and shell chips stuck together rather like the dwelling tube of a caddis fly larva, and thread-like structures extend from the top. Removal of the trunk after death would leave a trace resembling *Skolithos*.

Very commonly dwelling burrows take the form of a U, an arrangement with obvious advantages since it allows a one-way current through the burrow. Sea water, bearing oxygen and food, may enter one end and faecal matter can be carried away out of the other end. The actual morphology of some U-shaped tubes, with a mound at one end and a funnel at the other, passively causes ventilation currents to flow through the burrow without any effort on the part of the inhabitant. In other cases, such as the polychaete *Arenicola*, undulations of the body create currents when needed. U-shaped burrows are very common and illustrate well the difficulty of identifying the producers of traces. Amphipod and shrimp-like arthropods, a variety of polychaete worms, acorn worms (*Balanoglossus*), and *Echiurus* all produce U-shaped burrows. Thus traces of nearly identical morphology can be produced by very different animals. Equally, the polychaete *Polydora ciliata* forms irregular U-shaped burrows in soft sediment as well as distinctive more regular U-shaped borings in shells and limestones. When densely crowded together it is difficult to detect the U-shape of many *Polydora* burrows. Thus this one worm may produce several different types of dwelling trace. U-shaped fossil burrows are usually divided into two types, *Arenicolites* and *Diplocraterion*, according to whether internal connections exist between the two parallel tubes of the U. There is no reason to suppose that both types may not have been made by the same animal.

Complex burrows, rather like rabbit warrens, are produced by the shrimp *Callianassa*. They reach the surface in several places and usually have an anastomosing horizontal network in which tunnels branch and reconnect irregularly. Passing and turning places and brood chambers are developed. Where the sediment is particularly loose, *Callianassa* produces balls of mucus-impregnated sand and plasters these onto the burrow walls. Complex fossil burrows with and without these pellet-like linings (*Thalassinoides* and *Ophiomorpha*, respectively) are known in Mesozoic and Tertiary strata. Moulted parts of callianassids have been found in such burrows as far back as the Palaeocene. The two traces are usually accepted as the work of one animal, a callianassid shrimp, and it is often possible to see one type leading into the other.

Dwelling borings differ from dwelling burrows only in that they penetrate hard, rather than soft, substrates and, as in the case of *Polydora*, both may be made by the same animal. Usually boring requires more effort and specialized mechanical or chemical action. Simple tubes are produced by boring bivalves and some worms, U-shaped borings by *Polydora*, and complex networks of interconnected polygonal chambers by the sponge *Cliona*. Algae and fungi produce a variety of filamentous irregular tubular borings. Borings may or may not be *in situ*. If they penetrate solid rock, as in the case of the terebelloid worm borings in the surface of the chalk at Harefield, Middlesex, they are obviously *in situ*. Where they penetrate small objects like pebble and shells, the objects themselves may have been subject to transport.

Bivalves which bore into solid rock often produce flask-shaped borings that are larger inside than at the opening, because the animal grows within the bore-hole and enlarges it as necessary. Only the siphons protrude through the opening for feeding and breathing. Bivalves like *Zirfaea* and *Pholas* use mechanical action and the anterior end of the shell is ornamented with numerous ridges and platelets. Sand grains often lodge in this ornament, which enables the bivalves to penetrate rocks that superficially appear to be harder than their calcite shells. Where these bivalves penetrate sandstone, for example, the sand grains are usually only loosely cemented together. *Zirfaea* normally bores into softer substrates like consolidated clay or peat beds and its shape changes in response to the hardness of the substrate. As one would expect, short stubby borings, enclosing short fat bivalves, occur in harder substrates. On the other hand *Lithophaga* (plate 9A)–whose name means literally 'rock eater'– which has a smooth shell, bores using a chemical attack. Except for the circular cross-section, there is nothing in the morphology of the shell to suggest that *Lithophaga* is a borer. *Zirfaea, Pholas* and other pholadid genera which bore mechanically, have extensive gapes in the shell: anteriorly for the protrusion of the foot which effects the boring rotation and posteriorly for the extension of the siphons. The anterior adductor muscle, which in normal bivalves is entirely internal and is used to close the shells, in pholads has migrated to an external dorsal position and pulls the shells open against the side of the borehole during the rotary boring action. This exposed muscle is attached to distinctive plates on the external surface of the shell and is itself covered by accessory plates. Thus the shell morphology of pholads is very distinctive and, since the shells are trapped within the borings, is potentially preservable. Unfortunately such bivalve borings aid the erosion of solid rocks and tend to be self-destructive. Even so, *Lithophaga* and pholad borings are known back at least to the Jurassic.

When an animal living in or on sediment is covered by a sudden influx of fresh sediment, as happens after storms for example, it will try to climb up through the new sediment layer to make contact with the surface again, and so produce an escape structure. Tube-dwelling infauna may show extensive, rather irregular tubes running through several layers of sediment with the tube more obvious and regular at certain intervals. This is the result of rapid upward burrowing after the deposition of a new layer followed by consolidation of the burrow walls when a new stable level is reached. Furthermore, if the sediment level remains fairly constant for a period, a certain amount of 'dirt' will inevitably penetrate the burrow. Most burrow dwellers simply plaster this dirt onto the burrow walls and in doing so may line the burrow with orientated grains or emphasize the walls by adding grains of a different colour or texture. Thus we can often distinguish those parts of the burrow that were dwelt in for extended periods from those parts which were simply escape structures. Although the total length of the burrow may not reflect the length of the inhabitant, the dwelling part may well do so and we may also have an indication of the rate of sedimentation. If a single burrow penetrates several layers, any layers above the top of the initial dwelling tube are likely to have been deposited during the lifetime of the inhabitant: one to several years in most cases, rarely if ever over fifteen. Some U-shaped burrows of the *Diplocraterion* type show a complex history of yo-yoing up and down as the sediment level changed with repeated erosion and deposition.

Although pebbles and corals bored into by bivalves may be moved by currents, the majority of the examples discussed above occur *in situ*, either in or on loose sediment or within solid rock. Many other traces occur in small objects which are very likely to have been moved between death and burial. These traces may not be *in situ* and include feeding, parasitic and dwelling traces. Feeding traces include teeth marks, predatory borings of snails, or even just a characteristic damage to a shell. For example, the crawfish *Palinurus vulgaris* preys on the common whelk, *Buccinum*, by breaking away parts of the shell back from the aperture, thus opening it up for more than a whorl. Thrushes and the beetle, *Badister*, also produce characteristic damage to land snail shells, although these are less likely to be preserved as fossils. Sea birds feeding on sea urchins and large bivalves may produce a characteristic indentation by tapping with their beaks.

Predatory gastropods of the families Naticidae and Muricidae prey on bivalves by boring small round holes through the shell, inserting a proboscis and devouring the bivalve body inside. Shells with these characteristic circular holes are common on many present day shores and are also known as fossils. Snails of the two families make slightly different types of boreholes. Naticid boreholes have a bevelled portion on the outside, while muricid holes are more straight-sided. Both types are recognizable in fossil shells.

Evidence of parasitism is preserved on many fossil echinoderms. Modern crinoids are subject to parasitic attack by copepod crustaceans and myzostomid worms, both of which bore into the skeletal tissue and cause the formation of various galls and swellings. Similar swellings on fossil crinoid stems are well known in the Palaeozoic from the Ordovician onwards. Pyramidellid snails bore into modern crinoids producing hemispherical pits and similar pits occur in Palaeozoic crinoids and cystoids from the Ordovician to the Carboniferous, although no fossil pyramidellids are known from the Palaeozoic. A more satisfactory relationship (from the crinoid's point of view) existed between Palaeozoic crinoids and platyceratid snails.

The latter apparently fed on crinoid faeces without causing any great inconvenience to their hosts. Nevertheless examples are known where both the shell of the snail and the upper surface of the crinoid cup have been modified during growth to produce a closer fit between the snail and the crinoid. Even when separated from their hosts, platyceratid snails are easy to recognize by their shape and modified growth lines.

Dwelling traces not preserved *in situ* include borings of bivalves in pebbles and, in particular, borings of the sponge *Cliona*, algae and fungi which typically penetrate shells rather than solid rock. Barnacles and various worms also regularly inhabit living and dead shells. Characteristic L-shaped barnacle borings in belemnite guards have given a clue to the swimming habits of the belemnites. Some belemnite guards have randomly orientated borings and are usually broken. Borings on the broken surfaces confirm that these belemnites were bored into *post mortem*. Others are complete and have their borings orientated more or less parallel to the length of the belemnite. Barnacles feed by moving hand-like organs through the water and filtering out any suitable particles. The orientation of the borings in the belemnite guards is such that the gentle forward movement of the belemnite would have aided feeding currents for the barnacles, while the violent backwards escape movements would have folded the barnacle's feeding organs safely down into the boring. Had the orientation of the boreholes been reversed, the rapid backwards escape movement of the belemnite would have damaged the barnacle's feeding organs by bending them the wrong way.

The sponge *Cliona* bores into shells, eventually destroying them. The initial boring is a small circular hole but, once inside the shell, *Cliona* excavates a series of connected polygonal chambers. The shell may look relatively undamaged externally, while all that remains inside are the thin walls between the chambers. Similarly some algae and fungi bore into shell material and eventually reduce it to powder. The algae are usually confined to the shallow parts of the sea into which light can penetrate, the so-called photic zone. They produce very fine-scale disintegration of the surfaces of skeletal grains forming micrite envelopes, that is the grains appear to be coated with a very fine-grained (micritic) veneer. Boring by algae is probably the most effective agent destroying shell material in shallow seas.

A different sort of trace is left by epifaunal brachiopods. Almost all brachiopods are attached to something, often a shell, by a flexible stalk called the pedicle. The pedicle often penetrates the substrate

PRESERVATION HISTORY – HOW LIVING THINGS BECOME FOSSIL

slightly at the point of attachment, producing a characteristic set of radially arranged pits.

This review of trace fossils shows that they may have varied preservation histories and should not be dismissed as 'mere traces'. It is true that in body fossil terms they preserve the least information of any mode of preservation. However I hope I have shown that in ecological and behavioural terms they are some of the most useful fossils we know.

Comparison of the relative abundances of different types of living organisms and different types of fossils reveals some marked discrepancies which are not entirely due to evolution and extinction. To be sure there are no living dinosaurs or ammonites, but equally insects, worms and jellyfish which are so common today are very rare as fossils. However they do occur as fossils occasionally and we know that jellyfish and worms had evolved at least by the Cambrian and insects by the Carboniferous, six hundred and three hundred million years ago, respectively. Thus although these groups have a long fossil record, it is a very meagre one. This is so because they have a low preservation potential, i.e. the likelihood of them being preserved as fossils is very small. There are at least three aspects to preservation potential: the morphology of the organism, where it lived and its original abundance. Generally the three operate independently. The most basic aspect of morphology is the presence or absence of hard parts. Organisms with a skeleton or shell have a much greater potential than those without. Jellyfish never occur as body fossils because, being about 98 per cent water, they have virtually no tissue that could be preserved. Some worms have hardened jaws (scolecodonts) which are quite common as microfossils. The presence of scolecodonts within the borings at the top of the chalk near Harefield, Middlesex was used to identify the borings as those of a terebelloid worm, *Terebella harefieldensis*. As with jellyfish, the main body of most worms is very rarely preserved because it is all soft tissue, but the calcareous tubes secreted by other worms as protective dwellings are not at all rare. Related to this aspect of preservation potential is the time between death and burial. However brief this interval, hard parts of organisms are more likely to survive it and become buried. Even if it does become buried, soft tissue may decay away leaving no impression of its former existence in the sediment.

The length of the interval between death and burial and what happens during this interval is related to where organisms live. Those living in areas actively undergoing erosion are much less likely to be preserved than those living in areas where sediment is accumulating. This may be independent of the presence or absence of hard parts. For example, limpets and periwinkles, which are so common on our rocky shores, have thick and heavy shells which resist the battering they receive from the waves. Nevertheless they are relatively rare as fossils because after death they are subject to the same erosive action of the waves for a relatively long period and even their massive shells succumb and are destroyed. On the other hand, infaunal organisms, like bivalves, are already buried in life and when they die may well remain within the sediment in their life position without any further disturbance. As we have seen many surface and internal traces can only be preserved in quiet areas where sediment is accumulating without disturbance. Clearly infaunal organisms living in areas of deposition have a much greater preservation potential than epifaunal organisms living in areas of erosion. Since land areas are constantly undergoing active erosion and freshwater habitats like lakes are geologically temporary sites of deposition, we can generalize that land and freshwater organisms have a lower preservation potential than most marine organisms.

Original relative abundance plays some part in preservation potential. Obviously if an animal is exceedingly rare it is less likely to be preserved than one that is abundant. Sooner or later an individual of an abundant species will find its way somehow to a site of preservation. If we consider modes of feeding we can see that this may introduce a bias into the fossil record. Ecologists (people who study the relationships of organisms to each other and to their environments) sometimes construct food chains with the primary producers (plants) at the base of a pyramid, herbivorous animals in the middle and major predators at the apex of the pyramid. The idea is most simply illustrated using familiar terrestrial animals. If a lion needs to kill at least once a week and its prey needs an acre of grazing land, then just over fifty acres can support at most one lion, fifty deer and millions of grass plants. If the scarcity of lions is such that their preservation potential becomes virtually zero, then they, and other major predators, which are clearly the rarest animals in any ecosystem, may never become fossils. Turning to the fossil record of marine animals we find that it is inevitably biased in favour of filter-feeders, because they lie near the bottom of the food chain pyramid, and against major predators like fish, cephalopod molluscs and mammals, because they are near the top. Any reconstruction of past communities must take this sort of bias into account.

PRESERVATION HISTORY – HOW LIVING THINGS BECOME FOSSIL

The preservation history of any fossil generally has two parts, pre- and post-burial. Pre-burial history includes all the things which befall the organism between death and burial such as transport, erosion, disintegration, attachment of epifauna, destruction by boring organisms, and so on. Post-burial history includes reworking, disturbance by burrowing organisms, diagenetic changes like the solution or replacement of the original skeletal material and compaction, as well as distortion by earth movements. Different aspects of the preservation history may be of interest to different specialists. A limestone petrographer may be more interested in the diagenetic history, while a palaeoecologist will need to know the pre-burial history in detail. Indeed for many geological purposes knowledge of the interval between death and burial is vital. Interpretations of past climates, temperatures, environments or communities are all dependent to a greater or lesser degree upon an understanding of how closely the preserved fossil is to its original living environment. On the other hand, for correlation purposes fossils which are widely dispersed, during life or after death, are the most useful. Many studies of preservation history have attempted to find out if a fossil is *in situ* and, if not, to estimate how far it has moved since death. The reasons for this are obvious. If a fossil is *in situ*, we can use evidence from the enclosing sediments as well as associated *in situ* fossils to build up a picture of its living environment. If it is not *in situ*, but we can estimate the amount of transport, then evidence from sediment and so on may still be helpful. Some groups of fossils, particularly those with many skeletal parts, lend themselves to such analyses. A couple of examples will suffice.

Bivalve molluscs pass through a series of stages of disintegration between death and destruction which are relatively easy to recognize in fossil associations. When *in situ* they will be preserved with both valves (shells) articulated and in life position. Alternatively the valves may gape slightly and the shell not be in life position, indicating exhumation but little transport or possibly just disturbance by infaunal organisms or scavengers. At a later stage of decay the valves will gape more widely, opening to 180° when the ligament is rotten. This can only happen when the valves are lying on the surface as the sediment will resist any movement of buried valves. We may therefore expect attachment of epifauna or attack by boring organisms. The distribution of epifauna or borings over the shell often reveals its orientation on the sea floor and its gradual burial by accumulating sediment. In areas of strong currents the shell may be moved more or less continually, preventing the attachment of epifauna and borers but abrading the surface.

Soon the ligament will rot completely and the two valves, once separate, may have different hydrodynamic properties. Counts of right and left valves in fossil assemblages often reveal ratios which deviate markedly from the original 1:1. Individual valves may also show a preferred orientation due to currents. Further transport will eventually damage the individual valves and result in the formation of shell chips. Finally these chips may become so small as to be eaten by a deposit feeder or to dissolve away completely. A similar course of events befalls brachiopods, which also have two valves, and any palaeoecologist who comes across fossil assemblances rich in either group will automatically start assessing where this process of disintegration was stopped by the final burial of the fossils.

Complete crinoids with arms, cup and stem all preserved are relatively rare fossils, but stem fragments certainly are not. Even if only stem fragments are preserved one can still use them to estimate the degree of disturbance of past environments. The crinoid columns, as the stems are often called, are made of a whole series of washer-shaped discs, called columnals, which in life are held together by ligaments. In Palaeozoic limestones they are often so abundant as to constitute most of the rock. Columns may be preserved as long continuous segments made of several tens or hundreds of columnals. In such cases very little decay of the ligaments could have occurred between death and burial. Long sections of columns may show preferred orientation, as they do in the Carboniferous Limestone at Halkyn Mountain, Clwyd, where 'T' and 'V' orientations (figure 17) give a clue to current directions. Alternatively very few, short, articulated sections of column may survive, indicating that almost all

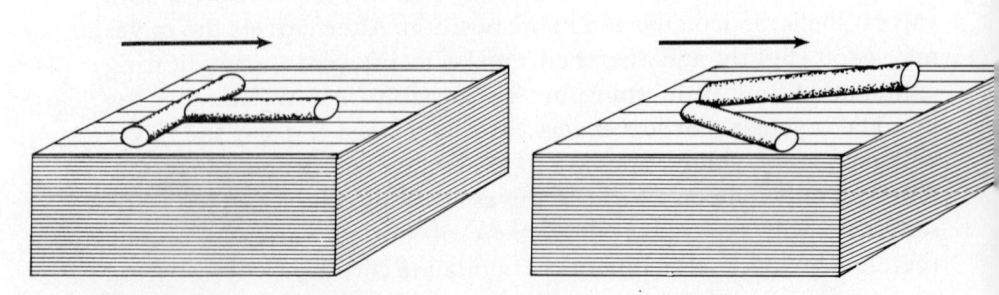

17. 'T' and 'V' orientations of cylindrical fossils which indicate current directions. In both cases if the currents flowed in the opposite direction the shells would tend to roll apart.

the ligamental material decayed before burial. Finally the individual columnals may separate and some of these may be abraded and broken so that only small pieces remain. Where crinoid stems are still *in situ* one would expect to find root and attachment structures associated with them, but not necessarily the cups which may have floated or drifted away on separation from the stem.

If more or less complete echinoderms are preserved, the order of disintegration can sometimes be deduced from the frequency with which structures are still preserved. In the Tremadoc cystoid, *Macrocystella*, the membrane over the anal opening (periproct) ruptured first and its plates were lost. The next part to separate was the distal stem, followed by the brachioles (feeding organs) and lastly the proximal stem. After that the individual plates of the cup and stem disarticulated. All stages of this process can be seen in material from the Shineton Shales in Salop. Thus again we may trace a series of stages from complete animals to isolated broken fragments and use these to estimate the time interval and distance travelled between death and burial. Where preferred orientations indicate current directions, we may even infer the direction of travel.

Ultimately, as a final step in unravelling preservation history, we may be able to infer the cause of death. Shells bored by predatory gastropods indicate the cause of their makers' demise. An ammonite bitten by a mosasaur, a large extinct marine lizard, has been recorded and we know that the mosasaur took eighteen bites before leaving this shell to sink to the sea bottom. Damage to echinoderm tests during life does not cause breakage along the sutures between the plates or along calcite cleavage planes and can thus be distinguished from *post mortem* disintegration or post-diagenetic collection damage. In fossil crinoid columns for example, cleavage planes indicate recent collection damage; separation of undamaged columnals along their articulation surfaces indicates *post mortem* rotting of ligaments; and irregular breaks indicate damage in life or at death.

Clearly there are numerous ways to detect transport of fossils between death and burial and even to estimate the amount of disturbance. This is important because if we can detect fossils that are *in situ* we may learn a great deal more about their living environment from the sediments in which they are buried.

Chapter 2

Evidence from sediments

Rocks are broadly classified into three main groups: igneous rocks which are formed by the cooling and crystallization of molten rock material called magma; metamorphic rocks which have been so altered by heat and pressure as to become recognizably new rocks, but not to the extent that they melt and form a new magma; and sedimentary rocks which are derived from pre-existing rocks by weathering and erosion. Since most fossils occur in sedimentary rocks we need only concern ourselves with the last group.

Weathering goes on all over the world as soon as rocks are exposed at, or near, the surface. It is the mechanical and chemical breakdown of rocks into smaller particles that affects pre-existing sedimentary rocks as much as igneous and metamorphic rocks. The products of weathering are solutions and insoluble residues. The solutions tend to accumulate in the oceans, causing the saltiness of sea water, and ultimately may form chemical sedimentary rocks (evaporites) in areas of high evaporation. Since the brines from which evaporites precipitate are usually too concentrated to support any life forms – the Dead Sea is a well-known example – fossils are rarely found in chemical sedimentary rocks. The insoluble residues are also carried down to the sea as the mud, silt and sand in rivers and form clastic sediments. Other sediments are largely or entirely composed of organic remains so that we call them organic sediments. In time chemical, clastic and organic sediments will become solid rock, but we need consider only the latter two types.

Lithification (changing sediments to rocks) is achieved by diagenetic processes which affect sediments as much as fossils, producing similar changes. Diagenesis may involve no more than the addition of a cement, usually calcite or silica, which binds the loose sedimentary particles together to form a solid rock. Equally, it may form new structures, like concretions, or even totally alter the composition of a rock, as happens when a limestone is changed to dolomite, a process which may destroy all trace of fossils and original sedimentary structures within the rock. We need to understand the diagenetic history of sedimentary rocks in just the same way that we need to understand the preservation history of fossils and for the same reasons.

No universally accepted classification of sedimentary rocks exists. Clastic sediments include gravels, sands, silts and clays. The most important organic rocks are limestones and coal. They will be dealt with separately, but in all cases the composition, textures and structures of the rock must be considered. Everything that can be deduced about the origin of a sedimentary rock is covered by the term provenance. Since most sediments do not accumulate at the sites of weathering and erosion, their particles must have undergone some transport and they finally settle out in a depositional environment. As a broad generalization, the composition of a sedimentary rock reveals information about its provenance; the textures about the degree and medium of transport; and the structures about the depositional environment. Since those fossils which are not *in situ* (the vast majority) are likely to have been transported along with the other sedimentary particles, we need to consider how to find out about the provenance and transport of sediments as well as the nature of the final depositional environment. This chapter deals with the information that the composition, textures and structures of sedimentary rocks reveal about their origin and formation and how this information can be used to reconstruct the original life habitat of fossils.

Probably the two most important aspects of the provenance of a clastic sediment are the geology of the source area and its climate. The source area of present-day sediments in the Thames Estuary is the entire drainage basin of the Thames, including all the Jurassic, Cretaceous and Tertiary rocks between the source north of Cirencester and the estuary. Not surprisingly many former deposits of the Thames consist of flint gravels derived from the chalk, flint being one of the most resistant rock types in the entire Thames drainage basin; and therein lies the key to discovering the geology of the source area of any sediment. Even if we could no longer trace the course of the Thames, we would know that it drained a chalk area because of the derived flint gravels. With gravels the method is simple. You collect a large representative sample of pebbles, identify the different types and record their relative abundances. The different types of pebbles indicate which rock types were exposed in the source area and their relative abundance is a crude measure of the exposed area of each rock type. For example, the Lower Triassic Budleigh Salterton Pebble Bed in Devon contains abundant pebbles of an Ordovician quartzite which still outcrops in Brittany. It also contains very rare pebbles of Dartmoor Granite, indicating that this Permian igneous intrusion had already been exposed to erosion in Lower Triassic times. The sources of the Budleigh Salterton Pebble Bed seem to have been to the south-west and west, and included a larger area of Ordovician quartzite than of Dartmoor Granite. Clearly the ability of rocks to resist erosion will also affect their abundance in a gravel. Soft rocks like clay and chalk will not last long, while flint, quartzite and granite will be much more durable. This too can be helpful because pebbles of soft rocks cannot have travelled far. If chalk or limestone pebbles are found in a gravel, their source outcrops must have been close by.

With sands the method is more difficult because most sand particles are quartz and could have come from sedimentary (sandstone), igneous (granite) or metamorphic (acid gneisses) rocks. However a small proportion, often less than one per cent, of all sands is composed of other rare resistant minerals such as zircon, garnet, rutile and tourmaline. Fortunately these minerals are all more dense than quartz and can easily be separated from it by immersing the whole sample in a suitably dense liquid, like bromoform. The quartz floats, while the small heavy mineral fraction, as it is called, sinks and can be collected. Once the heavy minerals have been separated in this way, the procedure is more or less the same as for gravels. Some minerals are characteristic of only one type of rock. Kyanite, staurolite and sillimanite, for example, are all metamorphic minerals and their presence usually indicates metamorphic rocks in the source area. Other minerals, like garnet, may occur in both igneous and metamorphic rocks and, of course, all metamorphic and igneous minerals may be deposited in one sedimentary rock which may itself become subjected to a second cycle of erosion. We must examine the whole suite of minerals to see if it includes typical igneous or metamorphic assemblages and particularly look for wear and weathering which indicate that minerals have already been through at least one cycle of erosion and deposition and hence that the source area included sedimentary rocks as well. The suites of heavy minerals in different sandstones will vary according to their source areas. Even within the same sandstone different source areas may be recognized on their heavy mineral suites. The Cretaceous Wealden Sandstone of southern England, for example, appears to have had three main source areas, one to the west, one to the north-west and one to the north-east, each representing major river drainage basins.

Examining the composition of a gravel or the heavy minerals of a sand not only reveals what rock types were exposed in the source area, but may also tell us where the source area lay, if the source rocks are still recognizable, and approximately how much of each rock type was exposed. The state of weathering of the constituent particles may reveal something of the climate of the area as well.

Mechanical weathering, the physical breakdown of rocks, is usually distinguished from chemical weathering where changes of chemical composition are involved. Both are substantially influenced by the prevailing climate but in different ways. One of the most important agents of mechanical weathering is 'frost wedging'. Water percolates into small cracks in the rock and expands when it freezes, opening the crack a little further, so that when the ice thaws again a larger amount of water will seep in. Repetition of freezing and thawing will eventually split the rock. Angular blocks of rock are split from cliffs and accumulate at the foot as scree or talus slopes. One might expect that frost wedging would be most effective under conditions where freezing took place at night and thawing during the day. Such conditions occur regularly on mountains in Britain, but there are no actively accumulating scree slopes in this country. Quite likely the severity of a night frost is insufficient to penetrate deep into rocks. Alternatively it may be that under conditions of prolonged severe frost ice crystals actually grow within the cracks. Either way, the large scree slopes of British mountains are relics of the Pleistocene glaciations when the climate was much colder than it is now. Frost wedging is characteristic of arctic or montane climates.

Chemical weathering involves reactions such as hydration, oxydation, carbonation, the addition of water, oxygen and carbon dioxide, respectively, as well as the chemical solution of rocks. An increase in temperature of $10°C$ roughly doubles the rate of any chemical reaction. Clearly between polar and tropical climates and between summer and winter there will be significant changes in the rate of chemical weathering. Since hydration is a significant part, it follows that chemical weathering proceeds most rapidly in hot, wet (tropical) climates, less rapidly in arid areas, and slowest of all in cold dry climates. When chemical weathering proceeds to completion only the most insoluble and unreactive constituents of rocks, aluminium and iron oxides remain and they give rise to the bauxite (aluminium oxide) and laterite deposits of tropical regions. In the production of most clastic sediments, chemical weathering is arrested by deposition and burial long before completion and the maturity of sediments is a measure of how far it had proceeded. Immature sands contain angular chips of rock and fresh minerals including felspars and micas as well as the ubiquitous quartz. Mature sands on the other hand contain quartz almost exclusively, as well rounded sand grains.

Thus we can conclude that mechanical weathering predominates over chemical weathering in cold and perhaps arid climates, while the reverse is the case in wet tropical climates. However climate has another indirect effect on rates of weathering because of its control over vegetation cover. In areas of dense vegetation, forest for example, the plants protect the soil and underlying rocks from erosion. They also add humus to the soil which acidifies rain water. So while good vegetation cover retards mechanical weathering, it actively aids chemical weathering not only by the leaching action of roots and 'humic' acids, but also by reducing the rate of erosion, thereby exposing the rock particles to chemical attack for a longer period. In areas with virtually no vegetation (deserts, high altitudes and high latitudes) there is nothing to retard run-off of surface water, and the erosive action of flash floods in deserts, or spring melts in glacial and montane areas, is immense. In such areas the cycle of erosion, transport and deposition is rapid, and very immature sediments result. Maturity is one aspect of a sediment's composition. It reveals information about the climate of the source area and possibly the depositional environment as well. Arkoses, for example, are immature sandstones containing common felspars, and usually indicate desert environments because felspars are particularly susceptible to hydration. Arkoses are unlikely to have been deposited in permanent bodies of water, even seas adjacent to deserts like the present-day Red Sea, because the felspars would decay in the sea water. Immature sediments, like arkoses, suggest conditions involving little transport and rapid burial. Textures reveal even more about the transport of sediments.

Sedimentary rock textures relate to the individual particles of a sediment and include the size, shape, orientation and surface features of the grains, all of which may be modified significantly and characteristically during transport. Sediment particles may be moved by water (in rivers or the sea), wind and ice, each of which imparts characteristic textures to the resulting sediment. Size is

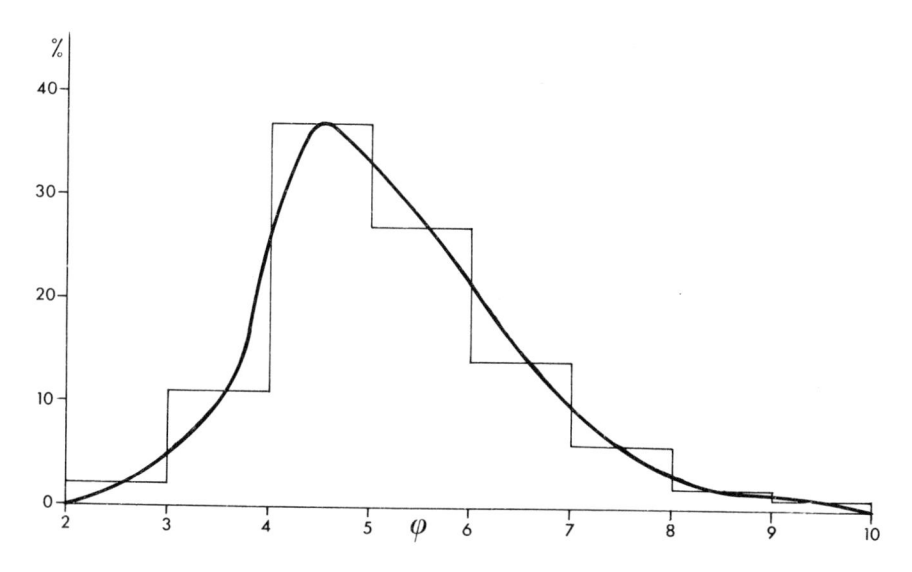

18. A histogram for loess, a wind-blown deposit. Note that the largest particles are less than ¼ mm. diameter (2 phi) and that there is a long 'tail' of 'fines', characteristic of wind-blown deposits. (Redrawn with permission from W. C. Krumbien and L. L. Sloss, *Stratigraphy and sedimentation*, 2nd edn, 1963, p. 98, W. H. Freeman & Co., San Francisco, USA.)

perhaps the simplest textural feature with which to begin. We are not only concerned with the sizes of individual particles, but the whole range of particle size within the sediment, a property known as the sorting. Poorly sorted sediments have a wide range of particle size; well-sorted sediments a narrow range. Different techniques are used to investigate sorting, depending on the size range involved. For large particles like pebbles direct measurement is feasible; usually length, width and breadth are measured on each pebble for a representative sample. For finer sediments like sands, special sieves with graded meshes are used, while silts and clays are allowed to settle in water. The sediment is thoroughly stirred up in water and its density measured with a hydrometer. As the sediment settles out, largest particles first, the density of the fluid decreases and is measured at intervals. A simple formula allows conversion of density measurements and settling times to particle sizes. The process of investigating the sorting of a sediment is called mechanical analysis and the results are usually expressed graphically as a histogram (figure 18). Earlier this century a sedimentologist called Wentworth tried to get a consensus of opinion on the use of terms such as 'sand

WENTWORTH SCALE

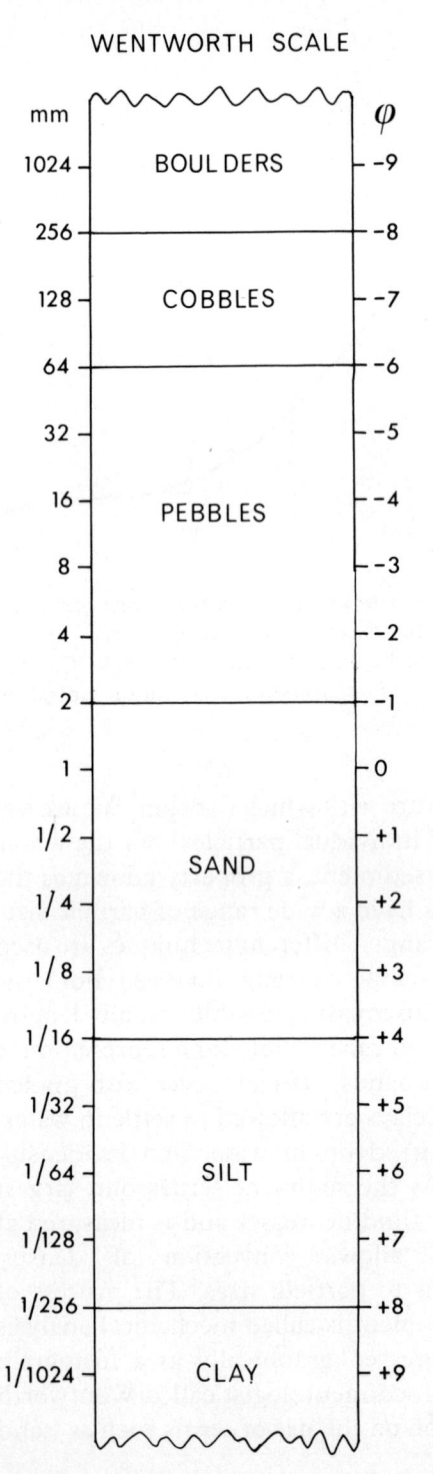

mm		φ
1024	BOULDERS	−9
256		−8
128	COBBLES	−7
64		−6
32		−5
16	PEBBLES	−4
8		−3
4		−2
2		−1
1		0
1/2		+1
1/4	SAND	+2
1/8		+3
1/16		+4
1/32		+5
1/64	SILT	+6
1/128		+7
1/256		+8
1/1024	CLAY	+9

19. Wentworth's scale of sediment-particle size with mm. and phi scales. Note that on an arithmetic scale in mm., all sand, silt and clay would lie in the first two units, while at least 256 units would be required to include the smallest boulder. (Redrawn with permission from W. C. Krumbien and L. L. Sloss, *Stratigraphy and sedimentation*, 2nd edn, 1963, p. 98, W. H. Freeman & Co., San Francisco, USA.)

grain', 'pebble' and 'boulder',[1] and the results are now known as Wentworth's Scale (figure 19). With the possible exception of 'granules' (2–4 mm.), all Wentworth's divisions are now widely accepted. Note that the size divisions in Wentworth's scale are logarithmic not arithmetical, i.e. they double or halve rather than increasing or decreasing by a fixed amount. This is largely for convenience: the arithmetical scale necessary to illustrate the smallest boulder would need at least 256-mm. divisions and yet would include all silt, sand and clay in the first two such divisions.

The transporting medium, water, wind or ice, affects sorting and the total size range. Wind can whip up good sandstorms but barely rolls granules and never moves anything larger. Furthermore, fine silt and clay-grade particles are carried up in suspension in dust storms, but sand grains bounce along, a method of transport known as saltation, and rarely rise more than 1 m. above the surface. Wind very effectively separates (sorts) different-sized particles, leaving large grains unmoved to form lag gravels, accumulating sands in dunes and carrying silt and clay away in dust storms. The dust eventually settles out with rain and forms characteristic deposits called loess. Wind-transported sediments, loess and dune sands, are exceedingly well sorted (figures 18 and 20). Water has a similar

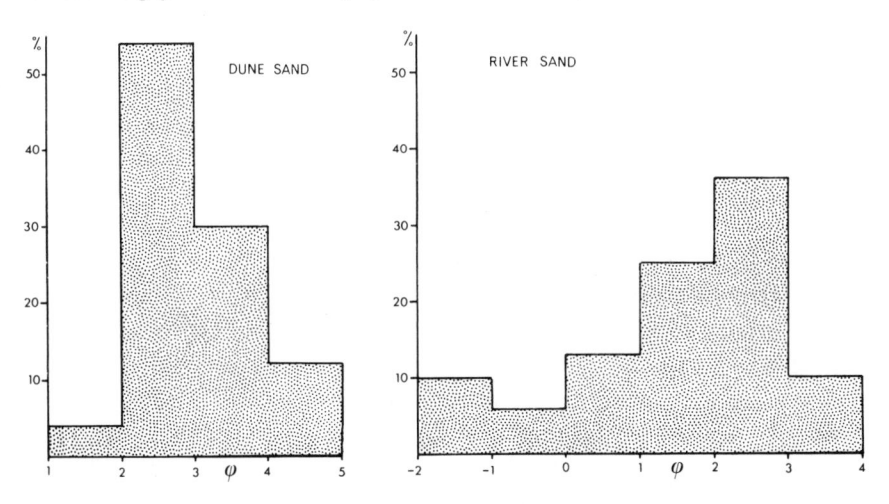

20 and 21. Mechanical analysis histograms of dune sand and river sand. Note that the dune sand is better sorted since it spreads over only 4 phi units. The river sand not only spreads over 6 phi units, but has two peaks. This is typical of river sands and especially gravels. (Redrawn with permission from W. C. Krumbien and L. L. Sloss, *Stratigraphy and sedimentation*, 2nd edn, 1963, p. 98, W. H. Freeman & Co., San Francisco, USA.)

sorting effect, but is able to move much larger particles including boulders. On beaches where the waves wash back and forth continually, the sorting action of water operates very efficiently and beach sands and gravels are as well sorted as dune sands. In rivers a phenomenon called 'bypassing' occurs where fine particles are carried past the larger stationary ones. Often some fine particles become trapped in the spaces between the larger particles, and river gravels typically have sand between the pebbles. As a result river deposits usually have a bimodal distribution of sizes (i.e. two peaks on the histogram, figure 21). Finally ice is immensely viscous compared with wind and water and will move anything in its path from clay to small hills. Ice has virtually no sorting action whatsoever. Ice-deposited sediments are always poorly sorted, a factor which led early geologists to christen many glacial deposits 'boulder clay' since they contained both boulders and clay particles.

The transporting medium has further effects on sediment particles. During transport by wind and water, particles impact on each other and the sharp corners or edges tend to be worn away. Particles may also become more spherical, but not always. During transport by ice however, particles are ground against each other and they tend to split or chip, producing fresh sharp edges. Grains which have undergone a great deal of transport by water or wind are likely to be highly rounded; those which have undergone little or no transport, such as screes, or were transported by ice, tend to be highly angular. The degree of transport need not necessarily relate to the total distance between source area and site of deposition, for example beach sediments may travel millions of miles up and down the beach by wave action without any movement along the beach away from the source. In river deposits however, roundness is broadly correlated with distance from source.

Sphericity is a measure of how closely a particle approaches the shape of a sphere. With an ideal homogeneous rock, particles may become almost spherical as some flint pebbles do. If, however, the rock has a preferential tendency to split, as slate does, a spherical shape is never even approached and slate pebbles are always tabular. Sphericity is thus not as closely related to transport distance as roundness is; however, non-spherical particles are useful in orientation studies. When ice transports sediments it tends to align the long axes of pebbles parallel to the direction of travel and this has long been used by glaciologists to study the detailed directions of ice movement. Similarly beach pebbles tend to become imbricated, overlapping like tiles on a roof, with those higher on the beach overlapping the ones below. Rod-shaped particles may be aligned parallel or perpendicular to the current direction and we have already seen that orientation of cylindrical fossils may reveal current directions. In this context the fossils are no more than non-spherical sediment grains and the same arguments can be applied to inorganic sediment particles. One final comment with regard to pebble shape. Although wind cannot move pebbles, it can and does alter their shape by the sand-blasting effect of blown sand. Such shaped pebbles, ventifacts, are good indicators of wind erosion and, if they have not been disturbed, reveal prevailing wind directions.

Recent studies using the scanning electron microscope (the SEM) have revealed that sand grains acquire surface textures characteristic of the transport medium. The crushing action of ice produces fresh conchoidal (curved) fracture surfaces all over the grains. Impacts under water or wind transport produce various cracks and pits, but since water is more viscous than air, wind transport produces distinctive impact marks. In deserts some sand grains become highly rounded and are referred to as 'millet seed grains'. This texture seems to be caused not by impact during wind transport but by repeated solution in, and evaporation of, desert dews. Minute amounts of silica dissolve preferentially from sharp corners and edges, but re-precipitation occurs in the last refuges of the evaporating dew, usually in hollows or cracks. Whatever causes this smooth surface texture and rounded grain outline, it is characteristic of desert conditions, and the occurrence of millet-seed grains in the Permo-Triassic Penrith Sandstone, for example, is used to interpret this rock as a desert deposit. Geologists have long puzzled over why the chalk seas were so free of terrigenous sediment. The presence of rare millet seed sand grains in the chalk has led to the suggestion that chalk seas were bordered by deserts and there were no streams to bring the terrigenous sediment down to the sea. Surface textures of pebbles are also useful. The characteristic 'chatter-marked' patina of flint pebbles on a beach is due to constant collisions, during wave action, which produce abundant small surface cracks. Ice-transported pebbles usually bear scratch marks while ventifacts have a polished surface texture known as desert polish.

Sedimentary textures give a good indication of the conditions of transport. Used in conjunction with the composition they reveal a great deal about the provenance of a sediment. The best interpretations rely on as wide a range of evidence as possible and sedimentary structures may help confirm ideas derived from examining composition and texture.

Structures are large-scale features of sedimentary rocks more easily studied in the field than in hand specimens. Primary sedimentary structures form *during* deposition while secondary or diagenetic structures follow deposition. Tectonic structures, like folds and faults, lie outside the scope of this discussion. The most ubiquitous and obvious sedimentary structure is bedding and, as with trace fossils, we may distinguish internal structures within beds from bedding plane structures which formed on the original sediment surface. Bedding itself is so familiar that we are apt to overlook its significance. Where there is a compositional change across a bedding plane, as when sandstone overlies limestone for example, the bedding surface marks a change in the type of sediment supplied to the site of deposition. Such a change may result from purely local circumstances such as a shift in a distributary channel of a delta, or it may indicate a regional change in the level of the land or even a worldwide change in sea level. It is only rarely possible to determine the cause of a single lithological change, but when the whole sequence of changes is considered over a wide area, plausible environmental reconstructions can be developed. Bedding planes do not always accompany lithological changes and regularly occur within the same rock type. Each bedding surface must represent a break, however slight, in the deposition of a sediment. Diagenesis may obscure some bedding surfaces and enhance others, while weathering may reveal bedding planes that are entirely hidden on fresh surfaces. It is unwise to assume that all individual beds represent a single depositional event, but many do. Rates of sedimentation vary from several metres overnight in storm deposits to perhaps 1 mm. per century or less in deep sea sediments, so that even when a bed does represent a single depositional event, its thickness may reveal little about how long it took to accumulate. Indeed many geologists regard the rock record as being composed more of gaps, represented by bedding planes, than actual rock.

Close examination of bedding surfaces may reveal evidence of prolonged time lapse between adjacent rock units. Sometimes sediments are lithified soon after deposition and form hardgrounds, or at least firmgrounds. Often encrusting organisms colonize such surfaces and borers may also penetrate them. The harder and better-cemented 'chalk rock' horizons in the Middle and Upper Chalk of western Europe represent such surfaces and are often overlain by hard chalk pebbles with encrusting oysters set in a normal chalk matrix. Sequences of colonization of hardground surfaces have been deduced with later encrusters overgrowing the early colonists and borers penetrating encrusting shells as well as the underlying hardground. Not all time breaks occur at hardground surfaces however. Channel structures which are common in delta deposits represent miniature unconformities where a period of erosion intervenes between two sets of deposits, and are revealed by the way they cut down into the underlying beds. Where the beds above and below an unconformity are parallel, it may be very difficult to detect the time gap other than by using the fossils to date the rocks above and below. In central Indiana Middle Devonian rocks overlie Middle Silurian rocks without apparent break, and the unconformity surface is no different from other bedding planes above and below. The break can only be demonstrated palaeontologically.

Bedding surface structures may tell us something of the time intervals between beds as well as revealing details of the environment. They include ripple marks, rain pits, mud cracks, flute and groove casts, and of course, the surface traces of organisms which we have already considered. Ripple marks form under gentle current action in shallow water. When the currents oscillate back and forth, as waves do, symmetrical ripples form and are generally aligned parallel to the shoreline of a shallow sea or lake. Where the back-and-forth motions are not in exactly the same direction, two sets of cross-cutting ripple marks may form, producing a diamond-shaped pattern known as interference ripples. Asymmetrical ripples form in one-way currents and the steeper face of each ripple lies down-current. When the waters become extremely shallow, as at the limit of high tide on a gently shelving sea shore, the washing of the waves may truncate the tops of the ripples, producing flat-topped ripple marks. All these features can be found in fossil ripple marks and interpreted by comparing them with modern examples. The preservation of ripple-marked surfaces, which are common sedimentary structures, is a puzzle as one would expect that the next tide would destroy them. We can be certain, however, that the interval represented by a rippled surface in a marine sediment must be at least one tidal cycle.

Rain pits form on any sandy beach during a shower and in Britain anyone who has been to the seaside for a holiday must have seen them even if they failed to notice them. Raindrops do not penetrate far into water, although rain pits can form under a centimetre or two of water. Normally they indicate exposed land surface. At least one Triassic series of dinosaur footprints records the animal walking into a shallow lake in the rain. The water's edge can be located exactly by the change from a rain-pitted surface to a ripple-marked surface with truncated ripples. The dinosaur's footprints are themselves slightly pitted on the land surface and become obscure in the water, indicating that all three features formed at the same time. The dinosaur walked into a temporary lake which then dried out, preserving the surface features before they were buried under a fresh influx of sediment. The time interval represented by this bedding surface was probably not very long. Had the sands dried out completely and been exposed for a prolonged period, one would expect them to have been blown away by the wind.

A similar time interval must be represented by most mud-cracked surfaces. Clay minerals, the major constituents of clays, absorb water and swell when wet. Conversely they shrink as they dry out. When layers of wet mud are deposited and then exposed they dry and crack into polygonal patterns and the edges of the polygons often curl up slightly. Fossil mud cracks are very common sedimentary structures and indicate shallow water and intermittent desiccation.

Flute and groove casts are less familiar structures than ripple marks and mud cracks. If sediment is stirred up by an earthquake or spring flood it produces a more dense mass of turbid water which will flow down any slope on the floor of the sea or lake. Such turbidity currents often scour the underlying sediment surface as they pass, producing a variety of asymmetrical scallopings (flutes) or grooves caused by particles dragging past. When the turbidity current stops flowing sediment settles out and fills the flutes and grooves. Since the surface layers of the underlying bed are often clay, after lithification they flake off; we usually examine the underside of the overlying turbidite bed, which reveals casts of the original flutes and grooves. Care is required in interpretation, but flute and groove casts may be used to determine the direction of the current which in turn reveals the original palaeoslope of the depositional basin.

Turbidite deposits also produce a characteristic internal structure called graded bedding (figure 22). While the current is flowing, sedimentary particles are kept in suspension by the turbidity, but when the current reaches the bottom of the basin and stops moving the particles settle out with the coarsest being deposited first. An individual graded bed shows a sharp contact with the unit below, and coarse grains at the base gradually becoming finer-grained upwards. In a series of turbidites the base of each bed is defined by a sharp

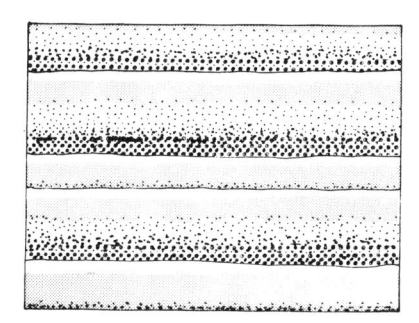

22. Graded bedding. Note the abrupt change from fine to coarse at the base of each unit, but the gradual change from coarse to fine upwards through each unit.

change from fine-grained sediment below to coarse-grained sediment above with a gradual change from coarse to fine within each unit. Each individual graded unit represents deposition from a single turbidity current. The unit may have been deposited in a few hours at most; the time interval between units could be anything up to decades or even hundreds of years. Graded bedding and flute and groove casts usually occur together and indicate relatively deep water deposition. Turbidites are also poorly sorted, have angular grains and are immature sediments.

Another internal structure is cross bedding (figure 23) in which within a single bed there are numerous cross beds lying at an angle to the main bedding. Cross bedding comes in a variety of forms, but all indicate current action – it is sometimes called current bedding – and the currents always flowed down the slope of the cross beds. Cross beds form in a delta front where topset, foreset and bottomset beds can be distinguished (figure 23A). Flooding often erodes the topset beds, and the resulting truncation of the foreset beds above is useful in recognizing the 'way up' of overturned sedimentary rocks. Cross bedding also occurs when dunes migrate (figure 23B). Sand is blown or washed (migrating dunes also occur under water) up the long slope and tumbles down the lee slope when the stable angle is exceeded. This produces planar cross beds which can be distinguished from the slightly curved cross beds of delta deposits. In rivers cross beds form which are curved or trough-shaped, with their surfaces sloping in from the channel sides as well as downstream (figure 23C). Other types of cross bedding are also known. Suffice it to say here that different types of cross beds can be used to recognize specific environments, and that all cross beds indicate local current directions

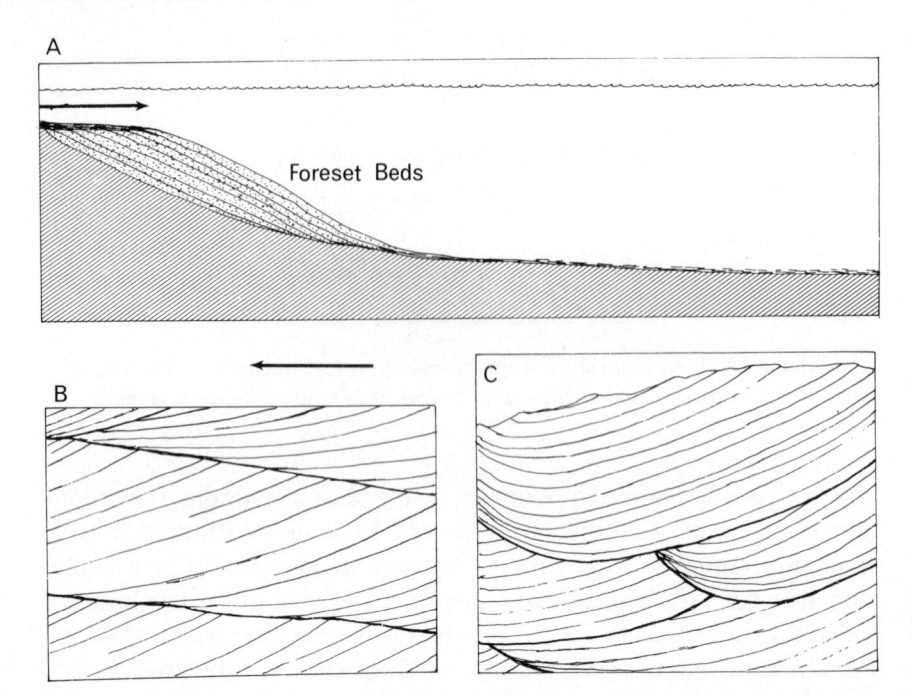

23. Cross bedding. A. As formed in a delta with current direction indicated. B. A cross-section through cross bedding to show inferred current direction. C. A transverse section through trough cross beds of a river deposit. In this case the current was flowing towards the observer.

at the time of deposition. Since currents fluctuate and rivers meander, when reconstructing palaeocurrent directions from cross beds, it is best to use as many examples as possible.

Secondary structures form after deposition and are generally less useful in environmental interpretations than primary structures. Nevertheless some form so soon after deposition that they can be relevant for our purposes. Without some diagenetic structures like concretions, the fossil record would be much poorer.

A variety of structures arises from the compaction and de-watering of freshly deposited sediments. Clays in particular hold large amounts of water when first deposited, as much as 70 per cent by volume, and the weight of overlying sediments gradually squeezes this out. When clays are overlain by sands the upper layer may sink down into the clay because it cannot support the weight of the overlying sand. After lithification the clay will flake off, revealing a very irregular lower surface to the overlying sandstone. These casts of the clay surface are called load casts and generally show no preferred orientation, unlike flute and groove casts. Because all of these structures are best seen on the under surface of overlying beds, they are collectively known as sole structures. If the de-watering continues rapidly, small springs may burst through the overlying sediments producing sand volcanoes.

On the continental slope, or any other sloping depositional surface, sediments impregnated with water may become unstable and slump downslope. Slump structures are not at all uncommon in sedimentary rocks and can be distinguished from tectonic folds by their irregularity and because they only effect the slumped horizon, not the beds above or, more importantly, below. If the slumping continues rapidly downslope, mixing occurs and a turbidity current results. Earthquake shocks, which often initiate slumping and turbidity currents, may also cause small-scale faulting in sediments, and an excellent example occurs in Ordovician mudstones on the foreshore north of Girvan, in Scotland. Again these can be recognized as original because they are local in occurrence and do not affect the beds below. When lightning strikes the ground it generates tremendous heat. In sand dunes it fuses the sand together into a tubular structure with a star-shaped cross-section. Unlikely though it may seem, fossil examples of lightning strikes are known in the New Red Sandstone of the Isle of Arran.

Early diagenesis may produce new structures of which concretions are the most common. We do not yet understand all the processes involved in the formation of concretions. In the simplest case a concretion is the local cementation of a sand or clay into a solid lump. Possibly the whole bed was not cemented because there was insufficient cement, but equally it may well be that the conditions which caused the deposition of cement were only locally present within the bed. In either case, we do not know why concretions form exactly where they do. Some occur in layers parallel to bedding; others are scattered irregularly through the rock. Some are almost perfectly spherical, suggesting equal growth in all directions out from a centre, while others are all sorts of irregular shapes. Some, but by no means all, concretions in clays contain cracks or partitions (septaria) inside, which seem to represent shrinkage cracks. The septaria are widest in the centre of the concretion and narrow to nothing towards the outside so that the external surface is usually entire and they are only revealed as septarian nodules when split open. Shrinkage must have been maximum in the centre and least at the outside surface, but we do not know why, nor do we know why some concretions are, and some are not, septarian. The septaria are often lined with secondary diagenetic minerals, calcite being the most common. Finally some concretions, like the flint nodules in chalk, involve a total change in chemical composition. Flint is almost pure silica; chalk almost pure calcium carbonate. Flint occurs in nodular bands parallel to bedding, as scattered nodules of any shape, as laminae which follow bedding or faults, and in Norfolk large irregular tubular flints which lie perpendicular to the bedding are known as paramoudras.

It is often stated that concretions form around organic remains and that these potential fossils initiate the concretion-forming process. While this is probably true in some cases, anyone who has sought fossils in concretions will know that most are barren. Even when fossils are only found in concretions and nowhere else within a formation, we do not know that this reflects their original distribution. Fossils, like the wood mentioned in chapter 1, which are well preserved within a concretion but no trace of which remains outside, clearly indicate that concretions may preserve fossils from later diagenetic changes which would otherwise destroy them. When fossils are confined to concretions it could simply be because those outside have not been preserved. This is certainly the case with the Essex fauna in the coal measures of northern Illinois. Here traces of soft tissue, which would undoubtedly otherwise have been destroyed, are preserved in concretions, but this does not necessarily imply that the fossils had anything to do with the formation of the concretions. The presence of such well-preserved fossils within concretions gives a clue as to the time of formation of the concretions. At least the initiation of the Essex fauna concretions must have occurred before the soft tissue of the organisms had completely decayed away, and hence very soon after deposition. In most clays concretions form before compaction since fossils within them are not crushed while those outside are. Similarly concretions which have been eroded from the banks are found in the bottoms of channels indicating that they formed before the channelling occurred.

Sedimentary structures of all types may be useful in reconstructing past environments of deposition. They may indicate water depth (graded bedding, ripple marks), current directions (flute casts, cross bedding), periodic exposure (mud cracks) or land surfaces (rain pits), and so on. Bear in mind, however, that they reflect conditions at the moment of deposition or soon after. As a result, taken alone, they may be misleading. The Permo-Triassic or New Red Sandstone in Britain is accepted as a desert deposit and this is undoubtedly correct. In the

Wirral, and probably elsewhere, most sedimentary structures in the New Red Sandstone indicate deposition by flowing water. The most obvious structure is cross bedding, but others include mud-flake conglomerates, armoured mudballs and slump structures. Wherever cross bedding is well exposed, as on the shore off Red Rocks, Hoylake, we see trough cross bedding which is characteristic of deposition by water flowing in channels. The mud-flake conglomerates contain flakes much too large to have been moved by wind and they usually form when rapidly flowing water breaks up mud cracks. Armoured mudballs develop when lumps of wet clay are rolled by water and pick up any solid object they touch until they are covered with sand and pebbles, while the slump structures indicate sands saturated with water. Clearly there was a lot of water around when the New Red Sandstone was deposited. The answer to this anomaly lies in the fact that deserts are not entirely devoid of water and that tremendous amounts of erosion, transport and deposition occur during the rare flash floods that follow a rainfall. Most of the structures we see were imparted to the sediments during these infrequent floods. The armoured mudballs and mud-flake conglomerates are perhaps the key to this environmental interpretation. Mud-flakes and clay balls break down very quickly if agitated in water. They cannot have travelled far or all trace of them would have long since disappeared. If we look more closely we find millet-seed sand grains coated with iron oxides which give the rock a rusty brown colour (a colour that geologists call 'red', hence the term New Red Sandstone) and other features indicative of desert conditions. Elsewhere the New Red Sandstone contains evaporites and calcretes which indicate prolonged exposure to conditions of high evaporation. There is no doubt that it is a desert deposit, but the sedimentary structures nevertheless indicate deposition by running water. This serves as a useful example of the need to consider all features of clastic rocks when making environmental interpretations.

The most important organic sedimentary rocks are limestones, and they differ in two important respects from clastic rocks. First, the major constituents are usually produced within the basin of deposition and secondly, because calcium carbonate is so soluble in water, diagenesis is much more important in carbonates than in clastics and the final rock is often more a diagenetic product than a product of the original constituents. The concepts of provenance and transport have different connotations when applied to carbonates, and limestone composition, textures and structures differ from those of clastic rocks and have different meanings. Nevertheless they may be equally useful in reconstructing the environment of deposition.

Chemically all limestones are composed of calcium carbonate, but it is the mineral rather than the bulk chemical composition which is important in both limestones and clastic sediments. Calcium carbonate of organic skeletal fragments occurs in three principal forms, the physical and chemical properties of which vary and so affect the early diagenesis of carbonate sediments. The minerals are aragonite and high and low magnesian calcite. Aragonite is always very pure calcium carbonate, is unstable at normal temperatures and pressures and much more soluble than calcite. In what is geologically a short time, thousands of years at most, aragonitic skeletal grains convert to calcite or dissolve away completely. Since the aragonite was pure originally it produces calcite of high purity. The conversion to calcite may involve no change in crystal size, each crystal originally secreted by the organism changing from aragonite to calcite. This mode of conversion preserves in great detail the fine fabric of the original organic skeleton. Alternatively much larger new crystals of calcite may grow *in situ*, so-called neomorphic spar, and often faint traces of original shell fabrics are preserved. As a third alternative, the aragonite may dissolve away entirely, leaving a void which is subsequently filled with calcite cement. In this case the cavity fill usually has a radial fibrous fabric with the crystals growing inwards from the margins of the cavity. Clearly the three modes of diagenesis preserve differing amounts of information about the original skeletal grain. Purely or partly aragonitic skeletons are secreted by molluscs (chitons, gastropods, bivalves, cephalopods and scaphopods), corals and many algae, among others.

Calcite is more stable than aragonite, but still much more reactive than the silicate minerals of clastic rocks, and is able to accommodate other elements into its lattice structure. Thus we find that organic calcite skeletons fall into two groups – low magnesian calcite where the magnesium content is generally three per cent or less, and high magnesian calcite with twelve to seventeen per cent magnesium. High magnesian calcite is the less stable of the two and loses its magnesium content early in diagenesis, reverting to almost pure calcite usually with little or no change in fabric. Low magnesian calcite skeletons may resist diagenetic changes right down to the present. High magnesian calcite occurs in all echinoderms, many algae and some foraminifera while low magnesian calcite is characteristic of brachiopods.

EVIDENCE FROM SEDIMENTS

Aragonite and high magnesian calcite that go into solution in sea water are often re-precipitated in the same form as early marine cement. Indeed these seem to be the only forms of calcium carbonate precipitated from sea water. In fresh water however, both aragonite and high magnesian calcite go into solution and all precipitation is of calcite rich in iron, ferroan calcite. Staining with various chemicals facilitates the distinction of aragonite and the various forms of calcite so that the cementation history of a limestone can be recognized in some detail.

Fabric refers to the size, shape and orientation of constituent crystals and is analogous to the texture of sedimentary rocks. At least originally, all the particles of a limestone, skeletal or otherwise, had a primary fabric of their own and this often enables us to recognize their nature in thin section. One example already quoted in chapter 1 is that of echinoderm plates which all behave as single crystals of calcite. Other groups of organisms may have lamellar, prismatic, or granular fabrics or combinations of these.

The textures of limestones may include the features described under clastic sediments: limestones, like all other rocks, are subject to weathering and erosion. The older terms 'calcirudite', 'calcarenite', 'calcisiltite' and 'calcilutite' – respectively, limestone gravel, sand, silt and clay – are then appropriate and may be interpreted in the same way as siliceous gravels, sands, and so on. However, limestones with skeletal grains are usually polymodal with respect to grain size and each mode corresponds to a different source organism, not to sorting phenomena, while equigranular limestone may result from recrystallization as a granular spar and could hardly be described as well sorted. Recently Folk[2] and Dunham[3] have suggested new classifications of limestones based on textural features. Folk suggested that all limestones consist of allochemical grains (allochems for short), which include skeletal debris and other particles that arise within the basin of sedimentation but have been transported, and orthochemical cements which were precipitated in place. The prefixes 'allo-' and 'ortho-' mean out of place and *in situ* in this context. Folk recognized four types of allochems: skeletal grains, peloids, ooids and intraclasts (figure 24). Peloids are pellet-like particles of fine-grained (micritic) carbonate which in many, but not all, cases are faecal pellets of deposit-feeding organisms. Peloids may arise in other ways however. True faecal pellets are trace fossils and indicate an abundance of deposit-feeding organisms. They are unlikely to survive prolonged transport and are hence useful in

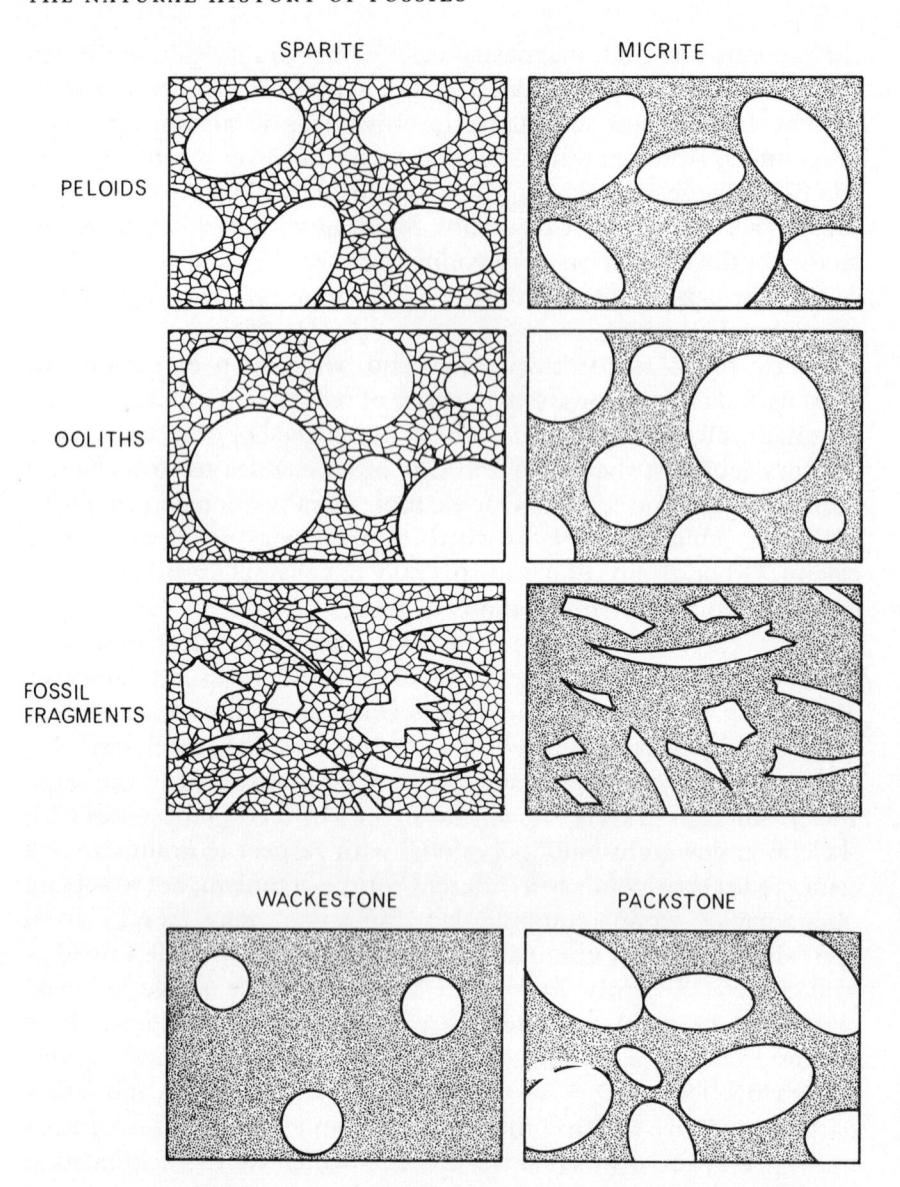

24. Sections to illustrate the Folk–Dunham classification of limestones. In Folk's classification the grains are either peloids, ooliths or fossil fragments (intraclasts are ignored here) and the matrix or cement is either sparite or micrite. Dunham emphasized the difference between matrix-supported grains in wackestones and grain-supported packstones or grainstones. Note that not all the grains will be in contact in a section through a packstone or grainstone. (Modified from R. L. Folk, *Mem. Am. Ass. petrol. Geol.*, **1**, fig. 3, p. 71, 1962.)

environmental reconstruction. Ooids are small, usually spherical, particles with a concentric layered structure around a central nucleus. They arise by precipitation of aragonite in agitated waters around the original nucleus. The grains are constantly moved by water currents so precipitation occurs on all sides – hence the concentric layering and spheroidal shape. Ooids usually originate in current-swept shallow seas, but may be deposited in other environments. Intraclasts are loose aggregations of other allochems eroded from adjacent weakly lithified sediments.

As far as cement is concerned, Folk recognized two types: very fine-grained (clay-grade) micrite and clear, coarse-grained crystals of spar. Putting the two constituents together, Folk coined new terms like 'biomicrite' for a limestone of organic skeletal grains cemented by micrite, 'oosparite' for a limestone of ooids in a spary cement, and so on. Dunham, with his use of the terms 'grainstone', 'packstone' and 'wackestone', introduced another concept which is a useful addition to Folk's classification and terminology. Not all micrites are orthochemical cements and it is often very difficult to distinguish original micrite, which was once aragonite mud, from micrite cement. Dunham distinguished grain-supported from matrix-supported sediments. In a grain-supported texture (grainstones and packstones) all the grains are in contact and represent the original material of the sediment. Any matrix (packstones) or cement (grainstones) merely fills the interstices between the grains. In a matrix-supported texture the allochems are so widely separated that they must originally have been supported by some finer-grained matrix. Micrite in a matrix-supported limestone, or wackestone, is likely to have been originally micrite. The distinction between grainstones and wackestones can also be related to conditions of deposition, with wackestones, particularly micritic ones, indicating quieter conditions. Care is necessary in the interpretation of rock slices. Grains will only be in contact at one point and a random slice will never pass through all the grain-to-grain contacts. Indeed a classical experiment was performed with an artificial 'cornflakes rock', in which the well-known breakfast cereal was cemented together. Slices through this experimental rock sometimes revealed no contacts between cornflakes but showed the extremely high original porosity of this 'sediment'. This experiment may seem rather artificial since cornflakes are particles of unusual shape, but some shell fragments, particularly those of irregular bivalves like oysters, do approach their shape. As a general rule if the particles are separated by their diameter or more it is a wackestone; if they are separated by a small fraction of their diameter it is a grainstone or packstone, while intermediate separations require careful interpretation.

Fenestral texture where large voids, or fenestrae, occur without apparent support from the matrix, is perhaps the most puzzling of limestone textures. In extreme cases large voids, often tens of centimetres across, occur in a pure micrite. The fenestrae are usually filled with spar but may be partly filled with micrite or silt-grade microspar which has a horizontal upper surface indicating a geopetal cavity fill. When the fenestra was a cavity, the micrite could not have been loose sediment or the cavity would have collapsed. Equally when the micrite was loose sediment, if it ever was, the cavity must have been filled with something or again it would have collapsed. One explanation is that the fenestrae represent spaces occupied by seaweed or other organic material which has since rotted away without trace, but not before early cementation bound the surrounding micritic muds together sufficiently to support the resulting cavity. Others have suggested the fenestrae are spaces protected by the skeletons of frond-like organisms such as bryozoans. The irregularity of the fenestrae, the absence of any trace of skeletal supports in many cases, and the fact that some micrite penetrated the cavities, all argue against these interpretations. Furthermore the spary filling frequently has a unique fabric, called radiaxial fibrous calcite, and it is difficult to see why this unique fabric should develop rather than a normal radial fibrous cavity fill. It has been suggested that radiaxial fibrous calcite represents recrystallized original marine cement, but this is by no means proven and the significance of the fabric remains obscure. Lithoherms, large mound-like structures which apparently grow *in situ* as solid rock and contain fenestrae, have recently been described from deep water in the Straits of Florida.[4] They may explain some features of fenestral texture. If the micrite was originally deposited as rock there is no problem of cavity support and the irregular shape of fenestrae may simply result from their being the last spaces not quite filled by the growing lithoherm.

As with textures, structures in limestones include some of the features of clastic sediments – coarse crinoidal limestones often show cross bedding, for example – as well as some structures unique to limestones. Broadly, limestone structures of physical origin are the same as those of clastic sediments and may be interpreted in the same way, while the unique structures are of biological origin, but there are exceptions. Biological structures include reefs, bioherms, algal laminations and stromatolites.

Organic reefs are structures which stand up above the surrounding sea floor and have a solid framework built up by living organisms. Present-day reefs are largely composed of corals and algae. Despite their reputation among sailors, they are very open structures with plenty of space within their framework. In most cases boring organisms are destroying the coral and algal skeletons as fast as they grow. Only very exceptional circumstances would preserve a reef as a skin diver sees it, the more so because the reef grows most vigorously in the most exposed situations. Complete coral heads are quite rare in demonstrable reef rocks, like the Key Largo Limestone of the Florida Keys. Even so, small coral thickets and patch reefs are known in the fossil record back to the Silurian at least. Most modern reef-building corals are hermatypic, in other words they are confined to warm shallow seas. The corals themselves are temperature-sensitive and cannot withstand more than a few days' exposure to temperatures below 18 C. Today hermatypic corals are confined to a belt between latitudes 30 N and 30 S. The tissue of the corals contains symbiotic algae, called zooxanthellae, which need light to photosynthesize like all other green plants, and this restricts the depth of water in which the corals can live. Ahermatypic corals are known and a few form reefs in deep waters, but these reefs usually contain a single species and could easily be recognized in fossil examples.

Modern corals belong to a group, the hexacorals (plate 15C), which arose in the Mesozoic. Whole reefs are often enormous structures and clearly must be preserved *in situ*. It is a reasonable assumption, supported by other lines of evidence, that Mesozoic and Tertiary coral reefs indicate clear shallow tropical seas. The Palaeozoic corals belong to two different extinct groups, the rugose and tabulate corals, and although it is unsafe to assume that they too were confined to the tropics, other quite independent palaeomagnetic evidence indicates that they were. It seems that coral reefs have always been characteristic of shallow warm seas, whichever coral groups formed the reefs.

Reefs can be formed by other organisms, including worms, octocorals, sponges, bivalves, and bryozoans, but they are usually much smaller structures than modern coral algal reefs. Fossil examples can be recognized and the principal frame builders identified. Bioherms, on the other hand, are mound-like structures which rose above the surrounding sea floor like reefs, but show no evidence of sediment-binding or frame-building organisms. The core of a bioherm is often a fenestral micrite which lacks bedding and is surrounded by flank deposits which dip off the core and in which geopetal infills indicate high original dips. In my experience bioherms are circular or oval structures with flank beds dipping off all round, and they vary in size from a few metres across to several square kilometres in area. They are the knoll reefs (or reef knolls) of the British Carboniferous Limestone, but occur throughout the Palaeozoic from the Lower Ordovician onwards. They often occur in belts on the edge of a platform or basin, as for example the Middle Silurian bioherms bordering the Michigan Basin in North America, or the Carboniferous bioherms in southern Ireland. The origin of bioherms is as puzzling as that of the fenestral texture which characterizes many of their cores. They may represent Palaeozoic lithoherms, but as far as I am aware no post-Palaeozoic examples have yet been reported.

Algae come in a variety of forms – after all, they represent several phyla of plants – and contribute to limestones in a variety of ways. Some, like *Penicillus*, secrete minute crystals of aragonite which on the death of the alga contribute to the aragonite mud of shallow tropical seas like Florida Bay. Others, like *Halimeda* have a framework of aragonite crystals which holds together after death and the platelets of this particular genus contribute to sediments as skeletal grains. Yet others, like *Lithothamnion*, secrete a hard porous rigid skeleton which rivals that of any coral for durability. These are the so-called 'coralline algae'. Many algae which never secrete any hard parts at all may produce structures in limestones simply by binding the sediment together. Limestones with very thin beds, laminae, are usually interpreted as algal laminates. Filamentous algae 'bloom' (multiply) in spring, forming dense mats coating the sediments of supra-tidal flats or lagoons. At other times of the year sediment accumulates, particularly after winter or tropical storms. The repetition of algal blooms and storm sedimentation produces a finely laminated structure in the resulting sediment. Algal mats will form under water, but in normal open-sea conditions, wave action destroys them. Algal laminates usually indicate supra-tidal or quiet lagoonal conditions.

During the late Precambrian and early Palaeozoic, mound-like laminated structures, called stromatolites, were abundant, but they become progressively rarer in younger rocks. They arose by the action of similar sediment-binding algae which formed mounds up to two metres in diameter, usually less, with a height of half a metre or more. In many Precambrian rocks they are the only evidence of life and for a long time there was disagreement about their organic origin. Recent examples have been found in Shark's Bay, Australia where the salinity of the water precludes the browsing molluscs and infaunal organisms which would otherwise destroy the mounds faster than the algae could bind them together. Presumably stromatolites were widespread and abundant in the Precambrian because there were few, if any, of the organisms which would destroy them. In Shark's Bay stromatolites occur near high tide level and their relief is related to the tidal range to which they are exposed. Fossil stromatolites not only indicate inter-tidal environments, but give an indication of the tidal range – which, incidentally, confirms that the moon was orbiting the earth in late Precambrian times. The currently accepted idea that the earth and moon have been partners in space since the formation of the solar system was seriously questioned in the years immediately prior to the collection of the first moon rocks, mainly on theoretical astronomical grounds. Stromatolites are not confined to limestones: the algae bind all sediment particles indifferently.

An interesting relationship between limestone solution structures and vegetation occurs in the Florida Keys. In shallow water off Big Pine Key nearly circular patches of *Thalassia* grass have been detected, and similarly shaped mangrove clumps occur in nearby lagoons. Investigation of these patches indicated that the plants were only growing where the recent sediment was much thicker, half a metre or more as opposed to a few centimetres in surrounding areas. The sediment had collected in solution hollows in the underlying limestone which formed when sea level was much lower during the last glaciation and the rock was exposed to subaerial erosion. Clearly the solution hollows control the distribution of the plants. However, along Islamorada Nature Trail on Matecumbe Key and elsewhere on Big Pine Key, solution hollows are forming preferentially down fossil coral heads of *Montastrea* at the present. The porous structure of the coral forms an ideal pathway for surface water. Equally clearly in this case it is the presence of fossil coral which is controlling the solution structures. It would be very interesting to know if the circular patches of *Thalassia* grass and mangrove are now growing on the sites of former coral heads.

Although there is a lot still to be understood, limestone structures, like those of clastic sediments, can be used in environmental reconstructions and are therefore relevant to the interpretation of the life habits of the fossils they contain so abundantly.

Coal, the other well-known organic rock, is composed almost entirely of organic material and represents the accumulation of vegetation in the coal forest swamps. The original vegetation is converted to coal by a process called distillation, in which the more volatile constituents like oxygen and hydrogen are driven off until only uncombined carbon remains. The rank of coal is a measure of this process, with high-rank coals like anthracite composed almost entirely of carbon. Distillation is aided by deep burial, heating and earth movements and is a subtle measure of diagenesis. In any one coal basin we find the more deeply-buried coals are of higher rank, while the same coal may increase in rank as it approaches a folded belt. In North America the products of Appalachian coalfields are generally of higher rank than those of interior basins like the Illinois Basin. Similarly in Britain the best anthracite comes from South Wales.

Coal exhibits different textures, which are related to the preservation history of the plant material. The dull parts of household coal generally represent broken-up plant debris, while the bright shiny bands are derived from woody material. Usually coal has been so compressed that little original plant structure remains, but occasionally charcoal-like pieces can be found. Coals, like other rocks, sometimes contain concretions, known as coal balls, which must have formed early in diagenesis since plant material within them is usually very well preserved and uncrushed.

Although coal has been, and still is, of considerable economic importance, for our purposes its main interest lies in the sequence of rocks within which it occurs. So far we have considered the information that can be derived from the sedimentology of individual rock types. However, sedimentary rocks occur in sequences and even subtle changes of rock type, for example from chalk to chalk rock and back again, may indicate changes in the environment of deposition. Thus we need to know how the environment was changing as we go up through the sequence. Even if a fossil was confined to one bed in a sequence, as coal plants tend to be, knowledge of what the beds above and below represent may help us interpret this fact. Fossils may be confined to a single bed because they only existed during the period of time during which the bed was being deposited. Alternatively the conditions necessary for their existence and/or preservation may have been confined to that bed. Consideration of sequences of

EVIDENCE FROM SEDIMENTS

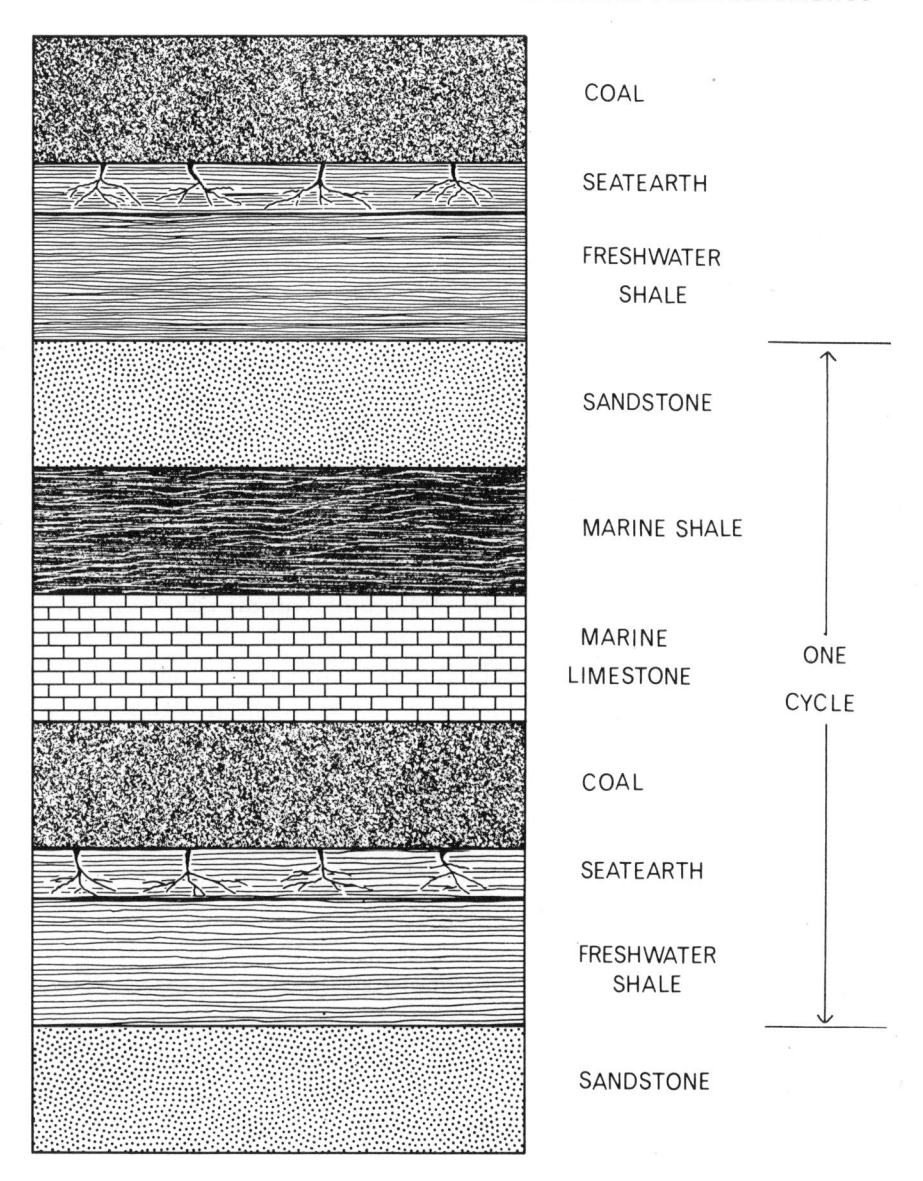

25. An idealized coal cyclothem. The cycle indicated starts with a freshwater shale which passes up into a seatearth with impressions of rootlets of the plants which formed the overlying coal. This in turn was overlain by a marine limestone, then a marine shale and finally a sandstone, before returning to the next freshwater shale at the beginning of the succeeding cycle. The cycle may be considered to begin at any level in the sequence and not all cycles are necessarily complete in a real coal measures sequence.

environments may help decide between these two alternatives and coal, which occurs in a well-defined sequence, is a useful illustration.

At first sight many rock sequences appear to be fairly random, while others show well defined rhythmic alterations or cycles. The regular repetition of muddy limestones and clays in the Lower Liass of the Dorset coast in England or of chalk and flint bands in parts of the Upper Chalk, are examples of regular alternations. Coal, on the other hand, is one unit in a regular sequence of several different rock types, and such cycles of sedimentation are called cyclothems (figure 25). The precise details may differ from place to place, and not all units of a cyclothem may be developed in every example, but the main sequence from coal through clays or limestone, deltaic sandstones, a seat earth and back to coal again, is generally recognizable.

The coal usually represents accumulation of forest debris *in situ*, and seatearths are typically penetrated by the roots of the coal forest vegetation. A very striking example of the root system of a coal forest tree is preserved in Manchester Museum. Not all coals formed in place, however; some represent accumulations of drifted plant debris in stagnant lagoons or pools. They can usually be recognized by the complete absence of any penetrating roots in the underlying rock which is likely to be a shale with freshwater bivalves, but certainly not a seatearth. Coal deposition ended when the area flooded bringing a return to marine or lagoonal conditions. So we find that the overlying clays or limestones may contain a variety of marine fossils or they may be packed with freshwater bivalves. In either case, this open-water environment was gradually invaded by an advancing delta which deposited the cross bedded sands that overlie the clays or limestones. When the delta had built up sufficiently it was colonized by coal forest vegetation. Roots penetrated the top of the delta sands to produce a seatearth, and the plant debris accumulated to form the next coal. This sort of sequence is repeated many times in our coal basins, although not all the coals are thick enough to exploit.

An obvious question is why did the cycle repeat itself? Once the coal forests became established why did they not go on growing for ever, or at least until the climate changed, making coal forest growth impossible? The answer probably lies in the concept of isostacy. We need to digress briefly to consider this idea, for it is relevant to virtually all environmental sequences, whether obviously cyclical or not. When a ship is loaded it sinks lower in the water until it has displaced enough water to compensate for the increased load. With anything floating in water, adjustment is almost instantaneous, but in a viscous liquid like treacle it would take longer. The uppermost part of the earth is called the crust and it 'floats' on the underlying mantle. Although the mantle behaves like a solid it will deform slowly under stress. It is analogous to a block of pitch, which will shatter like any other brittle solid if hit with a hammer but which will slowly flow downhill if left outside for several months or years. When part of the crust is loaded, for example by the deposition of vast thicknesses of sediment, it sinks slowly (over thousands or millions of years) to a new level. Equally, when other parts of the crust are offloaded as occurs with the erosion of high mountains, they will rise to a new level. Furthermore as the crust and mantle have an initial strength which must be overcome before any isostatic adjustment occurs, sediment may accumulate in a sedimentary basin for some time before the loading is high enough to start isostatic movements. Once the movement has started, however, it will continue until a new equilibrium is reached.

Confirmation of this theory comes from the geologically recent past. During the Pleistocene, great ice sheets, as much as ten kilometres thick, built up several times in high latitudes. During the glacial intervals, parts of the crust were loaded by these vast accumulations of ice and were offloaded again when the ice melted during the interglacial periods. The last major ice sheet began to retreat about twelve thousand years ago and the isostatic adjustment to this offloading is still going on in the areas most severely affected. In Europe isostatic uplift is greatest in Scandinavia, where the ice sheets were thickest and retreated last. The shores of the Baltic shelve so gently that slight uplift causes considerable retreat of the sea. Swedes living near the Baltic coast have been familiar with the idea that the land is rising for three or four hundred years. Perhaps the most convincing example occurs in the Great Basin of the western United States. Great Salt Lake, large though it may be, is but a small remnant of a Pleistocene lake, Lake Bonneville, which filled the entire basin during glacial periods. When fully established, Lake Bonneville eroded shorelines both in the surrounding hills and round islands within it, which can still be recognized today. Since water always 'finds its own level' this shoreline must have formed at the same elevation all round the lake, yet we now find it varying by as much as seventy metres or so, with the highest points on islands near the centre of the lake and the lowest in the most outlying bays. When the basin was full of water it sank under the load. As the water dried up the basin rose, most in the centre, least near the edges, and in

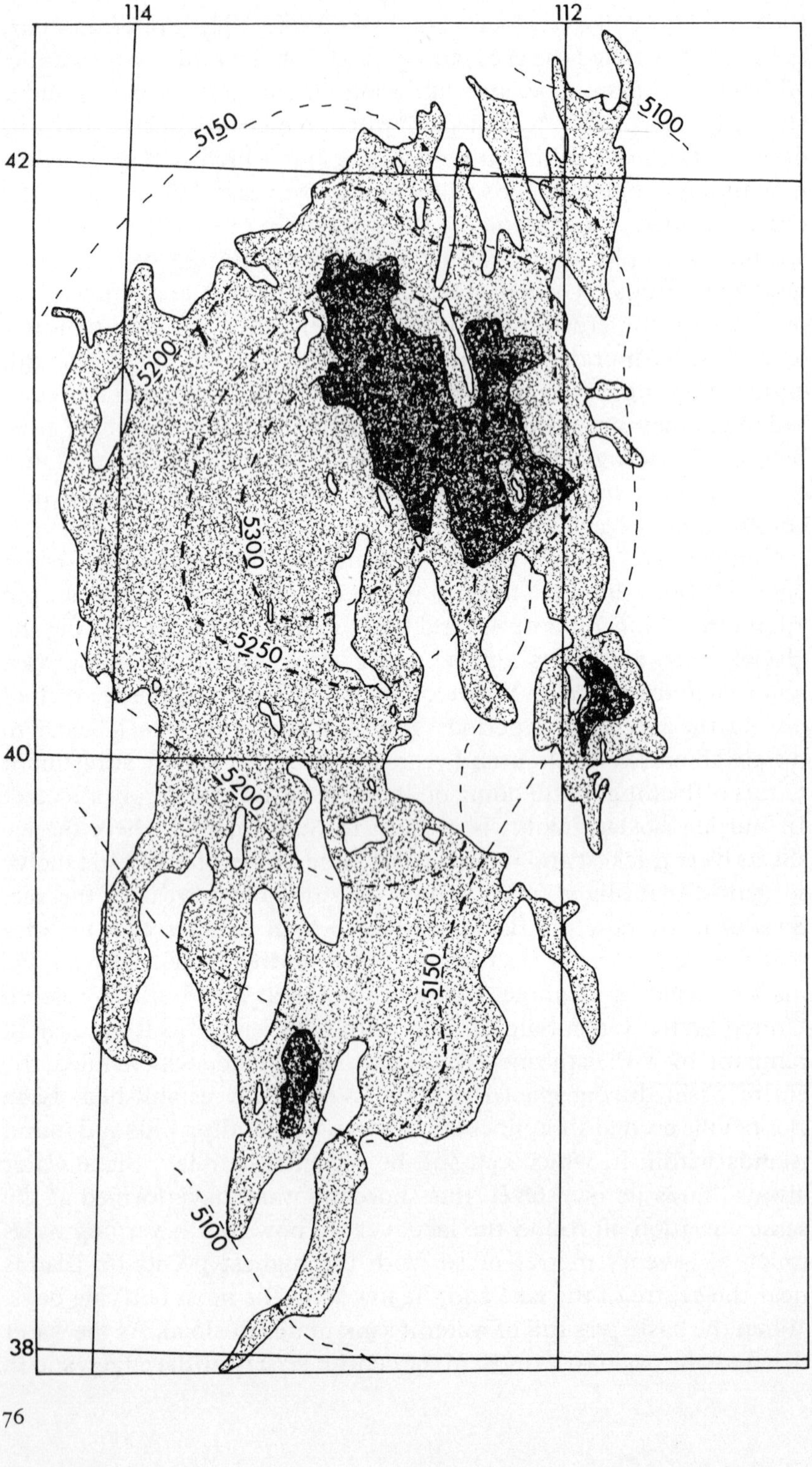
114
112
42
40
38
5100
5150
5200
5250
5300
5200
5150
5100

EVIDENCE FROM SEDIMENTS

so doing deformed the originally horizontal shorelines (figure 26).

To return to our coal cyclothem. The building out of the delta which underlies the coal is an episode of crustal loading. Presumably the delta built out until critical loading was reached, when the area began to sink. Sinking probably proceeded at a faster rate than sediment accumulation, particularly in coal forest areas where only the plants were contributing to the sediment, and so the area became flooded. Sinking continued until a new equilibrium was reached, by which time most of the area would have been under a moderate depth of water. Rivers continued to supply sediment during the sinking interval and would again begin building out deltas from the new shoreline after equilibrium was re-established, thus initiating a new cycle. This simple model explains many of the features of coal measures' cyclothems.

The details are, of course, more complicated. Delta distributary channels often shift their course and thereby alter the pattern of sedimentation in any one place. There is no reason to suppose that the deltas would build out in exactly the same way during each cycle. Near the shoreline the sequence is likely to be complete in most cycles. If a cycle is incomplete, sediments representing the flooding interval are likely to be missing. Equally, offshore the delta may not quite have reached the area and the coals may be thin or absent. Thus superimposed on the basic cycle are local details which make each cyclothem slightly different from its neighbours.

The thicknesses of all the beds within British coalfields increase towards the centres, indicating that each present-day coalfield was a separate basin during the deposition of the coal measures. By and large the sequence of cyclothems varies from coal basin to coal basin. Overriding these local sequences are occasional marine bands. They are thick beds with a fully developed marine fauna, and they are very

26. Isostatic uplift of the shoreline of glacial Lake Bonneville in the Great Basin of the western United States. The extent of Lake Bonneville is indicated by light stipple. Heavy stipple indicates present-day lakes, the largest of which is Great Salt Lake. The contours show the elevation of the shoreline in feet above sea level. As the glacial lake dried up it offloaded the crust which rose due to isostacy. Since the greatest loading was originally in the centre of the lake, this part has since risen most and the shoreline features are found over 70 metres higher up than at the northern and southernmost extremities of the Great Basin. (Source: Crittenden, *J. Geophys. Res.*, **68**, p. 559, 1963. Copyrighted by the American Geophysical Union.)

extensive: at least one can be recognized from South Wales to the Donnetz Basin in Russia. This extensiveness, together with the marine fossils, makes these bands very useful for correlation purposes. They represent something other than local isostatic fluctuations in land level and, since we know that the southern continents were undergoing glaciation at the time, the marine bands may well represent a worldwide rise in sea level caused by melting ice at the onset of an interglacial epoch. Thus the coal measures show purely local sediment variation as well as more regional patterns due to isostatic changes in land level and possibly worldwide, or eustatic, changes in sea level.

Isostacy has always operated, as far as we know, and one would expect other sequences to show its effects. In particular, if this isostatic model explains coal measures' cyclothems, it should also explain sediment patterns in other deltas. In fact it does. Deltas form in areas of very little tidal scour, and represent rather special conditions where small changes in water level may produce drastic changes in environment and sedimentation. Rivers draining into seas with an adequate tidal range have all their sediment redistributed by marine currents. The particles gradually work out towards the continental slope where turbidity currents may carry them into still deeper water. Thus in normal marine environments we cannot expect to find such an immediate response to isostatic changes. Nevertheless, isostatic and eustatic changes in sea level do affect sedimentary processes, and these effects can be recongnized. Uplift of land areas causes renewed vigorous erosion with a concomitant increase in sediment supply, while a rise in sea level causes aggradation of rivers with the silting up of drowned river mouths as is happening in the Dee Estuary at present. Less sediment may reach deeper waters and in some the water depth may be too great for wave action to disturb bottom sediments, producing deposits which accumulated in quieter waters. Past occurrences of the sea invading land areas are called transgressions; the reverse regressions. Cycles of transgression and regression are common in the rock record, although less obvious than coal measures' cyclothems. Often the regressional episode results in erosion and is represented by an unconformity rather than by a regressive sequence of rocks. In the Paris Basin the Tertiary deposits exhibit several transgressive–regressive cycles with the regressive phases, represented by complete retreat of the sea and the accumulation of freshwater sediments. Similar but less well developed cycles occur in the British Tertiary of the Hampshire and London Basins. In all sequences then, we can use the features described in this chapter to determine whether the water was deepening or shallowing as we go up the sequence. Repeating such analyses over a wide geographic area enables us to build up a picture of the palaeogeography of a region and how it changed with time.

Before leaving sediments one final point must be considered. The aim of the chapter has been to show how features of sediments may be used to reconstruct past environments so that we may infer from the sediments where and how fossils lived. Yet I have made reference to 'clays with freshwater bivalves' in interpreting coal measures' cyclothems. Do we interpret these fossils as freshwater bivalves because they occur in non-marine clays or are the clays non-marine because they contain freshwater bivalves? Questions such as these plague geological interpretations. In the case of the Cretaceous Wealden clays of southern Britain, the snails and bivalves belong to two living families, the Viviparidae and Unionidae, which are exclusively non-marine. Thus, although they could perhaps have adapted to freshwater since the Lower Cretaceous, we have at least this fact to suggest that the Wealden sediments formed in a freshwater environment. The coal measures' bivalves belong to extinct families, so not even this argument is available. How do we know they were non-marine? The answer is that we use as many lines of evidence as we can to confirm our interpretations. Coal measures' bivalves are similar morphologically to the present-day freshwater bivalves of the Unionidae. They show similar changes in shape with ecological station, as inferred from the sediments, to observed shape changes found in living unionids where the ecological station is known. Trace element studies of the clays indicate close similarities to modern fresh and brackish water muds rather than to marine clays. Although negative evidence, the complete absence of any marine fauna does not go against a non-marine interpretation, and finally the associations in which we find these bivalves are similar to those of living non-marine bivalves.

Chapter 3

Fossil communities and associations

The present distribution of organisms is far from uniform or even randomly variable. At all levels organisms are more or less closely confined to specific habitats, and groups of organisms to geographical areas. At a purely local level organisms occur together in communities. Members of a community may have a direct relationship to each other, as for example between predator and prey or flowering plants and pollinating insects, or they may simply occur together because their environmental requirements coincide. In the latter case there may or may not be competition for living space, food and so on, but little other direct interaction. Good examples of living communities can be seen by examining a rocky shore and an adjacent sandy bay at low tide. Most, if not all, of the seaweeds, limpets and barnacles found on the rocky shore are entirely absent from the sandy bay where bivalves, worms and heart urchins are common. Here we have two communities of living organisms which, in this case, differ mainly because of the nature of the substrate. Similar local communities are found on land, in freshwater and in the seas all over the world. The tendency of organisms to occur in local communities does not explain all features of their distribution. Habitats can be broadly grouped into terrestrial, freshwater and marine, and few species of animals and plants are able to live in more than one of these. Some land areas have been widely separated from each other for long periods of time, which allows independent evolution of their fauna and flora. For example we do not expect the freshwater faunas of Africa and North America to have much in common. Even in marine habitats which are directly connected we find changes in adjacent areas. One of the best documented is along the eastern seaboard of North America where faunas change from Newfoundland to the Caribbean. In this case climate is the principal controlling factor, and the diversity of organisms increases with increasing water temperature. If, however, we were to proceed away from the coast out into the Atlantic along the same line of latitude, we would find that the faunas and floras changed with depth. All photosynthetic marine plants would disappear long before the two hundred metre level, which is the maximum depth of light penetration in clear seas, but even the benthonic (bottom-dwelling) animal communities would also change markedly with depth. Finally, open oceans are as much a barrier to the dispersal of shallow marine benthonic organisms as are continents. Not only do the Pacific and Atlantic faunas and floras of North America have little in common, but those of the west and east coasts of the Atlantic differ significantly as well. Distribution of organisms are, therefore, affected by local environmental factors, by broader regional factors of climate, depth and marine versus nonmarine conditions, and finally by historical factors involving evolution in separate faunal provinces. Presumably the distributions of fossils were affected by similar factors when the fossils were alive. In this and the next chapter evidence for the association of fossils at all levels is reviewed, starting with small local fossil communities and working up to past faunal provinces and their relationship to continental drift and major climatic belts.

In discussing these various groupings of fossils I shall be using the three terms community, confederation and assemblage in particular meanings which ought to be defined at the outset. Fossil communities are representatives of the original living communities such as those of the rocky headland and sandy bay mentioned above. By definition fossil communities are *in situ* since whole communities cannot be transported intact. Fossil confederations are not necessarily preserved *in situ*, but retain some evidence of the original association between members. They are in effect mixtures of local communities which were originally controlled by more regional factors such as depth, climate and broad environment (e.g. marine versus nonmarine). Fossil assemblages are thoroughly mixed entities which involve elements of different communities or confederations. Alternatively the term 'assemblage' may be used where it is necessary to avoid any implication of community or confederation: just a naturally occurring group of fossils. In general fossil communities are most useful as aids to reconstructing original communities and environments; fossil confederations for reconstructing regional patterns; and assemblages in distinguishing faunal provinces, major climatic belts and for correlation purposes.

Detection of ancient communities requires that the fossils be preserved *in situ*. Where this occurs, the actual observed associations of fossils must reflect the original distributions of organisms when alive. Fossil communities are never complete, however, because the soft-bodied organisms are practically never preserved, and transient predators very rarely so. A cliff fall may bury almost an entire shore community, but is unlikely to trap shoreline-feeding sea birds while the soft-bodied worms and so on will most probably decay without trace. Using trace fossils, the concept of preservation potential and knowledge of the structure of present-day communities, we may attempt to reconstruct the missing elements of a fossil community. Even when fossils have been disturbed they may retain some elements of their original associations, and we may be able to distinguish members of different communities which have become mixed in an assemblage, as for example when free-swimming or-floating organisms like ammonites (plates 4–6) or graptolites (plate 11A) are preserved with benthonic animals and plants. It is always worth recording details of the occurrence and distribution of fossils, because only after this information has been recorded can it be evaluated.

Recognition of communities, and much other palaeontological field work, requires considerable powers of observation, which can be greatly helped simply by making a systematic checklist of points to look for, much as garage mechanics have checklists to ensure that cars are thoroughly serviced. As with many other branches of science, the successful interpretation of an assemblage of fossils may result more from asking the right question than from any brilliant flash of insight. For example, why are crinoids and platyceratid snails found together; why are the brachiopods clumped together in nests; and why are the trace-fossil burrows not found in the cross bedded sands? We are unlikely to ask this sort of question if we have not noticed such associations. Unless we put the right question there is virtually no chance of coming up with the right answer. Even if we guess the correct interpretation, there will be no detailed arguments to justify this intuition. Here is an illustration of the sort of observations that should be included on the checklist. They are divided into two sets of observations, the first (A) on individual species and the second (B) on evidence of associations. The precise order in which these observations are recorded is immaterial, but it is wise to get into the habit of recording them in the same order each time so as not to miss any out. Where appropriate each observation should be made on every single bed in a sequence. Field sketches of sections which include lithological information (rock type), thickness, and presence of faunal or floral elements condense an immense amount of information most economically, and are excellent memory aids when working through collections in the laboratory. One sedimentological manual urges sedimentologists to treat any outcrop as though they will never see it again and hence to record any information that is likely to be of the slightest future use. This is good advice for palaeontologists too.

A. Observations to be made on individual species

For each species check if the orientation of specimens is random within the rock, both with respect to the vertical as well as to compass directions, or if certain orientations occur preferentially. Random orientations may indicate transport or disturbance by scavengers or even infaunal organisms as they burrow past. Where a fossil species is more or less globular, random orientations may well result from original depositional attitudes after transport. Where it is cylindrical or tabular, random orientations with respect to the vertical are more likely to indicate disturbance by infauna. It is hard to imagine some specimens of such shapes being desposited on edge or on end, although occasionally ammonites were imbedded and preserved in a vertical position. Preferred orientations may result from original life positions, or reorientation by currents indicating transport. Each individual case needs to be examined carefully, but certain generalities may be stated. Life orientations will only involve complete skeletons and are often unstable positions for a particular shape. The brachiopod *Productus* and the bivalve *Gryphaea* have similar-shaped shells with one valve concave and fitting inside a slightly larger convex valve (figure 27). Large series of them are found with both valves preserved in a concave-up orientation, which is interpreted as their living position. They tended to live in muddy sediments, and as they grew the edges of the valves would have grown upwards, keeping pace with sedimentation. In other sediments we find large series of isolated valves preserved convex-up, which is the stable position for this shell shape and results from current orientation. Elongate infaunal fossil bivalves are often preserved end-on within the sediments – the razor shell, *Solen*, is a classic present-day example – and again this is likely to be a life orientation. With colonial animals like corals or bryozoa, the radiating growth of individual corallites or zooids reveals the life orientation. Changes of

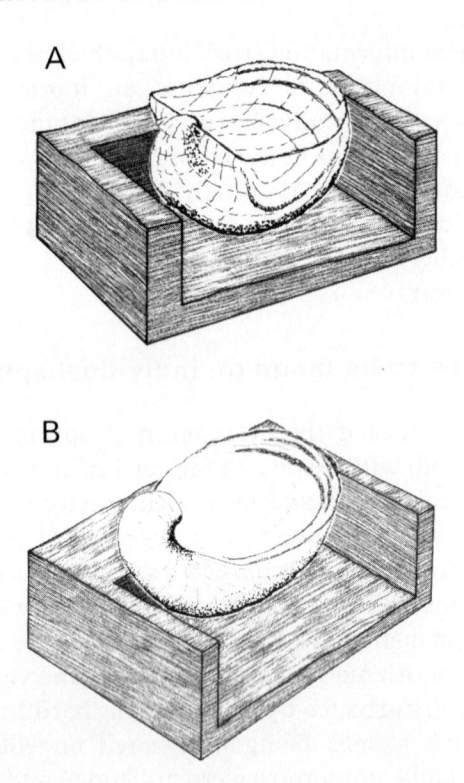

27. Reconstructions of the life orientations of A, the brachiopod *Productus* and B, the bivalve mollusc *Gryphaea*. Both lived with the shell edges just above the sediment surface. As the larger valve grew it maintained the edge just above the sediment level.

orientation in life are also recorded by changes in the growth directions of individuals within the colony. Morphology may give a clue to life orientation. Many diploporite cystoids (extinct primitive echinoderms) were attached directly by an attachment area and have the mouth and food-gathering organs at the opposite end. Where they grew on loose shell material their life orientation is obvious, although it is conceivable that some may have attached to the undersides of caves. Morphology should be used carefully, however. Cylindrical diploporites of the genus *Holocystites* frequently occur lying on their sides in the Osgood Limestone (Middle Silurian) of south-eastern Indiana.[1] One naturally expects this to be a death orientation, since the attachment is at one end of the cylinder and the mouth at the other. However, in all but one example that I examined the mouth

FOSSIL COMMUNITIES AND ASSOCIATIONS

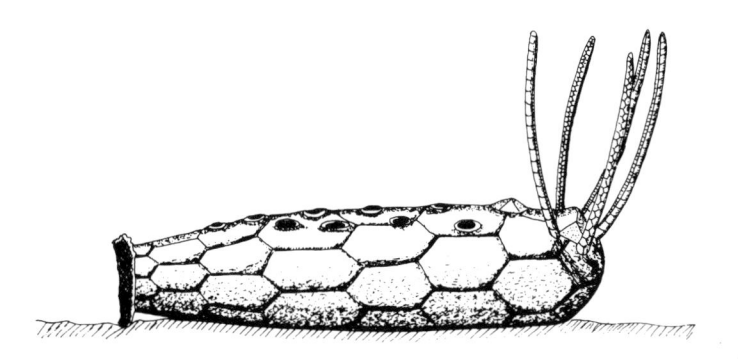

28. The inferred life orientation of cylindrical species of the Silurian cystoid *Holocystites*. Initially the cystoid attached itself directly to a fragment of shell on the sea floor and grew upwards. Soon it became unstable and fell on one side, but continued to grow. Gradually the mouth became reorientated to face upwards again and parasitic snails only bored into the upper surface of the test during the lifetime of the cystoid.

was offset to one side of the oral pole, and many specimens had hemispherical borings of a parasitic gastropod along one side of the test. If the specimens were orientated with the mouth upwards, all the borings were on the upper surface (figure 28). These cyclindrical *Holocystites* appear to have begun life growing upright, fallen over and continued growing while modifying the oral pole to bring the mouth in an upward directed position and then to have been parasitized by the snails. The modification of the test around the pits, and the reforming of the respiratory diplopores under the floors of the pits, both show that the cystoids were alive when bored into and that they did not succumb, at least not immediately, to the parasitic attacks. Pear-shaped species of *Holocystites* which occur in the limestone and succeeding mudstones generally managed to maintain their upright posture with the narrow end of the 'pear' buried in the sediment. They have pits bored all around the upper surface of the test, not along one side.

For each species check if the distribution is random or non-random, and observe whether specimens occur preferentially in clusters, as many brachiopods do, perhaps indicating original living groups. Most living brachiopods are attached to something, often another shell, by the pedicle. Clusters of brachiopods with the pedicle openings pressed closely against other shells in the cluster indicate a living cluster or 'nest' of brachiopods in life orientation (see, for example, plate 10B). Generally those examples on the outside of the cluster will be smaller and younger than the central ones. Other non-random distributions include the occurrence of specimens only at certain levels within a bed. The Middle Ordovician of eastern Tennessee includes alternations of clays and shelly limestones.[2] Brachiopods with flat valves are preserved only at the bases of the limestone beds. Immediately above the level of the planar brachiopods, more normal globular brachiopods, bryozoans, snails and other epifauna occur in a moderately diverse benthonic community. This repeated sequence has been interpreted as representing a background of mud accumulation. Periodically, flat-valved brachiopods settled and were able to colonize because their flat shells, acting like snow shoes, prevented them from sinking into the soft mud. Once these planar brachiopods were established, the pavement of their shells formed a solid substrate which other epifauna and epiflora could colonize. The establishment of algae enabled browsing gastropods to join the community, which was annihilated by an influx of fresh mud that smothered everything. The cycle was then repeated by the return of the next set of flat brachiopods.

Non-random distributions do not always indicate living groups. The diploporite cystoid *Trematocystis* occurs in the Osgood Shales of south-east Indiana immediately below the limestone horizon with cylindrical *Holocystites*. All the specimens are detached from their substrates, have lost the oral and anal cover plates and the feeding organs, are randomly orientated and sometimes damaged – all of which characteristics clearly indicate that they are not preserved *in situ*, yet they occur in clusters in an otherwise almost totally barren bed 15 cm. thick. On one occasion I collected nearly two dozen examples from a block about 65 cm. by 15 cm. by 19 cm. yet only one other specimen came from the several kilometres of outcrop along that particular creek. It is possible that these cystoids were attached to seaweeds in life and the cluster represented a group that were attached to one large seaweed, perhaps like the modern *Laminaria*. This would certainly explain why all specimens are detached from their substrates but have undamaged attachment areas. Nearer home, the Jurassic sea urchin *Nucleolites* occurs in similar clusters, also randomly orientated, in the Corallian oolites of Shellingford Crossroads quarry, near Faringdon, Berkshire. All the specimens have lost their spines and are filled with ooliths. They are equally clearly not *in situ*, but still show a non-random distribution.

The abundance of each species should be recorded. If specimens are *in situ*, then the abundance of the fossils must reflect their original frequency, although not all the specimens preserved on a single bedding plane need necessarily have been alive at the same time. Nevertheless, systematic recording of the frequency of each species in a standard volume of sediment, or a standard area of rock surface, enables us to recognize dominant, common and accessory members of communities or associations. Relative abundance also provides us with a finer guide to the ecological preferences of fossils than mere presence or absence. A fossil species may occur throughout a sequence of beds, but only be abundant in one bed. Such distributions may arise from selective preservation, or concentration in lag deposits, but equally they may arise from primary ecological requirements; the effects of selective preservation or concentration can often be recognized from sedimentological evidence.

When individual frequencies are recorded we may recognize associations which have few species, but many specimens (low-diversity, high-abundance associations) or those with many species each represented by a few individuals (high-diversity, low-abundance). Furthermore, from what we know of the feeding modes of the fossils concerned, we may be able to infer whether we are dealing with a community or an assemblage. For example, belemnites were most probably predators fulfilling a similar role to their modern relatives, the cuttlefish and squids. The occasional Jurassic beds with dominant belemnites cannot represent a community unless the belemnites were almost exclusively cannibalistic. Predators need prey and usually in numbers vastly superior to their own; they can never dominate a living community. Even if we did not know that belemnites and ammonites were free-swimming animals and hence cannot be preserved *in situ*, we could infer this from their modes of feeding and their abundance in Mesozoic clays.

In many modern communities adults and juveniles coexist, although this is not always the case and some animals have quite different habits and habitats as adults and juveniles. Butterflies are an obvious terrestrial example. In some Palaeozoic nautiloids, the ascoceratids, the juvenile shell is distinctly different in shape to that of the adult (figure 29) and when the adult shell was complete the juvenile portion was lost. This morphological change almost certainly indicates a change in life style; juvenile shells would have tended to adopt a vertical orientation because of the buoyancy of the gas-filled chambers, while the adult shells would have adopted a horizontal orientation. In the absence of direct evidence of a change

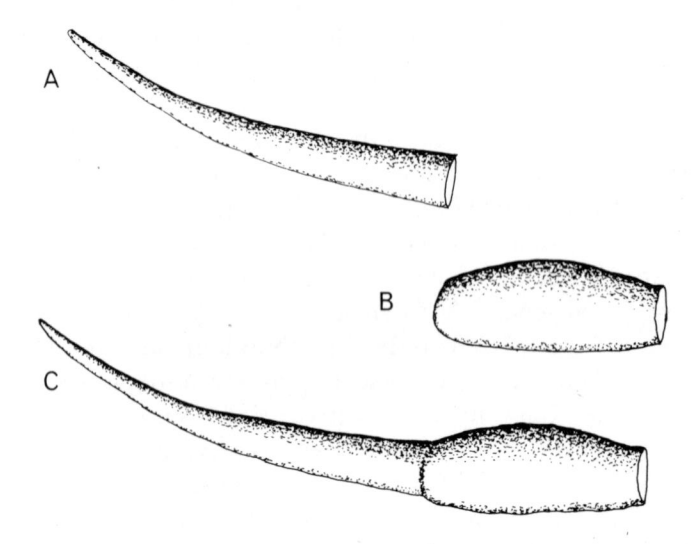

29. The shell of an ascoceratid nautiloid. A. The juvenile shell. B. The adult shell after loss of the juvenile portion (i.e. after decollation). C. A reconstruction of what the whole shell would look like if the juvenile portion had not been lost. Such differences in juvenile and adult shell shapes imply different modes of life at different stages of growth.

of life style between juveniles and adults, one would expect a thriving population to include all growth stages, and they should be sought when looking for fossil communities. For each species the size range should be recorded together with information about obvious changes between juvenile and adult shells. Many snails and ammonites modify the aperture of their shells when mature, while other snails and bivalves apparently continue growing until death. Where such evidence of adulthood exists, the proportion of adults to juveniles and any evidence of possible sexual dimorphism should be recorded.

Plotting size distributions on histograms or other frequency curves may reveal population structure or evidence of selective sorting by currents. Regularly polymodal curves (figure 30) may indicate annual generations, or in the case of arthropods, individual moults. Equally, absence of specimens outside certain narrow size limits may indicate their removal from, or failure to be carried into, the site of deposition by currents. In the latter case the sediments may contain structures and the actual fossils show preferred orientations due to current action. However, the smallest individuals are so often missing in what otherwise seem to be well-preserved fossil communities that it would be unwise to infer selective removal of juveniles in every single case.

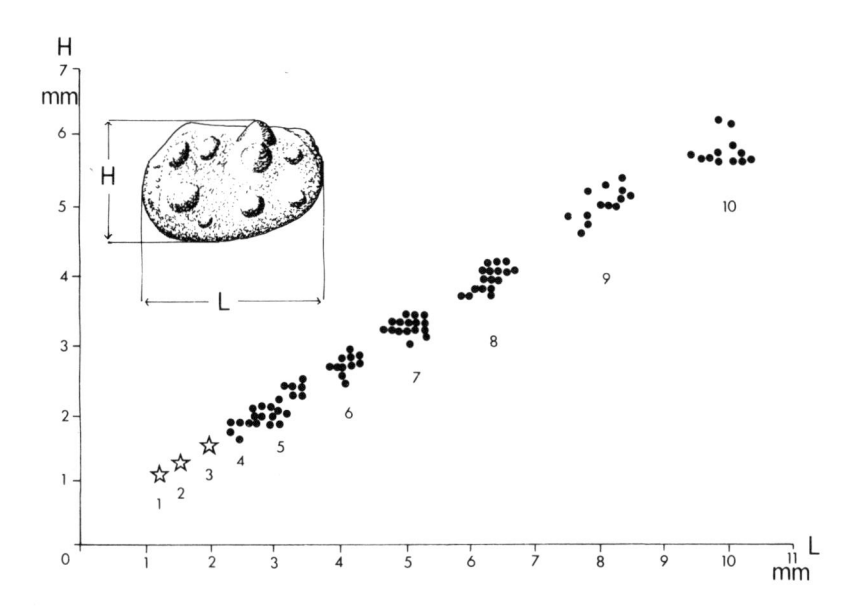

30. Moults (numbered 1–10) revealed by the size clustering of the carapaces of the ostracod, *Theriosynoecum fittoni*. (After I. G. Sohn and F. W. Anderson, *Palaeontology*, 7, fig. 2, p. 77, 1964. Copied with permission of the Palaeontological Association.)

Such size distributions can occur, for example, if the species breeds only in spring, and suffers little mortality in summer. If such a community was buried by a winter storm most individuals would be approximately nine months old (or twenty-one or thirty-three months, and so on) on death. In a species which breeds and dies annually, preserved individuals would be almost full-grown. In addition, many species do not breed every year; in others the spatfall may fail to develop. Annual recruitment to populations is common, but irregular recruitment is equally common, and the fossil record seems to preserve examples of both types of population structure.

Since arthropods moult, shedding their skeletons periodically and enlarging their size in brief spurts of growth immediately after moulting, any one arthropod leaves behind a number of potential fossils. There is no way of recognizing different moults of any one individual unless it happened to have a pathological abnormality which was repeated in each moult, for example a crab with nine legs. The chances of such moults being preserved, collected and recognized are infinitesimal. However, the distinction between whole skeletons which represent complete individuals, and partially preserved skeletons which may indicate either moults or individuals which were disarticulated after death, is relatively easy and should be made. In rare instances fossil arthropods are found with all the skeletal parts loosely associated in a characteristic orientation. Trilobites, for example, are found with the tail and thorax articulated, but the head separated and lying upside-down near the front of the thorax. These have been interpreted as undisturbed moults in which the old head was overturned as the trilobite crawled forwards out of the old thorax and tail. Such arthropod orientations are often referred to as being in 'Salter's position', after the nineteenth-century palaeontologist, J. W. Salter, who first suggested the possibility. After moulting, arthropods are very delicate and susceptible to predation. They swell up rapidly and then gradually the new skeleton hardens over a period of a few days or weeks. In the Middle Devonian Silica Shales of Sylvania, Ohio the trilobite *Phacops* is preserved in all stages of calcification following moulting. Interestingly this series of specimens allows the development of the lenses in the compound eyes to be studied.[3] The lenses are shed with each moult and new lenses have to be grown and calcified along with the rest of the skeleton. The development of new lenses follows exactly the principles first elaborated by van Huygens to correct for spherical aberration, a visual defect which causes blurred vision. Apparently, freshly moulted trilobites could see just as well as mature individuals between moults, a feature of obvious selective advantage to a trilobite in a vulnerable stage of growth.

Selective deposition of a particular size range of individuals is only one line of evidence for transport of fossils to form assemblages. Disarticulation, abrasion and other damage should also be sought to determine if species have been transported or not. Again, however, care is required in some interpretations. Ascoceratids with decollate shells (in other words with the top or juvenile part missing) are only one case of a fairly common phenomenon. Decollate shells occur in several unrelated groups of snails, while many other snails have shells which are abraded, covered with epifauna and bored into during the lifetime of the snail. Similarly bivalve shells are frequently eroded at the umbones, or beaks, in life. In both cases, the oldest parts of the shells will be most severely affected and the youngest parts free or nearly free of these effects. Abrasion during transport should act on any projection indifferently. The reverse case, where delicate structures like the spines of the brachiopods *Chonetes*, *Acanthothiris* and various productids are preserved intact, more positively indicates lack of transport. These and other delicate structures are too fragile to withstand any transport or even to be exhumed without damage.

Pathological abnormalities, such as damage and repair in life, parasitic attacks, or evidence of disease, are always worth recording. They may indicate aspects of the victim's life, such as predation or parasitism, or at least they may help to avoid mistakes in identification or reconstruction. Most artists' impressions of Neanderthal Man show a round-backed, stooping individual. Whilst this may be partly due to an unconscious feeling that he was an inferior 'ape-man', it is also partly because the first reconstruction of Neanderthal Man was made from the skeleton of a diseased individual who genuinely had a stoop. Jackson[4] used pathologically abnormal specimens of sea urchins with unusual numbers of radii (less than five) to show that the introduction of new test plates only occurred adjacent to the five ocular plates of the apical disc. Where only three or four radii develop, there are only three or four oculars.

Finally the distribution of epifauna or borings on shells of fossils should be recorded. Distribution may be random over the shell or show preferred associations which often reveal whether the epifauna attached *pre-* or *post-mortem*. Where the epifauna appear to have been attached before death, the life orientation of the host fossil may be deduced in favourable circumstances (see plate 6). The most obvious test for attachment before or after death is whether the epifauna are confined to parts of the shell which were exposed, or whether they coat parts of the shell, such as the inside, which were in contact with the living tissue when the host was alive. Clearly epifauna coating the internal surfaces of snail shells, bivalves or ammonites, and so on attached after death. Rarely non-predatory borers may penetrate to the inside of a shell during life, but the borings are covered over with mother-of-pearl by the living host. Epifauna growing over spine bases or the pore-pairs of tube-feet in sea urchins also indicate *post-mortem* attachment. Indeed I have yet to come across any example of what may be called 'casual epifauna' which attached to an echinoderm during its lifetime. Echinoderms were and are subject to a number of parasites and commensals, but seem to have been very effective at preventing attachment of passive epifauna.

Other examples exist of worm tubes with their apertures aligned along the edge of a brachiopod shell where the food-bearing currents entered the shell (figure 31). Presumably the worms were also filtering food from these currents. Auloporoid corals are known

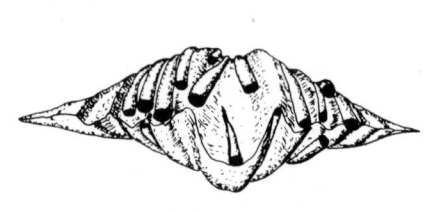

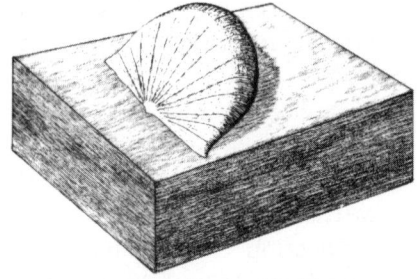

31. A spiriferid brachiopod covered with small worm tubes all orientated so that they open near the shell edges. The worms grew on the brachiopod while it was alive and probably themselves fed from the feeding currents created by the brachiopod. (After M. J. S. Rudwick, *Living and fossil brachiopods*, fig. 93, p. 162, Hutchinson University Library, 1970.)

32. The inferred life orientation of the Ordovician brachiopod *Rafinesquina*. Note that this is the opposite orientation to that suggested for *Productus* and *Gryphaea* (fig. 27, page 84). The orientation is inferred from the predominance of epifauna on the highest points of the convex valve and the frequent occurrence of undisturbed pavements of these brachiopods in this orientation in the Upper Ordovician of the Cincinnati region, USA.

where the colony terminates at a prominent growth line on the brachiopod shell, while the brachiopod continued growing. Something which was fatal to the coral interrupted the growth of the brachiopod but did not kill it. In these cases the epifauna were attached during the lifetimes of the hosts. Epifauna on the brachiopod *Rafinesquina* from the Upper Ordovician at Madison, Indiana are always more extensive and diverse on the convex valve than on the concave valve. The brachiopods are always entire with both valves together and preserved convex-up. Since in this orientation mud would have fouled the aperture, it seems likely that *Rafinesquina* lived with the straight hinge-line close to or within the sediment and the anterior edge raised up, as in figure 32. This interpretation is confirmed by the rarer epifauna of the concave valve which tends to be confined to a zone near the anterior margin.

Where epifauna attach in sequence, the order may be deduced by determining which forms have been overgrown by which other forms. The degree of growth also gives an indication of the rate of sedimentation or the interval between influxes of sediments. Tests of the chalk sea urchin *Micraster* often have juvenile epifauna near the

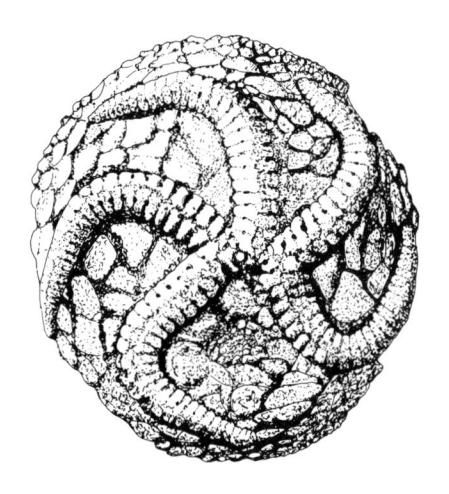

33. An edrioasteroid, an extinct group of epifaunal Palaeozoic echinoderms. (After B. N. Bell, cover illustration to Memoir 21, New York State Museum and Science Service, 1976.)

lowest parts of the test (in its burial attitude) and progressively more mature epifauna towards the top. The lowest individuals and colonies were overwhelmed by the accumulating chalk sediment before those on the higher points. Similarly two horizons for fossil edrioasteroids (rare extinct limpet-like echinoderms, figure 33) which I was shown in the Upper Ordovician of Cincinnati had slightly different histories. In both sites the edrios occurred on the convex (upper) valves of the brachiopod *Rafinesquina*, which formed continuous pavements in the muddy sediment. The *Rafinesquina* presumably colonized the mud, their initially flat shell shape acting like a snow shoe. When the brachiopods were established the edrios and other epifauna grew on their shells, often near the anterior edge which would have been the highest point of the shells according to my interpretation of the life position of *Rafinesquina*. In one bed the edrios were all small, up to 15 mm. diameter, complete and perfectly preserved. In the other bed the edrios were larger, 25 mm. diameter or more, and incomplete, often with only the marginal ring of plates remaining. In the first instance it seems the edrios were overwhelmed by renewed sedimentation whilst still juveniles and were buried alive. In the second case the edrios grew to maturity, bred, died and disarticulated before being buried by accumulating sediment. The time interval between attachment and entombment in the first case is unlikely to have exceeded two years and could have been only a few months.

Finally the positions of epifauna on their hosts may indicate aspects of the life habits of the epifauna itself. Some animals are strongly photophobic: they avoid light. Photophobic epifauna seek out dark crevices and undersides of stones as preferred attachment sites. Fossil epifauna, which are only found within shells, on the undersides of concavities or within crevices are good examples of this. Such crevice faunas have been described from the Middle Jurassic in Britain and elsewhere. Juveniles of one Triassic species of the bivalve *Lima* were similarly photophobic and are found preferentially in the cavity between the attached adult shell and the substrate.[5] Here the photophobia was of selective advantage since the juveniles were effectively brooded by the adult and gained protection from their crevice-dwelling habit.

B. Observations to be made on evidence of associations

Fossil communities include different members and the prime evidence for them must be the recognition of associations of *in situ* fossils. Merely going through the preceding checklist of observations on individual species will have revealed some associations; indeed, several of the examples quoted show not only a community, but a sequence of communities. The flat-valved brachiopods in the Middle Ordovician limestones of Tennessee and the *Rafinesquina* pavements in the Upper Ordovician of Cincinnati, Ohio and Madison, Indiana, formed pioneer communities on which later communities developed. In a sense the epifauna on a single shell form a micro-community within which competition for attachment sites is evident, and other relationships such as commensalism between the epifauna and host may sometimes be inferred. Nevertheless, in proceeding through a sequence of beds or working different outcrops of the same bed, systematic recording of associations is necessary. Associations may be arbitrarily divided into three categories, although combinations often occur. Associations of one type of fossil with another, associations of one or more types of fossils with a sediment type and associations of fossils with sedimentary structures are all three found, and are conveniently discussed separately.

Associations of fossils with fossils may be immediate and obvious or quite subtle. They may be universal or only developed in certain beds or at some localities. Wherever such associations are observed, the problems of interpreting the cause and possible relationships between associates arise. The Devonian coral *Pleurodictyum problematicum* is apparently always associated with a worm tube, *Hicetes*, in what seems to have been a commensal relationship, in other words one in which neither partner is harmed. In the Lower Silurian Manitoulin Dolomite of Manitoulin Island, Ontario, every single colony of the tabulate coral *Favosites* that I found was attached to the outer surface of a brachiopod shell; *Platystrophia* in most cases, but occasionally other genera. It may be that these brachiopods were simply the most commonly available substrates. However, hermit crabs are known to associate with sea anemones to the mutual benefit of both. The anemones gain food because the crabs are messy eaters, and the crabs gain protection through the deterrent effect on predators of the stinging anemone. Possibly the fossil corals became attached while the brachiopods were still alive and, at least initially, the two species lived in a similar symbiotic relationship. The small juvenile corals would benefit by attachment to brachiopods which were themselves fixed to the substrate, while the brachiopods might have gained extra protection. At least one modern solitary coral living in Scottish waters attaches to worm tubes preferentially. While the coral is still young the worm prevents it from being buried by shifting sediment because the worm will climb up to the surface each time it is overwhelmed. By the time the worm dies, the coral is large enough to maintain itself in a stable orientation and outgrow sediment accumulation. The *Favosites* colonies, which eventually overgrew the brachiopods entirely, could represent a fossil example of a similar phenomenon. The Palaeozoic gastropod *Platyceras* is commonly found associated with crinoids. In the vast majority of cases where the gastropod and crinoid are preserved in contact, the gastropod is attached to the crown of the crinoid over the anus. This association is usually interpreted as commensal, the gastropod living off the faeces of the crinoid but not seriously harming it. The gastropods were not apparently host-specific and are found on a variety of crinoids and even the occasional cystoid, *Caryocrinites*. This association began in the Middle Ordovician where *Cyclonema* is found on crinoid cups and continued through to the Upper Permian. Both the Palaeozoic crinoid groups (camerates, inadunates and flexibles) and the platyceratid gastropods became extinct at the close of the Palaeozoic.

All these associations are clear-cut, involve only two species and may be explained in terms of direct relationships between the partners. More diffuse relationships exist, as, for example, between many epifaunal organisms and their substrates. In the majority of cases epifauna settle on any available substrate indiscriminately. However, preference for certain surfaces does seem to occur. In the diploporite cystoid fauna of the Osgood Formation in south-eastern Indiana,[6] *Triamara*, which has the largest theca offering the greatest area for attachment and taking the longest time to become completely buried, generally has a poor epifauna. It has a rough surface covered with pits and holes. Some species of *Holocystites* and *Pustulocystis* have rough surfaces, but with tubercles all over them, not holes, and bear a moderate epifauna, while *Trematocystis*, which has the smallest theca but with the smoothest surface, carries the richest epifauna. The epifauna consists of the following groups in order of decreasing frequency: Bryozoa, crinoid attachment structures, worm tubes, sponges, the brachiopod *Petrocrania* and a solitary *Trematocystis* still attached to another example.

Finally there are associations which denote no particular relationship at all. These can be detected by simply recording all the fauna from each bed. It is quite likely that some loose associations would be overlooked, and computers are often used nowadays to check such data for all possible correlations. Using statistical techniques it is possible to determine whether the observed associations are unlikely to be due to chance alone. Such use of computers is a great help in detecting and evaluating associations, especially those involving more than two species.

Associations also occur between organisms and sediments. The Middle Ordovician sequence in Tennessee already quoted has virtually all the fauna confined to the limestone bands. Indeed in this case it is the presence of the fossils which caused the formation of the limestones. The Jurassic Bridport Sands of West Bay, near Bridport, Dorset, consist of alternations of well cemented sandstone bands and poorly cemented sands. Trace-fossil burrows of many types are strongly correlated with the sandstone bands, although such traces do occur in the sandy layers, but are less obvious. It could well be that diagenesis of the sandstones and subsequent weathering have enhanced traces in these layers but not in the uncemented sands. Alternatively the presence of abundant traces in certain layers of the sediment could have led to their preferential cementation. It is very difficult to decide between these two alternatives. The flank beds of the Upper Ordovician Boda Limestone bioherms in Sweden consist of bioclastic limestones intercalated with red and green shales. The faunas of the shales and limestones are markedly different when their composition is examined in detail.

Associations of organisms and sedimentary structures can be found in some instances. The pioneer Russian palaeoecologist, Hecker, has described short sections of crinoid columns orientated parallel to, and on the crests of, ripple marks.[7] The Carboniferous Limestone near Hope, Derbyshire contains a small bedded mound which resembles a gentle anticlinal fold. One bed which passes over the mound is rich in crinoid stems only over the crest of the mound, indicating that the mound existed when the crinoid stems were accumulating. Although the stems are now broken and disturbed, it is possible that the crinoids actually lived only on the crest of the mound. In the Carboniferous Drybrook Sandstone north of Drybrook in the Forest of Dean, abundant trace-fossil burrows occur in impure sandy and silty horizons, but are entirely absent from cross bedded clean sand units. The most likely explanation is that the infaunal burrow formers were unable to establish or maintain their burrows in the shifting washed sands represented by the clean cross bedded horizons.

Where the sedimentary structures are of organic origin, as with trace fossils, bioherms and reefs, there is obviously an association between organisms and the structure. Fragments of callianassid shrimps within *Ophiomorpha* or *Thalassinoides* burrows tend to confirm that the shrimps formed these burrow systems. Bioherms and reefs sometimes develop on pioneer communities which may not be immediately obvious as such, and certainly acted themselves as substrates for a whole host of organisms which are not found far from such structures. Bioherms which grew on mounds of crinoid stems occur in the Ordovician of Tennessee and Sweden. The Middle Ordovician Kullsberg bioherms at Amtjärn and Unskarsheden, Dalarna, Sweden, grew on the debris of crinoid meadows. The succeeding, Upper Ordovician, Boda bioherms occur on top of Kullsberg bioherms without exception, although at least one Kullsberg bioherm is known that does not have a Boda bioherm on top of it. The Kullsberg bioherms were annihilated and buried by muddy sediment which now forms the black Fjäcka Shale. Although completely buried, it seems the Kullsberg bioherms stood up as elevations in the Fjäcka Shale sea floor on which the alga *Palaeoporella* began to grow, forming the pioneer community of the Boda bioherms. The Middle Silurian Waldron Shale of Indiana and Tennessee has long been famous for its fossils, yet many sections in central Indiana are totally barren. The fossils are strongly associated with small, one- to two-metre-diameter bioherms. Even though they are disarticulated, it is easy to demonstrate that crinoid and blastoid cups are more common in the vicinity of these bioherms than elsewhere, while brachiopods were clearly attached all over the bioherms. In the Blue Ridge quarry, near Waldron, Indiana, the upper surface of the underlying Laurel Limestone is a hardground with a characteristic encrusting fauna of corals, bryozoa, an edrio and crinoid attachment structures. Within the Waldron Shale, crinoid cups, brachiopods and other epifauna are common at the base immediately above this hardground.

As a final comment on fossil communities, those of hardground surfaces, bioherms and reefs, or trace fossils in loose sediments, are the easiest to recognize as communities since they cannot have been transported. Others require careful evaluation to distinguish them from fossil confederations.

Fossil confederations, as defined here, are broader, more loosely knit groupings of fossils which still retain some evidence of original communality even though members of several different local communities may be mixed together. They are, so to speak, the next group up in a hierarchy of social order in fossils. For example, the sandy bay and rocky shore local communities mentioned earlier are themselves associated in being littoral, in other words intertidal, communities and therefore characteristic of the shallowest marine environments. Similarly offshore communities on sandy or muddy substrate may be equally distinct from each other, but are linked in being subtidal and occurring at similar depths on the continental shelf (as opposed to the continental slope or abyssal plain). Confederations may be depth controlled, climatically controlled or environmentally controlled. The littoral and shallow subtidal communities of the eastern seaboard of North America can be grouped into Caribbean, Carolinian, Virginian, Acadian and Arctic associations, each of which is a potential fossil confederation. Where some fossils are clearly not *in situ*, it is likely that the whole assemblage represents a confederation which may or may not retain sufficient evidence to allow recognition of its component communities. Most assemblages of fossils preserved in shallow shelf environments probably represent confederations if we can only recognize them as such. The complete mixing of fossils from different depths, different climatic belts, or marine and non-marine environments to form fossil assemblages (as defined here) is probably

FOSSIL COMMUNITIES AND ASSOCIATIONS

a rare event in shelf environments, although it may well happen where turbidites form.

The best examples of fossil confederations (which were, and still are, called 'communities' by their proponents) are the depth-controlled associations of brachiopods in the Lower Silurian of Wales and the Welsh Borderland, which Ziegler and others have documented since 1965.[8] Ziegler collected brachiopods from numerous localities in the Lower Silurian and recorded the associations he found. After a while a pattern of associations began to emerge with broad belts more or less parallel to the inferred Lower Silurian shoreline (figure 34). Furthermore, during the Lower Silurian the sea transgressed over land areas to the south and east and the belts of brachiopod associations migrated in the same direction, and at the same time, as the transgression. From this Ziegler

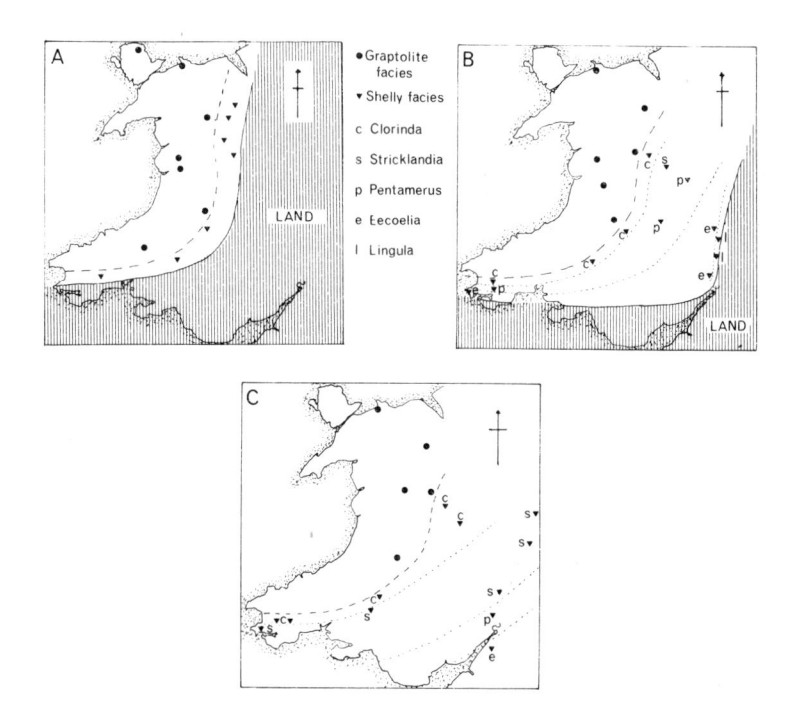

34. The distribution of Ziegler's Lower Silurian (Llandovery) brachiopod 'communities' in Wales. A. Positions during the Lower and Middle Llandovery. B. Positions during the early Upper Llandovery. C. Positions in the late Upper Llandovery. Symbols indicate the locations of the collections on which the 'communities' are based. The shelly facies is too narrow in A to indicate the separate 'communities'. (After A. M. Ziegler, *Nature*, **207**, pp. 270–2, 1965.)

concluded that these associations of brachiopods were depth-controlled, and he named them after prominent members of each association. They are, in order of increasing depth: the *Lingula*, *Eocoelia*, *Stricklandia*, *Pentamerous* and *Clorinda* communities. At depths greater than that represented by the *Clorinda* community, only graptolitic shales occur. It was soon pointed out that these associations of brachiopods are not communities in the sense used here, because the brachiopods are disarticulated, and have been transported. Furthermore the associations are apparently independent of the type of sediment and therefore of inferred original substrate. They are depth-controlled confederations – the original communities, which probably were influenced by sediment type, having been mixed but not to the extent that all trace of association has been lost. Some people have been reluctant to accept that the confederations are depth-controlled, and have argued that the original distribution of the brachiopods was substrate-controlled. Doubtless this was true, but it is difficult to explain the present distribution of the fossils in confederations parallel to the shoreline, and migrating with the transgression, on any other grounds than depth. It should also be emphasized that the whole aspect of an assemblage of brachiopods needs to be taken into account before it is possible to assign the assemblage to one of Ziegler's confederations. Species of *Lingula*, for example, occur at all depths. The mere occurrence of a *Lingula* does not imply the *Lingula* confederation, which was defined as being dominated by *Lingula* with *Camarotoechia* and the bivalve *Nucula*. Similarly, the brachiopod *Eocoelia* occurs in adjacent depth zones but dominates only within the *Eocoelia* confederation.

Since Ziegler's pioneer work, similar depth-controlled confederations of brachiopods have been recognized and named for the Upper Ordovician and the Middle and Upper Silurian and at other horizons.[9] Doubtless similar confederations of brachiopods occurred throughout the Palaeozoic and possibly the Mesozoic as well. Ziegler's original confederations were defined on brachiopods because brachiopods are the most common fossils in the Lower Silurian of the Welsh Borderland and because they were defined by a brachiopod specialist. Nevertheless, if the whole fauna is considered, the shallow water *Lingula* and *Eocoelia* confederations tend to be of low-diversity, high-abundance type while the deep *Clorinda* confederation is of high-diversity, low-abundance. This phenomenon of diversity increasing with depth is very widespread and well documented, although the occurrence of reefs and bioherms may alter the pattern locally. Certainly a similar pattern holds for the Appalachian Basin during Upper Silurian and Lower Devonian times, where the most diverse faunas occur centrally in the basin in what was still a relatively shallow shelf sea, perhaps analogous to the present-day North Sea. The Middle Ordovician of Wales and the Welsh Borderland and present-day seas also show this correlation of diversity with depth.

Communities living in marine and non-marine environments are totally different, and should give rise to completely different fossil assemblages. Recognition of past marine and non-marine environments depends to some extent on fossil evidence although interpretation of sequences of sediments helps. Fossil faunas and floras are usually recognized as marine or non-marine by comparison with those of the present day. Recognition of past marine faunas is relatively easy because a number of animal groups, including some whole phyla, are exclusively marine. Thus all living echinoderms, brachiopods, cephalopod, scaphopod and polyplacophoran molluscs, foraminifera and corals are exclusively marine. Sedimentary rocks rich in any of these groups are generally accepted as marine. Association of extinct fossil groups with these known marine groups allows us to extend the list so that all trilobites and graptolites, for example, are also accepted as having been exclusively marine. The mere absence of these groups is suggestive of non-marine conditions, but cannot be accepted as proof. Many species are intolerant of even slight fluctuations from normal marine salinity (35–6 per mille) and they are just as likely to be absent from an enclosed lagoon with above-average salinity as from a brackish or freshwater habitat. In the Mesozoic and Tertiary, freshwater deposits can be recognized by the presence of characteristic molluscs, ostracods and plants which belong to extant groups. While it is possible that they may have adapted to fresh water since their first appearance in the fossil record, they are unlikely all to have done so at the same time. The presence in the Jurassic of associations of viviparid snails, unionid bivalves, reproductive structures of the freshwater plant *Chara* and freshwater ostracods, just like those accumulating in present-day lakes, is strongly suggestive of precisely similar freshwater conditions. In the Palaeozoic, faunal comparisons are more difficult as we have seen with respect to Carboniferous non-marine bivalves.

Terrestrial floras are not difficult to recognize since they are dominated by vascular plants, which only form a very small proportion of marine floras and are rarely preserved in marine sediments. Marine vascular plants such as the eel grass, *Thalassia*, only evolved in the Tertiary and there were probably no Mesozoic and Palaeozoic marine vascular plants. Some of the earliest vascular plants known occur in the Lower Devonian Rhynie Chert of Scotland and are accompanied by very primitive insects. Terrestrial snails have been described from the Carboniferous. They have the aperture armoured with inwardly directed denticles, or teeth, which are very rare in marine snails at the present, but very common in all sorts of diverse terrestrial species where they apparently act as barriers to insect predators. Thus it seems that some members of the present-day terrestrial faunas had already adapted to life on land in the Upper Palaeozoic, but all Lower Palaeozoic faunas and floras are accepted as having been exclusively marine.

Where a non-marine environment is suspected, particularly in the Upper Palaeozoic, faunal diversity may help confirm the interpretation, although each case should be examined carefully on its own merits. Non-marine faunas tend to be of low-diversity, high-abundance types, if only because the exclusively marine groups are absent. This is particularly true of brackish-water communities in estuaries and salt marshes. Very few species can tolerate rapid fluctuations in salinity, and estuarine conditions may vary from almost fully marine to nearly freshwater with each tide. Fish, like salmon and eels which spend part of their lives in the sea and part in fresh water, generally wait for several days in estuaries to acclimatize before proceeding up river or out to sea. Those animals and plants which can tolerate rapid changes in salinity have few competitors and proliferate. A salt marsh in Britain will have at most only two or three species of snail and a similar number of bivalves, but these few species are often abundant. *Hydrobia ulvae*, a small deposit-feeding snail, occurs on estuarine mudflats in densities of several thousand per square metre.

The sequence of sediments often gives clues to the occurrence of non-marine environments even when fossils are absent. This usually comes down to recognizing a shallowing series of sediments and features indicative of shorelines or emergence. In the British Upper Jurassic, for example, the marine Portland Series is succeeded by the non-marine Purbeck Series. The precise transition is well exposed on Portland Island. The penultimate bed of the Portland Series is an oobiomicrite which contains oysters and giant ammonites, among other fossils, indicating marine conditions. It is succeeded by a three-metre-thick micritic bed, the 'shrimp band' of local quarrymen, which is generally unfossiliferous but has yielded occasional fragments of a callianassid crustacean which at the present day lives in low intertidal and shallow subtidal environments. Above this, the lowest beds of the Purbeck Series are finely laminated muddy micrites. Some bands have poorly preserved mud cracks and good ripple marks. They probably represent algal laminates and indicate supra-tidal conditions. Finally, three to four metres above the contact, beds with salt pseudomorphs occur. These indicate temporary conditions of evaporation, with salt cubes forming and producing impressions in the sediment. When the next influx of water and sediment arrived, the salt cubes dissolved leaving the sediment to fill the characteristic marks in the underlying lime mud. The sequence indicates a change from marine conditions through possibly a lagoon to supra-tidal mudflats with periodic desiccation. Even the marine conditions of the giant ammonite bed were probably already somewhat restricted since echinoderms, for example, which occur lower in the Portland Series, are absent from this horizon. The ammonites could have drifted in as their shells float after death, and oysters are known to be able to withstand conditions of reduced salinity. An interesting feature of this sequence, which is common in other similar sequences, is the absence of any clear indication of a shoreline or beach. Shorelines are such transient features that evidence of them is rarely preserved. Nevertheless, the sequence clearly involves a transition from marine to non-marine conditions. Similar sequences which involve a reduction in faunal diversity and concomitant shallowing have been used to recognize conditions of reduced salinity.

Interpretation of the above sequence, and so many others, depends on the use of evidence from both sediments and fossils. This leads me to consideration of the concept of facies. Facies are, in effect, generalizations about past environments and their communities, and usually depend for their recognition on both fossil and sedimentological criteria. An example will help to clarify the concept. In the Lower Palaeozoic, two broadly contrasting facies occur repeatedly from the Tremadoc upwards. On the one hand are thick sequences of sandstones, limestones and conglomerates with faunas dominated by shelly fossils such as brachiopods, molluscs, corals, bryozoans, echinoderms, and so on. This is the so-called 'shelly facies' and originated in shallow shelf seas. On the other hand there are thin sequences of black shales which contain nothing but graptolites – the graptolitic facies. Black graptolitic shales accumulated in deep water, offshore, where bottom conditions were inimitable to life so that no benthonic, shelly fauna could survive. The graptolites are believed to have been planktonic, and when they died their skeletons settled through waters of any depth. In shallow seas with shifting sediments the delicate skeletons were usually destroyed, but in deep quiet waters they accumulated to form the graptolitic shales. This contrast between deeper-water muddy sediments with faunas derived from the open oceans on the one hand, and shallow-water shelf sediments with shelly benthonic faunas on the other, can be seen throughout the Palaeozoic and Mesozoic, although the open-water faunas change. The shelly faunas remain shelly, but we find graptolitic shales in the Lower Palaeozoic, goniatite shales in the Upper Palaeozoic and clays with ammonites and belemnites in the Mesozoic. All three represent the deeper-water offshore facies, however.

Facies are not only controlled by depth. They represent specific conditions which are repeated in different places or at different times. Thus one can refer to 'reef facies' irrespective of the age of the reef or the particular frame-building organisms in the reef. Equally, carbonate facies can be distinguished from clastic facies, or marine facies from non-marine. The facies concept is analogous to the medical concept of a syndrome, a collection of symptoms not all of which may occur in any one patient and each of which may occur in several disorders but which, when they occur *together*, indicate a specific disease or malfunction. Not all supra-tidal mudflats have salt pseudomorphs or algal laminates in them as the Purbeck examples do. Equally however, birdseye limestones (a peculiar texture with irregular sheets and blotches of sparite in a micritic limestone), rain pits, and tracks and trails, are found in other supra-tidal areas and are absent from the Purbeck and, of course, supra-tidal facies may have terrigenous sediments like sands and clays rather than lime muds. Nevertheless a combination of several of these features is enough to indicate a supra-tidal environment.

Knowledge of the life habits of different fossils is often a great help in recognizing facies and assemblages. Mesozoic clays, for example, with a good fauna of pelagic ammonites and benthonic animals like snails, bivalves and corals, clearly have an assemblage of fossils. Open-ocean forms like ammonites and graptolites can never be buried in their living environment, and one would not expect to be able to detect their living associations. However, depth-controlled confederations of both have been described on a simple assumption. Suppose, for example, that at some time in the past graptolites lived in three associations controlled by water depth as in figure 35. Skeletons of members of all three associations would only accumulate together in sediments forming in the deepest water. In shallower water only the upper two associations would be represented, while near shore, in the shallowest environments, only the surface association would be preserved. Increasing diversity of faunas associated with increasing depth is known in some Ordovician graptolite occurrences, while in the Cretaceous of the western United States similar ammonite associations have been related to distance from shore and depth.

One rapidly expanding branch of palaeontology is concerned with the general synthesis of the sort of information outlined in this chapter. If we can recognize fossil communities and relate them to their environments, or deduce depth-controlled confederations, or sequences passing from marine to non-marine conditions, then we may assemble this information to produce maps showing past geographies, i.e. palaeogeographies. By considering all the evidence from sediments as well as fossils and their associations together, we can not only distinguish the sea from the land but plot in the positions of major rivers (using current indicators like cross bedding) and restore rock types and climates in the land area (from heavy mineral assemblages and sediment maturity). In the sea we can plot approximate depth profiles, identify shelf and basin facies, locate reefs, and so on. Indeed we can produce palaeogeographic maps which show all the sorts of detail found in a modern atlas. Furthermore, we can do this for each time interval in a sequence,

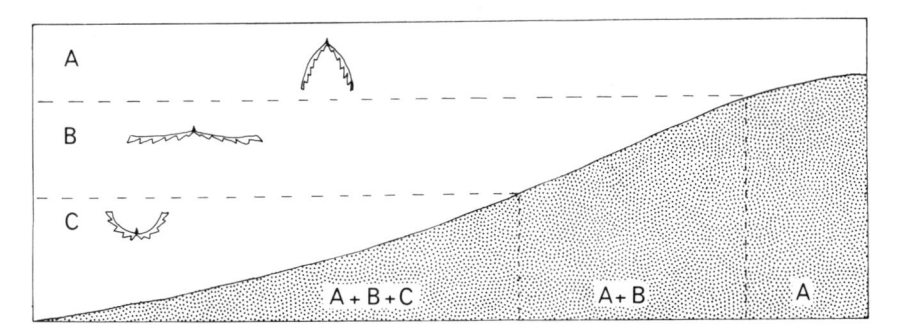

35. Possible depth-controlled confederations of graptolites and the resulting fossil associations. Only in the deepest sediments do members of all three confederations become buried together.

showing where and how the sea transgressed and retreated and, as Ziegler did,[10] how depth-controlled confederations of fossils moved with such movements of the sea.

At the levels considered so far, we may produce at most palaeogeographic maps for broad regions such as Europe and North America. As knowledge of the geology of all parts of the world increases, we may attempt to put these regional maps together for the entire globe. Attempts have been made in the past, but it is only within the last fifteen years or so that the importance of regarding geology as a worldwide subject has been realized and an understanding of past global patterns has emerged. This process is still only in its infancy. During the same period most geologists have been converted from regarding the positions of continents and oceans as having been essentially static in the past, to considering them as dynamic and their positions constantly changing. That is to say, the theory of continental drift, which has been around since the turn of the century, has only recently become widely accepted. Nevertheless, most geologists have yet to consider the possibility that the size of the earth may have changed, and meanwhile it is automatically assumed that it has not. The same incontrovertible evidence which shows that the continents and oceans have moved, also shows that the earth has expanded significantly during the last 250 million years, and probably over an even longer period.[11] Before outlining fossil evidence for past positions of continents and oceans or major climatic belts, it is necessary to review the evidence on which the present theory of continental drift is based.

Chapter 4

Faunal provinces and continental drift

Iron is not only the most magnetic and easily magnetized element, it is also abundant all over the earth's surface and occurs in almost all rocks. Not surprisingly all rocks are weakly magnetic. One way to make a permanent magnet is to heat a piece of iron or steel and allow it to cool in a strong magnetic field. As the metal cools it becomes magnetized in the orientation of the magnetic field. This type of magnetization is known as permanent magnetization because it can only be destroyed by reheating the metal or otherwise altering its internal structure. In an exactly similar manner, when an igneous rock cools it takes on a magnetization parallel to the earth's magnetic field at the time when it cooled. Unless the rock is reheated this remanent, or original, magnetization will survive to the present day and will furnish information about what the magnetic field of the earth was like when the rock cooled. Particles of sediment tend to be weakly aligned by the earth's magnetic field and, once cemented together, the resulting sedimentary rock will also have a weak remanent magnetization. Almost any rock, provided it has not been subsequently altered, can be used to study the earth's magnetic field at the time when the rock formed.

If an electric current flows through a wire it produces a magnetic field. By arranging large coils of wire in exactly the right configuration and passing precise amounts of electric current through them, it is possible to cancel out the earth's magnetic field completely and produce a 'field-free' area. A magnetometer can then measure the strength and orientation of the weak magnetization of any rock sample placed in the field-free laboratory. The procedure is basically simple. A cylindrical core is usually drilled from a rock, and its orientation is recorded. The sample is cleaned of any induced magnetization caused by the present-day magnetic field, by mild heating or rapid rotation in a weak magnetic field. Induced magnetization is only temporary, as for example in a nail picked up by a magnet which will itself attract iron filings, and it can be removed without seriously affecting the original remanent magnetization of the rock. The specimen is then mounted in the field-free laboratory and its remanent magnetization measured. Knowing the original orientation of the rock, for example with bedding horizontal in most sedimentary rocks, and the orientation of the magnetization of the sample, it is possible to calculate the orientation of the earth's magnetic field when the rock formed.

The present-day magnetic field of the earth is the same as that which would be produced by an enormous bar magnet nearly paralled to the earth's axis (figure 36) with a magnetic pole near each of the geographic poles. This is a dipolar magnetic field and it is assumed the earth's magnetic field has always had two poles. As everyone knows, anywhere on earth a horizontal compass needle points to the north magnetic pole. In addition to this, a compass needle free to rotate in a vertical plane that includes the magnetic poles will adopt a characteristic orientation which depends on latitude. At the north magnetic pole it will be vertical and pointing down into the earth; at the south magnetic pole it will also be vertical but pointing straight up into the sky; at the magnetic equator it will be exactly horizontal. Anywhere between either magnetic pole and the magnetic equator the needle will have a characteristic inclination (figure 36). Thus by measuring the original inclination of remanent magnetization we can tell not only in which direction the magnetic poles lay, but how far away they were.

Early in the study of palaeomagnetism two unexpected results were obtained. First the position of the magnetic poles appears to have changed with time, so-called 'polar wandering', and secondly the orientation of the magnetic field seems to have reversed periodically, in other words a compass needle which today would point to the north magnetic pole would have pointed to the south magnetic pole at certain times in the past. We do not yet understand how the earth's magnetic field is maintained, let alone how its polarity can reverse, but all current theories relate the magnetic field to the spin of the earth about its axis. The earth is believed to behave like a dynamo. If this is correct the magnetic and geographic poles have always been nearly coincident and, because a spinning object is very stable (the principle of a gyroscope), we believe that the orientation of the earth's axis, and therefore the positions of the magnetic poles, have always been the same in the past. From this it follows that the so-

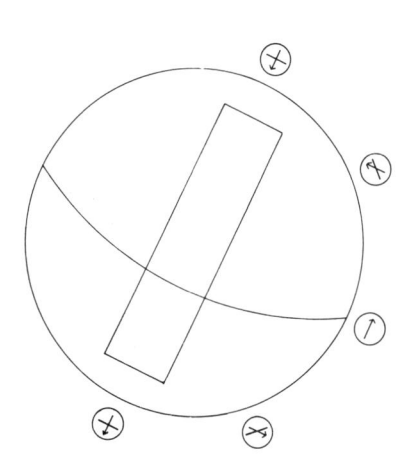

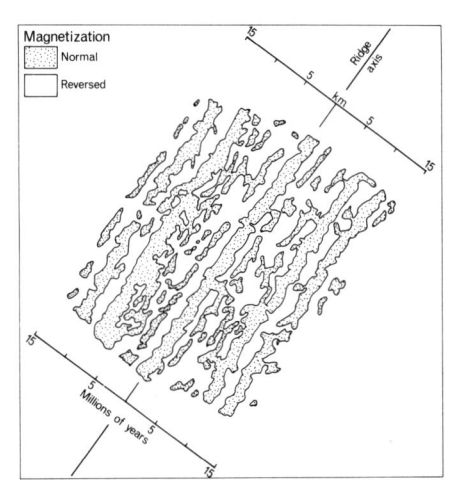

36. The earth's dipole magnetic field and the resulting magnetic inclination. A compass needle free to rotate in a vertical plane which includes the poles would adopt the orientations indicated at various latitudes. Hence we can use the inclination of palaeomagnetic samples to determine the contemporary latitude of the sample when it became magnetized.

37. The pattern of linear magnetic anomalies on either side of the Reykjanes Ridge in the Atlantic south of Iceland. Radiometric dating of the geomagnetic reversal timescale enables the rate of spreading to be calculated. It is approximately 1 cm. per year at this point on the Mid-Atlantic Ridge. (Based on fig. 6, 'Magnetic anomalies associated with mid-ocean ridges', by F. J. Vine, in R. A. Phinney (ed.), *The history of the earth's crust*, Princeton University Press, 1968.)

called 'polar wandering' is not due to movement of the magnetic poles, but to movements of the continents and oceans from which the rock samples were taken. The reversals of the magnetic field have enabled confirmation of this idea.

The theoretical strength of the earth's present magnetic field can be calculated for any part of the earth. The actual strength can be measured with a magnetometer and any difference is called the magnetic anomaly. Magnetic anomalies are positive when the observed strength of the field is greater than the theoretical and negative in the opposite case. Magnetometers can be towed from ships or mounted in aircraft, allowing rapid mapping of magnetic anomalies for wide areas of land or ocean. Over large regions of the oceans there are symmetrical sets of alternating linear positive and negative anomalies parallel to and on either side of the mid-ocean rift systems (figure 37). In 1963 Vine and Matthews[1] proposed that these linear anomalies were related to the remanent magnetism of the rocks in the ocean floor. Where the underlying rock was magnetized paralled to the present-day magnetic field of the earth its weak magnetism is added to that of the earth, producing a positive anomaly and, conversely, negative anomalies arise where the rocks were magnetized in the reverse orientation to the present-day magnetic field. Dating rocks with normal and reversed magnetization has produced a time scale for magnetic reversals (figure 38). Vine and

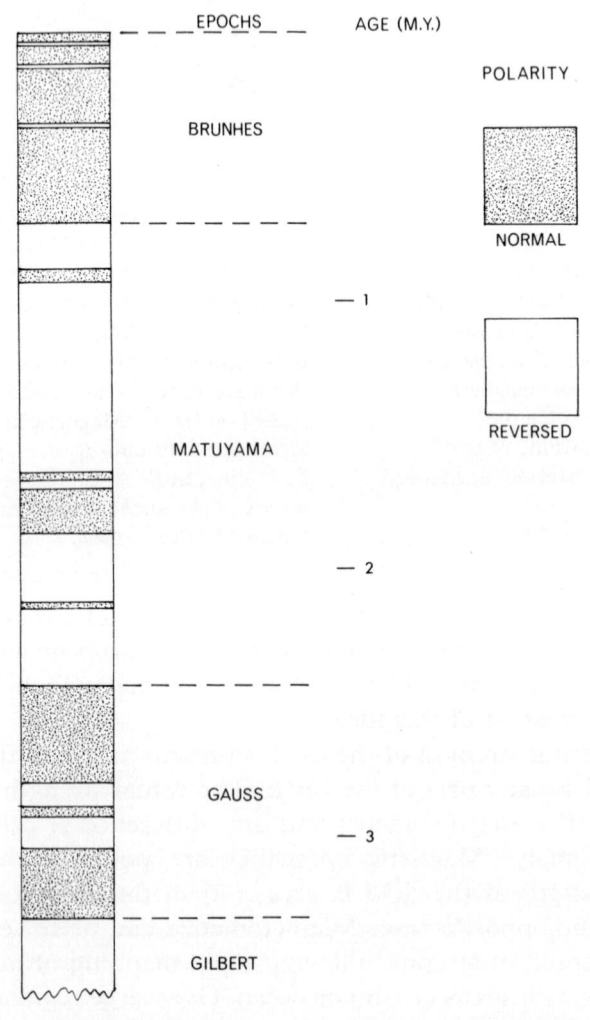

38. The magnetic reversal time scale for the last 3½ million years. This scale has now been extended back into the Mesozoic (approximately 100 million years).

Matthews postulated that new oceanic crust was formed during volcanic eruptions at the mid-ocean rift systems and gradually spread out from the rifts. After each eruption the rocks would cool and become magnetized parallel to the prevailing magnetic field of the earth which was sometimes normal and sometimes reversed. This explains why the magnetic anomalies are linear, parallel to and symmetrical about the mid-ocean rift system. They form a sort of stereo magnetic tape-recording of the history of the earth's magnetic field. Estimates of the rate of sea-floor spreading can be made. In the Atlantic, for example, rocks approximately one million years old occur fifteen kilometres from the Mid Atlantic Ridge on either side, which gives an average rate of spreading of three centimetres per year. Since Vine and Matthews' proposal, a great deal of oceanographic exploration has been carried out. Magnetic anomalies have been plotted for the greater part of all oceans, while the deep-sea drilling project has recovered rock samples and sediments from most regions of ocean floor. Relating the magnetic anomalies to the reversal time scale, direct radiometric dating of igneous rocks from the sea floor and fossil dating of the overlying sediments have all combined to confirm Vine and Matthews' hypothesis. Sea-floor spreading is now generally accepted as fact.

If new sea floor is created in the oceanic rifts, where does it all go? Assuming, as almost everyone does, that the size of the earth has remained constant, then for every bit of new crust formed in an oceanic rift an equal amount must be destroyed elsewhere. Earthquakes and volcanoes show a markedly non-random distribution over the globe (figure 39A). Not only do they occur along oceanic rift systems, but along island arcs, adjacent to ocean deeps and along major mountain chains. This distribution led to the theory of plate tectonics which suggests that the entire crust of the earth behaves as if it is composed of a few major (and some minor) plates (figure 39B) and that tectonic events (earthquakes, mountain building, and so on) occur only along the margins of these plates. According to this theory new oceanic crust is formed along ocean rift systems and old oceanic crust, which is more dense than continental crust, is dragged under the continents in subduction zones associated with deep ocean trenches. The Atlantic has 'quiet' margins. There are no ocean deeps, island arcs and, except along the Mid-Atlantic Ridge, few volcanoes and earthquakes. It follows that if the North Atlantic ocean floor is spreading at about three centimetres per year, then North America and Europe are separating by the same amount.

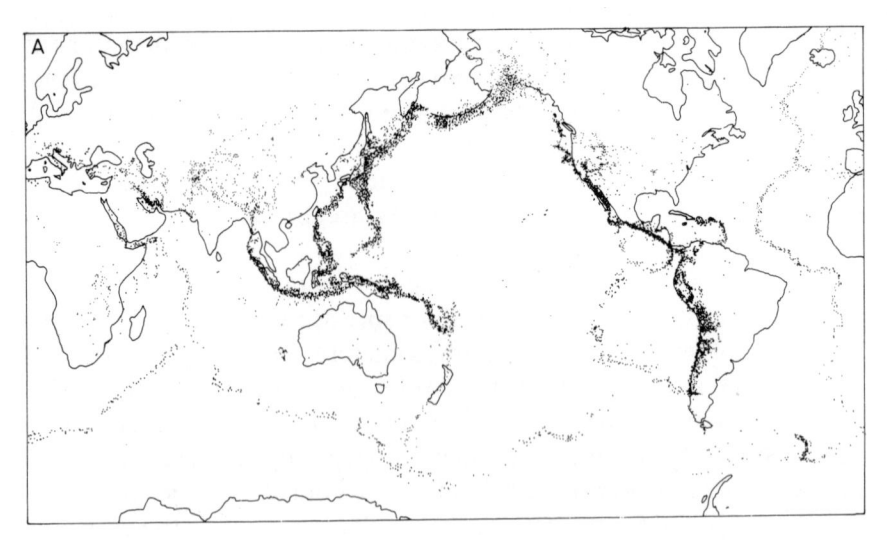

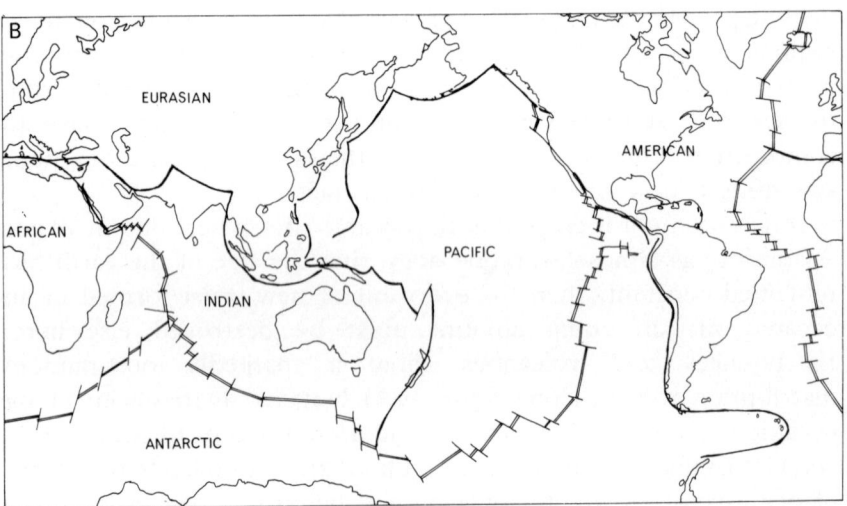

39. The distribution of earthquakes (A) and inferred plate margins (B) over the earth.

The Pacific, on the other hand, has active margins, the so-called 'circum-Pacific ring of fire', and includes many ocean deeps, island arcs, volcanoes and major earthquake zones. If North America is moving away from Europe, it must be getting closer to Asia on the other side (figure 40). Thus both the spreading of the Atlantic and Pacific sea floors is being compensated for by subduction zones around the margins of the Pacific alone. Although the Pacific sea floor is spreading, the ocean itself is actually getting smaller as the

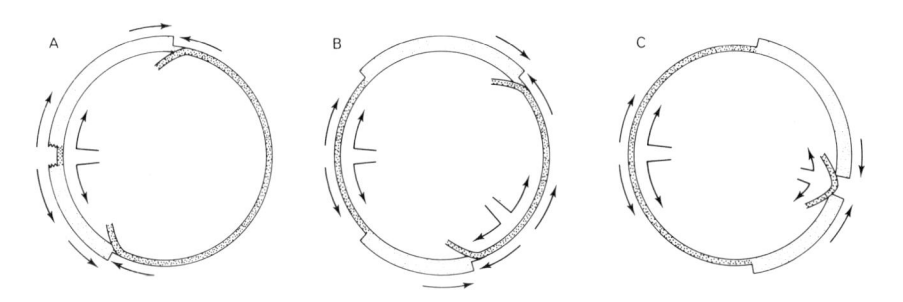

40. A simplified diagram to illustrate the drifting of continents around the globe. A. The position about 150 million years ago when the Atlantic Ocean began to open. B. The present-day position with the Atlantic spreading and the Pacific contracting. C. A projection into the future with the Atlantic at its widest and the Pacific almost closed.

continents bounding it ride over the oceanic crust. According to the theories of plate tectonics and sea-floor spreading, continents drift because they are pushed about by spreading ocean floors. At some times in the past continents drifted together to form supercontinents, and sediments deposited along the original continental margins became compressed into mountain chains. At other times continents have split apart into smaller fragments, but not necessarily along the lines of former oceans. The present-day continents are all made up of pieces which were attached to other continents in earlier times. Much of Scotland, Northern Ireland and western Norway, for example, was attached to North America in the Palaeozoic, while the Piedmont Province of the Carolinas in the United States was part of West Africa at that time.

As soon as a reasonable amount of information on the ages of parts of the ocean crust was available, it became possible to begin reconstructing the former positions of continents. To obtain an Eocene map of the Atlantic Ocean, for example, all one has to do is remove all the sea floor formed since the Eocene and then reassemble the continents on either side. North and South America were significantly closer to Europe and Africa during the Eocene. Incidentally, it is precisely this sort of exercise which has led Hugh Owen of the Natural History Museum in London to conclude that the earth has expanded significantly since Triassic times.[2] This is the furthest back in time that reconstructions can be made by direct methods since there is no known ocean floor older than Jurassic. Although moderately good reconstruction can be made for broad regions like the Atlantic, when attempts are made to reassemble accurate continental outlines over the entire globe, as Hugh Owen has done, gaps appear which cannot be accounted for by subduction. In conventional reconstructions of the Triassic Pacific Ocean, one such gap lies between Alaska and Asia; another lies between Australia and Asia. If the Bering Straits between Alaska and Asia were wider in the Triassic than they are now, then at some time since the Triassic the straits must have narrowed. Evidence of subduction zones and crustal compression ought to be found in the area. In fact, not only is there no such evidence, but, on the contrary, clear evidence of spreading and linear magnetic anomalies occurs. Exactly the same applies to the gap north of Australia. The conclusion that the world has expanded seemed inescapable and Hugh Owen has produced a series of world maps, all fitted to smaller globes, for various previous periods back to the Triassic when the earth was apparently only eighty per cent of its present diameter. We have no reason to suppose that the earth was not even smaller in pre-Triassic times. We can also see that not all the sea floor spreading of the present-day oceans is being accommodated by subduction, although I certainly believe that subduction does take place.

All this may seem far removed from palaeontology, but the oldest ocean floor present on earth today is only Jurassic in age and for any earlier time we cannot just remove ocean floor and reassemble continents. It is true that palaeomagnetic determinations of past pole positions will fix the latitude of a continent or continental fragment, but nothing fixes longitude, and continents may be assembled in a variety of positions. Continents may be looked upon as pieces of a jigsaw puzzle in which, to obtain a good fit, not only must the shapes match but the patterns must correspond as well. In the continental puzzle the pattern is indicated by geological structures, like mountain chains, and by faunal resemblances. At some times in the past, distinct faunal provinces existed, as they do today, and they help in reassembling former positions of continents. Furthermore, some fossils are climatic indicators and may be used to reconstruct former climatic belts. If we find polar and tropical fossil faunas side by side, the reconstruction would be doubtful to say the least. Indeed this last point may be used to test the assumption that the magnetic and geographic poles have always coincided more or less. Where palaeomagnetic determinations indicate a tropical latitude, the faunas should be tropical; where the latitude was apparently polar, the faunas should be polar, and so on.

In theory, recognition of past faunal provinces, even those of the early Palaeozoic, is easy. Fossil collections or published lists of fossils are compared. Where there are numerous fossils common to two collections, they probably belong to the same province; where there are very few or no common fossils, the two collections may have come from different provinces. This idea can be formalized for statistical treatment, and several different 'similarity coefficients' have been proposed. The simplest, 'Simpson's Index',[3] expresses the number of common genera (or species) as a decimal fraction of the total number of genera (or species) in the smaller fossil collection:

$$\text{Simpson's Index} = \frac{\text{Number of common fossils}}{\text{Number of fossils in smaller collection}}$$

A Simpson's Index of zero implies there are no common fossils at all, while a value of 1.0 implies that all fossils in the smaller collection also occur in the larger collection. Comparing every possible pair in a worldwide series of collections allows mapping of areas of high similarity which may represent past faunal provinces. Needless to say, computers are very useful in making these comparisons.

As always, in practice there are difficulties. First of all fossil assemblages are much more useful in recognizing provinces than fossil communities. If there really are no organisms common to the rocky-shore and sandy-bay communities used as examples at the beginning of chapter 3 and if they were preserved entire with no mixing, they might be misinterpreted as originating from different provinces. Certainly it would be difficult to argue that they belonged to the same province if they had no common fossils whatsoever. Of course fossil assemblages are much more common than fossil communities so that this difficulty is unlikely to cause confusion frequently, but it does mean that not all samples from within the same province will necessarily have high values of Simpson's Index when compared. It also means that low values of Simpson's Index may result from several different causes. The most obvious other cause is ecological. Comparison of non-marine and marine fossil assemblages, for example, will produce very few, if any, common fossils, although these are not normally regarded as faunal provinces.

Secondly, the fossil assemblages being compared should be of approximately the same age. If a Lower Palaeozoic collection of fossils is compared with a Tertiary collection, there will be no common genera, because of their vastly different ages. This problem is more serious than it might seem from the very obvious example just quoted and is a persistent cause of difficulties. We use fossils to date the rocks in which they occur (see chapter 6). We can only correlate, compare the ages of rocks in different places, if we can find the same fossils in different areas. Thus if we have two fossil collections which are completely different because they originally belonged to different faunal provinces, we can never be absolutely certain that they are of the same age because they have no fossils in common. This sort of difficulty occurs, for example, at the boundary of the Jurassic and Cretaceous in Europe. Ammonites, which are used to correlate the rocks of this period, appear to have occurred in two separate provinces: a Boreal province in northern Europe and a Tethyan province in the Mediterranean region. At present it is impossible to be certain that the boundary between the Jurassic and Cretaceous as accepted in Russia is the same as that accepted in southern Europe. Boundaries between faunal provinces are rarely sharp and the areas where faunas from two provinces mix are vital in correlation. In the Middle Jurassic in Britain we find ammonites from both the Boreal and Tethyan provinces mixed together and this helps greatly in correlation between southern and northern Europe, but towards the close of the Jurassic this critical area became a region of freshwater lakes and swamps so that no mixing of the marine ammonites was possible.

An even more subtle and persistent problem concerns the identification of the fossils. No one person can hope to travel all over the world collecting fossils of all ages and identifying them. Inevitably we rely heavily on other people's work. Yet published lists of fossils may be unreliable for all sorts of reasons. The same fossil may be known by different names in different parts of the world because no one has yet realized that it is the same. The blackbird, *Turdus merula*, has a different common name in every single European country in which it lives. To avoid this sort of confusion, scientists have agreed to give a Latin (or latinized) name to every living and fossil organism, to ensure that no two animals (or plants) have the same name and, where more than one name has been used, to accept the earliest as valid. This means that when a scientist discovers a new living or fossil animal, he must be sure first that it is genuinely new, that no one has described it before, and second, that the name he proposes to give it has never been used for any other animal. With the millions of living and fossil animals, this is very difficult, the more so because, for example, to find the oldest available name for a common European animal like the blackbird may require searching through literature in

1A. ABOVE A baby mammoth dima from Siberia which was only a few months old when it died approximately 44,000 years ago. The soft tissue has been preserved by a natural deep-freeze. The mammoth is just over 1 m. long. (From Robert F. Lundin, *J. Paleont.*, 52, fig. 1, p. 942, courtesy of the Society of Economic Paleontologists and Mineralogists and the author.)

1B. BELOW An Eocene fish from Italy. Here only the skeleton is preserved, but it is entire and there was no post-mortem disturbance of the fossil. The fish is 20 cm. long.

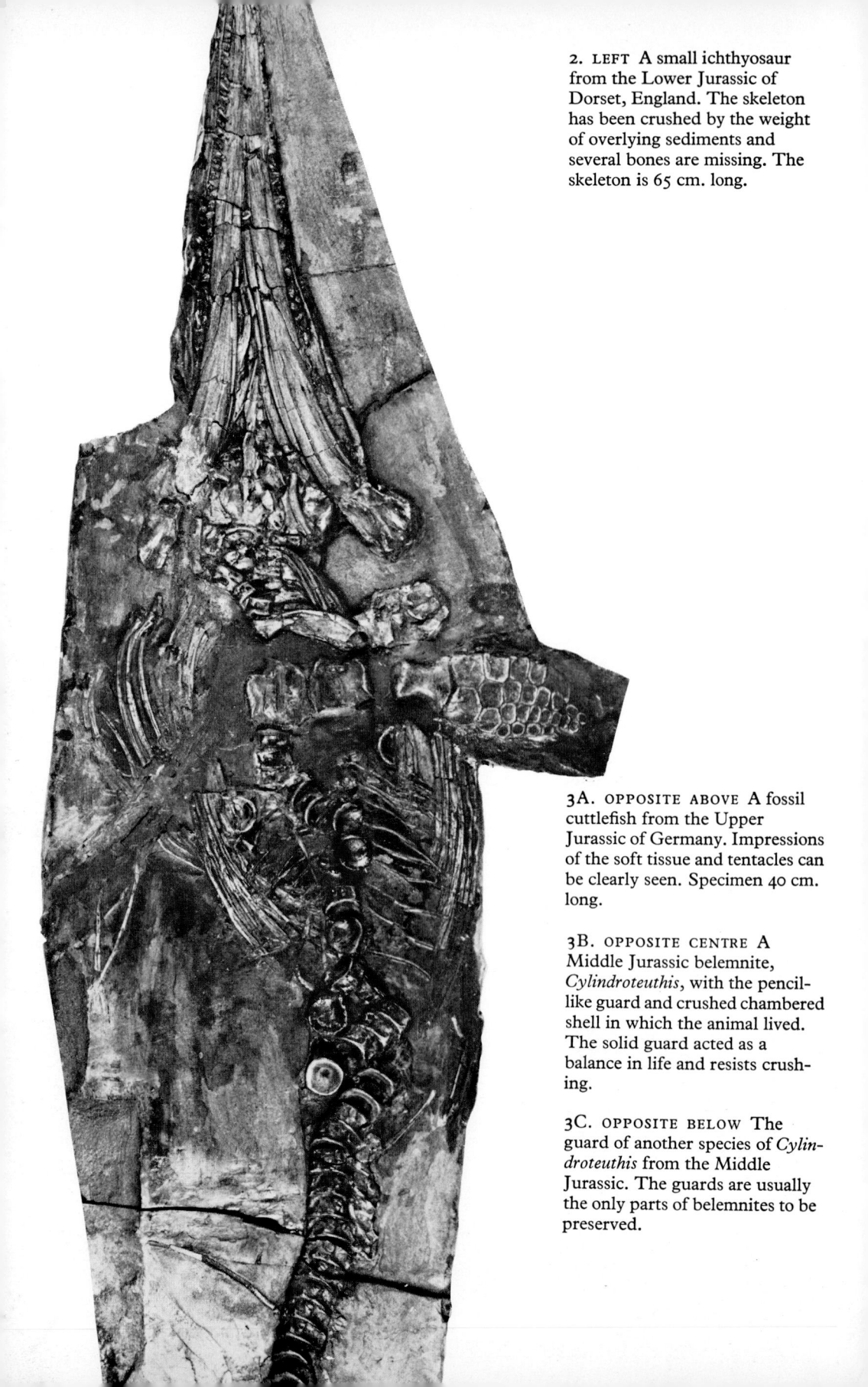

2. LEFT A small ichthyosaur from the Lower Jurassic of Dorset, England. The skeleton has been crushed by the weight of overlying sediments and several bones are missing. The skeleton is 65 cm. long.

3A. OPPOSITE ABOVE A fossil cuttlefish from the Upper Jurassic of Germany. Impressions of the soft tissue and tentacles can be clearly seen. Specimen 40 cm. long.

3B. OPPOSITE CENTRE A Middle Jurassic belemnite, *Cylindroteuthis*, with the pencil-like guard and crushed chambered shell in which the animal lived. The solid guard acted as a balance in life and resists crushing.

3C. OPPOSITE BELOW The guard of another species of *Cylindroteuthis* from the Middle Jurassic. The guards are usually the only parts of belemnites to be preserved.

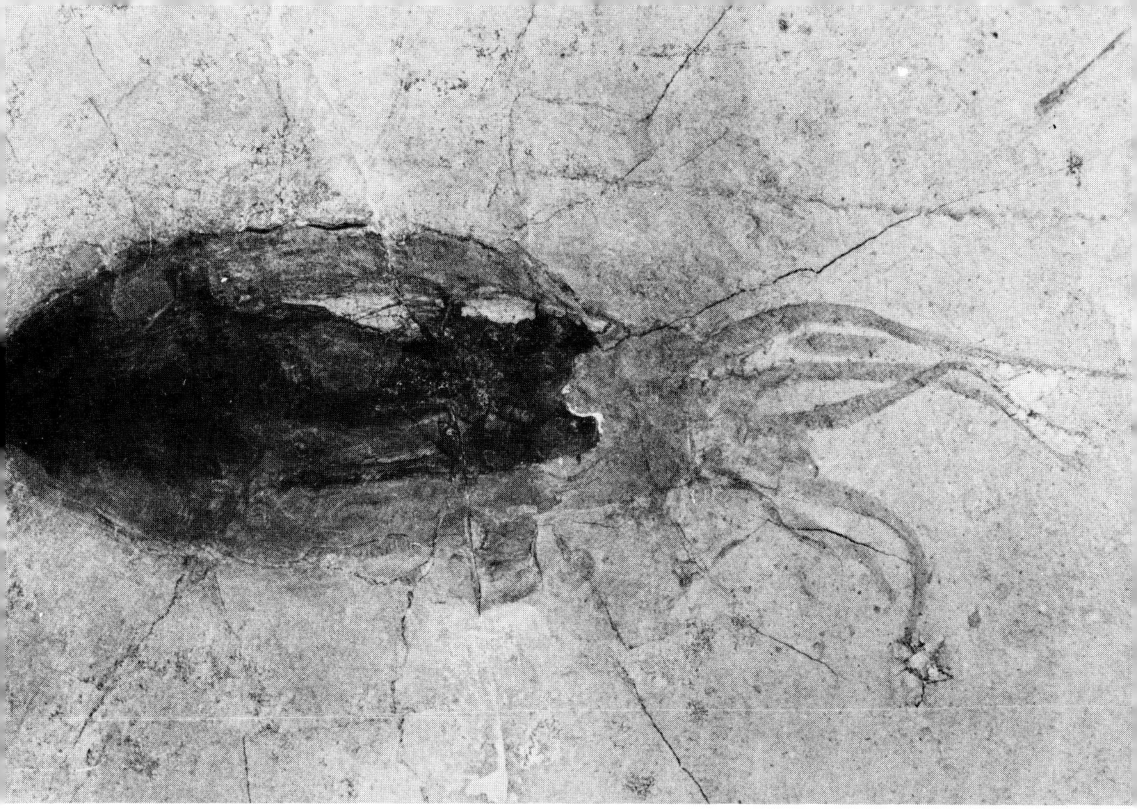

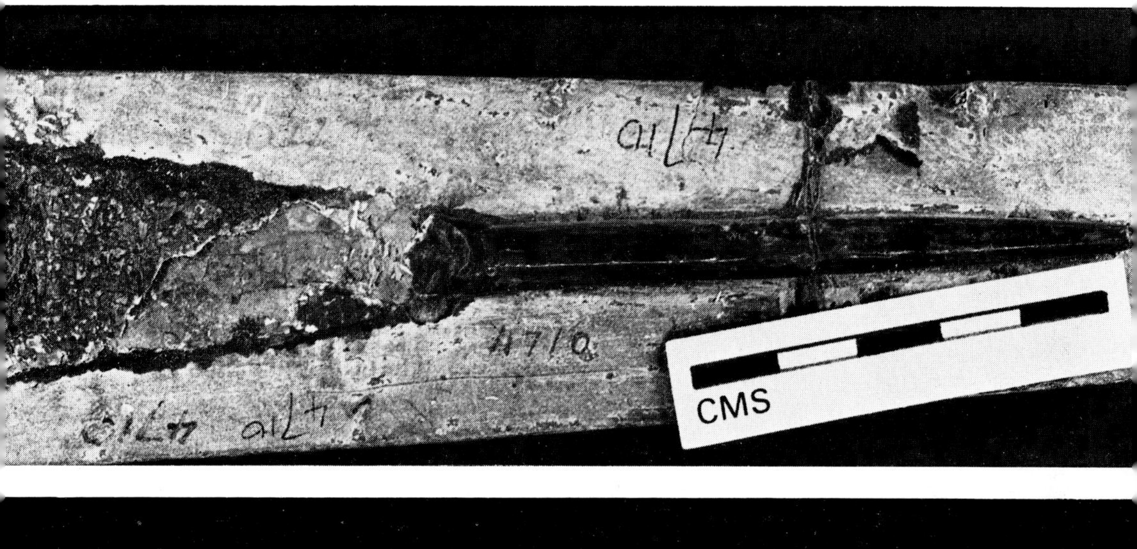
CMS

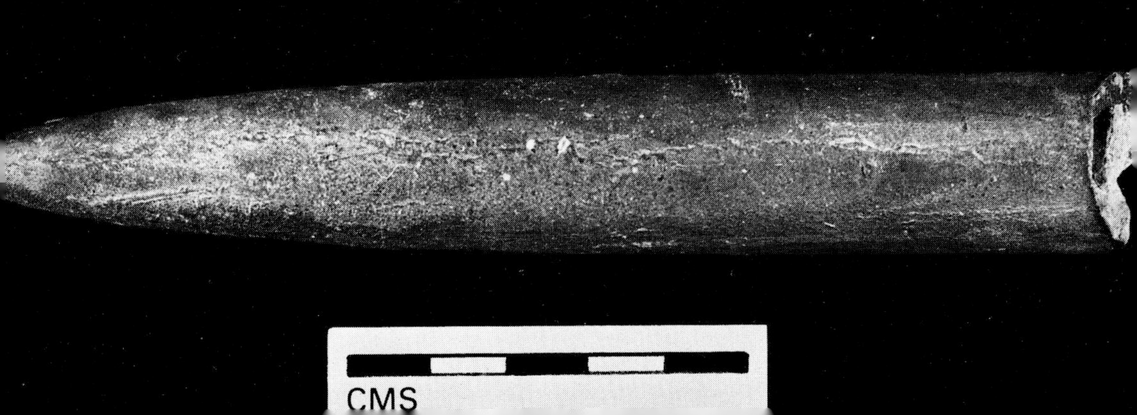
CMS

4. *Parkinsonia*, a large Middle Jurassic ammonite. This specimen has been polished to reveal the frilled suture lines which indicate where the internal chamber walls connected with the external shell. All the original shell has been removed. Original diameter 25 cm.

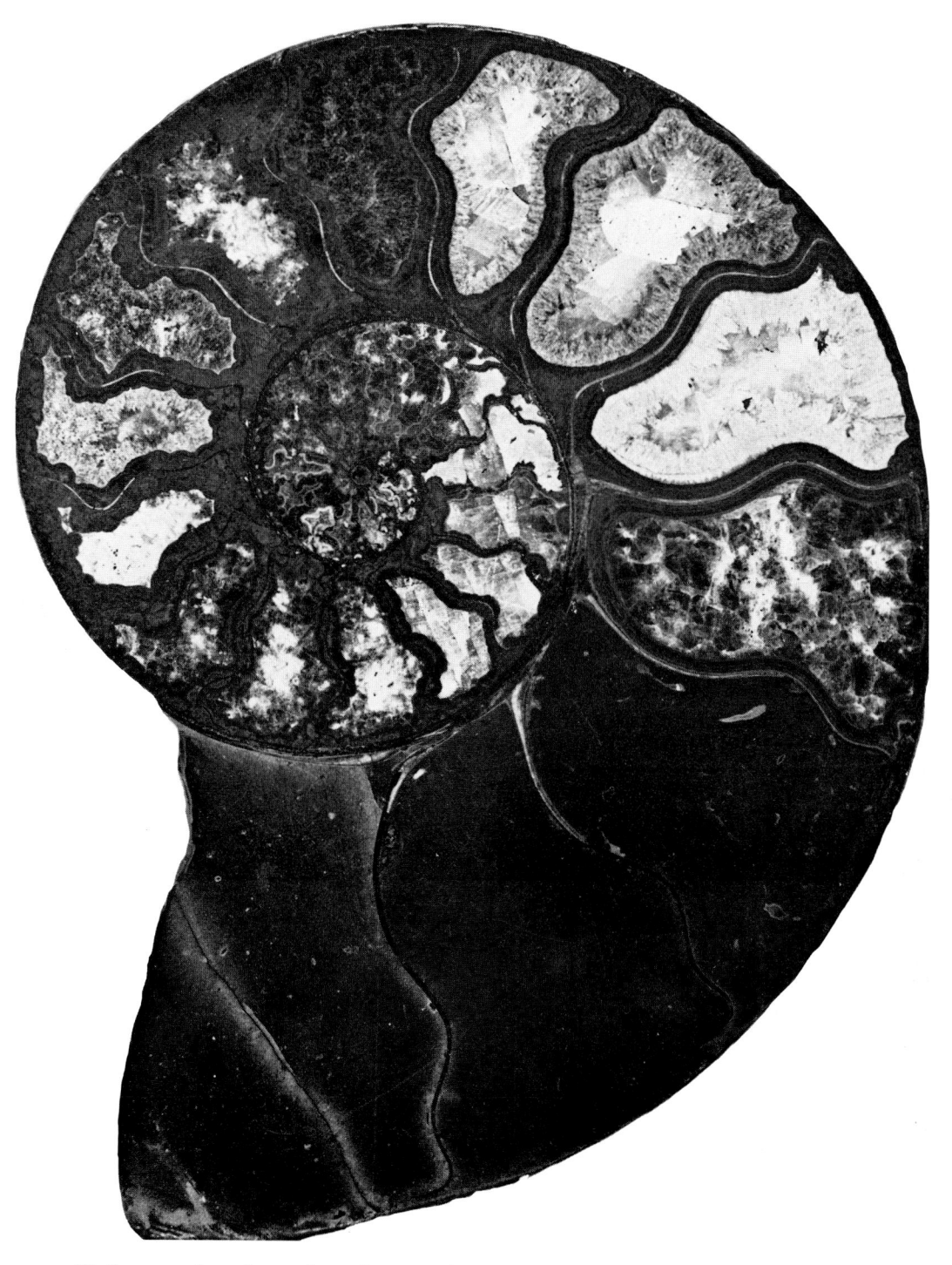

5. *Phylloceras*, a large Lower Jurassic ammonite sectioned to reveal the chambered shell and the complex history of diagenesis. The inner chambers have been filled with calcite crystals in four separate stages. Original diameter 20 cm.

6A. The Lower Jurassic ammonite *Dactylioceras* carved to resemble a fossil snake. A thriving trade formerly existed in these modified fossils at Whitby on the Yorkshire coast. Note that some of the original shell is still preserved in places and that the internal mould has the same ornament.

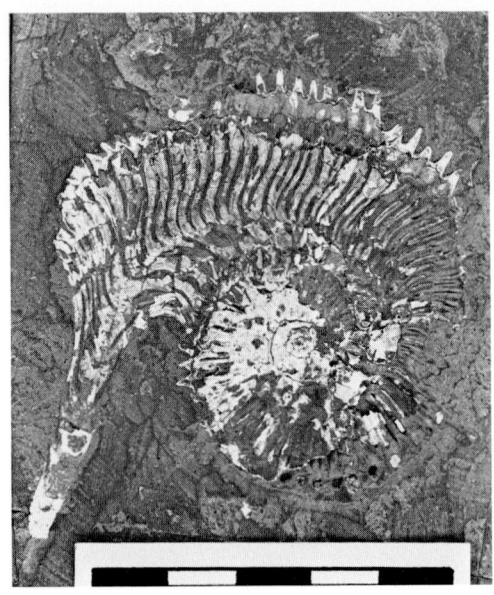

6B. *Kosmoceras*, a Middle Jurassic ammonite which developed lappets on the aperture at the adult stage. Ammonites with lappets are thought to have been males. This example still preserves traces of the original shell, but has been crushed by the overlying sediments.

6C. A section through another Middle Jurassic ammonite to show chambers either filled with sediments or only partly filled with calcite crystals. Sediment penetrated the inner chambers only in places where the shell was damaged before it was buried. Traces of the tube which connected the living animal in the last chamber with the first formed chamber can still be seen in this example.

7A. The Jurassic bivalve, *Trigonia*. In this example the original shell is preserved, but has been recrystallized. Traces of the crystal edges can be seen.

7B. Another example of *Trigonia* in which the shell has been dissolved away entirely to reveal internal structures. The fine tubes were formed by a burrowing organism before the sediment fill had hardened.

7C. *Arctostrea*, an Upper Cretaceous oyster with zig-zag shell edges. The zig-zags existed from the earliest growth stages and aligned currents on the gills to improve feeding efficiency.

7D. An Eocene bivalve, *Panopea*, with an enormous gape at the posterior end of the shell (right). Gaping shells indicate a burrowing or boring mode of life. Scales in cm.

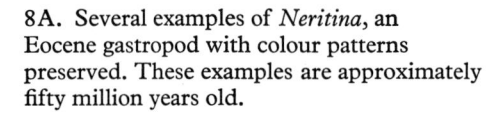

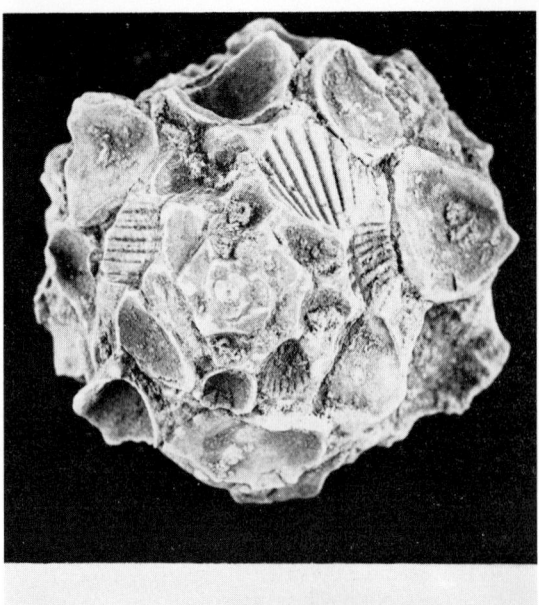

8A. Several examples of *Neritina*, an Eocene gastropod with colour patterns preserved. These examples are approximately fifty million years old.

8B. The remarkably well-camouflaged shell of the snail *Xenophora*. These snails attach pieces of other shells to their own as they grow. This camouflaging activity indicates that the snails lived on the surface of the sediment.

8C. A piece of Upper Jurassic Portland Stone with remains of many high-spired snails known locally as the 'Portland Screw'. In this rock none of the original shell material remains.

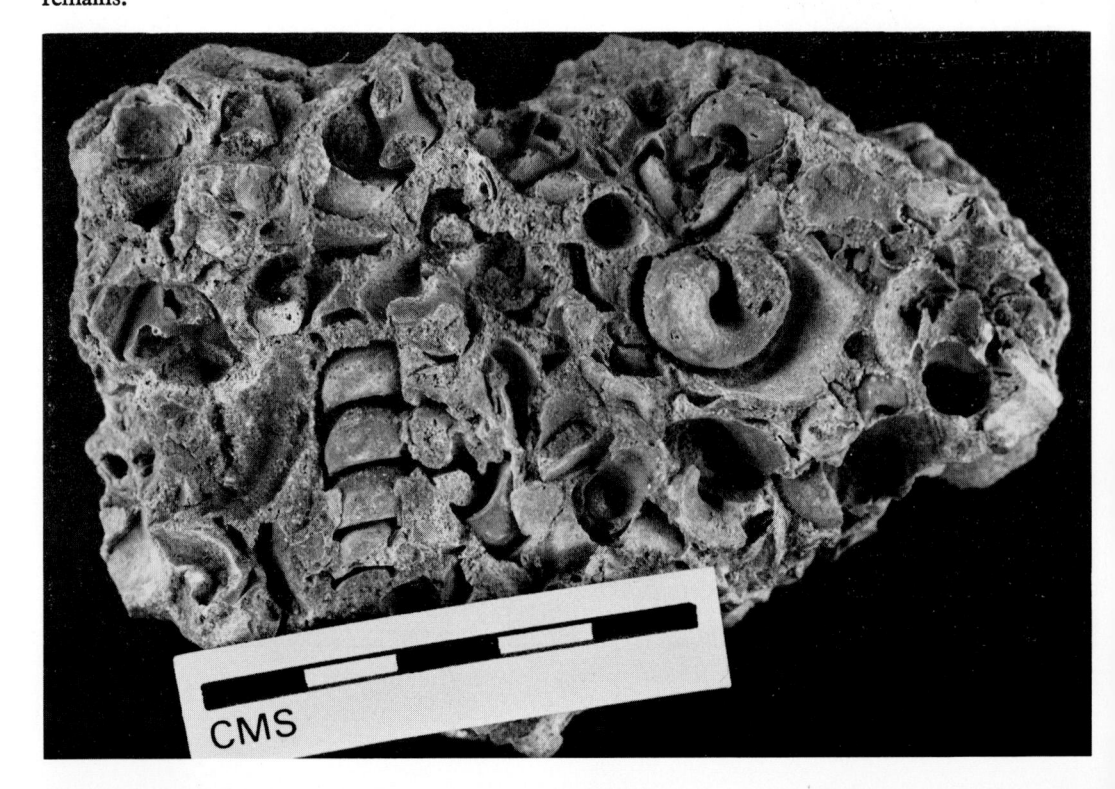

9A. RIGHT A piece of rock bored into by the bivalve *Lithophaga*. The shells of the bivalves remain within the borings in one or two cases (centre). Scale in cm.

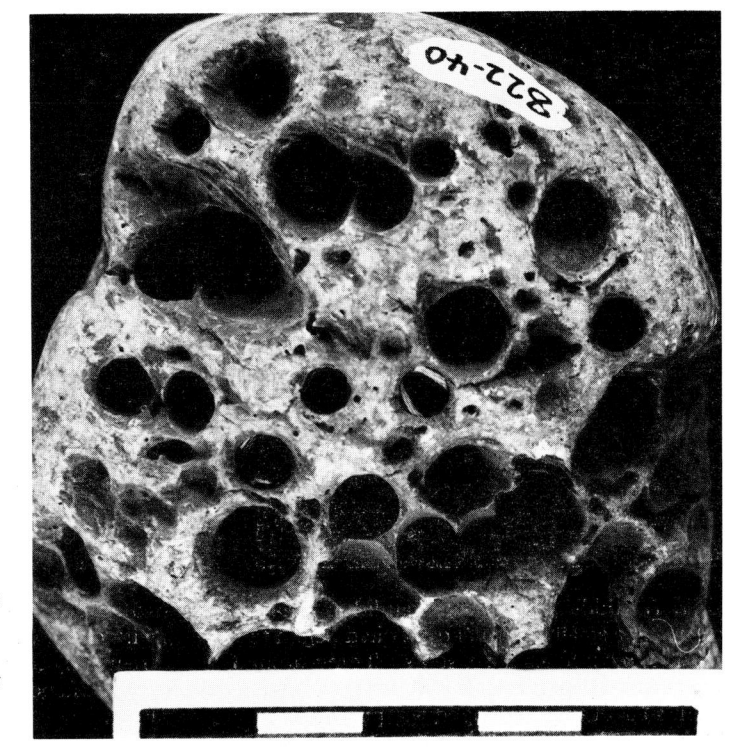

9B. BELOW A piece of Middle Carboniferous sandstone full of trace-fossil burrows. We do not know which animals made the burrows. The slab is 40 cm. wide.

10A. A Middle Jurassic terebratulid brachiopod on which a small epifaunal oyster had begun to grow (above). Since the oyster shell grew around the pedicle opening, we can infer that the attachment stalk of the brachiopod was present and hence that the oyster attached while the brachiopod was still alive. The brachiopod has the original shell preserved and shows very distinct growth lines.

10B. A 'nest' of terebratulid brachiopods with one rhynchonellid (top). Such 'nests' frequently represent original living clusters of brachiopods rather like modern mussel beds.

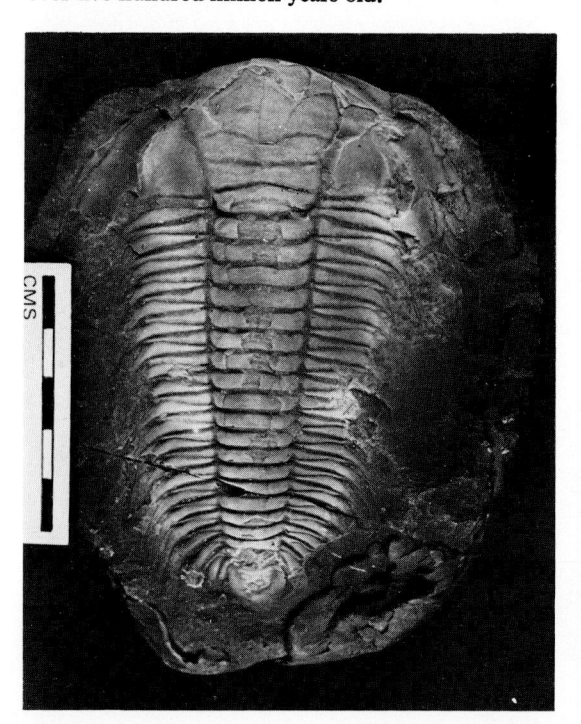

10C. The Cambrian trilobite, *Paradoxides*. A large complex arthropod with many segments, over five hundred million years old.

10D. The Silurian trilobite, *Calymene*. Neither trilobite can represent a moult stage since they are both complete skeletons.

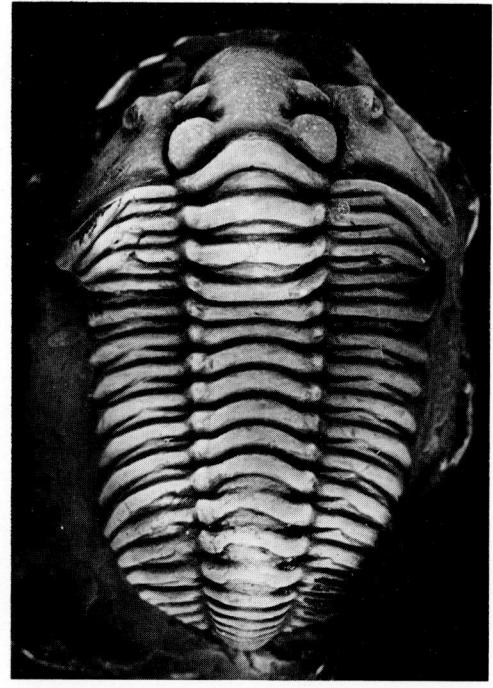

11A. An assemblage of the Lower Ordovician graptolites *Didymograptus*, from South Wales. Their preserved orientation is random and the colonies have been distorted by earth movements. They were originally all of approximately the same shape.

11B. *Chasmatopora*, a Middle Ordovician bryozoan colony from Estonia. Preservation of such delicate colonies implies very quiet conditions when the animal died and was buried.

11C. A 'crystal apple'. The Lower Ordovician cystoid *Sphaeronites*, from Sweden. These cystoids were distantly related to modern sea urchins and after they were buried the tests filled with calcite crystals growing in from the plates of the skeleton. This one has broken in half revealing the crystal filling.

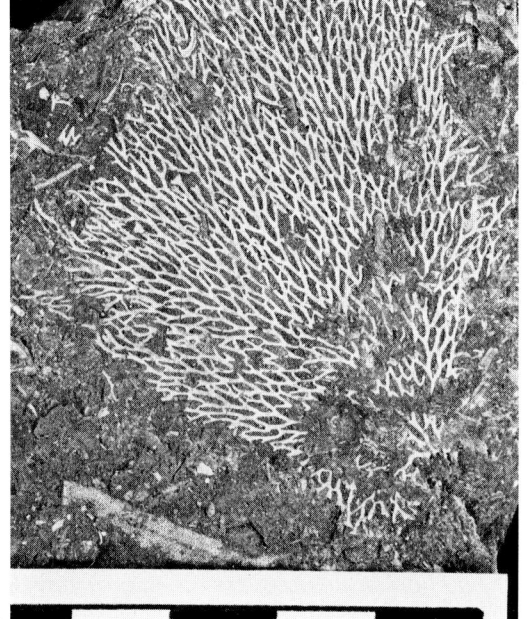

12A. LEFT A large slab of Upper Silurian rock from North Wales on which are preserved the remains of several crinoids (sea lilies). The consistent orientation of the crowns implies that they were all buried at the same time, probably by a sudden influx of sediment. The slab is 40 cm. wide.

12B. BELOW A slab of Lower Jurassic limestone covered with the crinoid *Pentacrinus*. Note the preservation of the delicate branching arms. Such specimens must have been buried immediately after death or the thousands of skeletal platelets would have soon separated. The slab is 20 cm. wide.

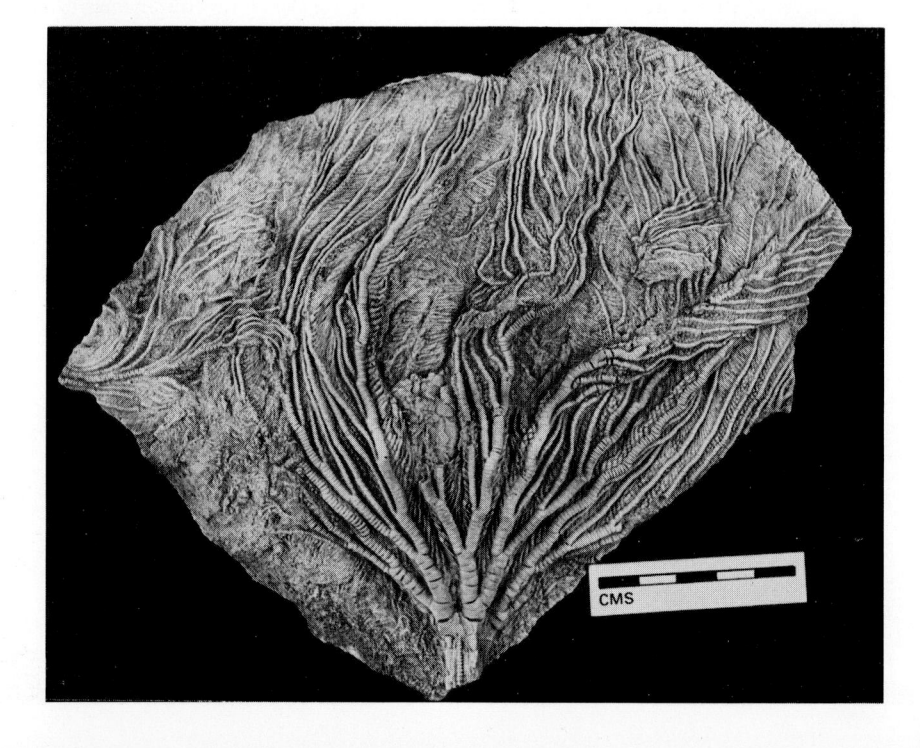

13A. ABOVE The regular Jurassic sea urchin, *Cidaris*. Note the five-fold symmetry of the test which in this example has been replaced by silica.

13B. BELOW LEFT The irregular sea urchin, *Clypeaster*. In irregular echinoids the five-fold symmetry has a bilateral symmetry superimposed upon it. In this specimen the original porous skeleton has been impregnated with calcite and shows cleavage planes where the skeleton has been damaged.

13C. BELOW RIGHT The sand-dollar, *Mellita*. The holes in the tests were filled with special spines in life which sieved the sediment and passed food particles to the mouth via grooves on the under surface. The small sixth hole worked the other way, passing faeces up from below to be left behind as the animal burrowed forward in the sediment.

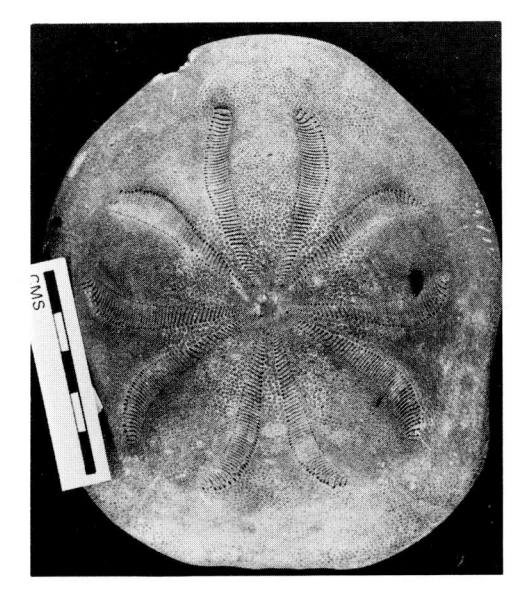

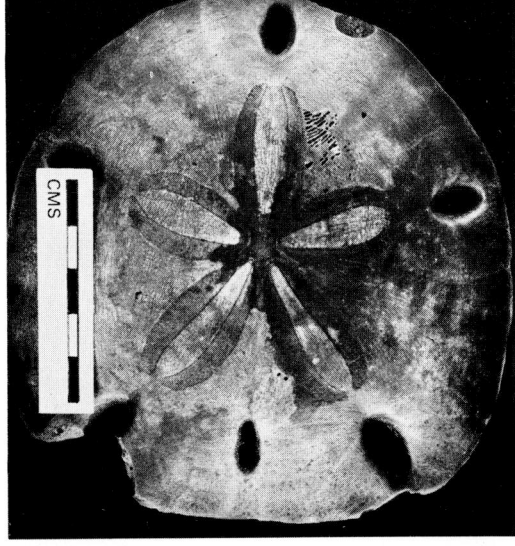

14A. A slab of Lower Jurassic rock with the remains of several brittlestars preserved on it. Starfish are frequently found in such 'starfish beds'. This one represents an example where the animals were overwhelmed by a sudden influx of sediment and were unable to exhume themselves. The slab is 30 cm. wide.

14B. A large slab of Middle Jurassic coral reef. Remains of several different small colonies are preserved together with other reef-dwelling organisms. The existence of such coral reefs in the British Jurassic has been used to argue that British waters were formerly much warmer than they are today. The slab measures 45 cm.

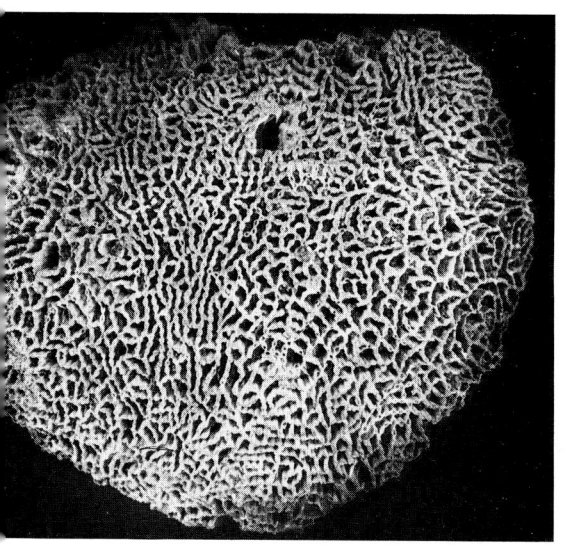

15A. LEFT The Silurian tabulate coral, *Halysites*, often called the 'chain coral' because the unique arrangement of corallites resembles the links of a chain. In this example the surrounding sediment has been weathered away so that the corallites stand proud much as they must have done when alive. Colony 10.5 cm. wide.

15B. RIGHT A polished surface of a Carboniferous rugose coral which reveals the detailed structure of the individual corallites. This specimen has been impregnated with calcite. Many such examples occur in the Devonian rocks at Petoskey on the shores of Lake Michigan where they are known as 'Petoskey Stones'.

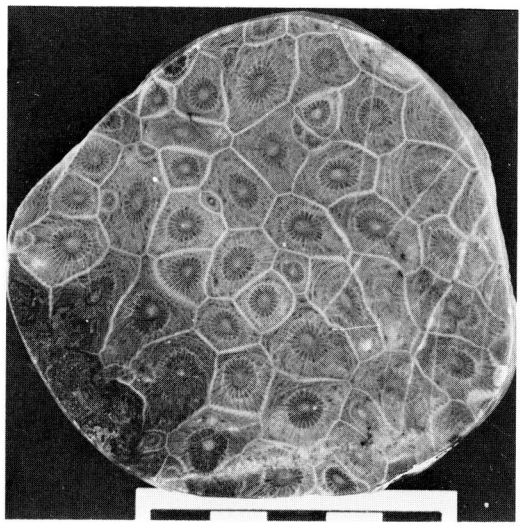

15C. LEFT A polished section of a Tertiary hexacoral in which the original skeleton has been both replaced and filled with opaline silica, but internal structures are exceedingly well preserved. Scales in cm.

16A. A frond of the Middle Jurassic gymnosperm *Williamsonia*, which, despite being 150 million years old, strongly resembles a modern conifer frond. The specimen is preserved as a carbonaceous film. Scale in cm.

16B. A section through a piece of fossil wood showing the tree rings. The specimen has been preserved by impregnation with calcite and is not crushed. The excentric form of the growth rings indicates that the wood came from a branch not the main trunk of the tree. Only vertically growing wood has nearly circular concentric growth rings.

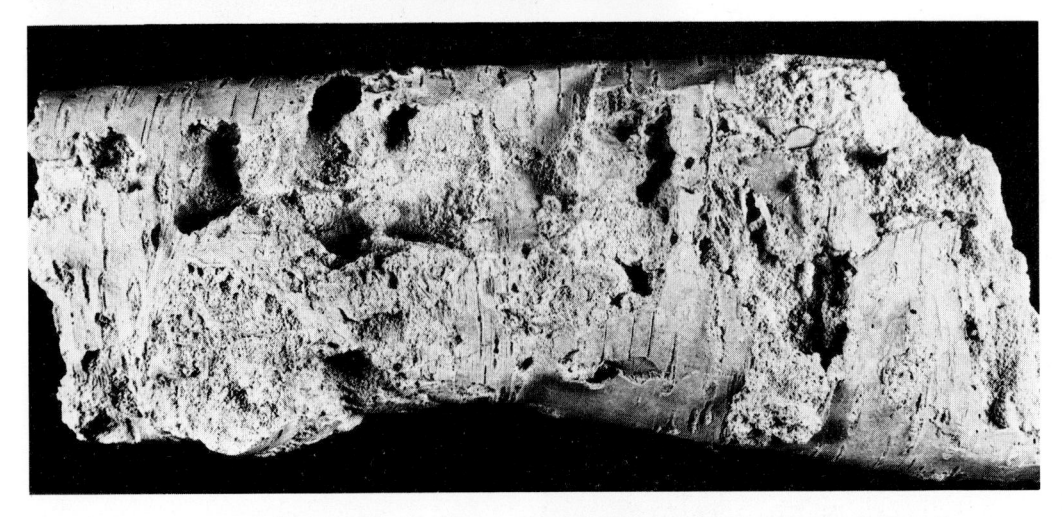

16C. The impression of the trunk of a birch tree, *Betula*, from the Caerwys Tufa, North Wales. The tufa formed from waters charged with calcium carbonate which oozed from the hills above Caerwys about eight thousand years ago. The trunk is 50 cm. long.

all European languages. Synonyms (different names for the same animal) and homonyms (the same name for different animals) are regrettably very common, and just as the same fossil may have different names in different countries, the same name may be applied to quite different fossils in different places. What Americans call sparrows belong in the thrush family (Turdidae) and are completely different from European sparrows which belong in the finch family (Fringillidae). The name is so entrenched now that American books on bird watching insist that European sparrows are not really sparrows at all, but it is very difficult to get a European to accept that! With formal Latin names for everything, this sort of difficulty should eventually be eliminated, but we still have a long way to go.

Specialists may disagree on classification. Two species may be considered, by one authority, to belong to the same genus but to be in widely different genera by another. Furthermore, there is a problem related to the time when the fossils were classified. As more and more new fossils (and living organisms) are found and described, their classification inevitably becomes more complex. Linnaeus, who founded the modern system of naming organisms, may have been able to use a handful of genera for all bivalves, but now there are thousands of genera arranged in numerous families and orders. Inevitably, time-honoured old genera are split up into new genera. What were subgenera become genera, genera become families, and so on to accommodate the ever-increasing number of organisms being described. Fossil lists published last century will contain many 'catch-all' genera and give a false impression of similarity, while a modern work may give an artificial impression of high diversity. The diversity may be equal elsewhere but masked by old, all-embracing names. This last problem of identification is no reason not to attempt to recognize past faunal provinces. If we wait until all the difficulties of naming and classifying fossils have been solved, nothing will ever get done. Like painting the Forth Bridge, by the time a major fauna is revised it is time to start at the beginning again.

All these difficulties can largely be overcome by not attempting to bite off more than can be chewed, so to speak. Most attempts to recognize past faunal provinces are based on single groups of organisms. One man may reasonably expect to become familiar with trilobites or brachiopods, for example, in his lifetime, particularly if he also confines his attention to one geological period. So we find that some of the best results have come from studies of Cambrian or Ordovician trilobites, Ordovician brachiopods, Carboniferous land plants, etc. No one person can be expected to identify everything correctly, but his or her mistakes are likely to be consistent and much less likely to distort the overall picture. Where one has to rely on published work, it is best if samples are available. This is one reason why specimens are deposited in museums. At the very least the fossils should be illustrated and nowadays no one relies on fossil lists alone for this sort of work.

Once experts have published interpretations of past faunal provinces based on two or more groups of fossils for the same period of time, it becomes possible to compare the results. Total disparity will cast doubt on some or all of the interpretations, but closely comparable results will greatly strengthen them. The fact that Ordovician trilobites, brachiopods and echinoderms show similar patterns of distribution, the boundaries of which change at similar times, is very difficult to explain in any other way than that they originally belonged to distinct faunal provinces. Indeed the pattern of distribution of Ordovician shelly faunas may be used to illustrate the successful search for past faunal provinces.

Early in the Ordovician the distribution of brachiopods shows distinct clustering into two faunal realms, an American and a European, which can themselves be subdivided into smaller provinces.[4] The American realm includes brachiopod faunas from north-west Scotland and north-west Ireland, both of which were part of North America in the Lower Palaeozoic. This pattern of distribution is maintained with little change until early in the Upper Ordovician, by which time the European realm shows a fairly clear subdivision into a Baltic province and a South European province. During the rest of the Upper Ordovician the area covered by the Baltic faunas expanded rapidly, displacing the American and to a lesser extent the South European faunas. By the latest Ordovician (Hirnantian) very uniform faunas occurred over much of the world, heralding the appearance of the almost completely cosmopolitan brachiopod faunas of the Silurian. The pattern of distribution for Ordovician trilobites is similar, although the details vary a little.[5] Five principal provinces, or faunas, can be recognized of which the American, Baltic and South European occupy very similar areas to their brachiopod counterparts. In addition there seems to have been a separate province in South America and Australasia and a South-East Asian fauna which shows some affinities with that of South Europe. Again this sort of distribution pattern remains stable throughout the Lower and Middle Ordovician until the early Upper

Ordovician when boundaries begin to shift rapidly and some provinces merge so that by the end of the Ordovician there is one cosmopolitan fauna worldwide. Although less numerous, Ordovician echinoderms also show a similar pattern of distribution and similar changes in distribution with time.[6] North American, Baltic and South European faunal provinces are quite distinct in the early Ordovician. Their limits are closely similar to the trilobite province boundaries. The South-East Asian echinoderm fauna shows affinities with that of South Europe, but there are, as yet, so few fossil echinoderms known from the southern continents that nothing can be said about a possible province to correspond to the South American–Australian trilobite province. Again by Upper Ordovician times and on into the Silurian, provincial boundaries become blurred and a cosmopolitan fauna predominates. Migration between provinces reached a peak in early Upper Ordovician times.

The favoured explanation of these distributions is that a large ocean existed between the Americas and Europe, Asia and Africa during the early and mid Ordovician. It acted as a barrier to the dispersal of shallow water benthonic fauna such as trilobites, brachiopods and echinoderms. This ocean was probably well established in Cambrian times and may have had its origins back in the late Precambrian. During the Ordovician the ocean began to contract, and by Upper Ordovician times it was sufficiently narrow to allow migration of some benthonic fauna. As it continued to narrow, more and more forms crossed between the shorelines and shallow seas on either side until by Silurian times thorough mixing had occurred. In more recent times a similar mixing of faunas occurred when North and South America became connected by the Isthmus of Panama. Northern placental mammals migrated into South America largely replacing the southern marsupial fauna, although a few conspicuous exceptions like the marsupial opossum have successfully migrated as far north as the Canadian border. An analogous faunal turnover occurred with Ordovician brachiopods during the Upper Ordovician when European (Baltic) forms almost entirely eclipsed the American forms and their descendents dominated Silurian brachiopod faunas. There was more of a two-way trade with echinoderms, but on the whole more forms migrated from Europe and Asia to America than came the other way. This Lower Palaeozoic ocean finally closed towards the end of the Silurian Period with the formation of the Caledonian and part of the Appalachian mountain chains.

Not all palaeontologists accepted these ideas completely. In particular it is known that towards the end of the Ordovician there was an extensive glaciation in North Africa, which lay close to the contemporary South Pole on palaeomagnetic evidence. Some workers[7] have argued that the lowering of sea level during the glaciation killed off the American brachiopods and European forms merely replaced the American species which had become extinct. Sea level changes undoubtedly affect shallow benthonic marine faunas and may well have caused some extinctions, but since the sea level changes would have been worldwide (eustatic) it is difficult to see why they should kill off American brachiopods completely while leaving European ones almost unscathed. To me it seems more likely that the European brachiopods eliminated the American ones in the Ordovician by competition just as the North American placental mammals replaced the South American marsupials in the Pleistocene.

Climate is another possible factor which may have determined past faunal provinces. The distributions of Ordovician conodonts[8] (microscopic tooth-like fossils of uncertain zoological affinities) and graptolites[9] (colonial hemichordates), both of which are thought to have been part of the plankton, appear to have been largely climatically controlled. It seems there was a widespread tropical fauna with more local colder faunas near the contemporary poles. Possibly some of the provinces described for brachiopods, trilobites and echinoderms were also climatically controlled. Certainly there is good evidence that the South European–North African faunas were cold to polar, while the Baltic and American faunas were more tropical or equatorial. The two European Provinces were probably separated at least in part by a climatic barrier. However, since both the Baltic and North America lay close to or across the contemporary equator, why are their benthonic shelly faunas not cosmopolitan as the conodont and graptolite faunas were? Indeed there seems to have been a difference between the provincial barrier separating North America and the Baltic on the one hand and that separating South Europe and the Baltic on the other. There is no more evidence for a substantial ocean between the Baltic and South Europe than there is for a climatic barrier between North America and the Baltic.

Whatever the correct explanation is, it must take account of the fact that three widely different elements of the Ordovician benthonic fauna (brachiopods, trilobites and echinoderms) show similar distribution patterns and changes in these patterns which occur at the same time, whereas two elements of the plankton (graptolites and conodonts) show a completely different pattern. Doubtless eustatic changes in sea level, glaciations and climatic barriers contributed to the precise details of these distributions, but the overall pattern of high provincialism early in the Ordovician and an increase in cosmopolitanism in the later Ordovician seems established at least for marine benthos. The barrier between North America and Europe seems to have been an ocean, all that remains of which is the Caledonian Mountain Chain, while that between the Baltic and South Europe may well have been climatic. Oceans do not form barriers to planktonic organisms, which may well account for the differences between the distribution patterns of Ordovician shelly and planktonic faunas.

Not all provinces are based on marine fauna. It has long been known that in the late Palaeozoic the flora of the southern continents differed from that of the northern continents. The distribution of the southern flora, known as the *Glossopteris* flora, after one of the characteristic plants, was used by early protagonists of continental drift to argue that all the southern continents (South America, South Africa, India, Australia and Antarctica) once formed a supercontinent called Gondwanaland. Through the upper Palaeozoic a progressive differentiation of flora seems to have occurred, from a cosmopolitan flora in the Devonian, through three provinces in the Carboniferous to five provinces in the Permian as the Siluro-Devonian supercontinents gradually fragmented.[10]

It seems, then, that not only can the worldwide distribution of fossils be used to recognize past faunal provinces, but that in the Palaeozoic fossil distribution is potentially the most useful test of both the existence of such faunal and floral provinces and their changes due to continental drift. Furthermore, we may be able to distinguish provincial barriers caused by drifting continents from those caused by climatic factors. This leads us to consider fossils as indicators of past climates.

If palaeomagnetic evidence indicates that in Ordovician times North Africa lay near the South Pole and Scandinavia near the Equator, can we recognize their respective shallow marine (shelly) faunas as polar and tropical, respectively, on independent evidence? Are there sediments or specific groups of fossils which are good climatic indicators? At the present, for example, most reef building corals, the so-called hermatypic corals, are confined to shallow water in tropical latitudes, i.e. between 30° north and south of the Equator.

Can we find similar climatic indicators for the Palaeozoic? The answer is that we can, but we need to interpret the evidence carefully and use as many different types of evidence as possible. An interpretation based on several fossil groups as well as on sedimentary criteria will be sounder than one based on a single line of evidence. This is even true of present-day corals. Not all corals, not even all reef-forming corals, are tropical. There is an extensive reef in deep water in the Skagerrak off Norway, but it consists of a single species whereas tropical reefs have many different coral species as well as tropical molluscs, arthropods, echinoderms, fish and marine algae associated with them. The sediments associated with tropical reefs are different from those which occur round cold, deep-water reefs like the one in the Skagerrak. First of all let us consider the types of sediments which are good climatic indicators and then the fossil evidence for climate. As is so frequently the case in geology, the arguments on which the interpretations are based are largely actualistic (or uniformitarian), involving comparisons of the present-day occurrence of sediments and organisms with past occurrences. However, as we shall see later, even estimates of past temperatures are possible.

Some sediment types are reliable as broad climatic indicators and a few of the most obvious will be considered here. At the present time the vast majority of carbonate sediments are accumulating in shallow tropical seas. In particular there are certain types of carbonate sediments which are good indicators of this environment. Modern coral reefs, which are largely composed of carbonate-depositing algae, the so-called coralline algae, as well as true corals, have already been mentioned. Potentially they are very good climatic indicators. A good 'reef rock' should immediately cause a field palaeontologist to look for other indicators of tropical climate. Ooliths are sand-grade particles with a concentric structure, and are formed by precipitation around a central seed grain in shallow agitated seas. The agitation causes deposits to form all round the grain and keeps adjacent grains separate. Ooliths are usually composed of calcium carbonate, but are sometimes formed of other compounds including economically important iron-bearing minerals. The best-known accumulations of ooliths in the world today occur on the Grand Bahama Bank in the Caribbean. A rock composed of ooliths is called an oolite and oolitic limestones are generally good indicators of tropical climates. They are less certain indicators of depth however. Ooliths may *form* in shallow seas, but are easily carried down into deeper waters, a process which is currently happening on the edge of the Grand Bahama Bank. A micritic limestone with occasional ooliths may well have formed in deeper water with the ooliths carried in from shallower environments. A clean spary oolite with current-indicating structures, such as cross bedding, is much more likely to be an *in situ* shallow-water rock. As with everything else, ooliths are not infallible indicators of tropical conditions. They form in agitated water where the conditions are right for precipitation. Large ooliths, called pisoliths (literally pea stones) form in caves and mineral springs in temperate climates. Thus oolitic rocks are not necessarily even marine, but since cave and mineral spring deposits are rarely extensive, true marine oolites can usually be recognized as such even without any fossil evidence to confirm their environment.

Many tropical algae, such as *Penicillus, Acetabularia, Udotea* and *Rhipocephalus*, secrete minute needles of aragonite (the unstable form of calcium carbonate) which, on the death of the algae, accumulate to form extensive deposits of aragonite mud. Most of Florida Bay on the Gulf Coast of the United States is floored with aragonite mud deposits. This aragonite mud is the source of much of the micrite in micritic limestones, having merely converted from unstable aragonite to stable calcite without any change in grain size. Extensive deposits of micritic limestone also probably formed in tropical climates. Indeed a suite of rocks dominated by carbonates, particularly shallow-water carbonates, is probably as good an indication of tropical conditions as one is likely to get from sediments.

At the opposite extreme, polar or glacial climates leave behind clear evidence in the form of glacial deposits which are collectively known as till. Tillites are fossil glacial deposits, several examples of which are known in the stratigraphic column. Tills are characteristically very poorly sorted, and include fresh mineral grains and pieces of rock which are broken and have sharp edges and corners and are hence very immature sediments; when present, large pebbles have scratched surfaces. Where large continental glaciers reach the sea, as around the coasts of Greenland or Antarctica, large pieces (icebergs) break off, a process known as calving. Any rock material incorporated in the iceberg will eventually sink to the sea floor when the iceberg melts. Sediments with exotic rocks of this sort occur off the coast of Labrador and are known as tilloids. Again fossil tilloids are known and their texture is so characteristic that it has been recognized even in the intensely metamorphosed rocks of the Highlands of Scotland. It is true that floating tree trunks also carry exotic rocks out to sea, but they are much less significant and can only occur in Devonian or younger rocks. Tillites and tilloids are known from the late Precambrian (Varangian) in Norway, Spitsbergen, Scotland and elsewhere; in the uppermost Ordovician (Hirnantian) of North Africa, Spain and Brittany and in the Permo-Carboniferous of the southern continents. Their distribution in the Permo-Carboniferous of South America, South Africa, India, Australia and Antarctica was one of the earliest lines of evidence for continental drift and was used to argue that these particular continents were much closer together at that time. The Ordovician tillites of North Africa are associated with many topographical features, like *roches moutonnées* and striated pavements, which indicate glacial action. They also occur close to the inferred South Pole and hence confirm the palaeomagnetic evidence.

'Red beds', an association of non-marine sediments, usually of a rusty brown colour, are perhaps the best indicators of arid climates. Although these may not necessarily indicate latitude and hence confirm palaeomagnetic data, at the present day most deserts occur between latitudes 20° and 40° north and south of the Equator. In arid climates chemical weathering, particularly hydration, is reduced by the lack of water, while erosion is increased by the lack of vegetation cover. Tremendous amounts of material are eroded, transported and deposited during flash floods which follow the infrequent rains in deserts. Immature sediments result, especially arkoses which are sandstones that contain the mineral felspar. Felspars normally decay by hydration. Desert sand grains have a characteristic surface texture, wind-faceted pebbles (ventifacts) develop along with distinctive sedimentary structures, including dune bedding, and they all indicate desert conditions. Above all, perhaps, most desert deposits are a rusty brown colour, due to the oxidation of iron compounds. It is this feature which has caught the eye of field geologists and given rise to the term 'red beds'. Again not all 'red' sediments are desert deposits, but when all compositional, textural and structural features are considered together, desert deposits are very easy to recognize.

As far as organisms are concerned the best-known and most widely quoted climatic indicators are coral reefs. They are confined to tropical waters because the corals are sensitive to temperature changes and succumb if even briefly exposed to water below about 18°C. Living in the tissues of the corals are unicellular algae (Zooxanthellae) which require light to photosynthesize like all other green plants. Hence these corals are confined to shallow water through which adequate light can penetrate. The same argument applies to the coralline algae which form half or more of the solid parts of modern coral reefs. Coral reefs are excellent indicators of tropical conditions, but even here there are limits to actualistic interpretations. The most common weakness of all actualistic arguments is that the further back in time we go the less sure are our interpretations. This is particularly true of palaeontological interpretations because the organisms will have evolved. The fossils may have been adapted to quite different conditions to those which suit the living examples. The reef corals of the Pleistocene Key Largo Limestone in Florida, for example, belong to the same species that still live in the offshore reefs today. The surf zone of the outer barrier reefs is dominated by the moosehorn coral, *Acropora palmata*. Behind the surf zone and in the patch reefs nearer shore *Montastraea annularis* dominates. The presence of *Montastraea*, but not *Acropora*, in the Key Largo Limestone of the Florida Keys shows that most of the Keys represent patch reefs which developed at a time in the Pleistocene when sea level was slightly higher. The Key Largo Limestone is associated with the Miami Oolite, indicating a similar climate to the present day. In this Pleistocene example where comparisons stretch over one to two hundred thousand years at most, quite precise interpretations are possible. Further back in the fossil record, the Upper Jurassic coral reefs of the Corallian deposits in Britain, for example, are probably tropical. They too are associated with oolitic limestones and, although all the coral species are extinct, they belong to genera and families which are closely related to living corals. They too probably had Zooxanthellae in their tissues and could well have been temperature-sensitive. All independent evidence suggests that they lived in clear, shallow, warm seas. If we go back further still, for example to the well-known Middle Silurian reefs of the island of Gotland in the Baltic or the Wenlock Limestone in Britain, climatic interpretations based on corals become much more uncertain. Fossil corals belong to three major groups: tabulate, rugose and hexacorals. All Palaeozoic corals are tabulates or rugosans, while all Mesozoic and younger corals, including all the living forms, are hexacorals. The rugose and tabulate corals became extinct at the end of the Palaeozoic. Thus all Silurian corals belonged to two major groups without close living relatives. It is no longer safe to *assume* that they had Zooxanthellae or were temperature-sensitive. In practice other features, including palaeomagnetic evidence, suggest that all Palaeozoic coral reefs and bioherms were tropical, but if we use palaeomagnetic evidence to confirm that the corals were tropical we cannot use the occurrence of corals to confirm the palaeomagnetic data.

Polar climates are more difficult to confirm on fossil evidence, but at least one example has recently been published. Most sea urchins shed eggs and sperm into sea water to reproduce. The only adaptation they possess to enhance successful reproduction is a chemical trigger to shedding. Once one adult starts to shed, it causes all adjacent mature adults of both sexes to shed, thus increasing the likelihood of successful fertilization. A few sea urchins brood their young and the females have special brood pouches in their tests. Brooding, or marsupiate, sea urchins are not characteristic of one family, but they are typically polar (Antarctic) at present. Philip and Foster[11] have recently described an extensive fauna of marsupiate sea urchins from the Tertiary of Australia and have used it to argue that Australia was nearer the South Pole in the early Tertiary than it is today. Interestingly, the earliest reported marsupiate echinoid from the lowest Tertiary of Denmark has recently been shown not to be marsupiate.[12] The depressions which were thought to represent brood pouches are artifacts of preservation. Possibly the only other known northern hemisphere example of a marsupiate echinoid, from the Tertiary of France, will also prove to be artificial.

Seasonal climates can be recognized in fossils by a variety of growth phenomena. It is well known, for example, that trees add rings to their wood each year. In a good season (for the tree) the annual ring is broad and in a bad season it will be narrow. Examination of tree rings not only tells us how old the tree is, but also reveals information about climate, about the history of the individual tree and even the orientation of a branch or trunk (see plate 16B). In a forest or plantation, if a large tree falls it allows more light to reach adjacent trees, improving their growth. Such rejuvenation can be detected in the annual rings of the adjacent trees. In favourable circumstances the felling history of managed woodland can be reconstructed from tree-ring studies. The rings of fossil wood record similar climatic information, but may not be *in situ*. Many bivalves and other shellfish show annual 'winter rings'. Again these indicate seasonal climates, the age of the shell when the animal died and its growth history. Usually growth in shells is most rapid early in life but falls off with age: the earliest winter rings are most widely spaced and the last most closely approximated. Accidents and other interruptions of growth may be revealed by departures from this pattern of regularly decreasing spacing of winter rings. These phenomena are described in more detail in the next chapter. Seasonal climates may be indicated by other features. Land snails may hibernate in winter or aestivate in dry periods. Many secrete an epiphragm, or lid, over the aperture when they do so. I have found two examples of the snail *Rumina decollata* in the Pleistocene deposits of Cala Salada, Ibiza, preserved with the epiphragms in place. Not only was the climate seasonal at the time, but the snails died during the dry season. Indeed one was crushed to death, but the aperture with its epiphragm was undamaged. Yet other terrestrial snails have a permanent structure, called the operculum, attached to the foot which is used to close the aperture of the shell when the animal retires inside. Some species which live in strongly seasonal climates have opercula that fit the aperture so tightly that the snails cannot breathe when they are closed. Special slits or tubes are developed in the shells to allow breathing when the snails shut up during the dry season.[13] Unrelated land snails have developed these breathing devices in the Caribbean area and South-East Asia. Their presence in Pleistocene deposits also indicates seasonal climates at the time.

Each of the preceding examples dealt with characteristic structures or taxonomic groups. We may also get information about past climates from the overall diversity and abundance of fossils, but it is perhaps more diffuse as other features, like salinity and depth, affect the diversity of marine organisms. Indeed one of the earliest attempts to use diversity gradients produced what would now be regarded as the 'wrong' answer. Stehli[14] plotted the diversity of Permian brachiopods at a number of localities and found that their diversity contours grouped better around the poles using present-day geography than the contemporary Permian palaeogeography deduced from palaeomagnetic evidence. As far as I am aware no other study of diversity gradients in fossils has yet demonstrated a clear increase in diversity from high to low latitudes. However, it is certainly true that many of the richest fossil localities lay in the tropics, as determined palaeomagnetically. In the Ordovician, for example, the richly fossiliferous deposits of the Ottawa–St Lawrence lowland and Cincinnati Arch in North America, the Oslo region of Norway and the Siljan District of Sweden, all lay close to the contemporary Equator. Rigorous numerical data on diversity and abundance have yet to be compiled with respect to palaeolatitudes, but on a subjective general impression density data do not go counter to the palaeomagnetic evidence.

To summarize, there are sedimentary and palaeontological indicators of climates, certainly the more extreme tropical and polar climates. Furthermore, as far as the present information goes, it tends to confirm rather than refute evidence derived from palaeomagnetism. It seems reasonably safe to accept both types of data since they are consistent.

Climatic indicators may be used, not only to confirm palaeolatitudes and palaeoclimates, but to test the reliability of uniformitarian (or actualistic) arguments about world climate. The classic example was Louis Agassiz's use of sediments and topography to demonstrate the reality of the Pleistocene ice age.[15] Agassiz was brought up in the Alps where glaciers still exist. He was familiar with the U-shaped valleys, tills and erratics of alpine areas and recognized them in other parts of Europe and North America where no glaciers now exist. He came to the inevitable conclusion that in former times glaciers had been much more extensive than they are now. This was, and is, a very significant discovery, since hitherto no one had suspected that major fluctuations in climate might occur. Indeed, it casts some doubt on the validity of actualistic arguments. If the climate of Wisconsin, Scotland or north Germany (for example) was so different only fifteen thousand years ago, who can say that the present climate of these areas is typical of past climates? So just how typical of the past history of the earth are present-day conditions? This question is very important because interpretations of the past which are based on *exceptional* present-day conditions are likely to be erroneous.

Before continental drift was widely accepted, it was often argued that past climatic fluctuations had been extreme. The discovery of a tropical fauna in the Devonian of Greenland, for example, was used to argue that the climate was tropical worldwide in the Devonian since it was assumed that tropical conditions had extended as far north as the present latitude of Greenland. Alternatively, the discovery of Ordovician glacial sediments in North Africa would have been used to argue that the world climate was intensely cold in the Ordovician because North Africa is now quite close to the Equator. Whole geological periods were characterized as tropical, glacial, temperate, and so on. Once continental drift was accepted, however, it became possible for a continent, or part of it, to have been near the poles at one time in the past and near the Equator at another time. It is possible, for example, that polar ice caps have always existed and any continent which happened to drift past a pole would have been glaciated. One could argue that world climate was always much as it is now with very little variation, such variation as apparently existed being entirely due to continents drifting into different latitudes at different times in the past. So can we test whether world climate has really changed all that much in the past? First let us look at climatic evidence from the Pleistocene which is the most recent geological period and therefore comparisons between it and the present are most likely to be valid.

Pleistocene climates are largely deduced by analysing the fossil pollen content of sediment samples. In a few favourable circumstances, lake deposits have been found lying between two tills (figure 41). A core is drilled through the lake sediments and samples examined every ten centimetres or so throughout the core. The first procedure is usually to estimate the percentage of tree pollen against non-tree pollen in each of the samples. Where more data are required, all the plant species represented by pollen are identified and their abundance recorded. In this way a fairly complete picture of the vegetation of the surrounding area can be inferred. If a complete sequence from glacial till through interglacial lake sediments and back to glacial till again is present, the ratio of tree pollen to non-tree pollen would produce a curve like that in figure 41B, with no tree pollen at the base when the ice first melted, a gradual increase to a peak in interglacial times representing forest conditions, followed by a reduction to nothing with the onset of the next glacial period. More detailed identifications of the vegetation reveal, further, that the first pollen to follow the glaciation represents a flora characteristic of the present-day tundra, followed by arctic birch and pinewood pollen and finally mixed deciduous woodland pollen only when fully

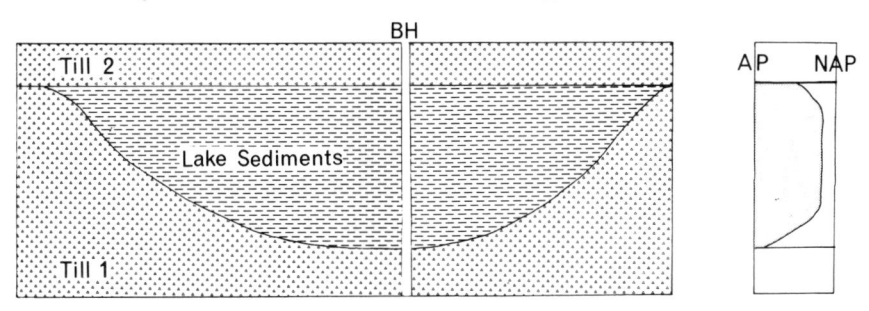

41. A. A borehole (BH) through interglacial lake sediments between two tills. B. The resulting pollen diagram showing the proportion of arboreal pollen (AP) and non-arboreal pollen (NAP) throughout the section. The arboreal pollen reaches a maximum during fully interglacial conditions.

interglacial conditions became established. Such sequences are in fact found and confirm that during the Pleistocene there were repeated advances of ice (glacial epochs) separated by interglacial epochs when the climate was as mild, or even milder, than it is today. Indeed, we may be in an interglacial epoch now. Slight differences in the precise sequences of pollen allow correlation of the different interglacial epochs, as we shall see in chapter 6.

It is now generally accepted that the Pleistocene Period included at least four major glacial epochs, but there is little evidence from earlier in the Tertiary for any glaciations at all, except in Antarctica. The Pleistocene seems not only to have been a period of relatively rapid and short-lived climatic fluctuations, but also to have been atypical of preceding periods.

In Morocco, Spain and Brittany all the Ordovician glacial and peri-glacial deposits are of uppermost Ordovician age, in other words Hirnantian. There is not much reliable palaeomagnetic evidence for the Ordovician, but all that we have suggests that Africa did not move very much with respect to the poles during the Ordovician. If this is correct one might expect evidence of glaciation throughout the Ordovician in Africa. The fact that the Ordovician tillites are confined to the Hirnantian not only confirms the glacial climate at that time, but indicates a climatic fluctuation, or glacial period, similar to the Pleistocene glaciations. Thus it seems that there have been distinct glaciations in the past separated by prolonged periods of more equable climate. Whether past glaciations were multiple events like the Pleistocene glaciation has yet to be determined. So far unequivocal glaciations are known to have occurred in the late Precambrian, Upper Ordovician, Permo-Carboniferous and Pleistocene, but we have not necessarily discovered them all. It does suggest, however, that the present conditions on earth and those of the last million years or so are far from typical of the preceding two hundred million years.

Once it was suspected that climate had fluctuated in the past it became desirable to know exactly how cold or warm it had been. Amazing though it seems, a method has been developed for estimating the precise temperature at which fossils lived and grew in the past. The method involves isotope chemistry so, before we discuss it, we need to digress briefly to consider what isotopes are and how they are used to solve geological problems.

All matter consists of atoms which are themselves composed of 'subatomic particles'. We need only consider three subatomic particles: protons and neutrons, which together form the nucleus of an atom, and electrons, which orbit around the nucleus. Electrons have very small mass compared with protons and neutrons so that almost all the weight of an atom lies in the nucleus. Protons and electrons are electrically charged particles; protons are positive, electrons negative. The precise chemical behaviour of an atom, the chemical element to which it belongs, depends on the number of electrons, which equals the number of protons. Atoms of each element are arranged in the periodic table according to their atomic number, which is simply the number of electrons (or protons) in the atom. Thus hydrogen, the lightest element, is entirely composed of atoms, with one proton and one electron, and has atomic number 1. Carbon atoms have six protons and six electrons and the element carbon has atomic number 6. Neutrons have no charge at all, but a mass almost equal to that of a proton. They do not affect the chemical behaviour of an atom, but they increase its atomic weight. If we compare the atomic weights of different elements we find that they correspond to the number of protons and neutrons in the nucleus. Many elements have atoms with different numbers of neutrons and therefore with different atomic weights. These are known as isotopes. Carbon atoms, for example, may have atomic weights of 12, 13 or 14. Since, by definition, all carbon atoms have six protons, these different carbon isotopes have nuclei with six, seven and eight neutrons respectively. Isotopes are atoms with the same number of protons, but different numbers of neutrons in their nuclei or, put another way, they are atoms with the same atomic number but different atomic weights. Isotopes are usually indicated by a superscript, for example ^{12}C, ^{13}C and ^{14}C for the three carbon isotopes.

Atomic structure and isotopes were only discovered this century. For as long as we have been able to observe them, isotopes have displayed two types of behaviour. Some have not changed at all – the so-called stable isotopes – while others change spontaneously into other isotopes with the release of energy. These latter are the radioactive isotopes, or radioisotopes. The change, or decay as it is called, of radioisotopes is discussed in more detail in chapter 6 because we use it to estimate the age of rocks. Here we are principally concerned with the stable isotopes of oxygen.

The stability of an isotope and the rate of decay of radioisotopes are normally independent of physical and chemical changes. However, very small changes in the proportions of stable isotopes can occur due to physical changes if the isotopes have atomic weights below about 40. Generally the lighter isotopes are more reactive. This slight alteration of the standard isotopic ratios is called fractionation, is frequently temperature-dependent and can be used for palaeotemperature analysis. The isotopes of oxygen, the most abundant element on the surface of the earth, are particularly useful. Oxygen has three stable isotopes, ^{16}O, ^{17}O and ^{18}O, which occur in a natural ratio of 99·76%/0.04%/0.20%. The ratio of $^{18}O/^{16}O$ is used because ^{18}O is more abundant than ^{17}O and the difference in its atomic weight compared with 'common oxygen', i.e. ^{16}O is greater. The ratio $^{18}O/^{16}O$ is therefore more sensitive to temperature changes and is more easily measured than $^{17}O/^{16}O$. Standard ratios of $^{18}O/^{16}O$ have been defined and are used to calibrate the mass spectrometers which measure isotopic abundances. One uses 'Standard Mean Ocean Water' (SMOW); another uses CO_2 released when a Cretaceous belemnite, *Belemnitella americana*, was dissolved in one hundred per cent phosphoric acid. Whichever standard is used, the $^{18}O/^{16}O$ ratio of a sample is measured and compared with the standard, and the deviation expressed in parts per thousand, i.e. per mille, ‰·$^{18}O/^{16}O$ of ocean water varies from about three per mille below standard at 30°C to three per mille above standard at 5°C. Clearly the differences are very slight and oxygen isotope ratios must be measured very carefully. Many organisms secrete calcium carbonate ($CaCO_3$) and so incorporate oxygen into their skeletons as they grow. Comparisons of the $^{18}O/^{16}O$ ratio of a skeleton with a standard should reveal the temperature at which the animal grew. If, for example, it is three per mille below standard the animal grew at 30°C. As usual the idea is very simple. In practice a number of assumptions must be taken into consideration and difficulties overcome.

First of all the $^{18}O/^{16}O$ ratio of water is not only temperature-dependent but salinity-dependent as well. This difficulty can be overcome by using only fossils which lived in open ocean environments where we *assume* the salinity has remained reasonably constant at approximately 36‰. Secondly, the $^{18}O/^{16}O$ ratio of skeletal calcite will yield valid temperatures only if the skeleton was secreted in equilibrium with the surrounding sea water, in other words if it has the same ratio as the sea water. Experiments with living animals and plants have shown that some, such as molluscs, do secrete their skeletons in equilibrium with sea water, while others, such as echinoderms, do not. As a result molluscs are very useful for palaeotemperature work, but echinoderms are virtually useless. Even if the skeleton is secreted in equilibrium with the sea water, the $^{18}O/^{16}O$ ratio of the original sea water must be known. In theory we ought to be able to assume that it is the natural ratio subject only to temperature and salinity variations. However, ice is enriched in ^{16}O. During a glacial maximum more ^{16}O than usual would have been locked up in the polar ice caps effectively enriching sea water in ^{18}O. Furthermore, if enough water were locked up in the ice caps, the salinity of even open oceans would rise slightly. So we cannot assume that the natural ratio actually occurred all the time in the past, particularly during Pleistocene ice ages. This difficulty is not as severe as it might seem at first. A value of the ratio $^{18}O/^{16}O$ is assumed for the sea water in which the fossil lived, taking into consideration all the relevant facts. This means that resulting palaeotemperatures are relative, but not absolute. For example if a palaeotemperature of 18°C is calculated, it is much more likely that the real temperature lay between 16° and 20° than below 5°. More importantly, *changes* in temperature are valid. Thus if analysis of growth rings reveals a seasonal temperature change of say 4°C, this is likely to be accurate although we cannot be absolutely certain that the actual temperatures varied from 16° to 20° or 17° to 21°. As with radiometric dating, the mere fact that a number can be given for the age or temperature of growth of a fossil gives the method an air of accuracy. It is wise to remember that both methods produce the best possible *estimates*, but neither yields absolutely accurate results.

Attempts have been made to arrive at absolute temperature determinations by using more than one thermometer, so to speak. Oxygen is not only incorporated into carbonate skeletons, but into siliceous and phosphatic skeletons as well. If the temperature curves for the $^{18}O/^{16}O$ ratios of carbonate, siliceous and phosphatic skeletons were known and if they intersected, then theoretically fossils with these different skeletal materials which grew together should yield a single unique value which fits all three curves. This would be the absolutely accurate palaeotemperature. Unfortunately after overcoming extreme difficulties a curve for the phosphate thermometer was determined but it has the same slope as those for silica and carbonate, so absolute temperatures still elude us.

Even ignoring the problems of absolute temperatures, the original behaviour of the organisms themselves may cause difficulties. Some organisms only grow above certain temperatures, some only at certain seasons. Temperature decreases very quickly with depth in modern oceans, so seasonal or diurnal migrations to and from depth may significantly affect $^{18}O/^{16}O$ ratios. Equally clearly, bottom-dwelling animals are of much less use than surface-dwelling animals in detecting seasonal variations in temperature.

Finally, diagenetic changes affect oxygen isotope ratios seriously. In an extreme case the original carbonate of the skeleton may be dissolved away entirely and replaced at a much later date by inorganic calcite precipitated from ground water. Clearly the oxygen isotope ratio of the replacement will reflect the temperature and salinity of the ground water and have absolutely nothing to do with the temperature at which the fossil lived. Once again it is impossible to overemphasize how essential it is to know the preservation history of a fossil *before* using it for any geological purpose. Even with less extreme diagenetic changes oxygen isotope ratios may be affected. Organic carbonate skeletons change from aragonite to calcite and from high magnesium calcite to low magnesium calcite relatively rapidly and in doing so may seriously alter their $^{18}O/^{16}O$ ratio. Hence palaeotemperature results from corals, gastropods and ammonites, which are predominantly aragonitic, and from echinoderms and some algae, which secrete high magnesian calcite, are suspect. Planktonic foraminifera and molluscs are probably the best sources of palaeotemperature data. Best of all are belemnites which were planktonic molluscs with massive skeletons that resist diagenetic changes longest of all.

Despite all the difficulties mentioned above, oxygen isotope ratios have been used to investigae palaeotemperatures back at least as far as the Mesozoic.[16] They yield what appear to be very reasonable results, which is a tremendous tribute to the skill and enterprise of the geochemists who have pioneered and applied the methods. Using planktonic foraminifera from deep-ocean cores taken in the Atlantic and Mediterranean Oceans, Emiliani[17,18] and others have been able to trace Pleistocene palaeotemperatures through the last million years or so. The cores have been dated using geomagnetic reversals and radiometric methods, and they show that surface waters of the Atlantic were as much as 10°C lower during glacial epochs than during interglacials. Oxygen isotope ratios of ice from deep cores bored into the Greenland and Antarctic ice caps have yielded a similar pattern of temperatures back over a hundred thousand years.[19] Mesozoic belemnites show seasonal changes with growth.[20] Summer and winter temperatures differed by 4–5°C and both indicate a more equable climate than that of the present day. An example is shown in figure 42. More surprisingly, benthonic

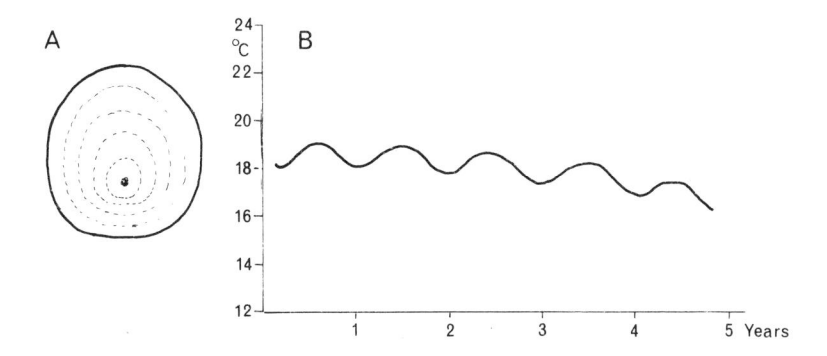

42. A. Section through a belemnite guard to show growth rings like tree rings. B. Palaeotemperature curve for a belemnite showing five seasons' growth and an overall slight decline in temperature.

organisms have yielded palaeotemperatures from the late Mesozoic through the Tertiary which suggest that deep ocean water has been cooling down more or less continuously since the Cretaceous. This probably reflects global climatic cooling together with the initiation and growth of the polar ice caps. If these interpretations are correct, the apparent cooling of the climate may have had unsuspected effects on oceanic circulation. The present-day pattern of oceanic circulation depends largely on the fact that cold, well-oxygenated sea water sinks at the poles and wells up again nearer the Equator. This circulation not only ensures that deep-ocean water is rich in oxygen, thus allowing many forms of life to survive at great depths, but the upwelling brings dissolved nutrients into the shallow seas where they contribute to the primary productivity of the plankton. The possibility that a different type of circulation existed in the Mesozoic opens up a whole new perspective on life in Mesozoic oceans.

So palaeotemperature analysis has produced some remarkable results in the short time that it has been feasible. We have been able to confirm the climatic fluctuations which accompanied the Pleistocene glaciations and have gained some insight into past climates as far back as the Mesozoic. It has also been possible to follow seasonal climatic fluctuations using the growth rings of belemnites in much the same way that tree rings record good and bad growing seasons. This leads us to consider what we can find out about growth in fossils and what use can be made of such studies.

Chapter 5

Growth studies

As we have seen in the case of palaeotemperature analysis, it is essential not only to understand the preservation history of a fossil, but also to understand its mode of life. Geochemists need to know whether the fossils they use for palaeothermometry lived in fully marine water and at what depth, as well as whether they have suffered diagenesis. Fossils were once alive and, whatever use is made of them, it is essential to know how they lived. When alive all fossils must have grown, as all living organisms do. Many fossils left behind them permanent records of their growth in their skeletons, which enable us to deduce precisely how they grew even though they have been dead for millions of years. Such growth studies are of intrinsic interest in themselves and they may also be used to investigate other aspects of the earth's history. We have already seen, for example, that marked seasonal changes in growth rates may be used to infer the former existence of seasonal climates. Where growth can be related to known fixed periods, it is possible to measure rates of growth or determine ages at death of fossils. Known growth rates may also be used to investigate the history of the earth's rotation and to estimate the intensity of cosmic bombardment of the earth's atmosphere, neither of which is a subject one would normally associate with fossils. As with so many other aspects of palaeontology, we need to understand first how *living* things grow before we attempt to interpret the evidence of growth preserved in fossils and, of course, it is the growth of skeletons which concerns us most since, in fossils, skeletons are all that is normally available for study.

Growth may be defined as an increase in size and complexity with time. Although changes in complexity are the province of development, it is normally impossible to separate growth from development and the two will be considered together. Growth of individual animals and plants is called ontogeny and may be distinguished from growth of colonial animals, which is often called astogeny. Since all the individuals within a colony have their own ontogeny, we will postpone consideration of astogeny until later in the chapter. All animals use one of three basic modes of skeletal growth, accretionary, moulting and growth with modification, which need to be understood before fossil evidence of growth can be used profitably. Different kinds of evidence are preserved in fossils exhibiting each type of growth and hence their usefulness varies with the mode of growth.

The first mode of skeletal growth is accretionary, whereby small or large increments are added to the skeleton (or shell) during life. In its purest form, all previous growth stages are retained in the skeleton, although occasionally some parts are lost by resorbtion or erosion during life. Accretionary growth is very useful in studies of fossils, because a more or less complete record of the growth of each individual is preserved in its skeleton. Accretionary growth is found in most mollusc and brachiopod shells, solitary and colonial corals, bryozoans, graptolites and, of course, the wood of trees. It is a very common mode of growth. The addition of each increment to the skeleton may be recorded by very fine growth lines. Alternatively, occasional interruptions of growth may produce thicker, more prominent, growth lines like the so-called 'winter rings' of bivalves. In either case, each growth line represents the former position of the growing edge of the shell at that growth stage. Thus we can see, for example, what the outline of a brachiopod was like when it was half-grown, or the shape of the aperture in a juvenile snail shell. In many organisms changes occur during growth. With accretionary growth, it is possible to determine when the changes occurred and whether they were sudden or gradual. The brachiopod in figure 2B (page 11) has fine ridges and grooves in each valve. By tracing these back towards the umbo (the first formed part of the shell), we can see that this species always had this ornament. In contrast, the brachiopod in figure 2A developed its gently folded shell edges associated relatively late in life because the associated ridge and groove are only developed near the edges of the valves. Similarly, the ammonite, *Kosmoceras*, in figure 43 modified its aperture edges only in the last stages of its growth. If a shell was accidently damaged in life, this may affect growth lines and once again the time and extent of the damage can be deduced from the preserved growth record.

The second mode of skeletal growth, moulting, is in complete contrast to accretionary growth and is characteristic of the phylum

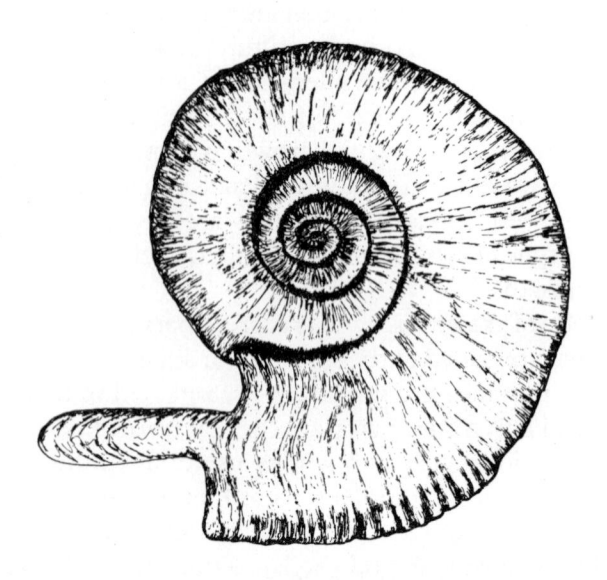

43. A crushed example of the Jurassic ammonite *Kosmoceras* which developed lappets at the aperture only when fully mature. (Re-drawn from an original photograph in Rhona M. Black, *The elements of palaeontology*, fig. 56, p. 96, Cambridge University Press, 1972.)

Arthropoda. In all arthropods (crabs are a familiar example) a complete external skeleton, or exoskeleton, is formed which is itself unable to grow. Periodically the animal sheds its entire exoskeleton, enlarges very rapidly and then gradually secretes a new skeleton to fit its larger body. Thus no one skeleton, at any growth stage, contains any record whatsoever of previous growth. In the extreme case of insects like butterflies, the adult stage may not even bear the slightest resemblance to any previous growth stage. This mode of growth is much less helpful to palaeontologists. A single fossil trilobite or crab cannot reveal anything about its growth or development, unlike a brachiopod or ammonite. To study growth in fossil arthropods it is necessary to have a whole series of fossils at all growth stages. Furthermore, any one arthropod will moult several times (perhaps up to a hundred times with some larger trilobites), each time shedding a skeleton that is a potential fossil. Thus it is theoretically possible for a single individual to give rise to many fossils. Palaeontologists who wish to reconstruct the relative abundances of different fossil species in former communities must make allowance for this; but who is to say precisely how many fossils result from each individual anthropod, on average or in any particular case? Growth of fossil arthropods can be studied if sufficient specimens are available. Under suitable conditions, all growth stages may be preserved in fine-grained sediments, like clays, and both growth and development can be reconstructed. Ostracods are small crustaceans which live within a bivalved shell, superficially like that of a minute bivalve mollusc. Their shells, or carapaces, occur in millions in many marine and freshwater deposits. By measuring the length and height of ostracod carapaces and plotting each measurement on a scatter diagram as in figure 30 (page 39), distinct clusters of points may become evident. Each dot represents one individual carapace and the clusters the variation in size (length and height) at each moult. After studying many such growth series of ostracods, Anderson[1] concluded that, in general, ostracods double their volume at each moult. A linear dimension, like the length of the carapace, would then be expected to increase in proportion to $\sqrt[3]{2}$ (approximately 1.2), which means that variation in length at any one moult must be very small if discrete clusters representing moults are to be recognizable. Indeed such clusters are very rarely recognizable in trilobites, so that we do not know exactly how many moults any one species of trilobite underwent.

Trilobites show not only size increase, but development as well.[2] They pass through four stages (figure 44) each of which may represent several moults. The initial stage, the *phaselus* larva, was first described in late 1978.[3] It strongly resembles the *nauplius* larva of modern Crustacea and its discovery will undoubtedly reopen the

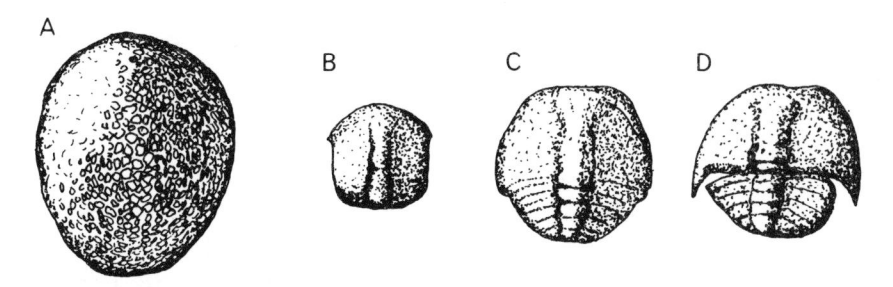

44. Growth stages of trilobites. A. The newly discovered *phaselus* larva. B–D. Growth stages of *Sao hirsuta*. B. Early protaspis. C. Late protaspis. D. Meraspis degree 0. Not to the same scale. (A after R. A. Fortey and S. F. Morris, *Palaeontology*, 21, fig. 1a, p. 826, 1978. Copied with permission of the Palaeontological Association. B–D after H. B. Whittington, *J. Palaeont.*, 31, pl. 116, figs 14, 16 and 20, 1957.)

debate about trilobite affinities. The next stage, protaspis, has a nearly spherical exoskeleton with no articulation whatsoever, although towards the end of the stage what will become the head and tail can be distinguished together with some other morphological features. The protaspis stage is followed by the meraspis stage which starts as soon as the articulation between the head and tail develops. The meraspis stage has a number of 'degrees' corresponding to the addition of thoracic segments. These are usually added one at a time, but occasionally a pair of segments may be released together. The meraspis stage begins with degree 0 with just the head and tail articulated on each other. Meraspis degree 1 has a single free thoracic segment between the head and tail, degree 2 a pair of articulated thoracic segments, degree 3, three and so on up to the full complement of thoracic segments, which is fixed for most species of trilobites. As soon as the full number of segments is complete, the last, holaspis, stage begins, but growth is not yet complete; holaspid trilobites may increase in length tenfold. In some species of trilobites one or more thoracic segments can be distinguished from the others by their size or the possession of spines. This enables us to recognize that during the meraspis stage, thoracic segments first form within the tail and move forwards until they are eventually released from the anterior border. The absence of any examples of one particular meraspis degree can provide information; for example, degrees 0–4 and 6–10 may be known, but no examples of degree 5, indicating that a pair of segments, 5 and 6, were released together. Unless this is known to have happened, each meraspis degree represents at least one moult and may represent more. We have, as yet, no way of telling if several moults occurred during meraspis degree 0, or degree 1, for example. If we accept the minimum number of moults, a normal trilobite with twelve thoracic segments moulted a dozen times in the meraspis stage alone and possibly underwent an even greater number of moults in the holaspis stage.

Moulting would seem to be a very inefficient mode of skeletal growth. First, a great deal of energy is expended in secreting a skeleton which is subsequently thrown away, and this is repeated several times during life – a type of waste familiar to parents chagrined when their growing children can no longer wear some perfectly good articles of clothing. To be sure, crabs for example resorb some of the material of their skeleton before moulting and use it again in the next stage; nevertheless, the majority is shed. In many, but not all, accretionary skeletons the whole skeleton is of use throughout life. The soft tissue of bivalve molluscs and most snails, for example, fills the entire shell at all growth stages, but that of ammonites and nautiloids does not. Even so, the vacated parts of the shell in ammonites and nautiloids were filled with gas, and acted as buoyancy chambers; they were therefore functional throughout life, although not filled with soft tissue.

Secondly during the critical period in which the new exoskeleton is hardened, recently moulted arthropods are vulnerable to attack. Crabs take a week to ten days before the carapace is fully rigid, during which period they do not feed and are very secretive, hiding under seaweeds or burying themselves in the sediment. Even then it may take twice as long again before the entire exoskeleton is completely calcified.

For both these reasons, waste of energy and vulnerability, one might predict that arthropods would not be a very successful group. However, nature, with her contrariness, has contrived to make them the most abundant and varied phylum of all. There are probably more species of arthropods than of all other animal phyla put together. If moulting is a disadvantage, it has not hampered arthropods. Indeed, it is probably a positive advantage because it confers the ability to re-design, so to speak, during growth. Thus butterflies not only look different from their larvae, but have a totally different mode of life. They are both the reproductive phase and the dispersal phase as well. With the ability to fly about, they can detect new colonies of food plants on which to lay eggs. They are thus able to adapt in one generation to ephemeral food supplies and seasonal fluctuations in climate. It is probably no accident that the insects, which include the groups where the contrast between larva and adult is greatest, are the most diverse of arthropods. Incidentally, this life cycle, with more or less static larvae and mobile adults, contrasts markedly with most marine organisms where the adults are sessile and the larvae dispersive. Again the insect life cycle is probably more advantageous. Dispersal of marine larvae is largely passive: they drift with the currents. Dispersal of adult insects need not be so: they are able to fly against light winds or rest if the wind is too strong and they have better-developed sense organs with which to take advantage of their surroundings. Insects may lay eggs where they choose, as it were; marine larvae settle by chance and most fail to develop because they settle in unsuitable places.

The third mode of skeletal growth involves constant modification as the skeleton develops. It is characteristic of vertebrates, but occurs, to a much lesser degree, in echinoderms as well. Vertebrate bone has associated with it two types of cells: osteoblasts, which secrete bone, and osteoclasts, which resorb it. Thus a slice through a thigh bone, for example, does not reveal concentric growth lines like tree rings, but a hollow marrow cavity which enlarges as the thigh bone grows. Such a completely enclosed cavity can only enlarge if the material surrounding it is dissolved away from the inside as new material is added to the outside. Even so, the existence of a marrow cavity merely proves that resorbtion occurs. After all, hollow trees also exist, but a section through a hollow tree will reveal the same growth rings that occur in a healthy tree, as well as evidence that they have been rotted away from the inside. Such growth rings rarely occur in bone structure. It is not just that the inside of a bone can be resorbed to enlarge the marrow cavity, but the whole structure of the bone itself can be modified during growth.

Bones, then, rarely carry any growth record and again palaeontologists who wish to study dinosaur growth, for example, must have bones from individuals of all sizes to do so. Growth with modification may seem as wasteful as moulting. A great deal of energy is used in secretion and resorbtion of the bone as remodelling proceeds during growth. However, this mode of growth allows the bones to be modified according to the stresses imposed on them in life. D'Arcy Thompson records how the engineer, Culmann, on seeing a section through the top of a thigh bone, realized that the fine bony sheets, or trabeculae, within the porous head of the bone follow exactly the lines of force stressing the bone. He had just analysed very similar stresses in a crane head he was designing and recognized the similarity (figure 45).

The ability to remould the trabecular bone enables the skeleton to adjust to changes in stresses that happen, for example, when a baby ceases to crawl on all fours and starts to walk. A dramatic illustration of the potential of growth with modification was Sédillot's puppies.[4] The main shaft of the tibia, the larger of the two bones of the lower hind limb, was removed, so that the smaller bone, the fibula, had to support the weight of the animals. Eventually the shaft of the fibula grew as thick or thicker than that of the tibia of normal dogs, having grown in response to the greater stresses acting on it. Significant quantities of trabecular bone are dissolved from the skeletons of astronauts in space and, although no astronaut has yet been up for long enough, it seems, by extrapolation, that there is a maximum safe limit to weightlessness beyond which an astronaut returning to earth

GROWTH STUDIES

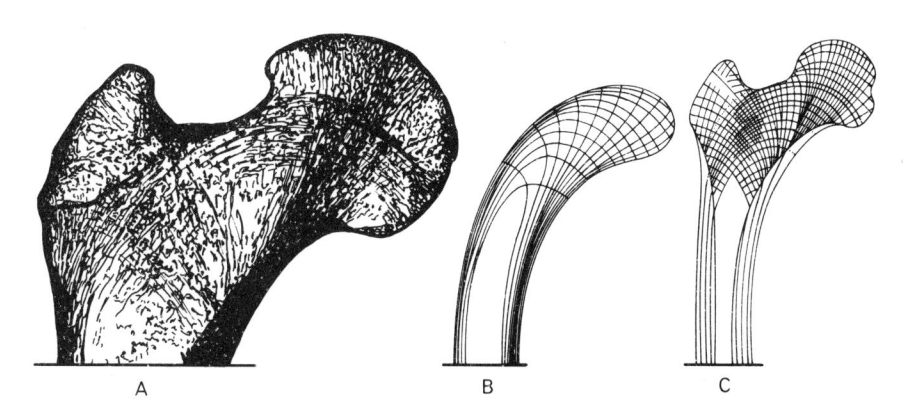

45. A. Section of head of the human femur to show trabecular bone. Stress lines of Culmann's crane (B) and the femur (C). (After Sir D'A. W. Thompson, *On growth and form*, rev. edn, figs 100–1, pp. 232–3, Cambridge University Press, 1963.)

would have bones insufficiently strong to bear his own weight. In old age, trabecular bone is dissolved by hormones, particularly in post-menopausal women. The common statement that an old lady fell and broke her hip is usually the wrong way round. What happens is that weakened by solution of trabecular bone, the head of the thigh shears off and then the old lady falls over.

Echinoderm skeletons also have associated osteoblasts and osteoclasts, but echinoderms seem to remodel their skeletons to the minimum necessary extent, and growth of most plates in any echinoderm is effectively accretionary. Echinoderms *are* able to resorb, for example enlargement of the central canal of a crinoid stem (figure 46) requires resorbtion, but they do so only rarely. The damage inflicted by parasites is often repaired with modification to the plate structure, as happened in the *Holocystites* specimens mentioned in chapter 1.

To summarize, there are three main modes of skeletal growth, accretionary, moulting and growth with modification, each of which

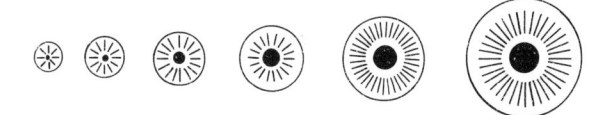

46. Growth of a crinoid columnal. In the largest stage the central lumen is as wide as the entire columnal was in the earliest growth stage. Enlargement of the central lumen can only occur by resorbtion.

preserves more or less information about growth in fossils and each of which confers certain advantages and disadvantages on the animals which exhibit them. Accretionary growth is the least wasteful of energy in most cases, but it is also the least flexible. In contrast, growth with modification and moulting are much more flexible but consume more energy. Although accretionary growth is generally the most useful in fossil growth studies and will be our main concern, growth of fossil vertebrates and arthropods can be investigated if sufficient numbers of specimens are available for study.

The next topic we need to consider I shall discuss under the general heading 'style of growth', for want of any better term. What I am concerned with here are several alternative possibilities in growth. For example, is growth slow and continuous or does it occur in discrete short bursts, as in arthropod moults? Does growth continue throughout life or is there, as in man, a well-defined adult size beyond which no matter how long we live we no longer grow? Finally, are there changes in shape during growth or are juveniles exact miniatures of adults? And, of course, can we recognize these alternatives in fossils?

Growth of different organisms may be discrete or continuous. Many bivalve molluscs and corals, for example, secrete daily or semi-daily growth increments to their skeletons. In bivalves this has been demonstrated by recording daily activities using time-lapse photography.[5] Not only do these organisms lay down daily layers, but the increments are often grouped into lunar fortnightly (i.e. tidal) cycles and annual cycles. Annual bands have been accepted in many bivalves for generations. They are usually marked by darker, more prominent growth lines, called 'winter rings'. The assumption that these growth lines were winter rings has only recently been confirmed. It seems that most bivalves produce the outermost, organic, layer of the shell at a more or less constant rate, but the winter increments to the underlying calcite layers are narrower than summer increments, and interruptions of growth also occur more frequently in winter. Thus the outermost layer thickens up in winter, producing winter rings. Other factors, such as damage, salinity changes, disturbance by storms (and marking for experiments on living bivalves), may also slow or interrupt growth. Some winter rings are caused primarily by repeated interruptions to growth in cold weather. Where true winter rings occur, a bivalve can be aged immediately and the season of its death estimated fairly accurately. If the original shell structure is preserved in fossils, sections may reveal the age even more precisely. Clearly organisms with accretionary growth, with no resorbtion or loss of skeleton by other means, and a continuous record of daily growth increments, enable palaeontologists to deduce a great deal about growth rates, population structures, mortality rates and so on of fossils.

Not all skeletons grow slowly and continuously. Certainly all arthropods do not, but even animals with accretionary growth and growth with modification may grow in sudden spurts separated by periods of standstill. Snails of the family Muricidae (figure 47C) characteristically grow forward a portion of a whorl in a very short period. For example, the American oyster drill, *Eupleura caudata*, adds half a whorl at a time, secreting a thin shell in about three weeks and then thickening this internally for a further four weeks. *E. caudata* apparently repeats this operation once or twice a year in the summer months.[6] In most muricids one third of a whorl is added at each growth period, but the genus *Biplex* adds half a whorl, while in *Hexaplex* and *Muricanthus* anything from a thirteenth or less up to one sixth may be added. Many other genera of snails grow in spurts, and I have myself kept a North African land snail, *Alabastrina quinquefasciata*, which added the last two-thirds of a whorl overnight, roughly quadrupling its volume in doing so! Even some bivalves show progressively more interruptions to growth as they get older.

Clearly, even within the same phylum (snails and bivalves are both molluscs), discrete and continuous growth may both occur. It is not safe to assume, therefore, that *all* bivalves grow continuously and add daily increments. From personal observations I know that not all snails grow in short bursts. The question is then, can we recognize these styles of growth in fossils? Where daily increments are added continuously, sectioning a bivalve or examination of the outer surface of a coral will usually reveal the increments. All we need are sufficiently well preserved specimens with the fine growth lines visible. Past positions of the aperture in muricid snails are indicated by thickenings of the shell often accompanied by various frills or spines (figure 47C). By counting these past positions of the aperture we can learn how many growth spurts occurred per whorl and how many in the entire lifetime of the snail, but not an absolute rate of growth since we do not know how long it takes to add one whorl to the shell, or even if each whorl added took the same time. Sectioning of a gastropod shell will also confirm the style of growth, again if preservation allows. Many snails which grow more or less continuously possess fine growth lines on the external surface of their

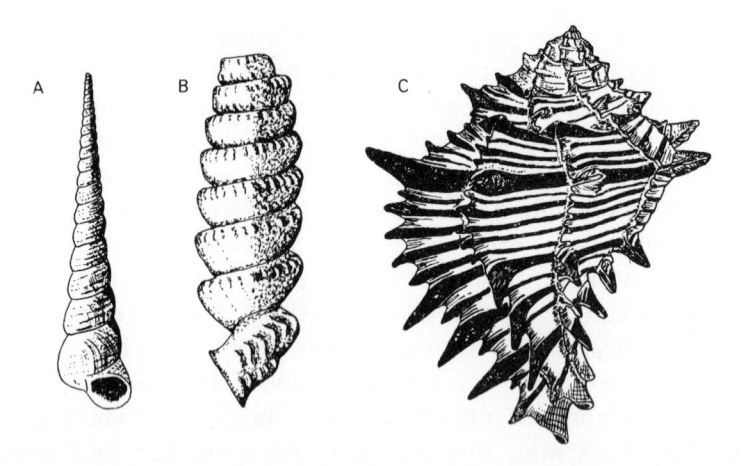

47. Contrasting styles of growth in snails. A. *Turitella*. Gnomonic growth with no fixed adult size. B. *Brachypodella*. Allometric growth with decollation and a single modification (uncoiling) at the final adult size. C. *Muricanthus*. A muricid snail with repeated bursts of growth followed by modified apertures. Not to same scale. (C after cover design of *Journal of Conchology* by D. Reid. Copied by permission of the Conchological Society of Great Britain and Ireland.)

shells. Thus in favourable circumstances one can deduce this aspect of the style of growth and possibly the rate of growth, even in fossils. So far as I am aware, no one has yet investigated this aspect of growth in brachiopods, *Nautilus*, the only living cephalopod with an external shell, or bryozoans. They are all very common fossils and until the basic work on living examples is done, we shall not be able to interpret growth in these fossils with confidence.

The second aspect of the style of growth involves recognition of a definite adult size or shape. Both extreme possibilities occur in nature. In some arthropods – butterflies again spring to mind – the adult phase bears not the slightest resemblance to any former growth stage and is of a definite size, within a narrow range of variation, in each species. Indeed we can separate some closely related species on size alone, for example the small and large tortoiseshell butterflies, *Aglais urticae* and *Nymphalis polychloros*. Less dramatic but equally distinct adult sizes are known in other arthropods like crabs and lobsters, as well as in some snails and ammonites, whereas most, if not all, bivalves, some snails and possibly many brachiopods grow throughout life right up to the moment of death. To be sure they usually grow more slowly as they get older, at least they increase in length more slowly with increasing age, but nevertheless they go on growing. A fixed adult size may be detected by measurement alone or it may be indicated by some skeletal modification. For example, in a normal human population large individuals (adults) outnumber small ones (children) because we are adult, as determined by size, for at least two and a half times as long (fifty to fifty-five years) as we are juvenile (fifteen to twenty years). A similar inbalance of juveniles to adults in a fossil population may indicate the existence of a defined adult size, but it may also merely reflect differential mortality rates at different growth stages. A Victorian graveyard, for example, may contain more children than adults, whereas a modern one will have far fewer children than adults, but neither can be used to argue the existence of a maximum adult size in humans. They simply reflect the changes in infant mortality over the last century. Similarly a randomly dredged sample of the freshwater bivalve, *Anodonta anatina*, from the River Colne in Buckinghamshire, showed a maximum adult size of approximately 80 mm. length, even though it is known that this bivalve grows more or less continuously until death. Larger examples from Nottinghamshire not only grow more each year, but live longer as well and still have a fairly well-defined maximum size of 120–30 mm. length.[7] Measurement of size alone in fossils is a doubtful criterion on which to recognize an adult stage. Unequivocal adults can be distinguished where they modify their skeletons, once only, at late stage of growth. Many snails, including most common garden species, do this, as did many fossil ammonites and nautiloids. In numerous examples of these the aperture is constricted in some way so that further growth is impossible without resorbtion of the modifications (figure 48). Yet other examples uncoil or reorientate the last parts of their shell, as in the small land snails, *Opisthostoma*, from the Far East or *Brachypodella* (figure 47B) from the Caribbean. The Cretaceous ammonite *Scaphites* (figure 49) is a well-known fossil example of this phenomenon.

The final aspect of the style of growth involves changes in shape of the whole, or part, of an organism during growth. When such changes do occur, growth is said to be allometric; when no change occurs (as for example in figure 47A), growth is said to be gnomonic, orthogonal or isometric. A gnomon is a geometrical figure which when added to another enlarges the original without altering its shape, hence enlargement without any change of shape is often called gnomonic growth. Examples are illustrated in figure 50 (page 149). In practice, allometric growth pervades everything and is regarded as the general case. The relationship between two parts of an organism can be expressed by the allometric growth equation, $y = \beta x^{\alpha}$, where x and

48. The modified T-shaped aperture of the brevicone nautiloid *Gomphoceras*.

y are measures of the two parts and α and β are constants. Using this equation, gnomonic or isometric growth can be shown to be just a special case in which the exponent $\alpha = 1$. Allometric growth is said to be positive when $\alpha > 1$, and negative when $\alpha < 1$. Allometry is so widespread that a general explanation of it must exist. Many, but not all, cases of allometric growth can be related to D'Arcy Thompson's[8] principle of similitude or proportionality. Numerous aspects of living things involve volume/area or area/length relationships. During growth, area increases in proportion to the square, and volume in proportion to the cube, of linear dimensions (i.e. $A \alpha L^2$; $V \alpha L^3$). Hence lengths do not keep pace with areas and volumes during growth. To give just two examples: food requirements are approximately proportional to body volume and, in a filter-feeding organism, food gathering capacity is proportional to the area of the filter. In the case of isometric growth, doubling the length of a filter feeder will increase the filter area by 4 (2^2), but the volume by 8 (2^3). Clearly unless the filter grows with positive allometry, starvation will set in at large sizes. Equally, the load-bearing capacity of limb bones is proportional

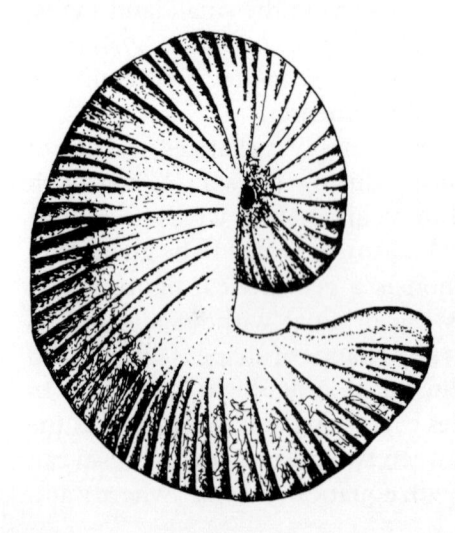

49. The Cretaceous heteromorph ammonite *Scaphites* which uncoils slightly at the adult stage. (Redrawn from an original photograph by W. J. Kennedy in A. Hallam (ed.), *Patterns of evolution as illustrated by the fossil record*, fig. 18–6, p. 272, Elsevier, 1977.)

GROWTH STUDIES

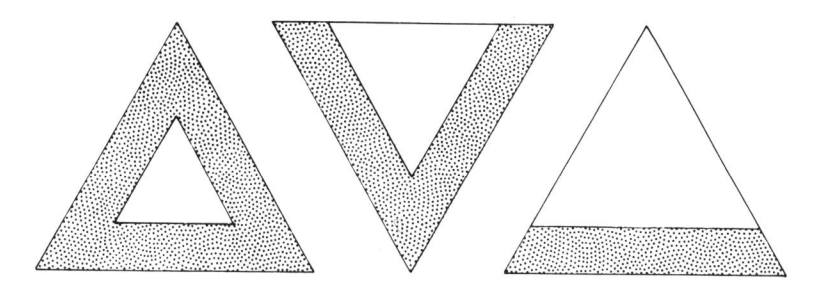

50. Gnomons to a triangle. Each stippled area enlarges the white triangle without altering its shape.

to their cross-sectional area, while their actual loading is related to body volume. Again, large mammals, like elephants, have proportionately thicker legs than a sparrow or kangaroo rat. Indeed if the latter were enlarged to anything like the size of the elephant, they would simply collapse under their own weight. In the sea, the weight of the body is taken by the displacement of water. There is no upper size limit due to load bearing factors, so that whales can grow many times larger than elephants. However, when they become stranded in shallow water, whales frequently suffocate because their rib cages cannot bear the weight of the body and collapse. Thus much allometric growth is what Gould[9] has called 'size required allometry'. These effects, incidentally, apply as much to engineering and architecture as they do to organisms. Gould has shown that the relationship between the periphery (a linear measure) and the floor space (an area) in English mediaeval churches follows the allometric growth equation very precisely,[10] mainly due to the requirements of lighting and structural strength. Indeed in more than one way the evolution of English Gothic architecture can be seen as the search for light.

Allometric and isometric growth can be detected in numerous fossils; one merely needs to measure two characters preserved in the skeleton. In theory, with accretionary growth allometry can be detected in a single individual. The shell of the brachiopod in figure 2A (page 11) shows allometric growth. In practice, even with animals that have accretionary growth, we tend to measure the final outline of a whole series of individuals of different sizes when investigating growth. The interpretation of allometric growth in fossils in terms of function is more difficult than just recording its occurrence, but it is frequently possible.

For example, Gould[11] has shown that the size and position of the muscle scars and the length/width ratio of the shell in several species of scallop (*Pecten*) all show allometric growth which tends to counteract an inevitable decrease in swimming efficiency with increased size. Large and small individuals produce the same propulsive force, but larger individuals need to travel more rapidly to keep off the bottom. The allometric changes all allow larger individuals to increase their propulsion. Similarly, the height of atrypid brachiopods increases with positive allometry, thus enabling more coils of the lophophore (the filter-feeding organ) to be packed within the mantle cavity. It is more efficient to increase the area of the lophophore by adding coils, rather than by enlarging existing coils. This allometric shape change tends to counteract the 'starvation effect' of increased size in filter feeders. The larvae of the silkworm, *Bombyx mori*, have a constant ratio of respiratory surface to body volume during growth. This is achieved by the trachea (the respiratory tubules) increasing in length and complexity with increased body size and tends to counteract the 'suffocation effect' of size increase. Allometric relationships are not confined to growth, but can be seen in evolutionary lineages too. Frequently their explanation is the same. Hypsodonty, having teeth with short roots and very high crowns, is a repeated evolutionary trend among large fossil herbivores. Since the amount of food that can be ground up by the teeth depends on tooth wear, while the food requirements depend on body volume, hypsodonty is an inevitable result of size increase. Large, high-crowned molars with complex folds provide the maximum amount of grinding action before they become worn. Elephants, with the largest food requirements of any living herbivore, have carried hypsodonty to the extreme. Not only do they have very large molar teeth, but they erupt only one at a time in each half of each jaw, and the last traces of an old tooth are worn away as the new tooth is brought into use, thus using the entire tooth, root and all. Finally, in considering growth of living things, brief mention should be made of the way in which new individuals are added in colonial organisms such as corals and bryozoans. Basically astogeny, the growth and development of colonies, is concerned with the different methods of budding new individuals from those already existing in the colony. The skeletons of common colonial organisms like corals, bryozoans and fossil graptolites all grew by accretion with little or no resorbtion and hence retain a record of their growth. Thus by sectioning a coral colony we may trace how new corallites arose.

GROWTH STUDIES

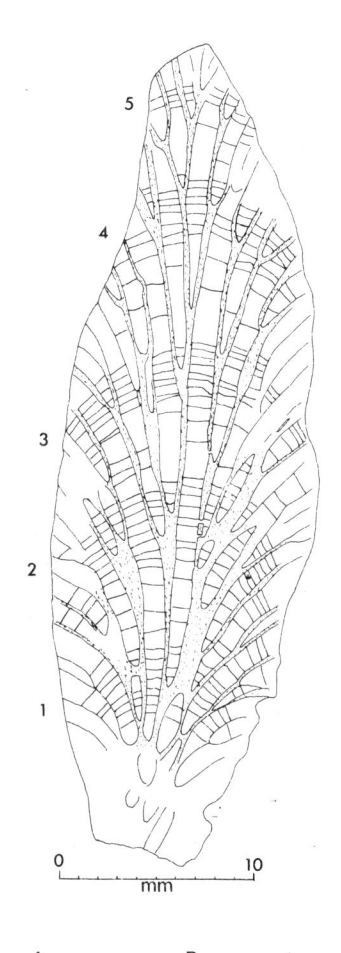

51. *(left)* A section through an Upper Silurian *Favosites* colony from New Creek, W. Virginia, showing seasonal growth, indicated by the variation in the spacing of the tabulae, and interstitial budding of new corallites. Five winter seasons are indicated and the colony grew approximately 7 mm. per year.

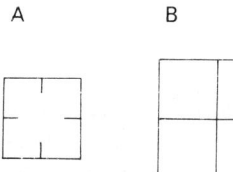

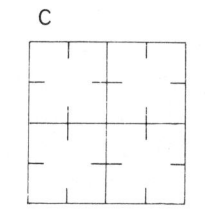

52. Colony increase in *Tetradium* as seen in cross-section. Each corallite divides into four daughter corallites as the septa lengthen.

Many different methods of budding are employed and they may be characteristic of different groups. For example, favositids, extinct colonial organisms that may be corals or sponges, generally bud interstitially (figure 51), new individuals being inserted between the existing ones. *Lithostrotion*, a rugose coral, often exhibits dendroid budding with new corallites arising like the branches of a tree, while *Tetradium* has septal budding (figure 52). Lack of space precludes a complete description of all modes of budding in all colonial organisms. Suffice it to say that a complete record is retained in suitably preserved fossils, and hence astogeny can be studied in fossils as well as it can be seen in living colonial organisms. Incidentally, coloniality overcomes some of the problems of size increase in solitary organisms. If an individual coral or bryozoan zooid can gather enough food and oxygen for itself, adding other similar individuals to a colony poses no problem of food gathering and so on since all the individuals can meet their own needs. Thus functional problems arising from an increase in size are minimized.

Growth studies inevitably involve a temporal aspect – either relative, such as when we compare a later growth stage (e.g. the adult) with an earlier one, or absolute, where actual growth rates may be determined. This leads me to a brief consideration of time and how it is measured. We take for granted the constancy of our familiar time units like the day or year, but evidence suggests that the length of the day has changed over long periods of time such as are represented by the fossil record. Furthermore, fossils provide some of the best evidence for this change.

Time is very difficult to describe adequately, let alone define, but two of its characteristics can be grasped immediately. First it is continuous, although we may arbitrarily divide it into units like seconds, years and millenia, and secondly it is as irreversible as our own growth. We can no more 'put the clock back' than we can 'recapture our youth'. Because it is continuous, measurement of time poses problems. We need to subdivide it into units whose length is equal, much as the divisions mark equal units along the continuous length of a metre rule. Two of the most obvious and most ancient units of time are defined by the period of rotation of the earth about its axis (the day) and the period of the earth's orbit about the sun (the year). Even these familiar units of time require some thought and experiment before they can be measured fairly accurately (as the pre-Gregorian calendars demonstrate!). The duration of daylight changes each day so that one cannot measure the length of the day exactly by the time from sunrise to sunrise, or sunset to sunset. We must start and end our measurement when the earth is in exactly the same position relative to the sun. The highest point reached by the sun each day is the most obvious position, and the length of the day measured from noon to noon should be accurate no matter at what time of year we make the measurement. Note, however, that such a basic measurement of the most familiar time interval not only requires an accurate clock to measure the passage of time, but a geometrical instrument to measure the elevation of the sun or, preferably, a star (and this discussion takes no account of the different length of the day measured with respect to the sun and stars). The measurement of time involves very much more than knowing how to read a clock. Equally, if we turn to the year, we know the date today because we have calendars. Without them, how could we determine how many days there are in a year? Once again we need to be able to recognize a fixed point in the orbit of the earth about the sun. The longest day or night or the two equinoxes, when day and night are exactly equal, represent such points. Counting the days from one midsummer's day to the next will give an approximate number of days in the year (365), but unfortunately the length of the year is not an exact number of whole days, so that now every four years we add an extra day to keep our calendars in line with the seasons, and even this needs further correction every four hundred years.

There are two reasons for raising this discussion of the measurement of time: first to emphasize that it is more complicated than it appears at first sight, and secondly to ask just how accurately it can be done. In order to measure time we must divide it into arbitrary units, but how do we know that the units are all exactly equal? Will today be exactly as long as yesterday? Will next year be exactly as long as this year? We can measure time (or any other continuous variable) increasingly accurately if we use progressively smaller units, just as we can measure the dimensions of a room more accurately in millimetres than in metres. The second is now the standard unit of time. There are 86,400 seconds in a day, which gives a reasonable number of units with which to measure the length of the day accurately. Provided any variation is random and not systematic, that is provided our clock is not speeding up or slowing down, slight differences in the length of each second ticked off by the clock will make very little difference to the accuracy with which we measure a day. Extending this idea, our most accurate clocks, atomic clocks, use the vibration of caesium atoms as units of time. A standard caesium atom changes energy states 9, 162, 631, 770 times every second, which provides adequate micro-units to measure seconds very accurately indeed! We now routinely time sporting events, for example, to a hundredth of a second, a time unit too short for us to distinguish unaided.

Seconds are artificial units of time whereas the day and the year are related to the motions of the earth. Once defined, the length of a second is fixed for all time, but the day and the year are only fixed if the motions of the earth remain constant. We may legitimately ask if there is any reason to suspect that systematic variations may have occurred in either the orbit or rotation of the earth. Gravitational attraction between the sun and the earth and between the moon and the earth causes the tides. When the attraction of both sun and moon combine (at full moon and new moon) the tidal range is greatest (spring tides); when they conflict, tidal range is low (neap tides). The crest of each tide passes right round the earth each day. Each time the tides encounter large land masses, considerable energy is dissipated in friction, which is probably slowing the earth down as it spins on its axis. At least, astronomers have believed for a long time that the earth is very very gradually slowing down as it spins, which means that the day is becoming very slightly longer as time passes. We have no reason to suppose that the process of slowing the earth's spin due to tidal friction has not been going on throughout earth history. On the other hand, we have no reason to suppose that anything has significantly affected the length of the year, that is the period of the orbit of the earth. Thus the year has apparently remained constant while the day has been getting longer. It follows that there must have been more (shorter) days in the year in the past than there are now. This may help to explain why there is such an irregular number of days in the year at present.

The theoretical idea that days get longer and hence that there are fewer of them per year now than in the past may be tested by examining growth records of fossils which produced daily growth increments and whose growth was accretionary. Bivalve molluscs and corals have been the main groups used. Such lines not only record daily growth increments, but are clustered into lunar (tidal) cycles. By simply counting these growth increments, Scrutton[12] demonstrated that the Middle Devonian year consisted of thirteen lunar months of approximately $30\frac{1}{2}$ days each, giving a total of about 400 days in the year. This compares with the present 13 lunar months of 28 days each in a 365 day year.

Although the basic idea that counting the growth lines in fossils will reveal the number of days in the year is simple, in practice all sorts of difficulties arise. The first counts that were made fitted astronomical theory well, but as the studies have widened all sorts of problems have been encountered, not only with fossil growth records but with the astronomical theory as well. Geophysical calculations have shown that tidal friction will account for only part of the slowing of the earth, which has been measured very accurately in recent years using atomic clocks. Furthermore, the slowing recorded for the past twenty years (using atomic clocks) is ten times the average for the past two thousand years deduced from accurate historical records of total eclipses, or even the past three hundred years since telescopes were invented.[13,14] However, what is certain is that the earth is slowing down, albeit not uniformly. The number of days in the year should have been larger in the past, but to determine this number accurately for any time in the past requires at least one well-preserved fossil with a *complete* growth record. It is the completeness of fossil growth records which is now questioned. Most information comes from bivalves so only these will be considered here.

Available evidence indicates that secretion of the shell of shallow marine bivalves is affected by both light and tides, the relative positions of which repeat every fourteen days. Shell deposition is interrupted by exposure at low tides in intertidal bivalves which consequently secrete semi-daily increments, not simple daily increments. Furthermore, since shell secretion takes place predominantly at night which occasionally coincides with low tide, intertidal bivalves frequently 'miss a beat', so to speak. Growth records with less than twenty-eight semi-daily increments for a fourteen-day period are the norm, not the exception. First then, it is necessary to distinguish semi-daily from daily increments in fossils before any count of the number of days in the year can be made. Since these have been confused even in the living common European cockle (*Cerastoderma edule*), care is required in interpreting fossil examples, but the missed increments are a useful indication of semi-daily growth. Even when semi-daily and daily growth increments can be distinguished, there is still the possibility of missed increments due to other random interruptions of growth. In some pectinids (scallops) the same shell may show a more complete record of growth laterally than on either the anterior or posterior regions,[15] while *Tivela stultorum* shows changes in the completeness of its growth record with age and latitude.[16] Juveniles have the most complete records, whereas individuals between twelve and twenty-three years old may possess only from 164 to 239 daily increments in a year's growth. Even among the more complete records of juveniles of one to eight years old, average daily increments per year vary from 350 at 35°N to 300 at 26°N. Indeed, Arctic bivalves grow for only three to five months per year, those off the coast of Maine (43° 50′N) for about eleven months, and south of Boston bivalves grow continuously, but even so random interruptions may cause the loss of ten per cent or more of their growth record. To provide adequate tests for geophysical or astronomical theories, the *exact* number of days per year is required, and at present it seems unlikely to be obtained by direct counting. However, the number of days per lunar fortnight can be determined and this indirectly yields estimates of the number of days in the year. Using these it has been possible to show that the number of days in the lunar fortnight has declined from fifteen and a quarter down to fourteen since the Devonian period. This infers a decline from about four hundred to the present three hundred and sixty-five days per year in the same time interval. Extrapolation back to Precambrian stromatolites,[17] which is very much open to interpretation, suggests perhaps eight to nine hundred days per year, two thousand million years ago.

Incidentally, as a spin-off from these recent investigations into bivalve growth, we may be able to reconstruct the ecology of fossil bivalves better. Inter-tidal bivalves may be recognized on their semi-daily growth increments which are slightly incomplete, irrespective of where they happen to become preserved. Furthermore, their positions on the shore may be determinable, since those low in the intertidal zone have the most complete records during neap tides while those higher up on the shore have more complete records during spring tides. Equally, with enough examples from widely scattered localities, latitudinal trends may be revealed by the completeness of the yearly growth record. In *Tivela stultorum* the total number of daily increments per year decreased with latitude (i.e. going towards the Equator). Furthermore, the number of thicker summer increments decreased rapidly while the number of thinner winter increments actually increased going towards the Equator. This is the exact opposite of what one might expect, winters being longer and colder in higher latitudes.

Finally, in considering growth studies and their application, mention should be made of the corrections to the radiocarbon time scale using tree ring counts, or dendrochronology. To a certain extent this pre-empts the general discussion of radiometric dating methods in the next chapter, but as radiocarbon dating depends to some extent on a unique set of assumptions which differs from those of all other radiometric dating methods,[18] it can be conveniently explained here. As we have already seen, isotopes are forms of the same element with different atomic weights because they have different numbers of neutrons in their nuclei. Some isotopes are stable, while others, the radioactive isotopes, decay spontaneously to different daughter isotopes. Carbon exists naturally as three isotopes, ^{12}C, ^{13}C and ^{14}C; the first two are stable, but ^{14}C decays spontaneously to ^{14}N (nitrogen gas). All radioactive decay, including that of ^{14}C, proceeds at an exponentially declining rate such that no matter how much one starts with, half decays in a fixed period of time, known appropriately as the half-life. Half-lives of different radioisotopes vary dramatically from fractions of a second to thousands of millions of years. That of ^{14}C is generally accepted as 5730 ± 40 years, although the figure 5568 ± 30 years has also been widely used. (We shall discuss briefly how half-lives are determined in the next chapter.) This means that starting with a fixed amount of ^{14}C, say 1 kg, half (500 g) will remain after 5730 years; after another half-life, a quarter (250 g) of the original amount will remain, and so on. Clearly after about a hundred thousand years virtually all ^{14}C would have decayed were it not being produced continually in the upper atmosphere by cosmic bombardment. Slow neutrons in cosmic rays react with ^{14}N atoms to produce ^{14}C and a proton. The radioactive decay of ^{14}C merely reverses this process.

Some of the ^{14}C in the atmosphere combines with oxygen to form carbon dioxide (CO_2) which in turn is incorporated into plant material during photosynthesis. Animals which eat plants also incorporate a small amount of ^{14}C into their bodies as do carnivores in turn. So all living tissue is slightly radioactive. On death no more ^{14}C is added to organic material, but the radioactive decay of ^{14}C continues. So if we sample some fossil wood or bone for ^{14}C we may estimate its age, up to a maximum of fifty to seventy thousand years, by which time the amount of ^{14}C remaining is so small as to be undetectable unless enormous samples are available.

Radiocarbon dating depends on three basic assumptions. First, it is assumed that there is an equilibrium between the production of ^{14}C in the atmosphere and its radioactive decay which has remained constant over the last fifty thousand years or so. If this assumption is correct, then the amount of ^{14}C in the atmosphere has remained constant. Secondly, another equilibrium exists between uptake of ^{14}C into living tissues and its decay, which we assume has also remained constant over the last fifty thousand years and has been independent of geographic location or the specific organisms involved. If this assumption is correct then all living tissue contains the same amount of ^{14}C at death. Hence if we know how much ^{14}C there was at death and we can measure how much remains now, we can calculate the time since death.

Finally, we assume that the sample to be dated has not been contaminated with any other source of carbon since death. This last assumption about contamination is general to all radiometric dating methods, but the first two are specific to radiocarbon dating and we must examine them further.

The first two assumptions depend in part on the rate of decay of ^{14}C being known accurately. No one has been around for six thousand years to measure decay of ^{14}C, so we can only measure the current rate of decay. It is assumed that decay of all longlived radioisotopes is regular and exponential. If we accept this assumption, measurement of the current rate of decay gives the half-life. We have at present no reason to question this assumption, nor any means of testing it accurately. Secondly, available evidence suggests that decay of all radioisotopes is completely independent of whether or not they are chemically combined, or of physical parameters like temperature and pressure. Thus ^{14}C decays at the same rate anywhere on earth, as elemental carbon (for example in charcoal), as carbon dioxide gas, or the calcium carbonate of shells, and so on. Thus if either equilibrium has altered at all, it is the rates at which ^{14}C is produced and incorporated into living tissue which have changed, not the rate of decay.

The neutron flux which produces ^{14}C is four times greater at the poles than at the Equator, and at any latitude it reaches a peak between 40,000 and 50,000 ft (12,300–15,400 m.). Despite this variation in production, ^{14}C is distributed evenly through the whole atmosphere within two years due to rapid atmospheric circulation. ^{14}C circulates more slowly in sea water, perhaps taking a thousand years to become distributed through the deepest oceans. Terrestrial plants from all latitudes yield similar results when analysed for ^{14}C, but marine shells are more variable. In areas like the coast of Peru where 'old' deep ocean water is upwelling, marine mollusc shells which were collected alive have yielded radiocarbon 'ages' of several hundred years because of their initially low ^{14}C content. Even more anomalous 'ages' can be found in freshwater shells, depending on the source of the dissolved bicarbonate ion $(HCO_3)^-$ from which their shells are secreted. In soft-water districts all the bicarbonate comes from atmospheric carbon dioxide, and radiocarbon ages are generally accurate. However, in limestone regions much of the dissolved bicarbonate comes from the limestone itself and has no initial ^{14}C content at all. Shells from such waters also yield anomalously high 'ages' because their initial ^{14}C content is too low. These facts, together with the tendency of all carbonate shells to undergo early diagenesis which may contaminate the original organic carbon, render ^{14}C dates from shells highly suspect and, in general, shells are only used where no other material is available. However, the second assumption is generally valid for terrestrial plant material, especially wood, and for bones.

The assumption that production of ^{14}C in the atmosphere has remained constant can be questioned on several grounds. First, much cosmic radiation originates from the sun and shows an eleven-year cycle corresponding to the sunspot cycle. Thus one would expect more ^{14}C to be produced during sunspot maxima than during sunspot minima. Even so it could be argued that cyclic production of ^{14}C on an eleven-year cycle would not seriously affect ^{14}C dates of thousands or tens of thousands of years. However, other data also indicate that production and incorporation rates have varied with time. Nowadays we have adopted as a standard the nineteenth-century ^{14}C content of the atmosphere because the increased burning of fossil fuels, coal and oil, which contain no ^{14}C, means that the ^{14}C content of the atmosphere has been declining since the industrial revolution began. This is known as the Suess effect. Equally, since 1945 atmospheric testing of nuclear devices and peaceful nuclear reactors have increased the ^{14}C content of the atmosphere. Although both these are man-made recent changes, it is also known from measurements of historically dated objects that between AD 1500 and 1700 the ^{14}C content of the atmosphere was two per cent above the nineteenth century standard (the de Vries effect). As yet we have no explanation for the de Vries effect other than an increase in cosmic bombardment.

More serious difficulties arise from anomalous ^{14}C dates for artifacts from well-dated archaeological sites and, of more direct interest here, from wood of known ages. Trees lay down a single growth ring each year. While woody tissue is growing ^{14}C is incorporated into it at a rate depending on the current ^{14}C content of the atmosphere, but once formed no further ^{14}C is added and decay proceeds as normal. A ^{14}C 'age' can be determined for wood from any part of a tree, while by counting the tree rings (and knowing the date of felling) the corresponding absolute age can also be determined. Thus any systematic errors in ^{14}C dating can be detected. Clearly the oldest trees available will provide the longest time span over which to detect variations in ^{14}C production. For this reason attention has been concentrated on the sequoia (*Sequoia gigantea*) which lives for up to 3,500 years and the much less impressive, but older, bristle cone pine (*Pinus aristata*), the oldest-known specimen of which is 4,900 years old.

Dendrochronology can be carried back even further than the age of the oldest living tree because tree rings record the sequence of good and bad seasons. By matching the records of dead timber with those of live trees it has been possible to extend dendrochronology back 7,500 years.[19] Further back than this varves can be used.[20] Varves are laminations in lake clays which are seasonal in origin. A relatively thick layer of coarse sediment is deposited after spring floods, followed by a thin layer of fine sediment in winter. Each pair of thick and thin layers represents a year's sediment accumulation. Varves have been used to check the ^{14}C time scale back for 15,500 years,[21] but earlier than this there is little evidence to test radiocarbon dates. Varves are themselves less accurate in testing radiocarbon dates than dendrochronology, because they cannot be dated directly by ^{14}C. Usually pollen zones or climatic fluctuations are used as an intermediate step. Thus if the beginning of a climatic change can be detected in a varve sequence and also dated using ^{14}C from another site, comparisons of the varve and radiocarbon 'ages' can be made. In most areas it is also difficult to trace varves right down to the present day. Even so, similarities in both varve and dendrochronological dating between 8,000 years before present (BP) and the present day imply that both dating methods are essentially accurate for this period.

Using varves and dendrochronology it can be shown that the ^{14}C

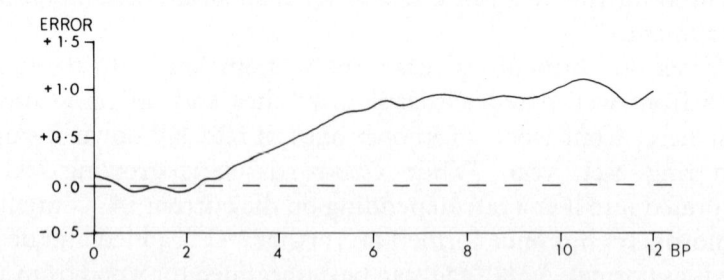

53. A graph showing deviations in the radiocarbon time scale. The dashed horizontal line represents the absolute age; the solid curve gives ages estimated from radioactive decay of ^{14}C. Scale in thousands of years. The curve indicates that between 10 and 12,000 years BP, ^{14}C dates are almost 10 per cent inaccurate. Scale from the present to 4,500 BP based on tree rings, remainder on varves. (After D. J. Schove, *Palaeogeogr. Palaeoclimat. Palaeoecol.*, **25**, fig. 2, p. 213, Elsevier, 1978.)

content of the atmosphere has deviated by as much as ten per cent from the nineteenth-century standard level (figure 53). Three possible explanations have been advanced: that primary radiation from the sun has varied with time; that fluctuations in the intensity of the earth's magnetic field have caused variations in ^{14}C production, because the magnetic field shields the earth from much cosmic ray bombardment; and lastly that climatic changes have altered the amount of carbon circulating in the atmosphere and therefore the amount of ^{14}C incorporated into plants. All three are quite plausible and could have acted in combination. Further research is needed to see if the deviations in the radiocarbon time scale correspond better with climatic fluctuations, or reversals of the magnetic field, or perhaps with some other feature.

As we have seen, growth studies not only tell us how fossils grew when they were alive; they also record other information about conditions on earth at the time when the fossils were growing. The idea that tree rings record climatic fluctuations as well as the age of the tree is not at all new. Even so, it is rather surprising to find, for example, that growth studies of fossils can be of use to astronomers in determining past motions of this planet and its satellite, the moon. All growth involves time, and the sorts of growth studies described in this chapter relate to very long periods of time. How do we know how old the earth is or that a particular fossil is three hundred million years old? We must now consider these questions.

Chapter 6

Time in geology

'These rocks are Silurian because they contain Silurian fossils.' 'We know these fossils are Silurian because they occur in Silurian rocks.' In their contexts both statements may be true. Fossils can be, and are, used to date rocks, but they are not the only method and sometimes the second statement is more appropriate to the situation. We can best understand the use of fossils in dating rocks if we trace the development of the geological column. Viewed from a twentieth-century standpoint, the development of the geological time scale seems a painfully slow process, but we have the advantage of hindsight and it is a tribute to the early pioneers that they got as far as they did with virtually no understanding of the underlying causes. Time scales and all history may be either relative or absolute. To comprehend basic processes, being aware of the relative order of events is often more important than knowing the exact dates on which they took place. This is certainly true in geology, and most of the geological column was established long before we had any accurate means of estimating the ages of the events in years. Relative dating merely determines which of two events preceded the other. A small number of simple principles is used in geology to date events relatively, and when put together they slowly and gradually formed the time scale we use today. As far as the use of fossils is concerned, two main principles, superposition and faunal succession, combine to form the key to historical geology, but as we shall see the others are equally important where fossils are absent. However, I shall start by considering the palaeontologically orientated principles.

Superposition

Nils Stensen (1638–86), better known to English language geologists as Steno, is credited with first expounding the principle of

TIME IN GEOLOGY

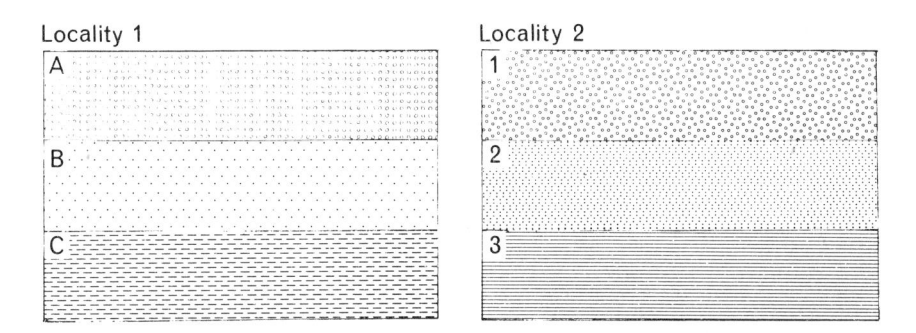

54. Superposition. At both localities the beds at the bottom (C and 3) are the oldest and those at the top (A and 1) are the youngest. It is impossible to determine age relationships between the two localities using superposition alone.

superposition in 1669.[1] He argued that, in a sequence of layered sediments, those at the bottom must have been deposited first and those at the top last (figure 54). Thus the relative ages of sedimentary rock layers can be determined *in any one locality* using this simple idea. Unfortunately, outcrops of rocks are not continuous. In most countries of Europe and North America and elsewhere in the world the vast majority of the rock is buried under soil or vegetation. Even in deserts where outcrops are more continuous, geological structures like faults and unconformities interrupt exposures. Thus we may know the relative ages of the rock layers within two exposures, but correlating between the two exposures is impossible using superposition alone. This situation remained for the next hundred and fifty years until in the early nineteenth century William Smith[2] in England, and Cuvier and Brogniart[3] in France, discovered independently that various strata were characterized by distinctive suites of fossils and, furthermore, that the suites of fossils always occurred in the same sequence wherever they were exposed. This was the second principle of faunal succession.

Faunal succession

Smith was an engineer and worked for canal companies in Britain. He travelled widely and eventually produced a geological map of most of England and Wales which is basically the same as that we use today. Although there is evidence that Smith had already formulated his ideas in the late eighteenth century,[4] it was not until the publication of his map in 1815 that the principle of faunal succession was widely publicized in Britain. In France, Cuvier and Brogniart were professional scientists at the Paris Museum. Cuvier was Professor of Comparative Anatomy and, although he was a zoologist, his comparative studies had led him to examine fossil vertebrates as well as living ones. In 1796 he demonstrated the existence of an extinct species of elephant (the Pleistocene mammoth) in the superficial deposits of the Paris Basin. This was itself a momentous discovery, since although some fossils were thought to represent extinct species, the world was so poorly known that it was possible to argue, as Lyell did later on, that apparently extinct species might still exist in deep oceans or unexplored parts of the world. It was however extremely difficult to imagine an undiscovered species of elephant, particularly one with long hair adapted to colder climates. Later Cuvier described more extinct mammals from the Tertiary deposits of the Paris Basin without realizing their different ages. When informed of possible differences in their ages, he joined his friend Brogniart, Professor of Mineralogy at the Paris Museum, in a series of traverses across the Paris Basin in which they discovered not only that each major formation, like the chalk, had its own characteristic fauna, but also that formations could be subdivided into beds on their faunal content. The publication of their results in 1809 introduced the principle of faunal succession to the French-speaking world, and thereafter much more attention was paid to the stratigraphic position of fossils. Incidentally, Cuvier and Brogniart's memoir[5] was also important as the first use of fossils for environmental reconstruction, and they demonstrated that the Tertiary strata of the Paris Basin contained alternations of marine and non-marine deposits by comparing the enclosed fossils with present-day marine and freshwater organisms.

When peace was restored to Europe in 1815, scientific travel became possible again, in particular between the two principal antagonists, Britain and France. In the same year William Smith published his map[6] together with illustrations of the characteristic fossils of each of his formations. Smith's map covered an enormous area compared with those of earlier workers on the continent and it is from this time that relatively rapid progress was made towards constructing the geological column as we know it today (figure 1, page 8). Parts of the column were recognized as having distinctive fossils and several formations were grouped together into new geological systems. Thus the Cretaceous System was defined and named after the French for chalk. Some systems were named after the areas in which the included formations (and their fossils) were first described. For example, the system below the Cretaceous, the Jurassic, was named after the Jura Mountains, the Permian after the Perm province of Russia and the Devonian from Devon. Even when the name of a system did not derive from the place of its first description, as with the Triassic, named after its three-fold division in Germany, or the Carboniferous, so called because it included the coal measures, type areas where the deposits were characteristically developed were defined – a practice still adhered to in the formal stratigraphy of the present. By defining type areas the problem of whether the rocks date the fossils or vice versa is settled once and for all. If fossils come from the Jurassic as defined in the Jura Mountains, they are of Jurassic age by definition. If similar fossils are found anywhere else in the world, the rocks containing them are Jurassic because they contain the same fossils as occur in the type Jurassic of the Jura Mountains, in other words because the fossils are of Jurassic age. Thus ultimately we can recognize Jurassic rocks anywhere in the world only by comparing their fossils with those from the Jurassic of the Jura Mountains. Very few fossils occur in every part of the world. So if some fossils which occur in British rocks are identical to those from the Jurassic of the Jura mountains, the British rocks are identified as being Jurassic. Other British fossils which are confined to these rocks must also be Jurassic and can be used to compare those of Spain (for example) with those of Britain and so on. And we know the Jurassic is older than the Cretaceous because wherever we find both together, the Jurassic underlies the Cretaceous.

Within twenty years or so of 1815, the geological column was established more or less as we know it today, using the principles of faunal succession and superposition. It is true that some difficulties were encountered, particularly with the older, more deformed rocks of Wales which lay below Smith's Old Red Sandstone formation. Adam Sedgwick, Professor of Geology at Cambridge University, and Sir Roderick Murchison, first director of the British Geological Survey, set off together in the early 1830s to unravel these rocks.[7] Sedgwick started at the bottom of the succession in Anglesey and worked upwards. He defined the Cambrian System. Murchison started at the top just below the Old Red Sandstone and worked downwards. Soon he defined his Silurian System.[8] Unfortunately it was not long before it became apparent that the top of Sedgwick's Cambrian System overlapped the base of Murchison's Silurian System. The two fell out and the controversy raged until after their deaths. Murchison had far better faunas to describe than Sedgwick and wider influence, but eventually the existence of a Cambrian System was accepted and in 1879 the disputed territory became Lapworth's Ordovician System.[9] This last system was by far the latest widely accepted geological system to be defined. With the exception of the Ordovician, the geological column of the 1840s resembled very strongly that of the present day.

With hindsight such disputes and the bitter feuds that attended them seem childish. However, lest we should feel too superior, it is worth pointing out that an equally vigorous dispute is still current as to whether the Tremadoc Series is uppermost Cambrian or lowest Ordovician. As far as I am aware no friendships have been broken and no bitter personal attacks made, but the protagonists of each viewpoint argue very passionately. Furthermore Lapworth's 'brilliant compromise' in creating the Ordovician System from the disputed series produced two boundary problems where only one existed before. To be sure there is general agreement about the Ordovician–Silurian boundary, but none yet on the Cambrian–Ordovician boundary. Currently boundary commissions are sitting to produce international agreement on all system boundaries and hopefully they will settle all such boundary disputes permanently.

The Lower Palaeozoic is not the only part of the geological column about which stratigraphic disputes have occurred. The Triassic–Jurassic boundary was a problem for some time. Although the disputed rocks, known as the Rhaetic Series, are now generally accepted as being uppermost Triassic, arguments were put forward for placing these predominantly marine sediments with the marine Lower Jurassic rather than with the predominantly non-marine Triassic. The Rhaetic was even proposed as a separate geological System between the Triassic and Jurassic. Another dispute in Europe raged over the Cretaceous–Tertiary boundary. In Britain there is a marked unconformity between the highest Chalk preserved and the overlying Eocene sands, gravels and clays. There is a very distinct break in both the fossil and rock types. This seemed to be the obvious place to draw a system boundary. However, in other parts of Europe, notably Denmark, there is a gradual transition between the Chalk and the overlying Tertiary sands and gravels. The boundary is much less obvious on lithological grounds, although, of course, the Chalk is still very distinctive. The main problem arose when it was discovered that the highest Chalk in Denmark, the Danian Chalk, lacked the ammonites, belemnites and many other fossils which were typical of Cretaceous, indeed Mesozoic, seas. Some geologists were reluctant to draw a system boundary, particularly one between the Mesozoic and Cainozoic eras, within a geological formation. However, as we shall see, formation boundaries always cross time lines and it is inevitable that in some places significant time boundaries will fall within a formation; so much so that current practice is to seek out places where the succession is both complete and fossiliferous and arbitrarily to select a boundary within this continuous sequence, the so-called 'golden-spike' approach. Once such a stratotype section has been defined, attempts are made to correlate all sections of a similar age with this type section. In the case of the Cretaceous–Tertiary transition, the best place to select a boundary is in Denmark and, in fact, the Danian Chalk together with the lowest of the overlying sands are now grouped as the Palaeocene, the lowest unit of the Tertiary rocks. Only the top-most part of the Palaeocene is found in Britain, mainly in Kent. Thus the British succession lacks the highest Cretaceous Chalk and most of the overlying Palaeocene. It is small wonder that the fossils and rock types differ so much and that the boundary is so easy to recognize in Britain.

This also emphasizes the problem of incomplete sections. The type sections of the geological systems were defined by the historical accident of where they happened to be described first. The type sections may be very poor for correlation purposes, as for example in the Devonian of Devon, much of which is poorly fossiliferous and all of which has suffered considerable tectonic disturbance. Furthermore, much of the Devonian of north Devon is non-marine and can only be correlated with the Old Red Sandstone deposits. Although the basic succession is probably known accurately, detailed correlation of the different sections is still a matter of interpretation. In such cases practical correlation is achieved by trying to correlate a richly fossiliferous and undisturbed sequence known elsewhere in the world with the type area. Thus the abundantly fossiliferous Devonian of New York State, the Michigan Basin or Iowa can be correlated broadly with the type Devonian of Devon and then the best of these North American sections used to correlate throughout North America.

Where type sections are incomplete the problem arises as to what to do with a more complete section discovered later. Generally these problems are overcome by defining only the base of a unit. Thus unit A extends from its base, defined as the first appearance of fossil X, for example, up to the base of unit B, defined as the first appearance of fossil Y. Any new strata found between the top of unit A as first defined and the base of unit B, belong in unit A. When the first section described is so incomplete that a whole new unit can be recognized, as happened with the Palaeocene, the new unit can be defined by its base and inserted in the sequence at the appropriate level. By this means the original geological column, which contained significant gaps, is gradually being made more complete. If somewhere in the world a complete section occurs for each part of the column, then eventually we may end up with a complete column. We have yet to achieve this, in my own view, although the column since the base of the Cambrian is certainly sufficiently complete for us to have a very good idea of the earth's history over this period.

The use of fossils to date rocks did not end with the establishment of the geological column. More and more refined methods were developed and stratigraphy, the branch of geology which deals with correlation, is a major part of the science and, some would argue, the most important use of fossils. Stratigraphy is often divided into three parts: lithostratigraphy, biostratigraphy and chronostratigraphy. Lithostratigraphy deals exclusively with rocks and is concerned with correlating incompletely exposed rock units. Biostratigraphy is concerned with the use of fossils to determine the age relationships of the rock units, while chronostratigraphy deals with the time units defined by the fossils. Although they are obviously related to each other, it is convenient to discuss them separately, and we need only consider the first two.

The basic unit of lithostratigraphy is the formation, a widely used term which has a precise meaning in stratigraphy. A formation is a unit of rock which can be mapped and distinguished from similar units by its character or lithology. Thus a distinctive sandstone unit which can be traced over a wide area may be given a formation name because it is easily distinguished from the underlying limestone and the overlying shale formations. Formations may be combined into groups or subdivided into members in a formal hierarchical lithostratigraphic classification. A code of stratigraphic practice has been formulated in North America[10] and is widely used in the more unexplored parts of the world. In Europe the stratigraphic code is less widely used, although the more obvious and least controversial parts are gradually being accepted. The difference in stratigraphic practice in Europe and North America is not due to perverseness or national pride, but to the different historical and geological settings.

In the continental interior of North America formations are often very widespread and classic 'layer cake stratigraphy' obtains. Western Europe, and particularly Britain, lies on the edge of a continent, and rock types, with very few exceptions, change rapidly over short distances. Formations are not as easily recognized, are much less widespread and more variable. Furthermore, of course, many of the names of stratigraphic units in Britain date back to William Smith and are so entrenched in the literature as to be self-perpetuating. For example, according to the code formations are supposed to be named after a place where they are well exposed, but terms like 'The Liass', 'The Cornbrash' and 'The Lower Greensand' will never be removed from British stratigraphy. Indeed, most European stratigraphy pre-dates any notion of a code of practice and is unlikely to be changed because one has now been formulated – even if the code were entirely non-controversial and universally accepted, which it is not.

Finally, before leaving lithostratigraphy, mention should be made of marker horizons and 'event stratigraphy'. Marker horizons in general are just very distinctive bands in a rock sequence that can be recognized over a wide area but are usually too thin to be considered as formations. They may be characterized by their lithology, such as a single band of volcanic ash in a series of marine sediments, or by their fossil content, as in a bed of corals such as occurs at the base of the Silurian Saluda Formation in south-east Indiana or the Carboniferous Limestone at Pentraeth, Anglesey, or Eglwyseg Mountain, North Wales. Some marker horizons, such as ash falls, represent instantaneous events, at least in terms of the length of geological time, and as such they are excellent time planes in stratigraphy. All storm deposits, volcanic ash falls and other eruptive deposits, lava flows, and so on, fall into this category. Some catastrophic kills of fossils are also events in this sense. Whenever such event horizons can be recognized they represent ideal time planes by which sections may be correlated. If recognizable, such events may be correlated worldwide. Dust from the explosive eruption of Krakatoa in the late nineteenth century was deposited worldwide and would be useful for correlating suitable deep-sea sediments of all oceans. 'Event stratigraphy' is simply an attempt to recognize and correlate such short-lived depositional events.

If all lithostratigraphic units were of the same age everywhere there would be no need for correlation using fossils, in other words for biostratigraphy. Unfortunately they are not, and Shaw,[11] in his

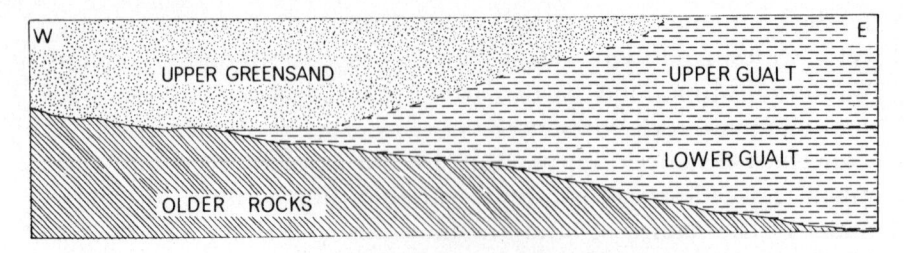

55. The diachronous boundary between the Gualt Clay and Upper Greensand in southern Britain. The transition took place much earlier in the west than in the east.

admirable book *Time in Stratigraphy*, goes so far as to establish as a principle the idea that the boundaries of all lithostratigraphic units deposited in shallow epicontinental seas *must* be diachronous (of different ages in different places). I cannot but agree with him. A particular rock type such as a sand (for example the Cretaceous Upper Greensand of southern Britain) will form where sand is supplied, if you like, in a sandy facies. At the same time, clay (for example, the Cretaceous Gualt Clay) may be forming elsewhere in areas where clay is the predominant type of sediment being supplied. Thus two sediments of different lithology may form simultaneously and, as time goes by, the boundaries between the different facies may shift. A lithostratigrapher will map out the limits of the sand as one formation, the Upper Greensand, and the clay as another, the Gualt Clay. Wherever we find them, the Upper Greensand overlies the Gualt Clay, but the transition takes place much earlier in the west than in the east. We know this because ammonites are used to date these Cretaceous sediments. The change from clay to sand takes place much lower in the sequence of ammonites in Wiltshire than in Kent (figure 55). This is just one instance of a diachronous boundary, but virtually all lithostratigraphic boundaries are diachronous, because of the very nature of facies. In the case above, the sand represented accumulation in shallower water nearer shore; the clay, deeper-water, offshore conditions. Whether clay or sand accumulated depended entirely on the relative position of the shore, the depth of water and the nature of the sediment supplied, in other words it depended on the facies.

Because we can assume that most lithostratigraphic boundaries are time-transgressive, biostratigraphy – the use of fossils to correlate rocks – is a major and complementary branch of stratigraphy. The basic biostratigraphic unit is the zone, but zones may vary considerably. At least three concepts are involved, mainly because stratigraphy is essentially a pragmatic discipline. Biostratigraphers collect fossils carefully and when they feel they can define a suitable zone they do so without worrying too much about what sort of zone it is. For all practical purposes this is perfectly all right. Nevertheless it is worth recording how the different types of zone are defined. The ideal zone, or biozone, is one defined by the total stratigraphic range of a species in an evolutionary lineage. Let us suppose, for example, that three trilobite species evolved one from the other in the sequence A, B, C. Then the total stratigraphic range of A would define biozone A, the total stratigraphic range of B, biozone B and so on. In practice such lineages are very rare and many biozones are defined simply on the total range of a species. It is assumed that the species spread throughout its geographical range almost instantaneously and, equally, that it became extinct everywhere at the same time. If these assumptions are satisfied, and especially if the species is part of a lineage, then the zonal boundaries correspond very well to time planes. It is hard to imagine species A evolving into species B at different times in different places.

The second widely used type of zone is the faunizone, where the aspect of the whole fauna is used to define the zone. Faunizones are, at least theoretically, less reliable than biozones, since they are likely to be facies-controlled and hence could be as diachronous as formations. In practice they are very useful and are widely used in correlation. Teilzones, which are less widely used, are defined on only part of the range of a fossil. They are useful locally and include some zones defined by overlap. A sequence with two key species, the stratigraphic ranges of which overlap, may be divided into three parts: a lower part with only the older species, a middle part with both and an upper part with only the younger. All three parts would be teilzones.

Zones are usually named after some characteristic or conspicuous fossil, known as the zone fossil. Zones, especially faunizones, may still be recognized even if the zone fossil is absent locally. This is certainly true of the coral/brachiopod zones of the Carboniferous Limestone in Britain, which were first defined in south-western Britain but are now applied even in Scotland. Certainly in the northernmost parts of the outcrop area some of the key species are totally unknown, but the zones may be recognized by general faunal similarity.

As with lithostratigraphy, there is a hierarchical classification of

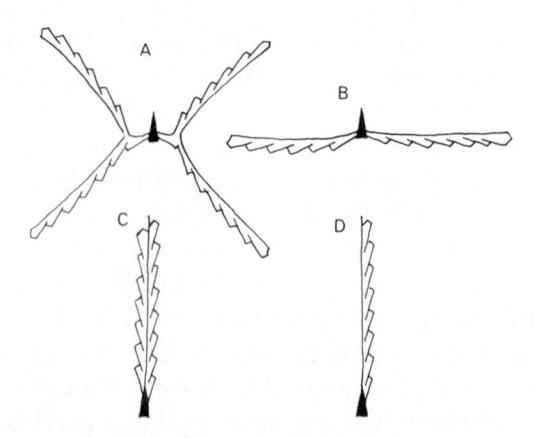

56. The sequence of graptolite faunas in the Ordovician and Silurian.
A. Tetragraptid. B. Didymograptid. C. Diplograptid. D. Monograptid.

biostratigraphic units. Zones may be divided into subzones, just as formations can be divided into members, and grouped into stages which are the finest biostratigraphic unit that can be used for intercontinental correlation. Even at stage level, faunal provinces may restrict worldwide correlation. Stages are characterized by faunas which have reached a particular stage of evolution so that although no species and few genera may be found all over the world, the general aspect of the fauna gives a broad indication of where it fits in the sequence. Graptolites, which are very useful for intercontinental correlation in the Ordovician and Silurian, went through a series of evolutionary stages which may be used to illustrate this idea, although none of the grades of graptolite evolution is actually used to define a stage. In the early Ordovician, graptolites had many branches, or stipes (figure 56). These were replaced by forms with only two stipes which hung down from the initial part of the colony, called the sicula. Later, biserial forms developed with the stipes growing up from the sicula and finally in the early Silurian, graptolites with only a single stipe appeared and displaced the earlier biserial forms. These changes affected not just one or two genera, but all the graptolites known to have occurred at any particular time. The faunas of most of the stages in the Mesozoic have this sort of character, but are dominated by ammonites rather than graptolites.

A quick perusal of a table of zones will show that certain types of fossils are used in biostratigraphy much more frequently than others. Gastropods and echinoderms like starfish are only rarely useful in biostratigraphy whereas graptolites, ammonoids and microfossils like foraminifera are very widely used. Consideration of the basic requirements of a good zone fossil will reveal why this is so. Biostratigraphers continually try to refine their correlations, in other words they try to recognize progressively smaller units of time over the widest possible area. We know now that the principle of faunal succession is due to the fact that organisms have evolved, although this was not realized when the idea was first promulgated. Organisms which evolved rapidly are more valuable in biostratigraphy since they can be used to recognize relatively small periods of time (currently down to about half a million years). Organisms which change little over long periods are much less useful in correlation. Secondly, the most refined sequence of zones is useless for correlation purposes if it cannot be recognized in the next county. Fossils which lived in a wide range of environments over a wide geographical area, or alternatively which were dispersed over a wide area after death, are also useful in biostratigraphy. Thus graptolites, which we believe floated in the open oceans, and ammonites, the shells of which floated widely after death, are very valuable for correlation purposes. Microfossils are generally useful because they are often widespread and, in particular, because they can be found in small samples of rock or sediment such as are recovered from boreholes. Indeed, perhaps the most useful fossils for biostratigraphic purposes are pollen grains. They are very resistant to decay; only oxidation attacks them. They can be spread by the wind and hence deposited in freshwater, marine or terrestrial sediments; and they are very small so that small samples of rock may yield large numbers of pollen grains. Palynology, the study of spores and pollen, is a very rapidly expanding branch of biostratigraphy. Incidentally, it is worth noting that the requirements of a good zone fossil are exactly the opposite of those for fossils which are useful in reconstructing ancient environments. Once again I cannot avoid restating the idea that whatever use is made of fossils, it is essential to understand the mode of life of the animals and plants which gave rise to the fossils in order to make sound interpretations.

By the 1840s, then, a geological column was established which was basically the same as that in figure 1 (page 8) and, by using fossils it gradually became possible to correlate rocks with a fair degree of accuracy. The dating was still relative, however. Geologists knew that the Jurassic preceded the Cretaceous, or that the *planorbis* zone was the lowest ammonite zone in the Jurassic, but they still had no idea how old any of these rocks were. Although fossils are still the simplest and most widely used method of dating rocks, where they are absent other criteria of relative age have to be used. It is worthwhile discussing some of these other methods briefly, because as we shall see later, they play an important role in relating radiometric ages in years to fossiliferous rocks. Most fossils occur in sedimentary rocks which cannot normally be dated directly by radiometric methods. Thus all the dates in years on figure 1 were related to the geological column using these simple principles.

Cross cutting relationships

This common-sense principle is best illustrated with one or two easy examples. Figure 57 shows a quarry section diagrammatically. The beds on the left of the section have been displaced downwards with respect to those on the right along a crack near the centre. Such a break in the rocks across which relative movement occurs is known as a fault, another common word with a precise meaning in geology. Consider whether the faulting preceded the deposition of the sediments, or vice versa. The sequence of beds is exactly the same on either side; they have merely been offset a short distance at the fault. It is much more plausible to assume that the sediments were originally deposited in continuous beds which were subsequently displaced by the fault, than the other way around. If the fault had been there first, some reason must be found to explain why sands accumulated on one side of a line, on the sea floor, but not on the other side until much later, by which time mud was accumulating on the first side which also appeared on the second side after a similar time interval, and so on. The latter interpretation is really quite

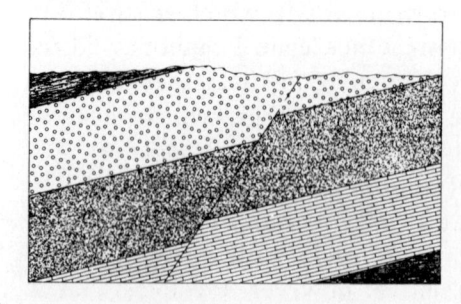

57. A section in a quarry with a fault offsetting the beds. The faulting occurred after the deposition of all the beds which have been offset.

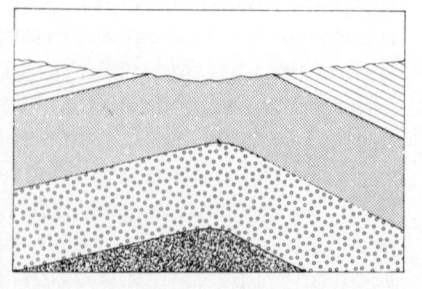

58. A section to illustrate folding. Again all the beds which have been bent are older than the folding.

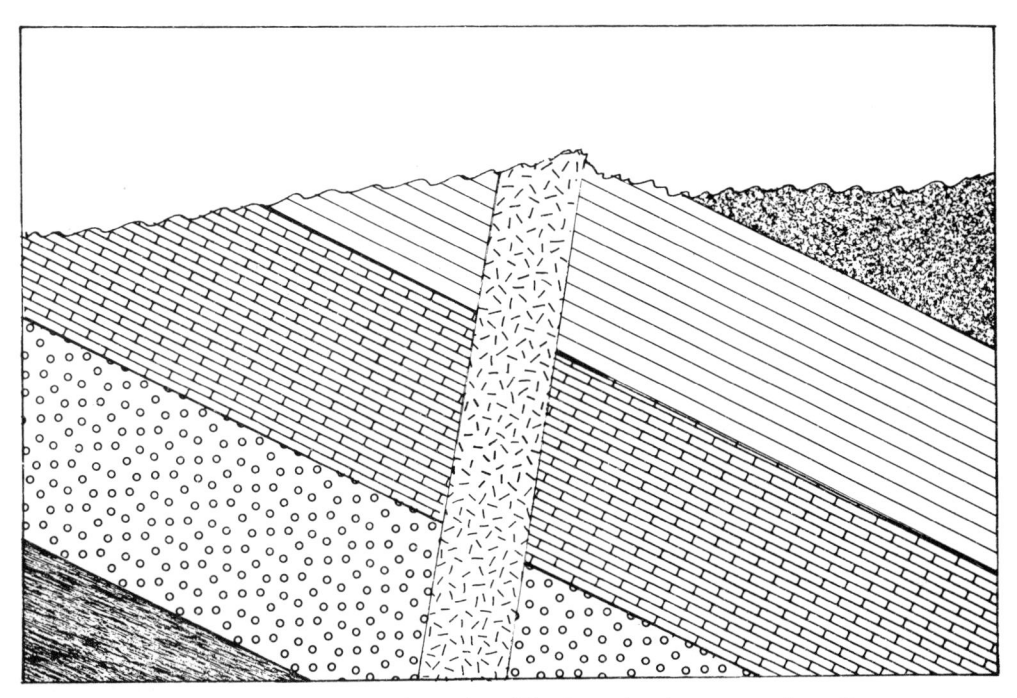

59. A section to illustrate an igneous intrusion. The intrusion is younger than all the beds through which it cuts.

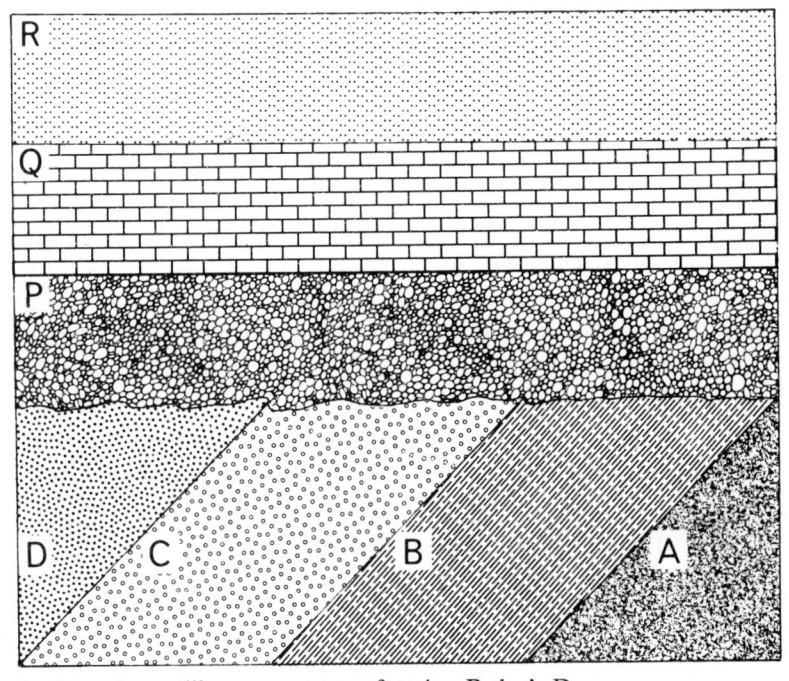

60. A section to illustrate an unconformity. Beds A–D were deposited, tilted and eroded before beds P–R were deposited.

ridiculous – the sediments must have been deposited before the faulting occurred. Figures 58–60 show similar diagrammatic sections in which the beds have been folded (figure 58), intruded by an igneous rock (figure 59), and eroded to form a break in the rock sequence known as an unconformity (figure 60). Again it is possible to date the relative order of events by the effects of the processes on the rocks. The folding in figure 58 must have occurred after the deposition of the youngest beds which are actually bent by the folds. The intrusion of basalt in figure 59 must have occurred after the youngest bed through which it passes was deposited. The erosion which caused the unconformity in figure 60 must be younger than the youngest bed which it truncates (bed D), but older than the oldest bed which passes undisturbed over the unconformable surface (bed P). We may state this general principle as follows: a geological event such as folding, faulting or erosion must have occurred after the deposition of the youngest bed which it affects and before that of the oldest deposit which is unaffected by it. This idea is simple and easy to apply. For your amusement determine the precise order of events in figure 61.

Way-up criteria

Superposition can be applied most easily to undisturbed rocks which are still horizontal and the right way up. In mountainous regions, rocks are often intensely folded and whole sequences of rocks may be overturned or vertical. In such cases it is necessary to recognize which was the original way up before superposition can be used. A whole host of such features can be recognized of which just a few examples will be given. Many involve the use of fossils, but at least as many can be found in unfossiliferous rocks as well. In particular, many sedimentary structures are good way-up criteria.

Where fossils are preserved in growth position their orientation may give a clue as to the way up. Many growth forms of colonial corals which branch or radiate upwards can be used, but it is essential to be sure they are preserved in growth position. This can usually be done by looking for as many examples as possible. Indeed, as a general principle, it is wise to look for as much corroborative evidence as you can find. One coral colony may have been preserved upside-down, but if there is a whole bed of corals all orientated the same way it is much more likely that they are in growth position. If sedimentary structures confirm the orientation indicated by the corals, the way up

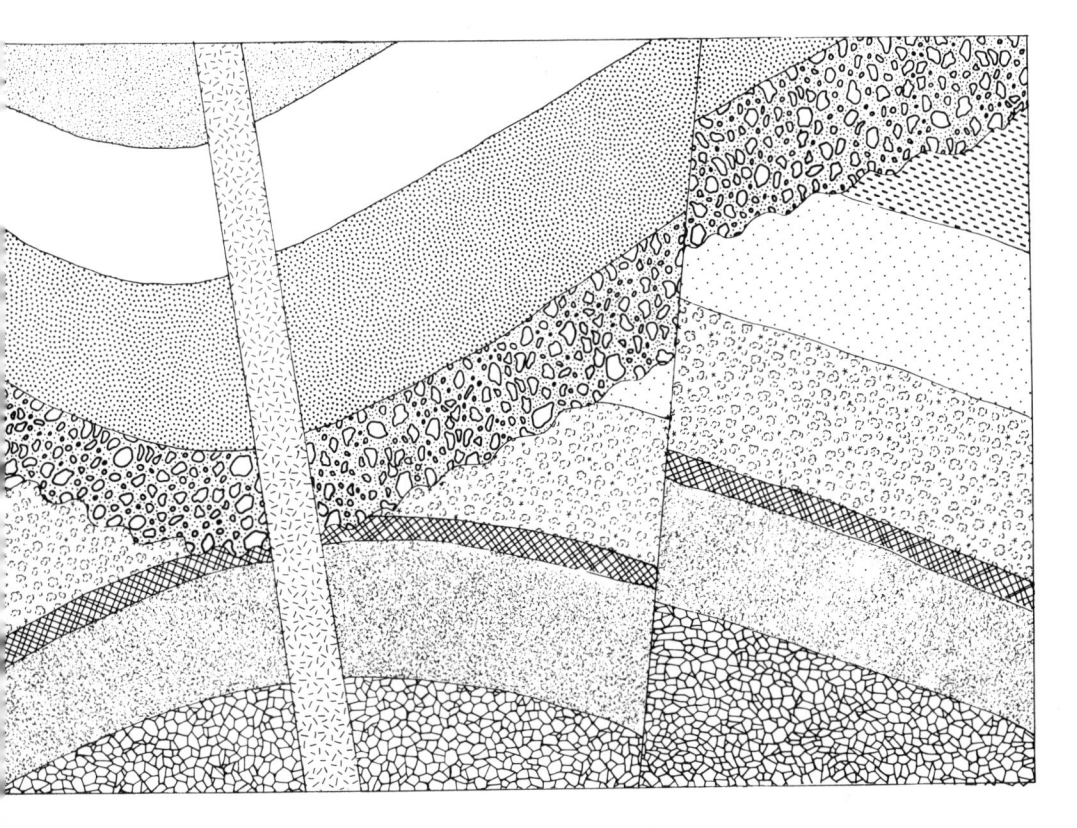

61. A complex section. Determine for yourself the order of events. Can you tell from the diagram if the fault is older or younger than the intrusion?

becomes even more certain. Geopetal structures in fossils are also useful. Fossils with chambers to their shells do not always fill completely with sediment. Where this happens the upper surface of the sediment inside may be used like a spirit level for it will originally have been horizontal. In most cases the remaining space in the chamber is filled with minerals, like calcite, so where we find fossils partly filled with sediment and partly filled with mineral deposits we can use these geopetal structures as a way-up criterion. Again it is essential to seek out a number of examples. Fossils can be, and have been, exhumed and reburied, in which case any geopetal structures will have random orientations. A series of parallel geopetal structures is necessary to be certain of way up.

Where fossils are absent, sedimentary and tectonic structures can be used instead. Perhaps the most obvious surface sedimentary structures which can be used as way-up criteria are footsteps, which

THE NATURAL HISTORY OF FOSSILS

always penetrate the bed below. Tracks, trails and some burrows all show this same feature of penetrating into the bed below. If they are turned upside down (figure 11, page 28), we can still recognize way up. Similarly, sedimentary structures of inorganic origin, like mud cracks, may be used on the same criterion. When mud dries out it cracks and tends to curl up. The next layer of sediment to be deposited will penetrate down the cracks and underneath the curled-up sheets, if drying has proceeded that far. Cross-sections through mud cracks will therefore reveal way up (figure 62). Graded bedding and cross bedding may also be used as way up criteria (figure 63). In most graded beds there is a gradual change upwards through the bed from coarse grain size to fine grain size and then a sudden change to coarse again at the junction with the bed above. Equally, where cross beds are truncated, the truncation is always at the top of the cross-

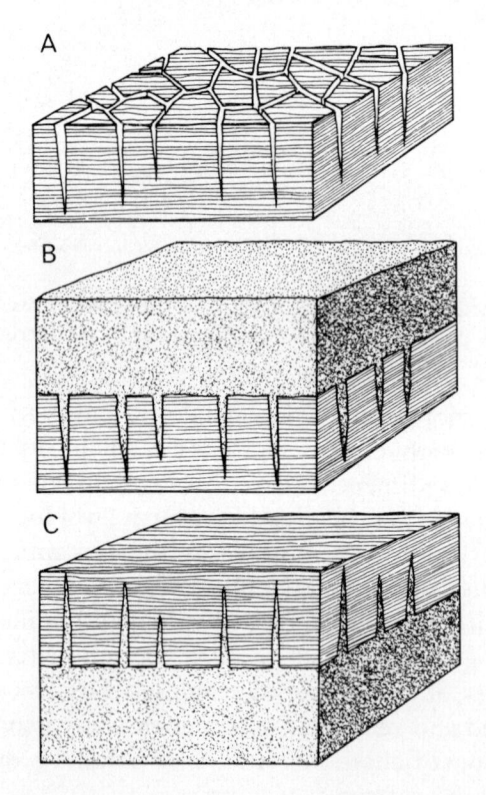

62. Block diagrams to illustrate the use of mudcracks to determine way up. A. The mud cracks form. B. A sand layer is deposited and penetrates *down* into the mud cracks below. C. Diagram B upside-down to show the sand penetrating *up* into the mud cracks.

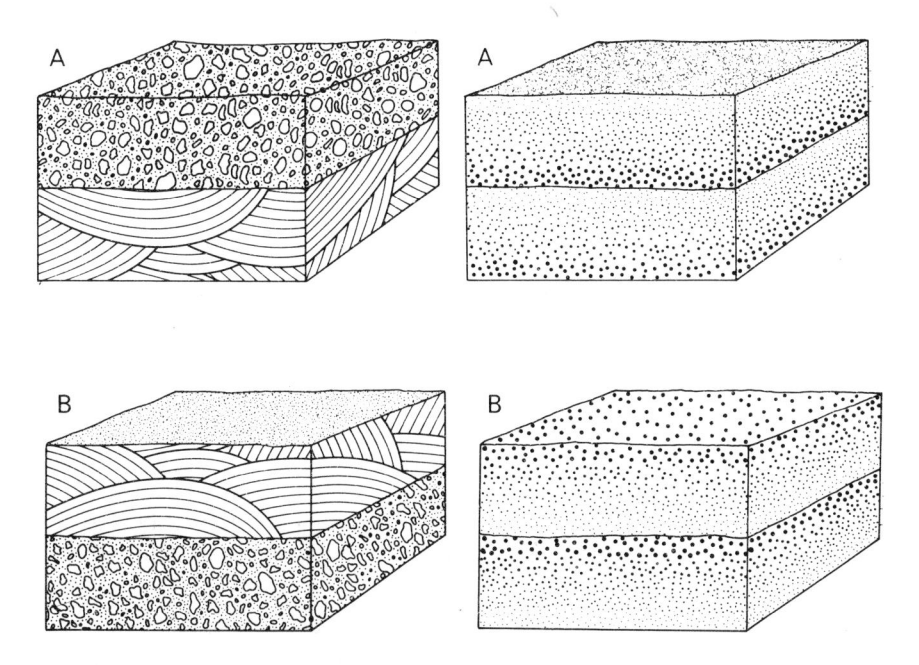

63. Cross beds (left) and graded beds. A, the right way up and B, upside-down.

bedded unit (figure 63). Once again, reverse grading (coarsening upwards) is known to occur rarely, so it is unwise to rely on a single example of any sedimentary structure.

Finally tectonic structures such as the various forms of rock cleavage can be used to determine way up. Broadly, if the bedding and cleavage dip the same way, the beds are the right way up when the cleavage dips more steeply than the bedding and upside-down in the reverse case (figure 64). In the rare event of bedding and cleavage dipping in opposite directions, more care is needed in interpretation, but it is still usually possible to arrive at way up. The best way to do this is to consider the two alternatives and see which makes more sense.

Using the above criteria, the correct succession can be determined even in highly deformed rocks, and cross cutting relationships can be used to date relatively the sequence of deposition, folding, faulting and so on. Even so, all these methods and all fossil methods involve relative dating. All tell us which of two events is older, but not how old either is. Long before any reliable methods of estimating the absolute age of rocks were developed, early geologists dreamed of

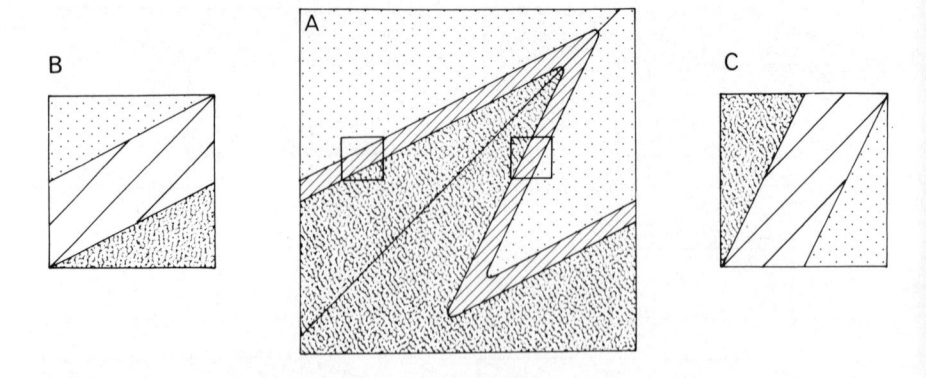

64. The use of bedding/cleavage relationships to determine way up. A. A fold with an overturned limb and axial plane cleavage developed in one bed. B. An enlargement of the normal limb showing cleavage dipping more steeply than bedding. C. An enlargement of the overturned limb showing bedding dipping more steeply than cleavage.

determining the age of the earth. Some early attempts yielded serious underestimates and are now of mainly historical interest. Nevertheless, it is instructive to see why these methods yielded false results.

The saltiness of the sea was one early method. Rivers carry down to the sea small amounts of dissolved salts. Evaporation of sea water returns the water to the atmosphere to fall as rain and feed the rivers again in a never-ending hydrological cycle, but the dissolved salts remain in the sea. Thus it was reasoned that if the sea was originally fresh and if one could estimate how much salt is in it now, and how much is added by rivers each year, one could determine how long it had taken the oceans to reach their current level of saltiness (approx. 3.6 per cent). This method yielded an estimate of ninety to a hundred million years, which at the time must have seemed an enormous interval. The figure is far too low because the calculations ignored all the evaporite deposits which have formed from sea water in areas of high evaporation. It is indeed true that rivers constantly add salts to the sea, but equally evaporation is constantly precipitating salts from the sea. An equilibrium exists between loss of salts in evaporite deposits and replenishment by rivers, so that the salinity of sea water remains more or less the same. What the early geologists determined was the residence time of salt in sea water, not the age of the oceans.

Another fairly obvious means of calculating the time since the beginning of the Cambrian Period (or any other Period for that matter) is to estimate the total thickness of rocks deposited since then as well as the average amount of sediment deposited in a year. Dividing the total thickness by the annual average thickness should give elapsed time. Again these calculated ages were low, because it is very difficult to estimate the amount of sediment deposited in one year. A storm may deposit several metres of sediment overnight, while another area may receive no net sediment for years. Equally, after ten metres or so of sediment has accumulated over a long period of time, a storm may remove virtually all of it and, of course, one metre of sediment may yield far less than one metre of solid rock. Fine-grained sediments, especially clays, are prone to compaction, which may reduce their thickness to a small fraction of its original value. Finally the method takes no account of the amount of time which is not represented by rock, of the gaps in the rock record. Some geologists believe the record is more gap than rock. Nevertheless, this method also yielded estimates in hundreds of millions of years, which at least made geologists think in terms of very long periods of time.

Charles Lyell, who was perhaps the greatest champion of uniformity, and Charles Darwin both made estimates of geological time. Darwin's was based on how long he thought it would take to allow evolution to proceed and he produced one of the rare overestimates of geological time spans. In 1859 he suggested that not less than three hundred million years had elapsed since the 'latter part of the Secondary Period',[12] compared with the present estimate of one hundred million years. Lyell dreamed of a statistical palaeontology way ahead of his time. He subdivided the Tertiary on the basis of the proportion of extant species of molluscs in deposits of different ages.[13] Lyell believed that the evolution and extinction of species were uniform processes which did not change rate. Thus, if two collections of fossil shells contained twenty per cent and forty per cent of extant species respectively, he believed the one with twenty per cent would be exactly twice as old as the other with twice as many living species. Although we now know Lyell's assumption that evolution and extinction always proceeded at the same rate is wrong, he was able to demonstrate that as much faunal change took place between the Upper Cretaceous and the Eocene as has since taken place from the Eocene to the present day.

Finally, I should perhaps also mention Lord Kelvin's estimate of the age of the earth (and the sun) on the basis of heat loss. In 1862 Lord Kelvin, then Professor W. Thompson, estimated the time since the solidification of the earth at not less than twenty and not more than four hundred million years.[14] Later in 1899, after considering the heat loss of the sun as well, he modified this estimate to twenty to fifty million years.[15] Lord Kelvin knew nothing of radioactivity (it had yet to be discovered) which provides the main source of heat in both the earth and the sun, so that his calculations could not possibly take this into account. We now know that Darwin's guess was somewhat nearer the truth than Lord Kelvin's detailed calculation, but it was Darwin who was forced to modify his estimate in later editions of *The Origin of Species*, because of the presumed reliability of Lord Kelvin's calculations. This is of more than passing interest in the present context. All science is based on some initial assumptions. In the case of Lord Kelvin's calculated age of the earth we now know the basic premises were wrong, therefore no matter how precise the mathematics, the answer was also bound to be wrong. One is reminded of the apocryphal story of the mathematician who 'proved' that bumble bees can't fly. His calculations are supposed to have shown that it was impossible for a bumble bee to generate enough lift by flapping its wings (fortunately bumble bees know nothing of maths). There is a natural human tendency to believe that mathematical calculations are somehow more reliable than logic expressed in words. Thus radiometric dates given in years are often thought to be more accurate than relative ages, in fact we *know* with absolute certainty that the Jurassic preceded the Cretaceous, but the current best estimate of fifty-five to sixty million years for the duration of the Jurassic is very much open to question. Radiometric dating is often talked of as *absolute* dating. In other words an accurate statement of dates in years as in recorded history. It is not. Undoubtedly it is the most accurate means we have of dating rocks in years and I have every admiration for the geophysicists who developed and refined the methods to their present high level of accuracy, but, as I am sure they would be the first to agree, they have yet to achieve perfection. Absolute dating is impossible at present, but radiometric dating is the only reliable means we have of estimating periods of time in the order of millions of years and upwards. Before we consider how this is done, it is worth mentioning why we need a special method of measuring very long intervals of time.

As we have seen, time never reverses and we measure its passing using arbitrary units such as seconds, weeks and years. For relatively short periods of time we can get more or less exact measures of time because we have clocks and calendars. If we want to know how old someone is, we can do so provided their date of birth was recorded. If we wish to know how long a recording lasts we can time the beginning and the end in just the same way that we record sporting events. These examples require that both the beginning and end of an event be recorded. We can measure lengths of time beyond a life-time so long as someone recorded the beginning. The date 1757 on a neighbouring building to my house reveals exactly how old the building is, although no one knows who the builder was. The point is that such accurate dating requires written records, which only go back about six thousand years. Beyond that we need a clock which does its own recording for us. Radioactivity provides just such a clock. With radiocarbon dating we assume we know how much ^{14}C there was to start with and we can measure how much remains. With all other radiometric methods we have a potentially more accurate method of discovering how much radioactive material there was initially. For example, the Uranium isotope ^{238}U decays to the lead isotope ^{206}Pb. For each atom of ^{238}U we start with, there will eventually be an atom of ^{206}Pb. So long as no Uranium or Lead is lost from or added to our sample the total number of ^{238}U and ^{206}Pb atoms equals the total number of ^{238}U atoms when the decay started. Thus we can measure both how much ^{238}U there was to start with and how much there is now. Indeed radiometric dating depends on the ratio of parent to daughter isotopes. After one half-life, half the parent isotope will have become the daughter isotope and the ratio will be 1/1. After two half-lives, three-quarters of the parent isotope will have decayed and the ratio will be 1/3. The amounts of various isotopes in a sample are determined in an instrument known as a mass spectrometer. Thus we can distinguish ^{206}Pb from ^{207}Pb, the daughter product of another Uranium isotope ^{235}U, ^{208}Pb, the decay product of a Thorium isotope ^{232}Th and ^{204}Pb which is nonradiogenic, or natural, lead.

Most of the radioisotopes used for dating rocks have very long half-lives, which is essential because the time periods to be measured are enormous. The following table records the principal isotopes used in radiometric dating of rocks, their daughter isotopes and half-lives.

Each radiometric method has its own limitations and strengths. As we have already seen, all radiometric methods depend on the samples not having lost or gained any parent or daughter isotope, the geochemical phrase for which is 'remaining a closed system'. The potassium–argon method (^{40}K–^{40}Ar) has a daughter isotope which is

Isotopes		Half-life	Useful time range
Parent	Daughter	(years)	(years)
^{238}U	^{206}Pb	4.50×10^{9}*	10^7 to origin of earth**
^{235}U	^{207}Pb	0.71×10^{9}	10^7 to origin
^{87}Rb	^{87}Sr	4.7×10^{10}	10^7 to origin
^{40}K	^{40}Ar	1.3×10^{9}	10^5 to origin
^{14}C		$5,710 \pm 40$	0–50,000

*10^9 is 1,000,000,000 years   **Currently estimated at 4.55×10^9 years

a gas. Even slight heating will drive off the argon, raise the K/Ar ratio and hence yield too low an age. However, potassium is relatively abundant in crustal rocks and a constituent of many common rock-forming minerals. Rubidium (^{87}Rb) is much less common, but occurs in the same rocks as potassium and has a solid daughter isotope, ^{87}Sr, while the uranium–lead method has the advantage of incorporating two separate isotopes which can be used to confirm each other, but is restricted in its occurrence and involves intermediate products including the gas, radon. It has been the most widely used method and is still popular. As with so many other geological investigations, we can be surer of our results if we use more than one method to get them.

Unless there has been some obvious sign of contamination or alteration, as in mineral veins or metamorphic rocks, we assume the rocks have remained a closed system. It is not always easy to test this assumption, so geologists tend to date samples by as many methods as are applicable. If three separate methods give the same age, it is highly likely that the age is correct. If, on the other hand, they yield widely different ages, at least two must be wrong. We then have to examine the geological history of the sample to see if we can detect which are likely to be the inaccurate dates and whether they are likely to be too high or too low. A sample from near a mineral vein with galena (lead ore) in it could have been enriched in lead, including ^{206}Pb and ^{207}Pb, hence yielding too high an age. On the other hand a sample that had been slightly heated might yield too low an age using the potassium–argon method. Often it is not easy to reconcile different isotopic ages, and many age determinations which do not agree with currently accepted time scales are simply rejected as wrong without our understanding fully why.

When discussing radiocarbon dating, I noted that man has not been testing the decay of ^{14}C for six thousand years in order to check the accuracy of the half-life (currently accepted as 5,710 ± 40 years). Nor has he, but we do have absolutely accurate historical records going back for about this time, and dendrochronological records as well. However, radiocarbon dating is the only radiometric method in which the ratio of parent isotope to daughter isotope is not used. This is simply because there is no way of distinguishing ^{14}N derived from the decay of ^{14}C from non-radiogenic ^{14}N which is present in enormous quantities compared with radiogenic ^{14}N. Thus we cannot test a six-thousand-year-old wood sample for the half-life of ^{14}C, because we have to *assume* how much ^{14}C there was originally and the amount assumed is open to at least a ten per cent fluctuation. In all other commonly used radioisotopes the half-lives are immensely long, so that no human existed a half-life ago and in some cases no life at all on earth. So how do we know that ^{238}U, for example, has a half-life of four and a half thousand million years? The answer is that we believe radioactive decay is always exponential, an assumption which has been tested repeatedly on short-lived radioisotopes, and hence all we need to know is the *rate* of decay of a known mass of ^{238}U to calculate its half-life. Even so the determination of half-lives is open to some error, and various different figures have been published for the same radioisotope. For example, two books I consulted in preparing this chapter gave the half-life of ^{87}Rb as 5.0 and 4.7 × 10^{10} years, respectively. The difference may not seem much, but 0.3 × 10^{10} is three thousand million years which is roughly two-thirds of the age of the earth!

To determine the decay constant (the rate of decay), a large amount of a radioisotope is stored safely and its decay measured using a geiger counter for as long as possible. A geiger counter is simply a device which detects decay of radioactive atoms, amplifies the decay to an audible sound and records how many decay events occur. Even so, for the longest half-lives an indirect method is used. A very old rock is selected, the age of which has been determined reliably by other radiometric methods. Then we have an equation relating three properties: the parent/daughter isotope ratio, the half-life and the age of the rock. Normally the first two are known and the equation is solved for the age. In the indirect method we assume we know the age of the sample and solve the equation for the half-life. This is probably at least as accurate as the direct method, for extremely long half-lives, but of course it depends on the age of the sample being known accurately. Meteorites, many of which yield ages of around 4.5 × 10^9 years, have been used for this indirect method.

Thus we know in principle how half-lives are determined and how the ratio of parent to daughter isotope yields the age of a sample, but we have yet to discuss the geology of radiometric dating. This is less exact than mathematics, but equally vital to the construction of a time scale in years for the geological column. All uranium, or for that matter any other radioisotope, is decaying to its daughter isotopes all the time, so why don't all radioisotopes simply yield the age of earth (or the origin of the universe)? The answer is that when a new mineral forms, for example a uranium silicate, only uranium combines to form the mineral. Any daughter lead around will form a lead silicate or at least some other mineral. Thus, in theory, at the time when a crystal of pure uranium silicate forms, only uranium is contained within the crystal, but thereafter lead will appear due to radioactive decay of the uranium. In practice the minerals are rarely pure and some allowance must be made for impurities of the daughter element. This adds a further uncertainty to radiometric dating, but there are means of estimating the original impurities, and the amounts involved are usually very small. Anyway, radiometric dating usually dates the formation of new minerals. Now new minerals develop as magma cools, to form igneous rocks, during the higher grades of metamorphism and during the diagenesis of sedimentary rocks. Thus we can date igneous rocks fairly easily, and metamorphic rocks provided the metamorphism completely destroys all trace of the original minerals, although there are ways around partial metamorphism which we need not go into here. Possibly we could date the cements in some sedimentary rocks, but they do not usually contain significant amounts of radioisotopes and, as they form at some unknown time after deposition of the sediments, they would only suggest a minimum age. The mineral glauconite, which contains potassium, forms in marine sediments during deposition and until recently promised to be the best means of dating sediments (and their included fossils) directly. However, it has subsequently been shown that at least four separate minerals are included under the heading glauconite, and all radiometric ages using glauconite are now considered suspect. If this view prevails, we have lost the only method of dating sedimentary rocks directly. Sediments may contain radioactive minerals, but since they were derived from pre-existing rocks we would simply determine the average age of these pre-existing rocks, not the age of deposition.

This being so, we have to date sedimentary rocks indirectly, and it is here that simple cross cutting relationships become vital. If, for example, we were to get a radiometric age from an igneous intrusion like the one in figure 59 (page 175), we would determine a minimum age for the rocks it cuts. Equally, an intrusion truncated by an unconformity would provide a maximum age for the overlying rocks. Thus sequences of sediments can be dated radiometrically by bracketing them between dated igneous rocks, but obviously the accuracy of the bracketing depends on the frequency of igneous activity. If a series of Silurian strata overlies a Precambrian granite dated at two thousand million years and is intruded by a Pleistocene dyke dated at half a million years, this does not help to date the Silurian very accurately. The best place to determine radiometric ages is in interbedded volcanic and sedimentary rocks. If we have a sequence of several lavas within fossiliferous marine shales, for example, we can date the shales using the fossils and the lavas radiometrically, thus perhaps bracketing individual zones between radiometric ages. The closer the radiometric ages are to each other, the finer the dating. Even so we usually want to know when a geological period began and igneous rocks do not always occur exactly where we want them in the column. When they don't we fall back on rates of sedimentation. If, for example, we know two dates above and below the Ordovician–Silurian boundary, say 445 and 415 million years, and the boundary lies one-third of the way up the section between the two igneous rocks, there is a strong temptation to divide the period between the two dates (thirty million years) by three and add that amount (ten million years) to the older date. We would thus conclude that the Ordovician–Silurian boundary was 435 million years ago. It is for this reason that after seventy-odd years of radiometric dating we still put wide limits on some system boundaries. The Ordovician–Silurian boundary cannot be dated to within ten million years and is usually accepted as 430–40 million years.

Just as we can only date sedimentary rocks indirectly, the very ancient rocks of the Precambrian, many of which have been intensely metamorphosed, generally yield ages of the last period of metamorphism to affect them. Thus the oldest rocks in Britain, the Lewisian gneisses of north-west Scotland, yield two groups of ages at approximately 2.6×10^9 and 1.6×10^9 years. These represent two separate phases of metamorphism and we have no idea how old the original rocks were. All we can say is that the older, the Scourian, must have formed well over 2,600 million years ago. If some of them were sediments, they were derived from even older pre-existing rocks. It is for this reason that the oldest rocks yet found on earth, which are about 3.8×10^9 years old, are still almost a thousand million years younger than our best estimates of the age of the earth itself. Thus because metamorphism and erosion alter and remove rocks, we have no direct evidence of the earliest period of the earth's history. It is a fair question to ask how we know the earth is significantly older than the oldest rocks. We have two lines of evidence for dating the origin of the earth. First astronomical evidence strongly suggests that all the planets, satellites and meteorites in the solar system probably formed at the same time. Many meteorites give ages of around 4.5×10^9 years. They also have consistent lead isotope ratios which we think are the original ratios that existed when the meteorites (and hence the earth) formed. If we know the original ratio of, say, ^{206}Pb to non-radiogenic ^{204}Pb and we can estimate the present ratio we can tell for how long ^{238}U has been decaying on earth. By the same argument the ^{207}Pb/^{204}Pb ratio gives an estimate of the length ^{235}U has been decaying on earth, and the method can be applied to other radioactive isotopes as well. These ratios gave the widely quoted figure of 4.55×10^9 years for the age of the earth, which closely agrees with the oldest rocks on the moon and the oldest meteorite ages.

Finally we can use the ratios of isotopes to date the so-called 'nuclear synthesis'. In other words the origin of at least our bit of the Universe. The mere fact that radioisotopes with half-lives of 10^9-odd years still exist, puts an upper limit on this event of no more than 10^{10} years. If ^{235}U, for example, with a half-life of 0.71×10^9 years, had been synthesized over 10^{10} years ago it would long since have decayed to lead completely. Evidence for the former existence of radio-isotopes with medium-range half-lives is found in meteorites. They are enriched in ^{129}Xe, the decay product of ^{129}I, which has a half-life of 1.64×10^7 years and is no longer known as a naturally occurring radioisotope. Isotopic ratios currently give a best estimate for the age of the universe of 5.6×10^9 years, but as the methods involve a great many assumptions we should not be too surprised if this figure changes considerably in the future.

To summarize then, radiometric methods are not absolute, but are the most accurate means we have of estimating the enormous spans of geological time. Their accuracy depends on the accuracy with which we know the decay constant, the sample having remained a closed system and, of course, the accuracy of the determination in the laboratory. This latter is usually expressed in the date, for example 500 ± 30 million years implies that if the same sample were re-run in the same laboratory there is a ninety-five per cent probability that the age would fall betwen 470 and 530 million years. Finally, as far as determining radiometric ages for the fossiliferous geological systems (collectively known as the Phanerozoic) is concerned, we still have to rely on simple principles of cross cutting relationships, and the accuracy of the date depends to a very large extent on the geological setting of the sample. For all these reasons, the dates in figure 1 have been, and will probably continue to be, subject to considerable refinement.

We have now seen how rocks are dated and correlated using fossils and radiometric methods as well as how the geological column was originally built up. This gives us an appreciation of the enormous span of geological time and the tremendous changes that have taken place on earth during this time. In the next three chapters we will consider how these changes were placed in an evolutionary context and follow the actual course of evolution as revealed by the fossil record.

Chapter 7

Faunal succession and evolution

We have seen how the geological column was gradually built up to its present form and how radiometric dates were added to it. We have also seen how the development of the geological column revealed a succession of life through time which, one might suspect, inevitably led to the formulation of a theory of evolution. In fact this did not happen, and the development of the theory of evolution by means of natural selection is beset with paradoxes. Cuvier, who denied that evolution had taken place, laid the groundwork for understanding the fossil evidence which supports evolution. Charles Darwin, to whom most people attribute 'the theory of evolution', convinced the scientific world of the fact of evolution, but was much less successful in convincing it of his theory of natural selection. Darwin realized the value of fossil evidence, but found little to support his ideas in the fossil record and was forced to argue that the record was extremely incomplete, just as Lyell had done before his conversion to evolution when he was arguing against it. The discovery of the mechanism of inheritance by Mendel was published in 1865,[1] long before Darwin died in 1882, yet it was not discovered by the scientific world until 1900. Thus the development of our ideas about evolution was not the straight fight with the Church that it is usually made out to have been. It was a complex process which, at times, was almost as slow as the development of the geological column, and this should have been the prime stimulus to evolutionary theory anyway. From the point of view of a palaeontologist, the meagre contribution that the study of fossils has made to evolutionary ideas is perhaps the biggest paradox of all. So I shall try to trace the history of evolutionary theory to establish how significant fossils are.

Cuvier, as we have seen, demonstrated the former existence of an extinct elephant, the mammoth, in 1796,[2] by detailed comparative studies of the Indian and African elephants and fossil bones. He believed in the functional integration of species. They were real entities, not arbitrary divisions in a continuous spectrum of organic life, and they worked because all their organ systems were admirably designed to perform their vital functions cooperatively, just as all parts of a machine are designed to ensure its smooth running. Cuvier could not conceive of modifying a working system without reducing its efficiency. As a result he was naturally disinclined to contemplate evolution. Perhaps he was impressed by the need to modify so many parts of the organism simultaneously to keep it functional, just as enlargement of the cylinders of a petrol engine will not improve its performance unless the piston and piston rings are also enlarged, by which time the crankshaft and connecting rods may need strengthening to take the increased loads, which in turn may mean a larger crankcase, and so on. At any rate, because of his strongly functional approach, Cuvier did not accept that modification of species had taken place. However, he did demonstrate extinction and concentrated more on the fates of 'old' species rather than on the origin of 'new' ones. To Cuvier there were three possible fates to an existing species: evolution, extinction or migration. In the case of large land mammals like elephants, he could not believe in migration which left him with evolution and extinction as *alternatives*. All his experience and belief in functioning organisms led him to reject evolution, whereas he had demonstrated that extinction was a fact. He could demonstrate that the mammoth differed from both the Indian and African elephants by at least as much as they differed from each other.

The question inevitably arose that if the mammoth was also a functional animal, adapted to a cold climate, why did it become extinct? This is a question to which we still have no satisfactory answer. Further research in the Pleistocene deposits of France showed that not just the mammoth but a whole fauna of mammals had become extinct. This, together with growing evidence that there had been recent changes in northern Europe (that were later recognized as evidence of the ice age) led Cuvier to propose that a violent 'revolution', like the recent French revolution, had overtaken the earth, extinguishing the old fauna and supplanting it with a new one. He was not very clear as to how the new fauna appeared, but his concept of violent changes in earth's history catastrophically destroying whole faunas found considerable following, especially as it was discovered that some mountain ranges were quite recent geological events, not the most ancient as had been formerly believed.

Progress in his research demonstrated yet older faunas, and so Cuvier modified his single revolution into a whole series of revolutions.

Cuvier's comparative studies led him to recognize four fundamental *embranchements*, what we would call phyla, in the animal kingdom. Within these he could recognize classes, which he might have conceded were arranged in some order of organization, but he could not see any way to compare different phyla and was very much against an 'order of creation'. Reptiles and mammals might be compared, but molluscs and vertebrates never. Because of this background, he reacted violently to the rather diffuse ideas of Lamarck,[3] and later Saint-Hilaire,[4] on evolution. These ideas were published long before Darwin's and were poorly grounded in detailed morphology or stratigraphy. Cuvier used all his powers of argument and his prestige to denounce these ideas and has largely been branded as an anti-evolutionist ever since. However, Cuvier's detailed anatomical and stratigraphic studies were essential to the discovery of the succession of life. It was largely his work which showed that the Mesozoic was dominated by reptiles, while mammals were confined to the Tertiary. Indeed in a public lecture as early as 1801, he had already stated that the older his fossils were, the more distinct they were from living animals. Cuvier, perhaps more than anyone other than William Smith, was responsible for the discovery of the succession of life through time, but it did not lead him to suggest a theory of evolution, although this may seem an inevitable corollary to us with our twentieth-century viewpoint.

Cuvier's views were readily accepted in early nineteenth-century Britain, perhaps for two reasons. First the editor of the English translation of one of his major works had added his own comments and equated Cuvier's Pleistocene revolution with the Biblical Flood.[5] Thus Cuvier's researches were seen as confirming biblical scripture, an exercise which was still popular in Britain. Secondly his functional studies revealed how the Creator had designed his creations to fit them for their mode of life. Functional studies such as those of Richard Owen, first Director of the Natural History Museum in London, were almost acts of worship in revealing the infinite wisdom of God. Cuvier's functional studies were seen as yet more revelations of Divine wisdom.

Charles Lyell was much less enthusiastic about reconciling scripture and geology. He wished to divorce the two entirely and, after travelling widely in Europe, he was profoundly confirmed in his belief of gradual change over long periods of time producing gentle cyclical 'revolutions' like the motion of the earth around the sun, not the violent revolutions envisaged by Cuvier. Thus although everything was gradually changing, to Lyell it was also remaining basically the same. He set out to produce convincing arguments in favour of what we now call actualistic methods in geology, that is, interpreting the past by reference to present-day processes operating over immense periods of time. He believed firmly in a 'steady-state' earth in which processes operating today had always operated and *at the same general rates*. Because of this, and because evolution ran counter to a steady-state, he boldly denied that there was any evidence for a succession of life in the fossil record by arguing, for example, that the apparent absence of mammals in the Mesozoic was due to the incompleteness of the fossil record. (This is a familiar argument trotted out by everyone who finds that the fossil record does not agree with their own particular theories. I shall return to it later.) Lyell also argued that so little was known about the ocean deeps and unexplored regions of Africa and South America that many of the apparently extinct forms of life could still exist somewhere in the world. The discovery this century of the coelacanth, *Latimeria*, a type of fish thought to have been extinct since the late Cretaceous about seventy million years ago and the monoplacophoran, *Neopilina*, a type of mollusc believed extinct since the Devonian (roughly three hundred million years ago) emphasize that we still cannot ignore this particular argument. Incidentally, it was precisely this argument that provided the impetus for the great nineteenth-century voyages of discovery to sample the ocean deeps, like that of the *Challenger*. So initially Lyell argued against evolution because he believed in a steady-state world. When he changed his mind under the weight of evidence amassed by Darwin, it was still because of his steady-state beliefs. Darwin's gradual changes operating over long periods were preferable to Cuvier's violent revolutions.

On to this scene of rapidly increasing knowledge of the succession of life stumbled Alfred Russell Wallace, a biologist. Quite independently of Darwin he thought up the theory of natural selection and sent a paper outlining his ideas to, of all people, Charles Darwin to be forwarded for review. Darwin's friends realized that his own ideas must now be published. Rather than compete, however, he worked with Wallace and the two of them read a joint paper before the Linnean Society of London in 1858.[6] Darwin was now committed to publishing his own evidence which he had been amassing for years.

He produced an abstract of over six hundred pages of the much larger work he was planning, which became *The Origin of Species*, published the following year. (Incidentally, Darwin's 'Big Book' was eventually published in the 1970s.) With characteristic thoroughness Darwin compiled so much evidence in favour of his theories that most of the scientific world was convinced of the *fact* of evolution almost immediately, but his idea of natural selection was much less readily accepted in his lifetime.

Darwin and Wallace made two fundamental observations (one borrowed from Malthus's essay on population[7]) and from these they drew two conclusions which now seem inevitable. The simplicity of their ideas helps to convince us that they are basically sound. First they observed that all natural organisms tend to vary, no two individuals being exactly alike. Secondly, following Malthus, they observed that all living things tend to overproduce offspring. Far more young animals and seedlings develop each year than there is food or space for. Inevitably it follows that there will be competition among individuals for resources such as food, light and living space. Now because all organisms vary, Darwin and Wallace argued that some would be better able to compete than others and that only these would survive to produce the next generation. That is, there is a *natural selection* of the fittest in nature, which is in some ways comparable to the artificial selection made by man in animal husbandry or horticulture, but is not directed towards any particular end as artificial selection is. This last idea was their prime contribution to evolutionary theory. It is interesting to note that Wallace, who stimulated Darwin to publish, was a biologist and, even if Darwin had some geological experience, his main evidence came from living things, not the succession of life as revealed in the fossil record. This failure of palaeontology to advance evolutionary theory has continued to the present day, despite the fact that the fossil record is the main evidence for the actual history of life on earth.

Darwin was not unaware of the value of the fossil record. He devoted two chapters of his book to it,[8] but the first stressed the imperfection of the record. Like Lyell, Darwin saw things in the fossil record which did not agree with his theories, was unable to explain them and hence appealed to the imperfections of the record as a means of explaining them away. To be sure, the fossil record in 1859 was poorly known compared with the present (and we do not yet know all of it by any means) but the basic outline of the succession of life was as well established then as now. Darwin knew that trilobites were confined to the Palaeozoic and dinosaurs to the Mesozoic as well as many other features of the history of life. What Darwin sought, and failed to find, was evidence of gradual change. Fossils at all taxonomic levels from species to classes and phyla seem to appear suddenly in the fossil record. Evidence of 'missing links' was, and is, very scarce. Yet Darwin believed that descent with slight modification operating over very long periods of time gradually produced new forms of life. He sought direct evidence of gradual change in the fossil record, but found very little. We now believe that it is unlikely to be preserved anyway, not because the fossil record is so very incomplete, but because we believe that new species arise in isolated areas and in small populations. This means that unless the transitional forms are preserved and we happen to collect fossils from the small area in which they lived, we are unlikely to detect the changes. If after evolving into a separate species the founder population flourished and migrated into the surrounding areas, the fossil record will apparently show that the new species evolved suddenly. This is what seems to have happened more often than not.

Natural selection is so simple and elegant an idea that it is easily believable, but it all hinges on the selected characteristics being heritable. The fastest growing seedling will outstrip its siblings, overshadow them and eventually kill them. Only the fastest growing will survive to reproduce and seed, but how do we know that the resulting seedlings will themselves be fast-growing? Equally, if a long-necked proto-giraffe which could feed above the level of other herbivores mated with a shorter-necked female, would the offspring not have necks of intermediate length and hence be less competitive than their father had been? The absence of any knowledge of the mechanism of inheritance posed a serious stumbling block to the acceptance of the idea of natural selection. Again paradoxically, the evidence was published by Mendel in 1865,[9] but remained unnoticed until about 1900, long after Darwin's death. Darwin would undoubtedly have welcomed Mendel's discoveries because he was well aware of the possibility of averaging out desirable characters. Mendel showed that at least some characters were inherited in their extreme forms, not as an average of the parents' characters. For example, no matter what combination of black and yellow labrador dogs is selected for breeding, the puppies will always be either black or yellow. Intermediate colours and mixtures of black and yellow just do not occur. Not all characters are inherited in this clear-cut way, but nevertheless those that are allow natural selection to operate in its simplest form just as Darwin and Wallace envisaged. If, for example, yellow labradors were better adapted than black ones, selection would soon eliminate the black form. Indeed it has since been shown that selection pressures as low as one per cent are enough to ensure the spread of a particular gene. That is, if a hundred yellow labradors succeed in breeding for every ninety-nine blacks that do, yellow will eventually eliminate black.

Although natural selection was not widely accepted in his lifetime, Darwin was very successful in convincing people of the fact of evolution because of the weight of his evidence. Once converted, palaeontologists looked to the fossil record to document the actual course of evolution. Now the vaguely defined succession of life became the actual phylogenies, or lines of descent, of various forms of life. The classification of animals and plants was reorganized to reflect their evolution, and so-called phylogenetic or natural classifications were proposed for many groups. Attention was directed away from functional morphological studies like those of Cuvier and Owen, towards phylogenetic studies like those of F. A. Bather on echinoderms.[10] Had natural selection been accepted more readily one would have expected that functional studies, demonstrating the relative efficiencies of competing organisms, would have proliferated. Regrettably, it is only since World War II that a return to functional studies has become evident, and even these are rarely conducted against a background of natural selection because the idea is now taken for granted. Fortunately there are one or two exceptions.

Thus we can see that although the demonstration of a succession of life through time cried out for an evolutionary explanation, it played little part in the formulation of evolutionary theories. Although the fossil record is the only evidence for the actual course of evolution, it is rarely accepted in this light. Whenever its evidence disagrees with our theories, we always reject that evidence, hiding behind our insistence that the record is incomplete. Yet common sense cries out against this rejection of the evidence in the fossil record. To be sure it is incomplete and incompletely known. We are still discovering new species of fossils every day and will continue to do so for decades if not centuries to come. But if the fossil record is so incomplete that we must reject evidence which conflicts with one theory, how can we rely on the same evidence to support any other theory since the evidence is demonstrably suspect? We cannot have it both ways, accepting only the evidence with which we agree and rejecting that with which we

FAUNAL SUCCESSION AND EVOLUTION

disagree. We use fossil evidence to reconstruct past geographies, climates, faunal and floral provinces, we correlate using fossils and some of us use relative stratigraphic position to determine ancestor–descendant relationships. Most of what you have read in this book and much of what is to come would be nonsense if the fossil record were so incomplete that we must reject its evidence in favour of any theory. Science does not advance by forcing facts into predetermined theoretical pigeon-holes. The fossil record must be accepted as the truth – not the whole truth, but certainly nothing but the truth, for those who can learn to understand it. We must accept it for what it is and construct our theories around it. It has been our failure to do this, more than anything else, which has led to the poor contribution of palaeontology to evolutionary theory. The evidence is there, but we have been so busy apologizing for it that we have failed to realize what an immense treasure it represents. Incidentally, I should like to point out that the biological record is also incomplete and incompletely known. The extant species of any family or higher group do not represent all the species belonging to that family which have ever existed, and new species of living animals and plants are being discovered all the time. As far as I am aware no one has argued that we cannot use the biological record to test evolutionary, or any other biological, theories.

It is certainly true that the fossil record is incomplete and incompletely known, but just how incomplete? That is the point at issue. Can we see only the tip of the iceberg or can we see the iceberg with only the tip hidden from us? Most palaeontologists and geologists have accepted the incompleteness of the fossil record without any attempt to test how incomplete it is. Indeed, Shaw[11] is the only geologist I have come across who has done this, and he has demonstrated that for all practical purposes, we can rely on the ranges of fossil species for accurate correlation. Although correlation was Shaw's main concern, it follows that if the fossil record is reliable for this purpose, it is probably reliable for other purposes as well. Indeed the very fact that we can correlate, recognize faunal provinces, reconstruct past climatic belts and so on argues strongly that the fossil record is adequate for all our purposes. To cite ludicrously obvious examples, literally millions of Mesozoic and Tertiary fossils are known, yet not one of them is a trilobite. On the other hand hundreds of thousands, perhaps millions, of Palaeozoic trilobite specimens are known. If this distribution is due to the imperfection of the fossil record, as Lyell once suggested, why are all known trilobites confined to only one part of the record? How did they become unpreservable and where are they now? It is common sense and the simplest hypothesis to assume that trilobites only occur in Palaeozoic rocks because they only existed in the Palaeozoic. Equally in the Lower Cambrian we find either redlichiid or olenellid trilobites, but not both groups together. Again this cannot be due to the incompleteness of the fossil record, but to their original distributions in separate faunal provinces. Shaw has described simple statistical tests which formalize this argument and allow an estimate of the probability that an observed distribution of fossils is due to preservation failure or collection failure.[12] Obviously Shaw's tests will be more rigorous the larger the samples taken and I suspect that the failure of palaeontologists to follow Shaw's methods is at least partly due to the large sample sizes required. However, large samples are available in many instances, and anyway small sample sizes only reduce the rigour of the tests, not their general validity.

At this point we should perhaps consider how evidence from the fossil record is used. To my mind fossil evidence is of two kinds – absolute and relative, just as in dating – but in this case it is the absolute evidence which is unquestionable and the relative evidence which, to a large extent, depends on the completeness of the fossil record. The absolute evidence in the fossil record is simply the documentation of when and where fossils lived. If we find a single dinosaur bone in the Jurassic, we know that that particular dinosaur species lived at that time in the past. Similarly if we find fossils of tropical palms in Britain, we know that at some time in the past palm trees grew in more northerly latitudes. These are indisputable facts, allowing that the fossils are not derived or out of place, and they have increased our knowledge of the variety of past life. We all accept that trilobites, ammonites and dinosaurs lived on earth at some time in the past, even though none does now.

The second way in which fossil evidence is used is to compare parts of the fossil record in a relative way. For example, were Jurassic dinosaurs more common, more diverse, more widespread, than Cretaceous dinosaurs? Did ants evolve before or after butterflies? The answers to these questions depend heavily on the adequacy of the fossil record. Jurassic dinosaurs may *seem* to have been more abundant and diverse than Cretaceous ones simply because we have found more of them, or because more were preserved. They may seem more widespread because a greater area of Jurassic rocks is exposed at the surface in areas where dinosaur workers have collected. As a group, ants may appear to be older than butterflies because we have not yet found any Palaeozoic butterflies, yet there may have been thousands of Palaeozoic species originally. Thus the adequacy of the fossil record affects these questions, and it is just these questions which we need to answer if we are to correlate, recognize faunal provinces, divine phylogenies, or do most of the things which palaeontologists attempt to do every day. The question then arises, can we test the fossil record for its completeness? I believe we can, using several different lines of investigation.

The problem as I see it is to establish what proportion of all the species that have ever lived we know as fossils. Are we looking at the ten per cent of the iceberg that sticks out above water or the ninety per cent below the surface? Obviously some groups approximate to one extreme and others may get close to the other. There are probably a million or more species of insects alive today, but the fossil record of insects is meagre in the extreme. The fossil record of groups like worms, insects and jellyfish is undoubtedly nearer the ten per cent of the spectrum, but we already realize this and do not rely on them for everyday activities like correlation. The fossil records of shelly groups such as brachiopods, trilobites, ammonites and other molluscs may well be nearer the ninety per cent of the spectrum.

There are several common-sense ways of testing how incomplete the fossil record of any group is in addition to the idea discussed by Shaw. First, there are gaps in the record. Gaps occur where a fossil group is known from above and below, but not within, a particular horizon for whatever reason. Each gap represents a situation where we know that at least one fossil species existed which we have yet to find or which has not been preserved. As a test of the fossil record of cystoids, extinct Palaeozoic echinoderms, I plotted the record at series level of all families known from two or more series (figure 65). Obviously a family known from a single series may or may not have gaps in its record, but we cannot tell. At this level it turns out that on average for every five families known to have existed during any one series representatives of only four have actually been found. In fact, at this level, the fossil record of cystoid families is at least twenty-three per cent incomplete. That of modern groups of amphibians is at least thirty per cent incomplete using the same method at epoch level during the Mesozoic and Tertiary. These records must be even more incomplete for several reasons. First, I have observed a convention widely used in plotting such range charts: that the occurrence of a single specimen on one bedding plane is accepted as representing the

THE NATURAL HISTORY OF FOSSILS

	ORDOVICIAN					SILURIAN			DEVONIAN					
	T	A	L	L	C	A	L	W	L	G	S	E	E	G	F

65. The known stratigraphic occurrences of cystoid families in the Palaeozoic to show the gaps in their fossil record. Two-thirds of the families are known to have gaps in their records and the proportion of all gaps to the total record is approximately 23 per cent. (No account is taken of ages in years.)

entire period of the series. Thus the fact that sphaeronitids are known in the Arenig, for example, may reflect the presence of millions of specimens at all levels throughout the Arenig or just one specimen at one level. Equally there may have been families of cystoids which have yet to be discovered or ones which existed in the past but no representative of which has been preserved. Finally, there may be additional gaps beyond the known ranges of the familes which cannot be detected by this method, as in the case of families known from only one series.

This last case can be used as another test, however. If the fossil record were very incomplete, then one would expect to find only a single example of most families preserved. Suppose, for example, that on average each cystoid family had fifty species and that, on average, only one species of each hundred original species is currently known to us as a fossil. Then most families would be unknown to us and even the largest would be known by only two or three species at most (assuming the chances of preservation and detection were identical in all families). Thus the proportion of monotypic families and genera (that is, families containing only one genus and genera containing only one species) is a measure of the completeness of the record. To a certain extent this will reflect taxonomic practice. For example, Bather[13] classified the cystoid *Pleurocystites* in the family Cheirocrinidae along with *Cheirocrinus*, *Glyptocystites* and *Cystoblastus*. He acknowledged that all four genera were morphologically very distinct, especially *Pleurocystites*, and that each might be assigned to a separate subfamily but, as this seemed an unnecessary complication, he suggested that *Pleurocystites* might be placed in a separate family when additional genera were discovered. Nowadays we know of six pleurocystitid genera and the family is well established. Incidentally, we also know of six cheirocrinid genera and two each in the families Glyptocystitidae and Cystoblastidae. Despite this difficulty of taxonomic practice, I believe that the exercise is worthwhile if done by one specialist whose judgement is at least likely to be consistent. Making comparisons between major groups is much more hazardous, however. Fossils regarded as belonging in two separate genera by a specialist in one group might be regarded as merely two species of the same genus by a specialist in another group. I have often remarked that brachiopod genera make good species, which is very uncharitable to my colleagues who work on brachiopods, but underlines the problem. Another difficulty arises in that it is impossible to say what proportion of genera or families one expects to be monotypic anyway. In this I suggest we take the extreme view that no genus or family ought to be monotypic, if only because it simplifies proceedings. However, this is a logical viewpoint when applied to fossils. One species of a genus may be destined to found a whole dynasty of descendants, but we can only recognize this after the event. If it were a Silurian species which gave rise to an extant order, we would group it with the order as the very first example. If, on the other hand, it is a present-day species we might recognize it as somewhat different from the others, but we would most likely include it in the genus and family to which its immediate ancestor belonged. For example, if *Archaeopteryx* were the only known bird, we would probably classify it as an aberrant reptile with feathers. Thus it is possible to argue that distinctive genera or families can only be recognized as such when several species have evolved (as Bather did about the family Pleurocystitidae). Where the intermediate species are unknown or unpreserved, we have problematical fossils which are very hard to classify. Monotypic genera and families fit this category very well. To return to the fossil record of cystoids, there are twenty-four families in all; eight are monotypic, hence the record of a third of the known cystoid families is probably incomplete.

By the same token we may count the number of families or genera known from a single horizon. Here again, it is just possible that they originally lived for a very short time, but it is unlikely that a large number of families will have been originally confined to one level. As far as cystoid families are concerned, six out of a total of twenty-four, i.e. twenty-five per cent, are known only from a single series and hence are likely to have incomplete records.

Survivorship analysis offers yet another possible method of testing the fossil record. If extinction is a random process, like death, then fossil groups should show a survivorship curve like A in figure 66, with many short-lived, but only a few very long-lived, groups. Curve A in figure 66 represents a summary of the survival of all known cystoid families. It simply plots how many were still living after various periods of time, assuming they all start life at the same time. Thus of the initial twenty-four families, eighteen were still alive after one series, sixteen after two series, fourteen after three series, and so

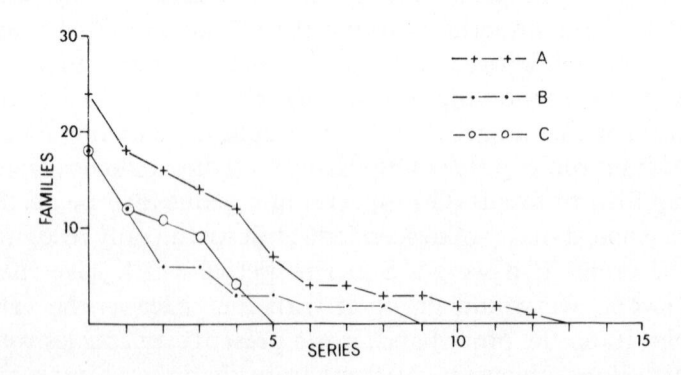

66. Survivorship curves for cystoid families. A. All families combined. B. The Caradoc cohort, that is post-Caradoc survivorship of all families known from the Caradoc. C. The Caradoc census, i.e. longevity of all families up to the end of the Caradoc. Curves A and B have the expected concave-up shape.

on. If the fossil record of a group were very incomplete, many, perhaps most, groups would be known from a single level and the first part of the curve would be very steep indeed. In the extreme all groups would be known from a single occurrence.

There are three methods of survivorship analysis, the cohort method, the census method and Lyell's method. Cohort analysis involves plotting survivorship of all the genera or families which originated at a particular time. Curve B in figure 66 shows the cohort curve for all Caradocian cystoid families. The method is analogous to following the life histories of all people born in, say, 1900. Alternatively, the census method involves tracing back to their origin all the groups that occur at a given time, like taking a census of the ages of all the people alive today. Curve C on figure 66 shows a census of survivorship of Caradocian cystoid families. The method Lyell used to define the Tertiary epochs is a third form of survivorship analysis, but it is less useful as a test of the adequacy of the fossil record. For either of the first two methods a very inadequate fossil record would produce distorted curves. For example, using the census method for the present-day fauna, the many groups which have no fossil record would oversteepen the first part of the curve. The cohort method removes this distortion, but even so if the fossil record were extremely incomplete even cohort curves would be oversteepened initially. In this case it is possible to say what the curve should look like if extinction operated randomly. Comparison of the theoretical curve with actual survivorship curves gives an indication of how incomplete the record is. Similar distortion would occur with Lyellian curves where the percentage of living organisms found in past periods would drop off very rapidly. Indeed the very fact that Lyell was able to use his method nearly a hundred and fifty years ago indicates that at least the record of the Tertiary molluscs must have been fairly good then and it is considerably better known now.

This leads me to consider just how good the record needs to be for our purposes. Shaw has argued that while striving for perfection is an admirable aim, in geology we cannot expect, nor do we need, to achieve this. Suppose, for example, we wish to know the exact stratigraphic range of a fossil species. To do this we must locate the first and last representatives of that species in the geological column. But we can only be certain that we have found the earliest (or latest) example when we have collected all the specimens that have been preserved. So long as one specimen remains in the rock there is a possibility that it will extend the known range. For correlation purposes it is not necessary to collect all preserved fossils; a reasonable sample will do. So what constitutes a 'reasonable sample' of past life and how closely does the fossil record approximate a 'reasonable sample'? An artificial example may help define what is reasonable.

Suppose a factory turns out coloured balls and each month a small sample is taken for quality control, put into a sack and dated. Suppose some of the sacks get lost and with what is left we set ourselves the task of finding out which colours were being produced and when. We may simplify things by assuming that the colouring substances were delivered to the factory in batches and once the batch was used up that particular colour would not be produced again. Just how small a sample would be needed? The answer depends on how many colours were produced at any one time and in what proportions, not on the total number of balls produced. Suppose in the first month ten colours were produced in equal numbers. Then a random sample of balls should contain roughly ten per cent of each colour. We would not be far off the truth with a random sample of ten balls, although it is *possible* that all ten would be the same colour. A hundred balls would be likely to contain all ten colours and would also give us a good estimate of the relative proportions of each colour. Note that the number of balls turned out by the factory is irrelevant. The sample size relative to the original proportions of each colour is what determines an adequate sample. If the original proportion of all colours was ten per cent, then a sample of less than ten could not detect all the colours, twenty probably would and a hundred would give a good indication of the relative proportions. If the lowest proportion were just one per cent, we would need at least a hundred balls in a sample before we stood much chance of detecting the rarest colour and up to a thousand before proportions could be determined with reasonable accuracy. If a unique ball were produced, we would only stand a fifty-fifty chance of detecting it if our sample contained exactly half that month's production, but it would hardly matter if we did not detect it since it would represent such a minute proportion of the total output.

Extending this analogy, we could still trace the history of production where a bag was missing because the same shades present in the preceding and following samples would tell us that those colours were still in production. Only the duration of production of colours which began or ended when the missing sample was taken would be uncertain, and those by only one month. Indeed we could probably build a reasonable picture of production with only one sample for each year, provided that most production batches continued for more than twelve months. So long as the sampling interval remained significantly smaller than the production duration, we would stand an excellent chance of detecting most colours and the lengths of their production to the nearest sample interval. Thus no matter how many millions of balls were produced, a sample of a hundred balls each year might be adequate for our purposes.

Turning back to the fossil record, we may estimate the average duration of fossil species as between a half and five million years or more. Thus provided we have fossil samples at intervals of less than half a million years, we should be able to detect most preservable species. As to sample size, provided our sample is greater than the total number of preservable species living in an area, we stand a good chance of detecting most of them. Furthermore, should we wish to do so, we can define exactly how large our sample should be to be ninety-five per cent certain that we have found all species present in a proportion of one per cent or more. Both percentages may be varied to suit personal preferences and Shaw has outlined the procedures.[14]

Of course things in the real world of fossils are not as simple as in the artificial example given, but for organisms with a high preservation potential small samples of a few hundred or at most thousands taken at intervals of one to two hundred thousand years would be adequate to build a fairly accurate picture of past life. Our sampling is well up to this standard for the more explored parts of the world. We have been mesmerized in the past by the astronomical chances against an individual's being preserved. Of all the millions of mussels on a mussel bank how many will ever become fossilized, let alone escape subsequent destruction by erosion or metamorphism and be found? But proof of the former existence of a species requires that only *one* specimen survive, be found and recognized for what it is. One example is adequate for absolute evidence, a modest sample of several thousands at most for relative evidence. Clearly in shelly groups with a good preservation potential, our samples are adequate. The incompleteness of the fossil record of cystoid families may be higher than usual for a shelly group. They are relatively rare and their skeletons fall apart very rapidly after death. Rapid burial is particularly necessary for their preservation, whereas this is less vital to the preservation of ammonites, gastropods, bivalves, brachiopods, and so on. The records of these groups may well be nearer the ninety per cent end of the spectrum. The estimates made for the completeness of the cystoid fossil record at family level suggest that it is twenty to thirty per cent or more incomplete, the corollary of which is that it is perhaps as much as seventy per cent complete. This is quite adequate for most of our purposes and again it can be tested.

If we repeated Lyell's experiment by ascertaining how many extant species there were in the Tertiary epochs, would we get the same result as he did? I suspect not. We would probably recognize a far greater proportion of extinct species, but I also suspect that the Lyellian curve for Tertiary molluscs would not have changed shape all that much. On the same lines, if the fossil record were very poorly known in, say, 1900 and much better known now, then an enormous number of new genera and families would have been discovered since 1900. This is another test which suffers from problems of taxonomic treatment, but in this case they can be overcome simply. If, for the purposes of illustration, we take families, we only want to know how many genuinely new families have been discovered, not just how many families have been recognized since 1900 due to refinements of systematics. As an example, the cystoid family Thomacystidae described by me in 1969[15] was based on a single new genus, *Thomacystis*, and is genuinely new in this sense. However, the Pleurocystitidae, which was not recognized by Bather in 1900, is not new because the type genus, *Pleurocystites*, had been known since 1854. Thus the present acceptance of the Pleurocystitidae as a distinct family results from taxonomic splitting. If we examine all cystoid genera known in 1900, and assign them to the families in which they are currently classified, we can see which families that have been accepted since 1900 are genuinely new and avoid the problem of taxonomic treatment. Of the twenty-four currently accepted families only two are genuinely new. The Polycosmitidae, with one genus and one species based on isolated plates, was described by Jaekel in 1918,[16] and the Thomacystidae, also based on one genus and one species, by me in 1969. (The specimens were found, but not described, nearly a hundred years before.) In the same time interval the number of *new* genera (defined in the same way as *new* families) was 35 out of a current total of 104, while the number of species has just about doubled, from approximately 210 to about 420 (figure 67). Revision of the entire cystoid fauna might well reduce the number of species, but it would probably affect pre- and post-1900 species alike. Thus while the number of known cystoid species has increased nearly twofold and the number of genera by half, only two new monotypic families have been described since 1900. Surely we

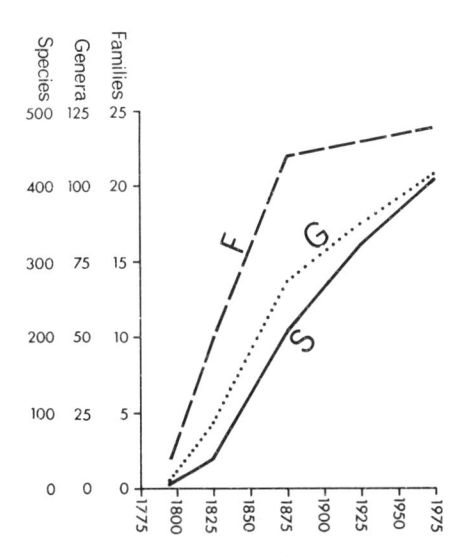

67. Graph of the increase in knowledge of cystoid families, genera and species since 1772 when the first examples were described. The curve for families (F) has flattened out since 1900, which suggests that there are not very many more families to discover. Those for genera (G) and species (S) are still climbing steeply, implying that many more forms remain undescribed.

must conclude from this that, despite our greatly increased knowledge of the cystoid fossil record, the broad outline of cystoid evolution was known in 1900. Also if the other estimates of the completeness of the cystoid fossil record at family level suggest it is twenty to thirty per cent incomplete, the last seventy-five years' collecting has done little to alter this, adding less than ten per cent of the known families. This suggests to me that we already know a pretty large proportion of all the cystoid families there are to know. Extending this idea to the fossil record in general, I would go so far as to say that a reasonable sketch of the history of life had already been drawn by the end of the nineteenth century and that all we have done since is to add colour, shading and detail, to what is still an incomplete portrait. However, well back into last century we could already see enough of the sketch to recognize it for what it is.

All of this discussion about testing the fossil record is for two purposes, one general and one particularly relevant to evolution and the succession of life, the main subject of this and succeeding chapters. First, I wish to stress that the fossil record is perfectly adequate for most geological purposes. Secondly, in tracing the history of life, that is, in constructing phylogenies, the fossil record is not only the sole test we have against which to compare our phylogenies, but it is also a rigorous and valid test. Only when there are the most compelling reasons should we produce a phylogeny which runs counter to the known fossil record. Obviously as we increase our knowledge of the fossil record we may need to modify our phylogenies, but this is still infinitely preferable to the more outrageous phylogenetic speculations that have been, and still are, published. In my own field of primitive echinoderms, one may cite the work of Haeckel in 1896,[17] which was pure fantasy unfettered by examination of actual specimens.

We have seen that despite the emphasis that the theory of natural selection puts on adaptation and fitness, the actual effect of the acceptance of evolution after Darwin was to direct palaeontological research away from functional studies towards phylogenetic studies. This change of emphasis was not absolute and vertebrate palaeontologists have managed to combine functional and evolutionary studies very well, perhaps because of the continuing tradition of Cuverian comparative and functional anatomy, perhaps because the functioning of these animals is so near to our own. It is much easier to envisage and analyse the problems of walking on all fours, for example, than to envisage the problems of a sessile filter-feeding brachiopod that lives all its life under water. Another problem of functional interpretations was that until recently they were not open to test. Two palaeontologists might suggest alternative functions for a fossil structure, but how were we to tell which of them was nearer the truth? All science advances by erecting hypotheses which allow predictions to be made that can be tested. Testing the predictions may cause us to confirm, modify or reject the hypothesis. In the latter case we erect a new hypothesis and try again. A great advance was made when a formal test of functional hypotheses was proposed by Martin Rudwick in 1961.[18] Rudwick suggested that an ideal design which would perform the proposed function with maximum efficiency, called a paradigm, should be formulated and compared with the fossil structure. The closer the comparison, the higher the efficiency of the fossil structure, and the greater the probability that it did indeed perform the suggested function. Now, if two palaeontologists suggest different functions for a fossil structure we can tell which of them is the better interpretation by comparing the fossil structure with the two appropriate paradigms. The paradigm which more closely compares with the actual fossil structure will yield the more probable function. So functional studies have recently been put on a more rigid scientific basis. Returning to phylogenetic studies, I think these should also be tested. Recently, two new approaches to phylogenetics have been proposed – 'numerical taxonomy'[19] and the 'phylogenetic systematics' of Hennig.[20] Numerical taxonomy attempts to measure the 'morphological distance' between organisms. The greater the difference in morphology between two species, the greater their morphological distance and, it is assumed, the less close the phylogenetic relationship. By measuring large numbers of characters in each species, it is possible to arrange the species in a branching network according to their morphological distance from each other. However, this branching pattern is not necessarily a phylogenetic tree since it does not contain any historical element. We may start with any species and produce a branching network from it. Thus any species is a potential founding ancestor. Hennig's ideas do not involve measurement of characters as the core of the method, but a formal logical system of classification. I cannot fault his logic, but again to derive a phylogeny using Hennig's methods one must be able to distinguish primitive from advanced characters and one must be sure that the groups being classified are monophyletic, that is derived from a single common ancestor. It is perhaps significant that both methods were developed largely in an attempt to classify groups, like insects, which have a high diversity at present but a poor fossil record. Both methods are inherently logical, but if we are to recognize a primitive character or a founding ancestor, surely we can only do this by reference to the fossil record?[21] As I hope I have demonstrated, for most purposes, including phylogeny, the fossil record is adequate. Indeed I would suggest here that phylogenetic studies will only be put on a formal scientific basis if they are tested, and the fossil record is the only possible test of ancestor–descendant relationships. Shaw has shown that for correlation purposes the total range of a species is as good a time line as we can get or need. He has also developed a systematic means of determining with reasonable certainty the total range of species by combining all the known ranges in separate sections into a single 'composite standard' section.[22] We need not discuss the method here, but if, after following his method, we find that two species have the stratigraphic relationship shown in figure 68, we can only conclude one ancestor–descendant relationship: a gave rise to b. The fossil record alone will not give us a phylogeny. It is true that in figure 68 a must be older than b, but it need not be closely related to b. Thus we need to determine phylogenetic

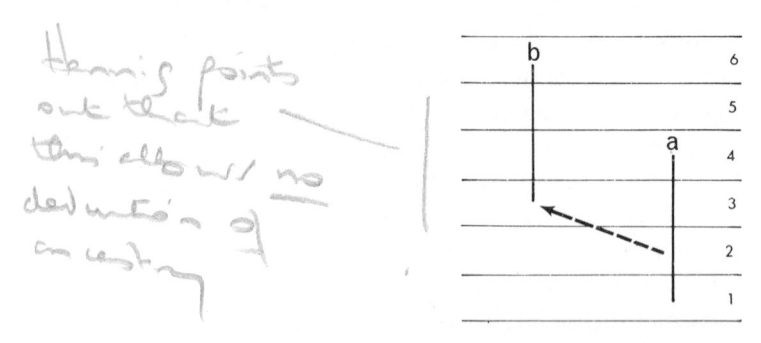

68. The inferred evolutionary relationship between two species with the stratigraphic ranges illustrated. In my opinion species **a** cannot have evolved from species **b** because it is known to be older.

relationships by traditional comparative morphology, by numerical taxonomy or by Hennig's methods, but the resulting phylogenetic trees can only be tested against the fossil record. Whenever we need to distinguish ancestor–descendant or primitive–advanced relationships, we must turn to the fossil record to find them. We may suggest these relationships on morphological grounds, as indeed we have to in groups with a poor fossil record, but we can only test the suggestions by reference to the fossil record.

So we may conclude that the fossil record is acceptable at face value. What, then, does it reveal about evolution in general and natural selection in particular? First it reveals that nearly all new groups, of whatever taxonomic level from species to phyla, appear suddenly. Secondly, it shows that evolution and extinction are not the uniform processes that Lyell believed them to be. There have been bursts of evolution (radiations) and mass extinctions (life crises) repeatedly in the past. Finally, although hardly any attempts have been made to find them, the fossil record is probably crammed full of examples of selection. It is worthwhile briefly reviewing the general pattern of evolution as revealed by the fossil record, as well as how to look for evidence of selection.

First, sudden appearances. A major controversy is currently raging as to whether the fossil record shows evidence of gradual transition or sudden changes. The debate is between the gradualistic view favoured by Darwin and recently defended by Gingerich,[23] a vertebrate palaeontologist at the University of Michigan, and the 'punctuated equilibria' model recently proposed by Eldridge and Gould.[24] Eldridge studies trilobites at the American Museum of

FAUNAL SUCCESSION AND EVOLUTION

Natural History, New York and Gould a wide variety of palaeontological problems at Harvard. Gingerich believes that sequences of fossil mammal teeth which he has investigated in detail show gradual changes in size which in some branching lineages lead to new species. At this point I should make clear that speciation is the appearance of new species in the sense that two arise where only one existed before (figure 69). Even if Gingerich is correct and his new species can be traced back to their points of origin (and even in his best data for the genus *Hyopsodus*, *H. simplex* and *H. miticulus* appear suddenly) the fact remains that most appear abruptly in the fossil record, many with no trace at all of an ancestral form. This sudden appearance of fossils has always been attributed to migration or the imperfections of the record. The species either evolved elsewhere and migrated in, or had a long period of prior gradual evolution not recorded in the fossil record. These explanations for the sudden appearance of most fossils have arisen because we expect the evolution of new species to be gradual, and when we find examples we seize upon them as proof of gradualism, ignoring the vast majority of cases which are sudden. For example, Gingerich has quoted another palaeontologist as saying, 'Whenever we do have positive

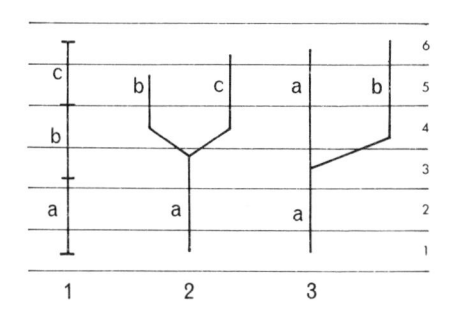

69. Speciation in stratigraphic lineages. In lineage 1 there is no speciation even though species **a** evolved into species **b** which in turn evolved into species **c**. At all times there was only one species present. In lineages 2 and 3 an initial species, **a**, gave rise to two species, **b** and **c** in lineage 2, **a** and **b** in lineage 3. In both cases two species arose where initially only one had existed. This is speciation in the present sense.

palaeontological evidence, the picture is of the most extreme gradualism.'[25] But surely this statement could be rephrased as, 'Whenever we find evidence of gradualism it is positive and should be accepted, but whenever we do not find it the evidence is negative and should be rejected'? This attitude might be defensible if the two alternatives, sudden and gradual appearances, were roughly equally common, but they are not. We are rejecting the overwhelming majority of cases in favour of the few that show what we expect to find. Why should evidence of gradual changes be so rare?

Eldridge and Gould have questioned whether we should expect to find evidence of gradual change even if natural selection is responsible for speciation. Their argument hinges on the precise way in which we now believe new species arise. In biblical times shepherds knew that large flocks were more healthy than small ones. This is because the effects of a deleterious mutation (a mutation is a new genetic arrangement that arises spontaneously) spread more rapidly and become entrenched in small populations but tend to be swamped out in large flocks. There is a natural tendency for large populations to remain fairly stable even under quite wide changes of environment provided, of course, the changes are not all in the same direction and prolonged. Random fluctuations in selection pressure are accommodated by large gene pools. Every species has a main area of distribution, towards the limits of which climatic and other factors reduce its ability to survive. We believe that new species arise in small peripheral populations of an ancestral species if they become isolated from the main population for long enough to allow them to become reproductively isolated from the parent species, even if they come back into contact again. We also believe that this may happen relatively rapidly because the peripheral isolated population is small, under considerable selective pressure, as it is near the limits of viability for the parent species, and new mutations could spread through it rapidly.

It has been pointed out that once a well-adapted species has evolved there will be quite strong selective pressure for it to maintain itself against genetic change and mutants will tend to be eliminated because they reduce its degree of adaptation. This concept of adaptive peaks explains why isolation mechanisms prevent cross breeding between species. The idea is that each species is adapted to its own niche better than any other competing species. Thus if two species cross-bred, any offspring would probably be less well adapted to either parental niche than the parents and would tend to be eliminated. The idea of adaptive peaks is not so different from Cuvier's ideas about the immutability of species, but is now in an evolutionary context. If a peripheral isolated population evolves into a new species with a slightly different niche from the parent species, on re-mixing both species may be able to maintain themselves since they do not compete for exactly the same niche. The consequences of this 'allopatric speciation model' are that in the fossil record we would not expect to find much evidence of the critical transition stages for at least three reasons: the changes took place rapidly, in small populations and in a small geographic area, all of which greatly reduce the preservation potential. Once the new species had evolved, the stabilizing tendency of large populations and adaptive peaks would tend to maintain it as it was. Hence Eldridge and Gould proposed their 'punctuated equilibria' model. They believe we should expect to find species which change little over long periods and then the sudden appearance of new species. If the new species out-competes an older species, then relatively sudden extinction ought also to occur. In my view the fossil record accords well with the Eldridge and Gould model. The rare cases which can be found to support Gingerich's point of view may well represent instances where the peripheral isolated populations have been preserved during their critical state of change.

If Eldridge and Gould are correct, then the fossil record is much less incomplete than we have been led to believe. The missing transitions represent only a small, but regrettably an important, proportion of past life. We should expect to find some evidence of gradual changes but it should be, and I believe is, the exception rather than the rule. In this view, although the fossil record does not reveal the gradual changes that Darwin sought, it is certainly not contrary to his idea of natural selection, and we need not accept Darwin's conclusion that the fossil record is very incomplete.

Even if the fossil record does not contain much evidence of the gradual changes implied by natural selection, it does contain direct evidence of selection, although very little attention has been paid to this critical point. In 1901 Weldon [26] made a classic investigation into selection among specimens of the European land snail *Cochlodina laminata*. He measured the width of the shell and the umbilicus (the small hollow about which the shell is coiled) and the appropriate lengths of the shell at each half-whorl for both adult and juvenile shells. Although Weldon presented his results in a manner which we now find rather unusual, he demonstrated that the juveniles were more variable than the adults. Here is classic evidence for the stabilizing tendency of species, since the extreme variants among juveniles apparently did not reach maturity and were unrepresented in the adult population; hence they would not be able to breed and pass their genes on to successive generations. Now this investigation was conducted using *shells* of recent snails, but shells are preservable, and exactly the same type of investigation could be performed on fossil molluscs with equal facility. Indeed, one of the very few cases where selection has been investigated in the fossil record involved a repeat of the same type of study on some populations of fossil oysters.[27] The ligament of these bivalves were preserved in some cases and showed growth bands so that members of the population could be aged. In this particular case the range of size reached by one-year-olds overlapped considerably with that of ten-year-olds, and so size alone was not a reliable indication of age. However, in many other cases size alone could be used and in any case, most bivalves show preserved annual rings and can be aged independently of size. Weldon's study of *Cochlodina* showed that measurements of the juvenile shell were more variable among individuals that died as juveniles than among individuals that reached maturity. The oyster study showed one character, number of folds in the shell, with the same stabilizing tendency; selection apparently favoured those shells with eight folds. It also suggested directed selection for maximum curvature of the shell, in other words selection favoured the most curved shells. Either possibility, stabilizing or directed selection, can be detected by this method; the point is that if the proportions of the population showing a particular character change between juvenile and adult states, selection is at work. The results can be made even more critical if the onset of sexual maturity can be detected in the fossils. This enables the fossil populations to be divided into immature and mature groups. However, the main point I wish to make is that provided one can collect fossils from a reasonably good population, the effects of selection can be investigated. Most examples of *in situ* communities on a bedding surface would meet this criterion. Inevitably, therefore, the fossil record must contain abundant evidence of selection. What is more, the effects of selection pressures on populations at one level, i.e. a bedding plane, can be compared up through a section or within suggested phylogenetic lineages to see if directed selection at the population level is reflected in actual evolution. If, for example, a number of populations of the same fossil species from different bedding surfaces all showed directed selection for larger size, one would expect the overall evolution of the fossils to show an increase in size.

The Eldridge and Gould model helps to explain the sudden appearance of fossil species, but it is inadequate to explain the simultaneous appearance of many forms of life (a radiation) or, for that matter, the sudden disappearance of many unrelated species (a life crisis). Before pursuing the point it is perhaps necessary to demonstrate that radiations and life crises are truly anomalous and not just coincidental random fluctuations in the fossil record. We can do this by a standard statistical technique. We suppose what is called a null hypothesis: in this case that the first appearance (or extinction) of a species is random. We can then predict the expected pattern of first appearances of new species and compare this with the actual distribution of first appearances. If they differ by an unacceptable amount – say there is only one chance in a thousand or even one in a hundred of finding the observed distribution from a random sample, then we reject the null hypothesis and conclude that the real distribution is genuinely not random. If we apply this test to the fossil record we find that some radiations and life crises are apparently genuine: they cannot be explained by random fluctuations alone.

An overall explanation for radiations is not too difficult to advance, but extinction is a problem both in particular cases and in general. Most radiations involve organisms which adapt to a new life style or a new environment. Initially there is little competition since the pioneers have the whole field to themselves and rapidly spread to occupy the available niches. Darwin's finches, those famous birds of the Galapagos Islands, are an excellent example of this. The pioneer population had the whole group of islands to themselves, and rapidly radiated into fourteen species from the original one. During the initial phase of colonization the most dramatic and rapid changes take place, but eventually, when all the niches have been filled, a new equilibrium develops and change is less rapid. Thus once the first sea urchins became able to burrow in the sediment in the Lower Jurassic a rapid radiation ensued and the infaunal, irregular echinoids soon became as diverse as the regular echinoids. Equally, when the first amphibians colonized land, they radiated into all sorts of niches until these were taken over by the reptiles with their amniotic eggs which freed them from the need to reproduce in water. The same may be said of the colonization of the air by birds or the development of flowers and specialized insect pollination, which allowed the radiation of the angiosperms in the Upper Cretaceous.

Life crises, or major extinctions, are much more of a puzzle and, perhaps because of this, more has been written about them. We can identify certain periods as general life crises: the end of the Palaeozoic and Mesozoic eras (the late Permian and late Cretaceous, respectively) are certainly two. Indeed, it is because of the major extinctions at these points that we choose them to be the boundaries of the eras. In addition to these general life crises, some fossil groups, e.g. ammonites, show life crises at other times as well. The ammonites nearly became extinct at the end of the Permian and also at the end of the Triassic. Only one or two families crossed the Triassic–Jurassic boundary to give rise to the immense variety of Jurassic and Cretaceous ammonites.

Suggested explanations of life crises abound: mountain-building episodes; changes in climate (the most popular explanation); fluctuations in oxygen levels in the atmosphere; sea level; the intensity of cosmic radiation; spread of toxins or trace elements, and competitive exclusion are among some of the more sane suggestions that have been advanced as general or particular explanations of extinctions. Perhaps no one explanation will suffice. Certainly it is extremely difficult to prove any cause in any particular case. A brief review of some examples will have to suffice.

Natural selection carries with it the idea of competitive exclusion. The organism less able to compete is eventually driven out of the habitat and may become extinct. The idea is simple and easy to understand, but very difficult to prove in the fossil record. This is at least partly due to the paucity of functional studies. If competitive exclusion is to be invoked, one ought to be able to demonstrate that the extinct group performed some vital function less well than the surviving groups. Only rarely has this been attempted. Even when it seems to be the obvious explanation, the fossil record does not always agree. For example, the reproductive system, parental care and warm-bloodedness of mammals are generally held to make them more efficient than reptiles. However, the radiation of mammals took place after the dinosaurs became extinct; they simply expanded to fill the vacated niches. Furthermore, if mammals *per se* are more efficient than reptiles, why are there still several thousand species of reptiles living on earth? The exact nature of competitive exclusion is not always clear in living examples. The introduction of placental mammals (dogs, rabbits, goats and so on) has had disastrous effects on many island faunas – even on the larger marsupials of Australia. Where dogs killed flightless birds or the goats overgrazed the vegetation it is easy to see what happened, but in many cases it is not at all clear what has upset the balance.

In most cases where placental and marsupial mammals have come into contact the placentals prove to be more competitive. In the Pliocene, North and South America were reunited and mammals migrated either way through Central America, marsupials northwards and placentals southwards. The resulting competition possibly caused the extinction of the widespread marsupial fauna of South America which so impressed Darwin when he visited South America with the *Beagle*. A few marsupial species, like the possum, have since spread as far north as the Canadian border. Similarly, Europe and North America appear to have been separated by a wide ocean in the Lower Ordovician. Brachiopods, among other fossils, evolved separately on either side, but when, towards the end of the Ordovician, they were able to cross the narrowing ocean, the European stocks almost annihilated the American. Most Silurian brachiopods can be traced to European Ordovician ancestors. Indeed James Valentine of the University of California at Santa Barbara has formulated this into a general theory.[28] He maintains that when there is a marked climatic gradient from the Equator to the poles and at times when there are many separate continental fragments, specific diversity will be high. For example an identical epifaunal filter-feeding niche may be filled by six separate species in shallow seas around six different isolated continents. Equally, the same basic niche may be filled by equatorial, tropical, sub-tropical, temperate and polar species, where a marked climatic gradient occurs. Thus the potential diversity is great. If two continents are brought together, two species occupying identical niches may come into contact and compete. More often than not we would expect one of them to exclude the other. A similar situation occurs when two firms merge: before the merger there were two company presidents, but afterwards there can only be one. So when the continents came together to form a supercontinent, and at times when the global climate was equable, specific diversity was low. When continents were separate and a marked climatic gradient existed, diversity was high. A change from the latter to the former conditions would give a period of major extinction.

The idea that changes in oxygen level may have caused extinctions is another worthy of mention. It was first seriously advanced by A. Lee McAlester of Yale University[29] and, although it has since been criticized, I still feel it has a simplicity which makes it well worth pursuing further. McAlester compared published figures for oxygen consumption rates with the rate of extinction for a wide range of taxa and found a good correlation. It is true that many data for oxygen consumption do not give details of temperature and body mass, which makes them notoriously difficult to compare, but the fact that a correlation was found suggests the data are not so unreasonable. If they were so poor as to amount to random numbers a negligible correlation would have resulted. McAlester's idea was that if the history of oxygen in the atmosphere was not one of steady gradual increase, but one of considerable ups and downs superimposed on the overall rise, then animals which use up oxygen most rapidly would be the most likely to become extinct during a period of decline in oxygen concentration. Hence the correlation between oxygen consumption rates and extinction rates. This idea would explain why totally unrelated groups such as dinosaurs and ammonites became extinct at the same time. It would also explain the fossil record of plants, which is generally one of continued progress without any life crises, in contrast to that of many animal groups. Plants produce their own oxygen and so would be much less susceptible to fluctuations in atmospheric oxygen content. In my view this idea needs further study and is a promising line of research. At least in fossil echinoderms it is possible to make estimates of oxygen exchange capacity.

The Permo–Triass life crisis is often attributed to a drop in sea level associated with glaciation in the southern hemisphere. During much of the Palaeozoic most continents were covered by shallow epicontinental seas. The area of these seas was enormous compared with the present-day continental shelf, and shallow seas support the richest marine faunas. If sea level dropped to the edge of the continental slope, the area of shallow sea would be drastically reduced and hence competition for living space greatly increased. It would also mean a much smaller chance of shallow-water organisms being preserved and found. The fossil record of bivalves across the Permo–Triass boundary has been examined and allowance made for the gaps. This is one of only two uses made of gaps in the record which I have come across. Even allowing for families which are known to have existed because they occur above and below, the Lower Triassic represents the lowest diversity of any part of the Permo–Triass.

Gaps may be used to distinguish genuine life crises from exceptionally poor preservation. The cystoids apparently had a life crisis in the Lower Silurian. Only one family of cystoids occurs in the Lower Silurian, and that known from only two or three species in two genera. Fourteen families occur in the preceding Upper Ordovician and eight in the Middle Silurian or younger rocks. At first sight the Lower Silurian seems to have been a time of life crisis for cystoids. However, eight of the families known in the Upper Ordovician survived beyond the Lower Silurian. Thus although the Upper Ordovician–Lower Silurian boundary saw a drastic reduction in cystoid diversity, it was nothing like the crisis it appears to have been. There were at least eight families of cystoids alive in the Lower Silurian somewhere in the world, even if their remains have not been preserved or have yet to be discovered. This was not a life crisis like that of the ammonites at the Triassic–Jurassic boundary when all but one or two families became extinct, but a massive preservation failure. Significantly, like the Permo–Triass life crisis, this Upper Ordovician–Lower Silurian crisis followed a glaciation. Perhaps the attendant lowering of sea level reduced the chances of preservation at least as much as it caused real extinctions.

We have now traced the development of ideas about evolution and considered the rather meagre contribution that palaeontology has made to evolutionary theory. On the way we considered the adequacy of the fossil record and concluded that it is in fact reliable for most purposes. If the fossil record is a reasonable sample of past life, it only remains for us to review briefly the main features of the history of life on earth, starting with the origin of life and progressing on to the emergence of terrestrial organisms, which ultimately led to our own appearance.

Chapter 8

The origin of life and early evolution

Once the idea of evolution has been accepted the obvious question, apart from actually tracing the history of life on earth, is the origin of life. For a long time this remained a complete mystery on which the fossil record shed little light. Less than twenty years ago when I first went to college the prevailing opinion was that there were no Precambrian fossils. Those objects claimed to be Precambrian fossils which were obviously organic were from doubtfully Precambrian rocks, while the organic origin of those that were undoubtedly Precambrian was questioned. Now we have quite a considerable Precambrian fossil record, but still it does not shed much light on the *origin* of life. We do have other lines of evidence which help suggest the most likely way in which life arose on earth, although there is a great deal we still do not understand. I shall consider first the general theories about the origin of life before going on to consider inorganic evolution.

All theories about the start of life fall into three categories. First there is panspermia, the idea that the seeds of life exist throughout the universe and when they fall on a suitable planet they develop. This is a very unsatisfactory theory because it begs the question. It may explain how life reached earth, but where did the seeds come from in the first place? Secondly there are theories which appeal to some supernatural intervention, of which special creation is the most familiar to those brought up in a Judeo-Christian tradition. Again these ideas are unsatisfactory from a scientific point of view, because they take as their starting point the assumption that something unique happened which is not open to normal scientific enquiry. All appeals to the supernatural, witchcraft and so on are really admissions of ignorance. We find it very difficult to admit that we do not understand something, even when it is patently obvious how little we know about it. Furthermore, religious beliefs are largely a matter of faith and faith is not subject to test like a scientific theory. The third group of theories suggests that life originated on earth by natural means, gradually evolving from non-living material. These ideas, since they do not invoke a suspension of normal physico-chemical laws, are subject to test and are therefore the most promising line of inquiry.

Before we discuss these theories in any detail we must have some idea of how life differs from non-living matter. One obvious attribute of all life is the ability to reproduce; another is the ability to react to stimuli. If we consider the chemistry of living tissues, we find nothing particularly strange in the elemental make-up of living things. The most common elements found in living matter are also some of the most abundant on earth, or indeed in the solar system (see the table below).

COMMON ELEMENTS IN LIVING THINGS

Elements	Order of abundance in the solar system
Hydrogen (H)	1
Oxygen (O)	3
Carbon (C)	4
Nitrogen (N)	5
Sulphur (S)	9
Phosphorus (P)	16

Living matter does not differ from non-living matter because it contains some rare and special elements, although it is the peculiar combinative power of carbon that enables the vast array of complex organic compounds to form. Organic chemistry is, in effect, the chemistry of carbon, while inorganic chemistry is the chemistry of all the other elements. This gives some idea of how much more complex the chemistry of carbon is, and most naturally occurring organic chemicals are biogenic in origin, in other words derived from living things.

If the elements found in living matter are commonplace, the compounds certainly are not. All living matter has several types of organic compounds which are not found in abiogenic, non-living matter. First and foremost are the proteins, an almost infinite variety of compounds with very large molecules, but all composed from twenty amino acids. There are also the nucleic acids, which control the mechanism of inheritance and protein synthesis as well. These too are enormous chain molecules in the famous double helix arrangement, but again all composed of only four nucleotide bases.

Other biogenic compounds include fats for storing energy, sugars and other carbohydrates which are a source of energy, and the adenosine phosphates which are involved in energy transfer. Now it seems clear that the first step along the road to life must have been the synthesis from abiogenic sources of the relatively simple amino acids, nucleotide bases, fats, carbohydrates, etc. which all life contains and without which the extremely large and complex molecules like proteins and nucleic acids could not have been formed. A classic experiment was carried out in 1953 which showed that such a synthesis was entirely possible. Before I outline the experiment, however, we need to digress briefly to consider what the earth may have been like when life first evolved.

Perhaps the simplest test we could devise to see if life can evolve from non-living matter on earth is to look for it happening at the present time. No one has yet found evidence of this, so we have concluded that the process no longer happens. Most evolutionary scientists believe that conditions on earth are no longer suitable for life to evolve – mainly because our atmosphere contains a lot of oxygen, but also perhaps because any organic molecules which got even half-way there would probably be eaten by something already alive. Oxygen is a very reactive element and will combine with metals like iron (as anyone with a rusty car knows all too well). All the free oxygen would soon combine with other elements if it were not being replaced continually by the photosynthesis of green plants. Thus before there was life there was no photosynthesis and very little free (uncombined) oxygen in the atmosphere or oceans. So we believe the atmosphere of the early earth was a reducing, not an oxidizing, atmosphere. Now the outer planets, those beyond the asteroid belt, have atmospheres containing ammonia (NH_3), methane (CH_3), hydrogen (H_2) and water (H_2O), and we believe this may well have been the composition of the atmosphere on earth when life evolved for the first time. If so, it contained most of the elements necessary for life to evolve. We assume there were electrical storms, that the earth received cosmic radiation and we know there was vulcanism. As it happens enough experiments have now been conducted to show that the exact composition of the atmosphere and the exact source of energy for the synthesis are not important. In the first experiment Stanley Miller, at the time a graduate student at the University of Chicago, heated water and passed the resulting steam into a spark chamber containing an atmosphere of methane, ammonia and hydrogen.[1] This combination of gases was subjected to an electric spark to simulate lightning, condensed and the water returned to the initial flask for reheating. This last part simulated rain falling into the early oceans directly or via rivers. Miller allowed the experiment to run for a week, by which time the water in the flask was a dirty brown colour. Analysis of the contents of the flask revealed several amino acids among other compounds. Since Miller's first experiment, others have been performed using slightly different atmospheric compositions and using ultra-violet light or heat as energy sources to simulate cosmic radiation or vulcanism. Virtually all simple organic chemicals necessary for life have been synthesized and some experiments even produced chains of amino acid molecules. Thus the first step towards life can be duplicated in the laboratory. We now imagine that these simple compounds were synthesized naturally in the primitive atmosphere and accumulated in the early oceans to form the 'organic soup' that the English biologist, Haldane,[2] and the Russian, Oparin,[3] suggested before World War II.

Now it is a very long way from organic soup with amino acids to self-replicating life forms. Let us just examine one step – protein synthesis. This happens in living organisms under the control of nucleic acids, often with the aid of enzymes which speed up chemical reactions in living things and are frequently proteins themselves. Nucleic acids are also involved in the mechanism of inheritance, and have the unique property of being able to duplicate themselves. The double helix consists of two chains of nucleotide bases with cross-links between each pair of bases in opposite chains. The structure is rather like a ladder twisted along its length with the sides of the ladder representing the chains of nucleotide bases and the rungs the cross-links between them. Now the cross-linkages are unique. If we label the four nucleotide bases A, B, C and D we find that A always links with D, and B always links with C. During reproduction the cross-links break down and the two chains of nucleotide bases separate. The two separate halves then complete the missing chain exactly because of the unique linkages. Any D on a chain which was originally combined with an A will attract another A and nothing else. Similarly a B will only link with another C. Thus each half of the original nucleic acid acts as a template or blueprint for the synthesis of the other half and eventually two new nucleic acid molecules are formed which are identical to the parent molecule. In a similar manner, the exact sequence of the four nucleotide bases acts as a blueprint for protein synthesis, slightly different sequences producing different proteins. So we are in something of a chicken and egg situation. If we had a nucleic acid molecule we could produce proteins and more nucleic acids and eventually life, but the only known source of nucleic acids is living things. So how did the first nucleic acids or the first proteins arise?

Nucleotide bases are somewhat more difficult to synthesize in the laboratory than amino acids, but it can be done and under conditions that we think occurred naturally on the early earth. So we can imagine the building blocks of both proteins and nucleic acids were present in the organic soup. There is a saying in statistics that given enough monkeys playing on enough typewriters, one of them will come up with the complete works of Shakespeare. The chances against the right combination of nucleotide bases coming together in the right order and at the same time to form the first nucleic acid molecule must seem equally astronomical. What is needed then, are ways in which the chances against synthesis can be reduced.

First, the chances of chemical combination are proportional to the concentration of the reagents. We can imagine that the chances of the vital synthesis taking place would be greatly enhanced if the organic soup were concentrated. This must have happened in rock pools and areas of high evaporation. Next, it is known that clay minerals have what are called base-exchange properties. They attract bases to their surfaces and they have complex silicate structures in which sheets of silicon and oxygen atoms are separated by bases. Thus if clays were present in pools of concentrated organic soup, it is possible that nucleotide bases might have been brought together in the right order to produce chains and possibly the first nucleic acid molecules. Finally, there is some evidence that abiogenic organic molecules more complex than those used by Miller in his experiment were already present in the primitive earth. This evidence comes from two sources: meteorites and Precambrian igneous rocks. One class of meteorites has long been claimed to contain organic chemicals. Unfortunately these claims have not been widely accepted, because until recently all the samples available had not been collected under circumstances that ruled out any possibility of contamination with terrestrial organic chemicals. However, material from the Murchison meteorite, which fell in southern Australia in 1969, has been very carefully collected and analysed. It not only yielded a surprisingly high concentration of amino acids, but some of them are unknown in terrestrial organisms, which rules out contamination as the source. The argument goes then, that if amino acids were present in meteorites, they and other compounds may already have been present on the primitive earth. The second line of evidence is that some igneous rocks contain oil, not as a contaminant filling cracks, but as a primary constituent. The oil can sometimes be found partly filling bubbles within crystals and was, therefore, part of the original molten magma. Furthermore, it is sometimes possible to show that this oil is apparently of abiogenic origin.

Many organic compounds exist with left and right handed spirals, one structure being an exact mirror image of the other. For some reason, living things often synthesize such chemicals with one of the two forms in a greater proportion than the other, whereas if we synthesize the same chemical abiogenically in the laboratory we always get a fifty-fifty mixture. We can tell if we have an unequal mixture of the two forms because a solution of the chemical will rotate the plane of polarized light, that is, light that has been made to vibrate in one direction only. What seems to happen is that both types of molecule affect the vibration of the light in equal and opposite ways. If the mixture is fifty-fifty, the effects cancel each other out, the light is unaffected and the substance is said to be optically inactive. If, on the other hand, the mixture is unequal, say seventy-thirty, then there is a net effect, the plane of vibration is rotated and the substance is said to be optically active. Thus optical activity is a good indication of the biogenic origin of an organic chemical and, conversely, optical inactivity suggests an abiogenic origin. The oils which are primary constituents in some igneous rocks yield inactive organic chemicals. We do not know how they became primary constituents of a magma, nor how old they were originally, because we can only date the time of cooling. Perhaps some of these abiogenic organic compounds were around early enough to assist the vital synthesis. We can see that there are still tremendous areas of ignorance, which I do not wish to minimize, but nevertheless we are now firmly convinced that some sort of gradual chemical evolution of progressively more complex macromolecules took place and led to the first forms of life on earth.

Initially the macromolecules would probably have been synthesized from simple organic molecules in the soup. However, there must have come a time when no more small molecules were available for synthesis. No further progress could have taken place until some means of trapping outside energy evolved. This was the probable stimulus for photosynthesis. Some organic compounds that contain magnesium are able to absorb light energy and release it for use in chemical reactions. The chlorophylls, which are responsible for the green colour in leaves, are the best known of these compounds and they are vital to photosynthesis in plants. Chlorophylls occur in little green organelles within plant cells, called chloroplasts. Although chloroplasts typically occur in plants cells, some evidence has recently been discovered for free-living chloroplasts. This would fit in very well with the theory that the organelles of all types of cells arose as independent bodies which found refuge within cells once the latter had evolved. So, once photosynthetic compounds arose there was a possibility of continuing the vital synthesis even if the organic soup was virtually depleted. Our ideas about how cells might have arisen are linked to concentration mechanisms.

When mixtures of amino acids are dried out and then remixed with hot water, tiny droplets form which are called proteinoid microspheres. They contain mixtures of amino acids which do not necessarily match the original mixtures, and some chemical reactions occur during the formation of the microspheres. Furthermore, the microspheres seem to have a double-layered outer coating which strongly resembles a cell wall. One can easily imagine the formation of microspheres in evaporite pools or volcanic lakes, and they are not the only possible means of producing cells or cell-like bodies. Lipoprotein vesicles are tiny droplets that form in scummy water when it is agitated, while coacervate drops form in colloidal solutions under the right circumstances. Colloids are chemicals in a finely divided state somewhere between true solution and a fine-grained suspension. They have rather special physico-chemical properties, such as the ability to set into gels or to produce coacervate drops. When coacervates form they may concentrate chemicals as much as ten thousand times and the Russian scientist, Oparin, whose life's work was investigating the origin of life, managed to make coacervate drops change under the influence of various enzymes.[4] In particular he made some coalesce and others divide just as living cells do in fertilization and growth. He even managed to produce photosynthetic coacervates by providing the right mixture of chemicals. Again, I do not wish to minimize the difficulties, nor areas of uncertainty, but these experiments certainly illustrate possible ways in which the first cells or cell-like concentrations of organic molecules could have arisen. Any 'protocells' which arose and developed their own photosynthesis would have had an advantage over pre-life forms in the organic soup (if it still existed) and they would have multiplied faster than the others. Of course cell division is a very complex process, and simply splitting coacervate drops is not all that is required. However, if the right combination of chemicals, including perhaps some nucleic acid, were to come together in something like a coacervate drop, then the splitting would have been better organized. A greater proportion of daughter drops would have survived intact in a state like their parents', and again natural selection would favour this combination over others. So we can imagine how the first unicellular organisms might have come about by some such mechanism, even if the precise details remain to be determined.

Once cells or even protocells were present in the early oceans, there would be the possibility of them 'dying'. Those that did would provide a concentration of useful organic chemicals as an energy source or building blocks for others. Thus any cell or protocell which could absorb concentrations of organic chemicals would be favoured, and the first 'organisms' of decay, like modern bacteria and fungi, might have developed. From these it would not be a large step to the first 'organisms' which broke down other 'organisms' before they were 'dead', that is the first diseases and eventually predators. Very early on we can imagine the development of the major elements of our present-day ecosystem, with photosynthetic cells being the primary producers, decay organisms reducing and recycling dead cells and diseases and predaceous cells absorbing and killing living cells.

If we accept that some process of inorganic evolution led to the first living organism, when did it occur? We now have good fossil evidence of primitive life forms from rocks over three thousand million years old. Clearly life originated on earth before this and after about 4,500 million years ago, when the earth itself formed. Unfortunately, between these limits there are few sedimentary rocks, and the oldest yet found, in western Greenland, are about 3,700 million years old. So the first eight hundred million years (which is two hundred million years longer than the time since the beginning of the Cambrian, when fossils first became abundant) has left no suitable rock record in which to look for fossils. Nevertheless, we can check the rocks we do have, not only for fossils, but for traces of biogenic organic compounds whose optical activity can be tested, and for distinctive isotopic ratios. Organic geochemistry is a growing branch of geology as a result of the search for the earliest traces of life on earth.

In chapter 4 we discussed isotopic fractionation and the use of $^{18}O/^{16}O$ ratios in palaeothermometry. Isotopes with atomic weights below about forty are separated (fractionated) slightly during chemical and physical changes, the lighter isotopes being more mobile. Attempts have been made to use isotopic ratios to detect the origin of life. Two main methods have been used involving isotopes of carbon and oxygen. Carbon exists as two stable isotopes, ^{12}C and ^{13}C. ^{12}C is the more reactive and enters living cells more rapidly during photosynthesis than ^{13}C. Since ^{12}C accounts for about 99 per cent of the carbon in atmospheric carbon dioxide, these isotopic ratios, like so many others, have to be determined very carefully. Nevertheless, it has been argued that sediments like limestones which are biogenic in origin should be enriched in ^{12}C compared with those which are entirely abiogenic in origin. Therefore if we measure the ^{12}C/^{13}C ratio in ancient rocks we may be able to trace the onset of photosynthesis. In South Africa, rocks of the Onverwacht Group, which are about 3,350 million years old, include a series of beds which show a significant rise in ^{12}C content. If the measurements are reliable and the rocks have not been contaminated, this may well date the onset of photosynthesis. Oxygen isotopes also show fractionation and are abundant in limestones. ^{18}O/^{16}O ratios not only reflect temperature, but organic activity as well. By the same argument, biogenic limestones should be enriched in ^{16}O, the lighter isotope, and measurements on ancient limestones suggest that by three thousand million years ago photosynthesis was running at about eighty per cent its current level. However, some geochemists have expressed reservations about the basic arguments.

So, if we accept the isotopic data, we think life evolved on earth perhaps 3,500 million years ago, although we cannot yet be precise about the date, and that photosynthesis began perhaps a hundred and fifty million years later. The earliest fossil remains yet discovered occur in the Fig Tree Chert of South Africa and are estimated to be about 3,000–3,200 million years old. Chert is a finely crystalline form of silica (SiO_2) and it preserves uncrushed minute organisms. Most of the earliest Precambrian fossils we know are preserved in chert deposits. The Fig Tree Chert contains two types of primitive life. One, as its name *Eobacterium* implies, is interpreted as the oldest known bacterium, while the other, *Archaeospheroides*, is interpreted as a spherical blue-green alga, not unlike modern examples of the coccoid group. Perhaps significantly, both bacteria and blue-green algae lack nuclei in their cells and are of a grade of organization known as prokaryotic. Prokaryotes are organisms with their DNA (deoxyribo-nucleic acid, the nucleic acid which controls inheritance) dispersed throughout their cells, which lack specialized organelles within the cells and are thought to be the most primitive living organisms. Since their cells lack definite nuclei, prokaryotes cannot undergo cell division of either reproductive (mitotic) or normal (meiotic) types, because such division requires that the genetic material be arranged in the chromosomes of the cell nucleus. Prokaryotes are regarded as more primitive than eukaryotes which have cell nuclei and include all forms of life other than bacteria and blue-green algae. If the biological affinities of the Fig Tree Chert organisms are correct, they are significant in the history of life not only because they are prokaryotic, but also because *Archaeospheroides* would have been photosynthetic. Indeed the Fig Tree Cherts have a $^{12}C/^{13}C$ ratio very close to that of modern algae. Hence we have possible evidence of primary producers and decay organisms among the first fossils.

Further up the Precambrian record in the Gunflint Chert of western Ontario, which is approximately two thousand million years old, a considerable flora of primitive blue-green algae has been recovered. One form shows what looks like a cell nucleus, although it could possibly be contamination. Two further features of interest are that the Gunflint Chert contains two organic chemicals, phytane and pristane, the most reasonable explanation for which is that they are decay products of chlorophyll. One may doubt the assignment of *Archaeospheroides* to the blue-green algae and hence that photosynthesis had developed by Fig Tree Chert times, but there can be little doubt that photosynthesis was well under way two thousand million years ago. Secondly the Gunflint Chert contains stromatolites which are sedimentary structures of algal origin and are the most obvious and abundant evidence of life in the Precambrian. Like the Fig Tree Chert, Gunflint Chert carbon isotope ratios are enriched in ^{12}C and close to those for living algae.

The next most significant event in the Precambrian seems to have occurred about a thousand million years ago. In Australia the Bitter Springs Chert has yielded a rich flora including some forms tentatively interpreted as fungi and others more certainly assigned to the green algae. Green algae are eukaryotes and, like fungi, capable of sexual reproduction. Even more remarkable is the green alga *Glenobotrydium aenigmatis*, which appears to include examples showing all stages of cell division, again apparently with cell nuclei preserved. The resemblance to cell division is so strong that it is very difficult not to accept the evidence for what it appears to be. So we think all the basic requirements for the evolution of sex existed by a thousand million years ago and that possibly sexual reproduction had already evolved by this time.

The advantages of sex are debatable! In its simplest form half the individuals (males) are unproductive, and only females produce offspring; but one effect it does have is to speed up the rate of evolution by diversifying the gene combinations on which natural selection can operate. In asexual reproduction a cell simply divides into two daughter cells, each of which has exactly the same genetic material as the parent. Each half of each DNA molecule simply replicates the other half. Unless something goes awry and a mutation occurs, no genetic change whatsoever takes place during asexual reproduction. This means that potential change can only occur as fast as new mutations arise, and many of these will be lethal or at least harmful and hence rapidly eliminated. With asexual reproduction the mutation rate puts an absolute upper limit on the rate of evolution. Indeed, it has been suggested that the earliest Precambrian fossils resemble modern living bacteria and blue-green algae because the rate of evolution of these primitive groups has been so slow. However, without wishing to be too cynical, in the case of simple spheres and rods and with only size and shape to go on, it is hard to imagine how the earliest fossils could look very different from, and yet still be interpreted as, algae or bacteria. Even so, life existed on earth for over two thousand million years before there is any evidence of a major radiation, and it may well be that asexual reproduction was one of the limiting factors. Put another way, the development of sex had a liberating effect on evolution.

All the genetic material of eukaryotes is contained in the nucleus. During all cell division the genetic material is organized into visible pairs of dark bodies called chromosomes. In sexual reproduction, as a cell divides one of each pair of chromosomes goes into each daughter cell but the other half is not then regenerated. Eggs and sperm have only half the chromosomes of other cells and when they combine at fertilization the normal number of chromosomes is completed. In this manner the fertilized egg derives its genetic material half from the father and half from the mother. Now unless the father and mother have identical genetic material, not only will they differ from each other, but the offspring will also differ from both parents. If we imagine the Adam and Eve of sexual reproduction, then their offspring would have a different set of genes from either parent and if they crossed back with the parents would produce yet more possible combinations of genetic material. By this means, genetic diversity of a population of sexually reproducing animals becomes very varied. Should a new mutation arise, it does not produce just one possibility but a range of possible combinations with existing genes. The rate of evolution is not limited just by the mutation rate, but by the rate of mutation and recombination together. In the simplest case a new mutation can produce three possible combinations, but very often a single gene affects a number of adult characters, and equally several characters may each be under the influence of a set of genes, not just one. So a new mutation may in fact have a wide range of possible morphological effects. Sexually reproducing organisms have a greater genetic variability on which natural selection can operate, and hence they evolve much faster than asexually reproducing organisms. This may well have been a contributing factor in the late Precambrian/Cambrian radiation.

During all this time the environment on earth was not static, but changed in direct relationship to the evolution of life. We have already seen that the early atmosphere was probably reducing and contained hydrogen, ammonia, methane and nitrogen, but very little free oxygen. The atmosphere is now almost entirely composed of nitrogen and oxygen. What brought about the change, and can we trace when and how? The most obvious and probably the most significant change was the release of uncombined oxygen by photosynthesis which probably started about 3,350 million years ago. While this was undoubtedly responsible for the change in the atmosphere from a reducing to an oxidizing state, the change did not happen overnight. Hydrogen is the lightest of gases and the gravitational attraction of the earth was probably insufficient to retain it. Most of it probably escaped into space, but even if it remained it would soon have combined with free oxygen to form water once photosynthesis began. The methane and ammonia were probably used up in biogenic processes or again oxidized by photosynthetic oxygen, which leaves just unreactive nitrogen gas, the major constituent of our present atmosphere.

Even with gases which are more dense than hydrogen, occasionally a molecule reaches escape velocity and passes out into space never to return. Small planetary bodies lose their atmospheres faster than large ones because their gravitational fields have lower escape velocities. For this reason Mars, which is slightly smaller than the earth, has the vestiges of a thin atmosphere while the moon, with one sixth of the earth's mass, has virtually none at all. However, this is not the entire story. Even earth would have lost much of its atmosphere were it not being replenished. The American geochemist, Rubey, first investigated the origin of the volatile constituents of the earth's atmosphere and oceans.[5] He calculated that there was an excess of volatiles way above anything that could be accounted for by the weathering of rocks. He noted that during volcanic eruptions volatiles form the greatest mass of volcanic products, although our attention is usually fixed on the lava and ash thrown out during eruptions. The gases include steam (H_2O), carbon dioxide (CO_2), sulphur dioxide (SO_2), hydrochloric acid (HCl) as well as compounds of fluorine (F) and boron (B). Rubey concluded that these excess volatiles, and particularly the water in the oceans, had come from de-gassing the interior of the earth. Now if Hugh Owen is correct in his suggestion that the earth has expanded significantly since the Late Precambrian,[6] the amount and type of vulcanism probably changed when the original continental crust first began to crack and the first ocean basins (in the geological sense) formed. Currently most vulcanism is along plate margins, so before sea-floor spreading and plate tectonics began, one can imagine much less volcanic activity. Even if Hugh Owen's ideas are incorrect, sea-floor spreading and continental drift are intimately related to the history of life on earth, first because they supply large quantities of the elements necessary for the continuation of life through de-gassing, and secondly because separation of continents has allowed the isolation and independent evolution of faunas, as with the marsupials in Australia, while at other times continental collisions have led to mixing of faunas, competition and extinction, as with the European and American brachiopods at the end of the Ordovician, or the North and South American mammals in the Pliocene.

To return to the history of oxygen in the atmosphere, we have seen that isotopic ratios and possibly direct fossil evidence in the Fig Tree Chert suggest that photosynthesis began between 3,000 and 3,500 million years ago. When it began, uncombined oxygen would have been released into the sea (bear in mind that we believe all life existed in the sea until the end of the Silurian, only four hundred million years ago). Even if we accept the older figure for the commencement of photosynthesis, for a thousand million years rivers had been carrying sediments and chemicals into the oceans which must have been chock full of all sorts of elements and compounds in a reduced state. One element which we know to our cost is very easily oxidized, is iron, but there must have been many others. The most likely first effect of free photosynthetic oxygen would have been to oxidize elements like iron dissolved in sea water. Bear in mind too that oxygen is only released by photosynthesis during daylight so that even if the early plants were able to release oxygen faster than it could be used up in oxidizing reactions, there would still have been all night for any surplus free oxygen to have combined with reduced substances. So initially photosynthetic release of free oxygen would not have affected the atmosphere at all.

Now in the mid-Precambrian, from about 3,000 to 1,800 million years ago, we have puzzling banded iron formations. Nothing quite like them is known in older or younger rocks and their mineralogy suggests that they formed under conditions which do not exist on earth today. Many are obviously banded, hence the name, and consist of alternating laminae of iron oxides and chert. The laminations resemble varves, and it has been suggested that they may have had a similar seasonal origin. In many parts of the world algae have a short burst of rapid growth, an algal bloom, followed by much lower population densities for the rest of the year. Blooms usually follow seasonal changes in the supply of chemical nutrients. For example, in high latitude lakes there is a seasonal changeover of water due to its peculiar property of being most dense at a temperature slightly above freezing point (at about $4°C$). During the cold winter season surface water is colder and less dense than that at the bottom which remains at about $4°C$. In summer the surface water is less dense, but warmer than the bottom water which in most lakes rises well above $4°C$. Each spring and autumn unstable situations develop in which warmer bottom water rises (spring) and colder surface water sinks (autumn) bringing about a complete turnover of water. The spring upwelling brings nutrients to the surface and this, together with the rise in temperature, results in an algal bloom. It is suggested that banded ironstones arose because seasonal algal blooms altered the oxygen concentration and precipitated iron oxides, while for the rest of the year normal silica deposition continued to form the interleaved chert laminae.

Now banded ironstones are known from 3,000 to 1,800 million years ago all over the world. Their beginning is close to the suggested onset of photosynthesis and their end coincides quite well with the first red beds. The onset of banded ironstone formation probably marks the point where photosynthesis had released enough oxygen to start the precipitation of iron oxides, and the end of their formation marks the point at which all the unoxidized iron in the sea water had been used up. As soon as the oceans were completely oxidized, oxygen would begin to diffuse into the atmosphere and start to oxidize iron at source. Thereafter iron compounds exposed on land surface would have begun to rust, producing that characteristic rusty brown colour which geologists call red. Today red beds form mainly in desert areas where strongly oxidizing conditions obtain. However, of course the entire land surface was desert in the Precambrian. So it is highly significant that the last banded ironstones occur at about the same time as the first red beds. This time, about 1,800 million years ago, marks the first appearance of significant amounts of free oxygen in the atmosphere. Again the surface of the earth must have been littered with reduced substances, so that we do not imagine atmospheric oxygen rose to anything like its present level immediately. However, at some time it must have reached the critical concentration of one per cent present atmosphere level (PAL). At this level, approximately 0.2 per cent oxygen, cosmic radiation in the upper atmosphere converts normal oxygen (O_2) into ozone (O_3) to form the ozone layer which absorbs most of the ultra-violet light that reaches earth from the sun. This critical level of oxygen concentration is sometimes called the Pasteur point. It is ultra-violet radiation which causes sunburn, so you can imagine how roasted we would become if we were exposed in shallow water or on land without the ozone layer. It is not yet possible to date accurately the time when the Pasteur point was reached, but it must have had several important effects. First, organisms sensitive to ultra-violet light would have been able to migrate into shallow seas and secondly new organisms which did not thrive on ultra-violet light could evolve for the first time. Significantly blue-green algae, which dominate the earliest Precambrian floras, are much more tolerant of exposure to ultra-violet light than other organisms and thrive on radiation doses which would kill us.

Two American atmospheric physicists, Berkner and Marshall, have developed a theory that the Pasteur point was reached shortly before the onset of the Cambrian when fossils first become abundant and that this accounts for the explosive radiation of organisms at that time.[7] Ken Towe, a geochemist at the National Museum of Natural History in Washington, DC has added yet another important idea about the rise in oxygen level and the Cambrian radiation.[8] He points out that without collagen, a unique structural material found in all multicellular animals, no hydrostatic skeleton like that of worms, nor any rigid skeleton with muscle attachments, could have evolved. Collagen is absolutely essential to most animals, for example it is collagen fibres which hold the individual plates of echinoderm skeletons together. It is so successful at doing this that when injured, the plates of living echinoderms fracture rather than separate. The synthesis of collagen requires large quantities of oxygen so Towe argues that natural selection would have operated against collagen synthesis or organisms with collagen while oxygen concentrations were low, but as soon as a reasonable amount of free oxygen became available, collagen synthesis could proceed, and with it the evolution of multicellular animals. Thus the reaching of the Pasteur point had many important effects on life, of which perhaps the most obvious is that it allowed aerobic (oxidizing) respiration, which is vital to almost all animals, unicellular or multicellular.

To continue with the history of oxygen in the atmosphere, the evolution of land plants in the late Silurian would have made available a significant area of land surface for photosynthesis, possibly raising atmospheric oxygen concentration sharply to something like its present level. We do not know if the rise in atmospheric oxygen was a steady increase as Berkner and Marshall originally indicated, or whether it fluctuated considerably as McAlester[9] has suggested. The fossil record does contain some hints about this, but it is difficult to be certain. For example, all classes of echinoderms known in the Ordovician have at least some representatives with specialized respiratory pore-structures, and the Ordovician was the period of maximum diversity for groups like the cystoids, which are characterized by the possession of pore-structures. Furthermore cystoid pore-structures were morphologically most diverse in the Ordovician and the group declined after the Ordovician. My overall impression is that competition for oxygen was a significant factor in the lives of Ordovician echinoderms, while thereafter competition for food seems to have been the main preoccupation, at least among sedentary filter feeders.

One last speculation about Cambrian trilobites. In the Upper Cambrian and into the Lowest Ordovician of the western interior of the United States, trilobites show several radiations followed by life crises, for which the term biomeres has been coined. Biomeres do not occur in later trilobite evolution. The only trilobites to pass through the crises are small agnostids (figure 70), trilobites with only two thoracic segments, and very similar heads and tails, and which are thought to have floated in near-surface waters. So the extinctions apparently wiped out only bottom-dwelling trilobites. Jim Stitt, of the University of Missouri, has suggested that the extinctions were caused by cold deep-ocean water upwelling onto the shelf where the trilobites lived and killing them.[10] The water, being cold, remained on the bottom and did not affect the free-swimming agnostids. If the water was not only cold, but devoid of oxygen, the effect would have been even more devastating and instantaneous as well.

One other aspect of the late Precambrian environment is the evidence for an extensive glaciation, the Varangian, which comes from widely separated areas and which palaeomagnetic data suggest was very intense, reaching into low latitudes. As the climate ameliorated after this those forms of life which had survived may have spread widely into new areas recently vacated by the ice. Whatever the reason, whether it was the evolution of sex, increased oxygen levels with their attendant affects, or climatic changes, firm evidence of multicellular animals appears in the latest Precambrian and, although it is known to have been moderately widespread and diverse, it is still meagre compared with the fossil record in the Cambrian. Let us now see what sorts of animals and plants the first multicellular organisms were.

The best known locality for late Precambrian fossils is Ediacara in South Australia and, not surprisingly, the fauna is known as the Ediacara fauna. Elements of the Ediacara fauna are known from South Africa and England, and it is now possible to correlate the uppermost Precambrian crudely on its occurrence. The animals in the Ediacara fauna include jellyfish, worms, sea pens (colonial organisms related to corals) as well as some others of unknown affinity. Although the sea pens were first described as algae, there are traces of spicules in some. U-shaped burrows and trails indicate that mobile animal life existed in the Ediacaran sea. The entire fauna lacks skeletons, except for the spicule impression in the sea pens and other isolated spicules which may have originated from sponges. The preservation of this fauna resulted from a happy accident. The animals were stranded on a fine mud or silt lamination which took up their impressions. Later sands covered the muds and retained all the details of the fossil impressions in the muds. The sands have since been cemented by silica to form sedimentary quartzites. Modern experiments have shown that the sand must have covered the mud within a few days at most or the delicate impressions would not have been preserved. As to the age of the Ediacara fauna, at Ediacara itself the fauna occurs in quartzites which are more than a hundred and fifty metres below dolomites with Lower Cambrian fossils. The Lower Cambrian fossils are identical to others of the same age from elsewhere in the world and quite different from the Ediacara fauna. Furthermore, elements of the Ediacara fauna are found in South Africa and at Charnwood Forest in Britain. The Charnian rocks are cleaved and intruded by uncleaved

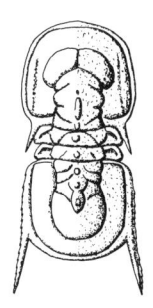

70. An agnostid trilobite. A group of Cambrian trilobites characterized by very similar heads and tails and only two thoracic segments. (After D. L. Clark, *Fossils, paleontology and evolution*, fig. 33-5, p. 84, Wm C. Brown, 1968.)

syenites. The syenites are identical to some others which intrude the Cambrian at Nuneaton nearby and which have been dated radiometrically at 684 ± 29 million years. Thus the Charnian rocks were slightly metamorphosed before being intruded by syenites which are probably nearly seven hundred million years old. An age of seven to eight hundred million years is accepted for the Ediacara fauna wherever it occurs.

Elsewhere in Australia and also in other parts of the world, trace fossils appear in the late Precambrian so that we do have widespread evidence of multicellular organisms in the Precambrian, but only in the last one to two hundred million years. All these traces, and the impressions of the Ediacara fauna, differ from the fossils in the Lower Cambrian and later rocks in that there is no evidence of solid skeletons: at most only spicules had developed. So one obvious explanation for the sudden appearance of diverse fossils in the basal Cambrian is that they rapidly acquired the ability to secrete skeletons, thus greatly increasing their preservation potential. This idea has long been the most popular explanation and, it was argued, the diverse forms of life that appeared in the Cambrian had a long Precambrian evolutionary history before they acquired skeletons. Here again we see the influence of the search for gradual changes. The absence of even trace fossils more than one to two hundred million years back into the Precambrian puts a limit on this 'long' pre-skeletal history. There is no doubt in my mind that multicellular animals had not evolved prior to about eight hundred million years ago at most. Even so, two hundred million years, from eight hundred million years ago to the beginning of the Cambrian, is a long time–time enough, for example, for the appearance on earth of all flowering plants, birds and virtually all mammals. So we can imagine that the last two hundred million years of the Precambrian saw the gradual evolution of multicellular organisms towards their eventual acquisition of skeletons and the first appearance of common body fossils in the lowest Cambrian. The Ediacara fauna gives us a glimpse into this world.

To understand a history as complex as that of life, we must draw upon theoretical considerations as well as all lines of evidence. Multicellular organisms, that is, animals and plants with more than a single cell in their bodies, are not only larger than protistans, but much more complex. They can differentiate their tissues, as in the wood, leaves, roots, fruits and tubers of plants, for special purposes and they can develop special organs or organ systems as in the gills, digestive tract, blood vessels and sense organs of animals. Protistans must perform all vital functions within their single cell. Among multicellular animals we can distinguish four significant grades of organization and, although the fossil record does not confirm their relative positions in animal phylogeny, we can suggest the evolutionary sequence on the basis of their complexity. Inevitably such an argument always assumes that none has become secondarily simplified. Of all multi-cellular animals, sponges (phylum Porifera) are the most simple in their organization. They do not possess distinct layers of tissue, and the only specializations they have are chambers lined with flagellated cells and, in some, a spicular skeleton. The flagellated cells possess a whip-like organelle, the flagellum, which beats to produce water currents, and they are very similar to free-living flagellated protozoans, some species of which are known to aggregate together to form spherical bundles, but disaggregate and go their own ways at other times. One can imagine a sponge arising by daughter flagellated cells remaining in contact after division and beating their flagella cooperatively to form water currents from which they extracted food and oxygen. Hence from their simplicity of structure and similarity to flagellate protozoans, we believe sponges were the earliest and simplest multicellular animals.

All other multicellular animals have their cells arranged in tissue layers and are collectively called metazoans. The next grade of animal organization is represented by jellyfish and corals (phylum Coelenterata). Coelenterates have two layers of cells, an outer skin or ectoderm and an inner skin or endoderm which is largely digestive. Between the two layers of cells there is a nerve net and some organic material, but no cellular material. This grade of metazoan organization is called diploblastic and contrasts with all other metazoan phyla which have three layers of cells and are described as triploblastic. In triploblasts there is a thick layer of cellular tissue, the mesoderm, between the inner and outer layers. The ectoderm forms the skin, the endoderm the lining of the digestive tract and all the other tissues like muscles, the heart and blood vessels, lungs, kidneys, liver, reproductive organs and even the skeleton in echinoderms and vertebrates, are all differentiated from the mesoderm. You can see that in many animals the mesoderm forms the main mass of the body. All the triploblastic phyla can be further divided into those with internal body cavities, or coeloms as they are known, and those without. Flatworms (phylum Platyhelminthes) characterize acoelomate phyla and are thought to be the most primitive of the triploblasts. Coelomate phyla included segmented worms (annelids), molluscs, arthropods, echinoderms, brachiopods, bryozoans, vertebrates and some other minor phyla. During their development coelomates show at least two different methods by which the coelomic cavities form, so these internal cavities may have arisen independently in different coelomate phyla. The possession of a coelom conveys distinct advantages. If it is fluid-filled, the coelom may act as a hydraulic system, which enables earthworms to move and bivalves to burrow, for example. Equally, circulation systems with fluids pumped around the body, carrying nutrients, oxygen and waste products, develop from coelomic cavities. Thus we think acoelomates preceded coelomates, which arose independently at least twice for functional reasons. This brief outline of animal organization will, I hope, show why zoologists think that protozoans gave rise to sponges on one hand and evolved independently through diploblastic to triploblastic organization on the other hand, the acoelomate flatworms having preceded the coelomate phyla. Regrettably the fossil record does not confirm this pattern for two reasons: first and foremost because the structures are all composed of soft tissue and therefore not normally preservable, and secondly, because even though skeletons are developed in some phyla and therefore we can infer soft tissue structures in fossils, other phyla, notably the flatworms, have not one single species with a skeleton and virtually no fossil record at all. Sponges *may* be present in the Ediacara fauna, while coelenterates are represented by the jellyfish and sea pens and the first coelomates by *Spriggina* and *Dickinsonia*, which are interpreted as segmented worms. Thus, it seems, already by Ediacara times sponges, diploblasts and coelomate triploblasts had evolved.

THE NATURAL HISTORY OF FOSSILS

Cellular organization reflects what we know about living metazoan animals, but the major change in the fossil record at the Precambrian–Cambrian boundary reflects the appearance of skeletons more than anything else. Annelids and coelenterates are fairly certainly represented in the Precambrian; sponges possibly, and one or two other fossils of uncertain affinities, may represent other phyla. In the Cambrian we find undoubted sponges, arthropods, of which the trilobites are the most distinctive but many other classes also occur: echinoderms (four classes in the Lower Cambrian), brachiopods and molluscs (snails, bivalves, cephalopods and several minor extinct classes), plus completely extinct phyla like the Archaeocyatha which were sessile filter-feeding organisms resembling sponges and corals but distinct from either group. Archaeocyathids underwent a major radiation in the Cambrian but did not survive the period. This relatively sudden appearance of many different types of animals reflects a major radiation, but it is known to us because all these diverse groups acquired skeletons at about the same time (the Cambrian lasted about ninety million years). The physiology of skeletal secretion is very different in the different phyla. The position (mesodermal in echinoderms, ectodermal in arthropods, molluscs and brachiopods) and composition (calcite in echinoderms, both carbonates, calcite and aragonite, in molluscs, carbonate or phosphate in brachiopods, carbonate or silica in sponges) differ, so it is hard to imagine that all these different animals acquired the ability to secrete skeletons as the result of a single event unless it was the development of collagen. However, collagen is as vital to flexible hydrostatic skeletons as it is to mineralized skeletons, so this cannot be the answer. It has been argued that the rise in atmospheric oxygen may have provided the right conditions for skeletization, but skeletons would not have evolved just because conditions were right for them. There must have been some positive benefit conferred by a skeleton before selection would operate. A rigid skeleton confers two main advantages on its possessor. First it provides attachment for muscles which can then operate against the rigidity of the skeleton, opening and closing shells, articulating limbs and so on without distorting the whole body. Secondly, if the skeleton encloses the soft tissue it provides protection. While it is true that in coelomates a hydrostatic skeleton will offer resistance to muscular distortion, it provides little protection. To be effective as a protective envelope, a skeleton should completely enclose the soft tissue without any gaps that predators or parasites could exploit. The skeletons of Cambrian trilobites, echinoderms, brachiopods and molluscs generally meet these requirements, although they are often not as efficient as later examples and we can trace distinct improvements in design during the Cambrian and Ordovician in most groups. Nevertheless Cambrian brachiopods, molluscs, arthropods and echinoderms were undoubtedly better protected than any member of the Ediacara fauna. Protection is not only required to ward off predators, but to survive the physical energy of the environment, for example in storms. Associated with skeletization is an increase in infaunal dwelling traces, many of which may have been made by animals without hard skeletons. Indeed R. B. Clark of the University of Newcastle has suggested that the acquisition of a coelom allowed the development of hydraulic burrowing techniques.[11] Be that as it may, the adoption of an infaunal mode of life would provide protection for animals with or without skeletons. Thus, to my mind, one big ecological change from the late Precambrian to the Cambrian is that faunas of the latter period have developed protective structures (skeletons) and behaviour (burrowing in sediments). This, in turn, is likely to reflect the evolution of mobile predators capable of consuming large metazoan prey. Of course other factors must also have been operating. In times of oxygen shortage, modern infaunal organisms come to the surface to breathe, so infaunal behaviour could not have developed until at least the shallow seas were pretty richly supplied with oxygen. The oldest infaunal burrows known are about eight hundred million years old, so we can assume that shallow sea water, into which light penetrates and in which algae could photosynthesize, was adequately oxygenated by this time. Thus the Precambrian–Cambrian transition saw several important developments. Multicellular animals arose and differentiated their tissues into the grades of organization we see now. Community structures developed with predator–prey relationships much the same as those we can recognize in modern oceans. As far as the fossils are concerned, the protective and structural advance represented by the acquisition of skeletons was by far the most obvious and important. It heralded the beginning of the Phanerozoic (visible life) era.

The timing of the appearance of major phyla has been the cause of considerable differences of opinion in evolutionary theory. In the first hundred million years of the Phanerozoic, from six hundred to five hundred million years ago, most modern phyla and classes appear, together with numerous extinct groups. This fact has led many workers to argue that a long Precambrian evolution occurred before the appearance of skeletons enabled the organisms to be preserved. However, we know, from the absence of traces that this early evolution could not have extended more than one to two hundred million years back into the Precambrian. Thus although a time span of three hundred million years is available, still it seems that the Cambrian saw the biggest radiation in the entire fossil record. Radiations are of two types, at low or high taxonomic levels. In low level radiations many new species, genera or even families develop which are effectively variations on a single theme or groundplan. The proliferation of infaunal, irregular echinoids in the Jurassic, or of flowering plants or birds in the Cretaceous, or mammals in the Tertiary, are all of this type. Alternatively, high-level radiations involve the near-simultaneous development of several different groundplans, and the Cambrian radiation of metazoans was undoubtedly of this type.

Some workers have questioned whether evolution, even of sexually reproducing organisms, could proceed fast enough to promote such a diversification of basic groundplans in such a short time. In answer I would say first that two to three hundred million years is not a short time. It represents almost the entire Mesozoic and Tertiary, during which very considerable evolution occurred. The difference is simply that most of Mesozoic and Tertiary evolution involved radiations of the lower type. Moreover, although major groups have evolved, such as birds, mammals, modern hexacorals and articulate crinoids, irregular echinoids, social insects and so on, they did not all evolve at approximately the same time. Secondly, with the natural tendency to over-produce, life will fill up all available space very rapidly. A farmer who ploughs a field and then leaves it fallow will find the most unholy crop of weeds growing within a season. Almost any seed which can get over the fence, so to speak, will survive because there is room for all. Indeed, many plants with wind-blown seeds are adapted to exploit just such opportunities. If the field is left, stronger-growing plants will overshadow low herbs, out-competing them for the vital resource of light, and eliminate them. In southern England, climax oak forest will eventually develop after several decades to a century. Now if we examine the fossil record we find that life has been increasingly successful as measured by the numbers of families or genera, except for the setback at the Permo–Triass life crisis (figure 71). Higher taxa, orders and classes apparently peak in the Lower Palaeozoic, and I believe phyla do too, but we have a tendency to

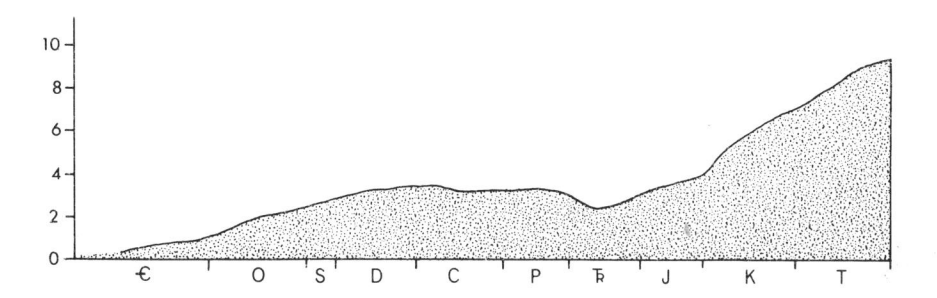

71. The estimated increase in the diversity of life through the Phanerozoic as indicated by number of families. Vertical scale in hundreds. Note that the overall increase was slightly interrupted by the Permo–Triassic life crisis. (After N. D. Newell, 'Crises in the History of Life', *Scientific American*, Feb. 1963.)

ignore small, very distinct groups early in the fossil record and not accept them as phyla. At any rate the basic groundplans of life were very much more varied in the Lower Palaeozoic than they are now. The best model to accommodate these facts is one of initial colonization during which competition and predation are low, followed by retrenchment as competition increased and eliminated the less well adapted. Those that are well adapted increase in numbers at the expense of those which were eliminated. This is exactly what happens in a fallow field and it is, I believe, what has happened in all major radiations. Once organisms have crossed an adaptive threshold (the fence round the field) they have the whole field to themselves, at least for a while.

Now it seems to me that at no time were the opportunities for life greater than in the late Precambrian and early Cambrian, when metazoans first appeared and the entire marine biosphere was open to colonization. Surely it is not surprising that a greater diversification took place at this time than at any other time in the history of life? The only really comparable opportunities since then have been the colonization of land, which gave rise to all terrestrial plant and animal groups, and the recovery after the Permo–Triass life crisis when modern corals and crinoids, among other groups, appear for the first time. The conquest of land gave rise to insects and flowering plants (and there are more species of insects than of all other animal phyla put together), and it all happened in the four hundred million years since the late Silurian. Viewed in this light, the Cambrian radiation is just what I would have expected.

So metazoans and multicellular plants probably arose in a spectactular radiation in the late Precambrian and early Cambrian, but how did they live? Can we say anything about the ecology of the Cambrian and did it differ from that of the present day? Certainly we can apply the same principles of ecological analysis to fossils of the Cambrian that we apply to those of any other system. We can look for *in situ* fossils and attempt to recreate the communities in which they lived. We can also use their morphology to elucidate their modes of life by seeing how they performed the vital functions necessary for survival. In one respect we have been immensely fortunate. The Middle Cambrian Burgess Shale of British Columbia has preserved in it a diverse fauna of soft-bodied organisms which completes the picture we can develop using the skeletized groups. The Burgess Shale fauna includes about a hundred and twenty genera of which arthropods are the most common, forming over one third of the total, although trilobites form only about ten per cent. The next most common groups are a number of worm phyla (together about 23 per cent) and sponges (18 per cent), while all the remaining eight phyla do not include more than five per cent of the fauna each. As far as major feeding types go, the arthropods represent all types, including major predators, to judge from the jaw-like gnathobases on the limbs, while the worms are mostly deposit feeders or scavengers and the sponges filter feeders. Thus we can see that the main feeding types of modern marine animals were present, although filter feeders do not dominate as they do from the Ordovician onwards. The only significant absence is of free-swimming predators like modern fish and cuttlefish. However, the Burgess Shale was deposited after a submarine avalanche (turbidity current) which swept the fauna into deeper water where it was preserved undisturbed. (Could this deeper water have been anaerobic, thereby retarding bacterial decay and allowing soft-bodied organisms to be preserved?). At any rate there is no reason to suppose that free-swimming organisms would have been caught up in the turbidity current and preserved at all. Like the agnostid trilobites in the later Cambrian biomeres, they could have escaped the catastrophe, so their absence in the Burgess Shale need not imply that this niche was unfilled. It certainly was filled by nautiloids by the earliest Ordovician.

If we look at other vital functions, it is possible to show an improvement in protection among Cambrian echinoderms and brachiopods and probably other groups as well. Lower Cambrian echinoderms have some or all of their plates imbricated, in other

THE ORIGIN OF LIFE AND EARLY EVOLUTION

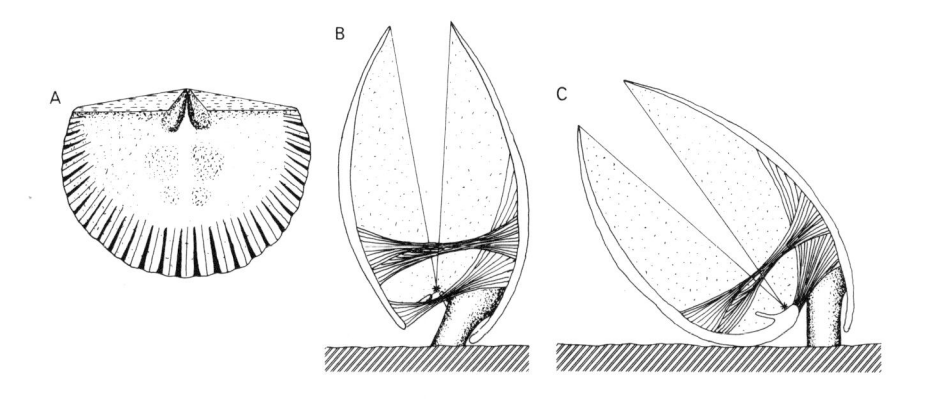

72. Increasingly efficient protection of the divaricator (opening) muscles in early orthids (A and B) and later brachiopods (C). Orthids have a large opening through which the muscles pass (B). In some later brachiopods (C) the point of attachment of the divaricator muscles is tucked into the larger valve and the muscles are better protected. (After M. J. S. Rudwick, *Living and fossil brachiopods*, figs 19b, 20, pp. 56–7, Hutchinson University Library, 1970.)

words they could move over each other slightly and were arranged like the tiles on a roof. Middle Cambrian echinoderms include the first with fully tesselated plates (abutting against each other like bricks in a wall) which formed a rigid skeleton. These plates grew larger and developed strengthening ridges by the end of the Cambrian. The earliest inarticulate brachiopods had thin shells with no hinge structures so that misalignment of the shells was a distinct possibility and a complex musculature was needed to operate the valves. Later, articulate brachiopods arose with more heavily mineralized shells and a hinge line which allowed opening and closing by a much simpler arrangement of muscles. Even here, however, the muscles used in opening the shell passed outside through a large opening and were somewhat exposed. They formed a sort of brachiopod Achilles heel. In the later Palaeozoic periods various modifications to the shell developed which shielded these muscles and, in forms without a straight hinge line, carried the site of attachment inside the shell (figure 72).

Filter-feeding echinoderms trap particles with minute soft-tissue tentacles called tube-feet. In the Lower Cambrian, tube-feet arose directly from the theca or, at most, arose from short finger-like

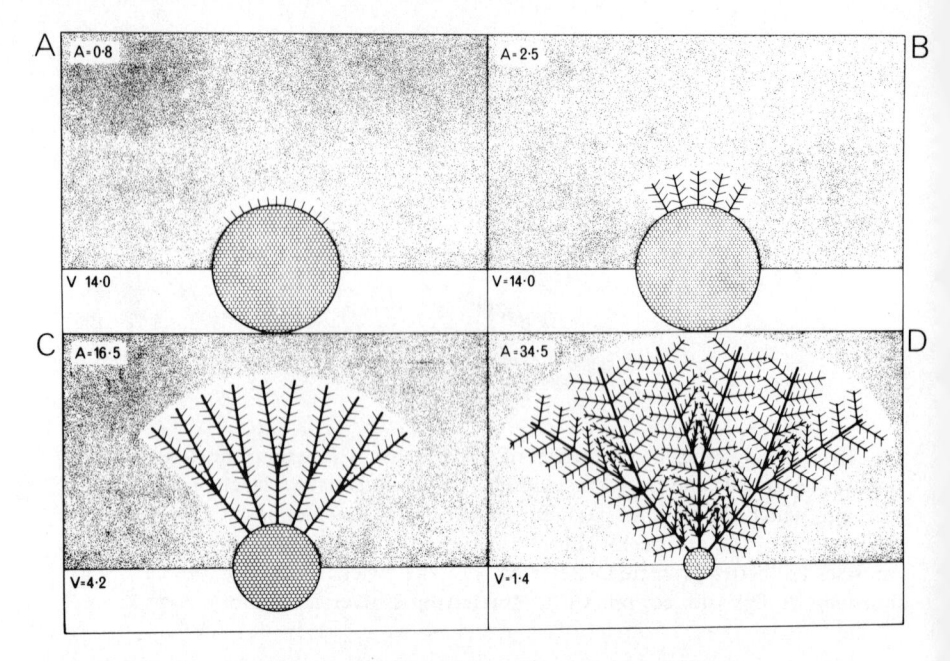

73. The increased efficiency of filter-feeding in Cambrian and Ordovician echinoderms. A. Helicoplacoid grade (Lower Cambrian) with just tube-feet arising from a large theca. B. Blastozoan grade (L. Cambrian–Permian) with tube-feet arising from short unbranched brachioles erect above a large theca. C and D. Crinozoan grade. C. An early crinoid (Lowest Ordovician–Permian) with moderately large theca and branched but non-pinnate arms off which tube-feet arose. D. An advanced crinoid (Upper Ordovician–Present) with very small theca and branched pinnate arms which support the tube-feet. These grades represent an evolutionary trend to increase feeding capacity while reducing feeding requirements. A and V are measures of food-gathering *area* and thecal *volume*, respectively, in arbitrary units. (After C. R. C. Paul, in A. Hallam (ed.), *Patterns of evolution as illustrated by the fossil record*, fig. 5, p. 138, Elsevier, 1967.)

processes called brachioles (figure 73A and B). By the beginning of the Ordovician, extensive branching arms had developed, which allowed a greater volume of water to be filtered and raised the tube-feet well above the level of the theca (figures 73C and D) In turn the theca was often raised off the substrate by a long flexible stalk.

Space precludes a great deal of discussion and these few examples must serve to emphasize two points. One is that the main functional features of many groups, certainly of the echinoderms, evolved early in their history. Very little new happened in echinoderm evolution after the Ordovician. Secondly, by analysing vital functions even in a very general way, it is possible to show how evolution reflects adaptation and hence test Darwin's views about natural selection. For example, all animals need some sort of protection and Cambrian echinoderms and brachiopods were less well protected than later forms. All animals need to feed, and Cambrian filter-feeding echinoderms were less efficient than Ordovician and later forms. Indeed, all animals must perform just six vital functions to survive: feeding, respiration, excretion, protection, growth and reproduction. Metazoans usually have special organ systems to perform these vital functions and sense organs which assist some of them. By analysing how fossils performed each function it is possible to build up a picture of their modes of life. The modes of life of individual species can, in turn, be assembled into an ecological picture or compared through time to produce a functional or adaptational evolutionary model. To my mind there is little point in documenting evolutionary changes using the fossil record if they are not interpreted in terms of adaptation or functional efficiency.

To summarize, life originated on earth between 3,000 and 3,500 million years ago by the process of inorganic evolution. Photosynthesis, with the attendant changes in the oceans and later the atmosphere as well, possibly started more than 3,000 million years ago, but was certainly well under way by 2,000 million years BP. Sexual reproduction probably evolved by a thousand million years ago and may have increased the rate of evolution near the Cambrian–Precambrian boundary when fossils first became abundant mainly due to the acquisition of skeletons, but also due to a genuine increase in the diversity of life forms. We need now to look at the last major event in the history of life – the emergence of life on land.

Chapter 9

Life on land

In the entire history of life on earth there have been three developments of fundamental importance. Although in my opinion the rise, or as Darwin saw it, the descent, of man is not one of them, the last of the three was the most important from our human point of view. The first and most fundamental event was the origin of life and the second the radiation of metazoans at about the Precambrian–Cambrian boundary which gave rise to the variety of animal phyla we know today. We have already discussed these and now pass on to the last, the emergence of life on land, which has given us our world. Scuba diving and other improvements in marine exploration have vastly increased our knowledge of the seas in recent years, but still our world remains essentially a terrestrial one: the world of birds, flowers and trees, pandas and pet rabbits, the slugs that eat our lettuces and the mosquitoes that plague us in summer. None of this world existed before the late Silurian, and all the vascular plants, reptiles, mammals, birds and insects arose as a direct result of the first colonization of land in the Palaeozoic. So in this last chapter I want to consider how life on land, or perhaps it would be better to say *in air*, differs from that under water, how various plants and animals have overcome the difficulties of life in air and, most important of all, why the land was colonized anyway.

So I shall begin with a comparison of marine and terrestrial environments to see what sorts of problems had to be overcome by the first pioneer organisms on land. Some of the problems are also involved in the transition from the sea to freshwater, often seen as the first step to life on land. I shall mention these where appropriate, but it was the transition to fully terrestrial life which posed the more serious difficulties and which is of prime interest to us.

As we have seen, all living creatures have to perform a small number of vital functions in order to survive, but the performance of these functions differs, sometimes considerably, in marine, freshwater and terrestrial environments. Anyone who has been thirsty on a hot day knows that water is vital to survival, and obtaining it on land is not always easy. Furthermore, it supports our weight when we swim so that we can relax or even sleep in a warm sea, but after a hard day's walking we need to 'take the weight off our feet'. These two properties of water affect all other vital activities and there are other problems affecting sense organs. We cannot see, hear or smell very well under water. All sorts of modifications were required to make the transition from water to air. Consider first the problem of respiration which is the most obviously necessary change in moving from an aquatic to a terrestrial mode of life.

Water contains only a small fraction of the amount of oxygen which is available in air. To obtain an adequate supply most aquatic organisms have special structures, gills, with extensive surfaces and a rich blood supply. Gills are usually delicate, feathery structures unable to support themselves out of water. A fish literally 'drowns' out of water in the same way we do in water. It cannot get enough oxygen because all its gill filaments are stuck together. The problem of breathing air is not so much a difficulty in getting hold of oxygen, because it is much more abundantly available than in water, but one of evolving a structure which will not collapse under its own weight. As far as vertebrates are concerned there was no difficulty at all. Several groups of early fish had already developed functional lungs well before the amphibians first appeared. Snails merely modified the mantle cavity in which their original gills were housed, oxygen diffusing through the wall of the mantle cavity instead of through the gill walls. Terrestrial arthropods developed small tubules within their body, called trachea, through which they obtain oxygen. These may be the only air-breathing devices which were exclusively developed for life on land. So in fact the most obvious problem of life on land was not as serious as it might seem. The problems of obtaining, and retaining, water on land are much more serious.

In a marine or freshwater habitat water is all around so obtaining it is no problem at all. Indeed for many freshwater animals, as we shall see, the problem is one of keeping water out. On land, however, water is at best only intermittently available and specialized adaptations have evolved to ensure adequate supplies. Among plants and animals there are two basic ways of adapting to the difficulties of water supply on land. One is behavioural, in which the organisms are either confined to damp locations or, as in the case of desert flowers which bloom after the occasional shower, live out their lives during brief wet spells. The other is to develop special modifications to ensure that water is stored or conserved during times of shortage. The most obvious example is the fleshy tissue of cacti. In the plant world, only the vascular plants have successfully developed structures to ensure water supply on land. All other terrestrial plants are more or less confined to wet habitats. For example, mosses and liverworts (the bryophytes) are not very well adapted to life on land. They have no special structures to obtain or transport water, rarely exceed thirty centimetres in height and are confined to wet habitats. They represent the plant equivalents of amphibians among vertebrates and are equally tied to water for reproduction. The vascular plants, on the other hand, have roots which are specialized to extract water and nutrients from the soil. They also have a vascular system, as the name 'vascular plants' implies, which consist of tubes within the stem that transport water up from the roots to the leaves where it is required for photosynthesis. Food manufactured in the leaves is also transported around the plant by the vascular system to feed growing tissues, including those of the roots. By means which are still not fully understood, vascular plants are able to pump water up against the pull of gravity as much as 120 metres in the tallest trees. The possession of roots and a vascular system has enabled the vascular plants to colonize all sorts of terrestrial habitats except the very coldest. Even the driest of habitats in deserts can be colonized by plants which either store water, as cacti do, or lie dormant as seeds until the rains come. These plants all belong to the last two major groups of terrestrial plants to evolve, the gymnosperms and angiosperms, both of which bear seeds.

In contrast to plants most animals have no organs which are primarily specialized to obtain water. They take it in with their food or by drinking directly. A few desert rodents do not normally drink at all but obtain their water from the carbohydrates in their food, which consists mainly of seeds. Invertebrates have been less successful in overcoming the problems of water conservation, and many are confined to wet habitats. All worms and gastropod molluscs have permeable skins and lose water rapidly in dry environments. Snails have shells into which they can retire and many seal off the aperture with a temporary lid of hardened mucus called an epiphragm. Others have retained the operculum, the permanent horny or calcareous lid which is carried on the back of the foot and which closes the aperture when the snail retracts. By means of the epiphragm some desert snails can survive periods of two to three years in a dormant state without emerging from their shells. One story has it that some specimens in a museum got up and walked away after several years on display, much to the astonishment of the curator! Certainly I have had snails from Spanish Morocco which remained dormant for a year before I discovered that they were alive. Slugs, which have no shell or just tiny vestiges of one, can only reduce water loss by behavioural adaptations, paramount among which is their great ability to distort their bodies. This enables them to squeeze into small crevices, including cracks in the soil or under the bark of fallen logs and so keep to the dampest locations during dry weather. Nevertheless, slugs are much more drought-sensitive than snails. Insects reduce water loss by having waxy skins through which very little moisture evaporates, but other arthropods like woodlice (isopods) have no such adaptations and again are generally confined to damp habitats. Among the vertebrates, amphibians are least well adapted since they have permeable skins, but reptiles, birds and mammals have their bodies covered with a generally impervious epidermis.

Water loss occurs not only due to evaporation from the body surface, but from other vital activities as well. Respiration, excretion and, in 'warm-blooded' animals like ourselves, temperature control by sweating, all involve water loss. Special adaptations have evolved in most terrestrial organisms to reduce water loss caused by these other necessary activities. Respiratory surfaces, by their very nature, allow diffusion through them and are generally kept moist anyway. As carbon dioxide diffuses out, so do water molecules. Unless the air surrounding the organism is saturated with water, is holding as much water vapour as it is able to, there will be a net loss of water during respiration. The condensation of our breath on a winter's morning is direct confirmation of this. Various mechanisms have arisen to reduce this loss of water. In the leaves of vascular plants are small pores, called stomata, which allow direct connection with the surrounding atmosphere. During respiration and photosynthesis gases diffuse into and out of the stomata, the entrances of which are surrounded by two guard cells. These are kidney-shaped cells which respond to atmospheric humidity. When the air is dry they straighten out and close the stomata. Of course closure of the stomata on a dry day not only conserves water but also reduces the rate of photosynthesis and respiration.

The adaptations of pulmonate snails to reduce water loss during respiration include the possession of a respiratory pore which is closed most of the time. Terrestrial (and some freshwater) snails take a gulp of air every few minutes, but otherwise the lung remains closed to the atmosphere. Some terrestrial snails have developed the lung as a secondary water store, and keep it partially flooded with water. Most terrestrial arthropods, including the ubiquitous insects, breath by means of a system of tubules, called trachea, within their bodies which open at the surface in spiracles. Like the guard cells on the stomata of leaves, the spiracles can be opened and closed to balance water conservation against respiratory needs. Man has taken advantage of this in some insect sprays which kill their victims by closing the spiracles permanently and hence choking the insects to death. Woodlice have 'pseudotrachea', a similar system of tubules, developed in what are the gills of aquatic forms. Although it has yet to be proved that the entrances of the pseudotrachea of woodlice can be closed, somehow they reduce respiratory water loss in dry conditions. Most vertebrates cannot close their respiratory orifices, but water loss is reduced in some desert-dwelling mammals by extensive folded mucous membranes in the nasal passages. Inhaled air evaporates moisture from the membranes thereby cooling them. The evaporated water passes into the lungs and is returned across the cooled membranes on exhaling. Because the membranes are cool, the moisture condenses again which gives off heat that is partly carried away by the exhaled air. Measurements of higher temperatures in exhaled air than inhaled air, both well above body temperature, show that some desert rodents may actually gain small amounts of moisture by this means; certainly they do not lose much. The drips that form on the ends of our noses in winter arise by the same process.

To a physiologist excretion is more concerned with the removal of the by-products of metabolism than with the voiding of that portion of the food which cannot be absorbed in the gut. Both involve water loss, but the former is related to the general problem of controlling blood concentration. Blood is a solution of various dissolved chemicals as well as a suspension of living cells, the corpuscles. The blood of many animals has a concentration very much the same as that of sea water, and this is sometimes taken to be evidence that animal life arose in the sea. Whatever its strength, the precise concentration is critical and significant variations from normal are usually fatal. All animals have mechanisms for controlling the concentration of their blood. In man it is the kidneys, and the process is called osmoregulation. We need to understand a little about osmosis itself before we can appreciate the differences in osmoregulation among marine, freshwater and terrestrial animals. All solutions consist of something dissolved, called the solute, in a liquid, called the solvent. When two solutions with the same solvent, such as water, come into contact across a semi-permeable membrane, the solvent migrates through the membrane from the weaker to the more concentrated solution until the concentrations are equal. This phenomenon is called osmosis. It does not matter what the solute is, or even if there is a mixture of solutes; osmosis takes place if the concentrations of the solutions differ. A semi-permeable membrane is one that allows solvent, but not solute, molecules to diffuse through it. It is this property, found in many plant and animal membranes, which explains osmosis, although it may seem mysterious at first sight. As an example, imagine a dilute solution containing ten per cent table salt in water, separated from pure water by a semi-permeable membrane as in figure 74. The membrane will allow water molecules to diffuse through it in either direction, but the salt molecules cannot pass through it at all. Now suppose in a given time ten water molecules diffuse through the membrane from the pure water to the solution. In that same period of time ten molecules will attempt to diffuse from the solution to the pure water, but as every tenth molecule is a salt molecule, only nine water molecules will get

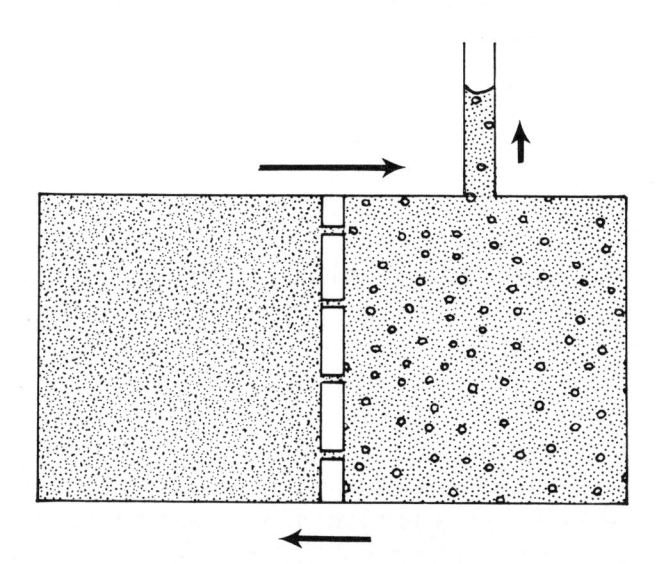

74. Osmosis. The level of fluid on the right rises because water can diffuse more rapidly from the left to right than the other way. The large solute molecules 'dilute' the solvent molecules in the solution to the right.

through. Thus in the time it takes ten molecules to diffuse from pure water to the solution, only nine molecules can diffuse the other way and the solution will have effectively gained a molecule of solvent. If you like to think of it that way, the salt has 'diluted' the water making less of it available for diffusion. So osmosis is just the process by which pure solvent diffuses through a semi-permeable membrane faster than solvent mixed in a solution and the difference in the diffusion rates, or the osmotic pressure as it is called, is directly proportional to the difference in concentration on either side of the membrane.

Now perhaps we can see why blood is the same concentration as sea water. In marine animals this means that diffusion of water will take place at equal rates into and out of the animal so that it need not expend any energy at all maintaining its blood concentration. Marine animals only need to clean their blood so that their 'kidneys' are purely excretary organs. In fresh water, which is never pure, but contains a minute amount of dissolved salts compared with sea water, a problem of osmoregulation occurs. Sometimes the problem is avoided, as in the freshwater mussel, *Anodonta*, which has very dilute blood of the same concentration as the rivers and lakes in which it lives. Such weak blood is not very efficient at transporting oxygen or nutrients, however. The difference in blood concentrations of freshwater and marine animals is the main reason why they cannot move freely between the two habitats. A freshwater animal plunged into the sea is desiccated by osmosis as the water diffuses from its dilute internal fluids to the more concentrated sea water. On the other hand a marine organism, or an animal with concentrated blood, placed in freshwater has its internal fluids continually diluted by osmosis and will swell up and burst. So any freshwater animal which has blood more concentrated than its surroundings must continually pump water out of its body against the natural osmotic seepage. Its kidneys must act like the bilge pumps of a leaky old ship fighting a never-ending battle against invading water. Such kidneys are adapted to maintain blood concentration as well as to remove impurities from the blood. Fish like salmon and eels which spend part of their lives in both fresh water and the sea usually wait for a few days in estuaries modifying their blood concentration to adapt to the change in environment. Salmon which pass from fresh to salt water store urea, the main by-product of metabolism, in their blood until the concentration reaches that of sea water. Again I emphasize it does not matter what is dissolved so long as the total concentration is the same as that of the surrounding fluid. On the return journey urea is pumped out of the blood to dilute it again. Freshwater organisms armed with a kidney that can retain or pump out water are to some extent preadapted to the transition to land. This is one of the reasons why some scientists believe the transition to land was made via fresh water.

If we drink a lot it isn't long before our kidneys react and we need to pass water. The urine is dilute and osmoregulation is the main function performed. If, on the other hand, we haven't had a drink all day and it has been hot so we have sweated a lot, we will pass very little urine and it will be concentrated. Excretion is then the main function and our kidneys are so efficient that they can produce urine which is more concentrated than the blood, thereby saving water. Birds are even more efficient and excrete metabolic by-products in the form of uric acid which is voided with very little water indeed. Most is excreted as minute crystals. Thus the tendency to desiccate on land necessitates an efficient kidney even if the skin is impermeable to water.

The danger that an adult terrestrial organism will dry out on land is even more marked for a single cell and this applies to genital products, eggs and sperm, just as much as it does to free living protozoans. Most marine invertebrates and many fish reproduce by simply shedding vast numbers of eggs and sperm into the sea and relying on chance for fertilization. The only behavioural modification they exhibit which enhances the chances of successful fertilization is simultaneous shedding. Sea urchins and starfish, for example, release a shedding substance with their genital products which stimulates other mature adults of the same species in the immediate vicinity to shed as well. The fertilized eggs of most marine invertebrates develop into larvae covered with tiny hair-like structures, called cilia, which beat continuously and keep the larvae afloat for a period of a few days to a few weeks. So the sea water provides not only the medium for fertilization but the mechanism of dispersal as well. The planktonic larval stage is vital to the dispersal of sessile marine organisms like corals, or brachiopods, but is just as important to those which can move slowly as adults, like snails and bivalves. On land fertilization just cannot take place this way although many plants rely on the wind for dispersal. Wind pollination, which most closely resembles marine fertilization in that pollen is just shed, depends on the sperm being packaged in a special waterproof capsule, the pollen grain. Even in fresh water a ciliated larval stage is not too effective as a means of dispersal since it may be swept down stream into the sea. Certainly dispersal could only be downstream. Freshwater animals tend to suppress the ciliated larval stage or pass through it within the egg capsule as many freshwater snails do. Freshwater mussels of the family Unionidae have developed a very ingenious means of overcoming the dispersal problem. They produce a small bivalved larva, called a glochidium, which parasitizes fish. Since fish naturally swim upstream the glochidia tend to be dropped upstream at the end of their parasitic phase. In the female mussel, eggs pass to the gills where they are fertilized and brooded until the glochidia are fully developed. Glochidia are released when a fish approaches or, sometimes, when the temperature rises. In the presence of a fish they flap their valves vigorously, shooting out a sticky thread. If the thread touches a fish it sticks and the glochidia hitch a ride. At least one fish repays the compliment and broods its young in the gills of freshwater mussels. The freshwater mussel *Dreissena*, which lives attached to piles and rocks and strongly resembles the marine mussel *Mytilus*, retains the free-swimming larval stage and is thought to have adapted to fresh water relatively recently. *Dreissena* can only live in lakes and slow-flowing canals as a result of its larval development.

Even if dispersive larvae are a disadvantage in fresh water, fertilization itself is as easy as it is in the sea. On land, fertilization poses serious problems, and requires specialized structures and complex behaviour patterns in both animals and plants. Bryophytes (mosses and liverworts) are confined to damp places because they rely on water for fertilization. The sperm are motile and literally swim to the eggs in the thin film of water on the surface of a wet plant. Dry out the plant and reproduction just cannot take place. Mosses have alternation of generations in which one form of the plant, the gametophyte, produces eggs and sperm for sexual reproduction, while the other form, the sporophyte, produces spores which are dispersed by the wind and represent an asexually reproducing phase. In mosses most of the plant that we recognize is the gametophyte, so called because it produces gametes, that is, eggs and sperm, and the sporophyte is represented by the small capsules hanging above the moss at certain times of the year. Ferns are close to the most primitive vascular plants and have overcome some of the difficulties of living on land by reversing the sizes of the sporophyte and gametophyte. The large plants we recognize as ferns are the sporophytes and can live in dry habitats, as bracken, *Pteridium aquilinum*, does on heaths. Nevertheless, the small gametophyte generation is still confined to damp places. In land plants the real breakthrough came with the appearance of pollen and seeds. Pollen grains are minute, very resistant capsules which contain individual sperm and protect them from desiccation. Pollen can be cast to the wind just as sperm is shed into the ocean. Flowering plants have also taken advantage of insects to disperse their pollen. However it is transported, on arrival at another flower the pollen grain grows a minute tube which penetrates the ovary and allows the sperm to fertilize the ovules or eggs. Botanists regard the pollen tube as all that is left of the sexually reproducing generation of plants like mosses and ferns. The main flowering plant is the spore-bearing generation and it produces two types of spores, microspores, i.e. pollen, and megaspores called ovules, which develop into seeds after fertilization. The seeds are themselves an excellent adaptation to life on land since they can survive desiccation, cold and other hazards much better than any plant can.

The problems of reproduction on land are no less for animals. The main problem is one of getting sperm transferred safely to the eggs and has been overcome by copulation. Although copulation and internal development occur in some marine and freshwater animals as an alternative reproductive pattern to shedding, it is absolutely vital to, and universal among, terrestrial animals. Copulation not only requires special organs to effect the transfer, the penis of males and the vagina of females, but also highly modified behaviour. Recognition of the opposite sex of the same species becomes important. From the point of view of survival, it is a complete waste of time courting an animal of another species. In those species which have sexual phases, recognition of a partner who is ready to mate also becomes important. Sex attractants are used by most insects and a newly hatched female moth is said to be able to attract a mate over a distance of two or three kilometres. Sexual reproduction on land has opened up the whole gamut of courtship displays, which are such a feature of birds and mammals but are also found in numerous invertebrates, such as the fiddler crabs, *Uca*. Some slugs of the family Limacidae go through the most unbelievable courtship and copulatory antics. Courtship behaviour has led to sexual selection where individuals of whichever sex displays or assumes the aggressive role (usually but not always the male) are selected by the opposite sex, not necessarily because they are the fittest, but because they are the most attractive. However, an unfit male is hardly likely to survive long enough to display in the first place. It is interesting to note that although a successful male may wind up with a large harem and defend it vigorously against the approaches of other males, it is the females who actually choose to become part of the harem. In the male-dominated world of the nineteenth century T. H. Huxley, Darwin's strongest supporter, doubted the validity of Darwin's arguments about sexual selection because he didn't think that females were able to make such a choice!

Perhaps because of the difficulties of mating on land, many invertebrates mate only once. The male transfers a packet of sperm which is retained by the female and used to fertilize all her eggs over the entire laying period. Other terrestrial invertebrates, such as most slugs and snails, are hermaphrodite, having both male and female reproductive organs in the same individual. When snails mate, both partners act as male and female. Sperm packages are transferred to both partners, which then go their own way, each to deposit fertilized eggs. The problems of reproduction on land do not end with successful fertilization. If eggs are deposited they must be kept moist, and we find the whole range of behaviour from total abandonment at laying to the intense parental care of bees or humans. In vertebrates the great step forward, comparable to the development of pollen and seeds in plants, was the appearance of the amniotic egg. The eggs of amphibians, like frogspawn, are just unprotected cells in a jelly-like mass. The eggs of a reptile or bird have a tough but porous outer shell, lined inside with a special membrane, the amnion, which allows respiratory gas exchange but conserves moisture. This development freed vertebrates once and for all from the need to return to water to reproduce. Nature with her perversity has ensured that some amphibians behave atypically. Most have courtship displays and some internal fertilization. The European salamander even bears live young, but nevertheless most amphibians, fossil or recent, are only able to reproduce in water. The possession of warm blood requires that most birds incubate their eggs, while mammals have adopted the alternative of internal development and bear live young.

The second effect of water is to give support or buoyancy to the body. As we have seen, this not only affects the main body but delicate organs like gills as well. Support for the main body of a plant comes from the development of woody tissue in the stems and branches. The largest seaweed, the giant kelp *Macrocystis*, is said to reach two hundred metres in length but has no support problems; nor does a whale, for that matter. In contrast, the tallest trees reach 120 metres and rise on massive trunks anchored by extensive root systems. Wood is a natural example of a class of materials called *composites*. Composites combine the strength of a brittle component, like glass, with the resilience of a softer bonding medium like resin, as in fibreglass, a man-made composite, to produce a material which is both stronger and more resilient than either component alone. The ultimate strength of a composite is determined by the shape and orientation of the brittle component, which may be granular as in concrete or tar-macadam, fibrous as in fibreglass or wood, or sheet-like as in laminated plastics or plywood. In a fibrous composite the strength is directly related to the length and orientation of the fibres. Wood has fibres arranged in three dimensions. Short fibres radiate out from the centre of the trunk, while longer fibres and the water-carrying vessels are arranged along the length. Now it is more difficult to break across the fibres of any fibrous composite than to crack between them. Anyone who has done any carpentry knows that wood has a grain to it. This simply reflects the greater strength needed to resist stresses imposed by the trunk bending along its length in the wind. Almost all skeletal materials in the organic world are composites of one sort or another.

For animals, emerging on land produces load-bearing problems which become progressively more severe the larger the animal. Furthermore, as D'Arcy Thompson pointed out earlier this century,[1] these problems increase exponentially. The weight of an animal is proportional to its volume, while the load-bearing capacity of a bone, for example, is proportional to its cross-sectional area. Double the size of the animal and its strength increases fourfold, but its weight goes up eight times. Since most invertebrates are small, lack of the support given by water is rarely a problem for them. Spiders may adopt the most unsuitable means of supporting their bodies on widely splayed legs, without overtaxing the strength of their limbs (figure 75), but most terrestrial vertebrates could not take up such a position even briefly. If we consider only support, the legs of early amphibians

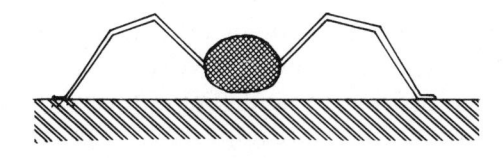

75. The gait of a spider in front view. The body is suspended from the legs. If spiders were much larger the legs could never take the strain of this posture.

and reptiles were not well adapted to life on land. They were splayed out at the sides and most of the time the bodies rested on the ground. We can see this still in newts and lizards which raise their bodies off the ground to run, but soon tire and for most of the time rest their weight directly on the ground. Advanced reptiles like dinosaurs, as well as mammals and birds, adopted a much more efficient load-bearing posture with the legs swung under the body; this is also related to changes in locomotion.

The backbone and limb girdles are also modified in terrestrial vertebrates as part of the support system for the body. In quadrupeds the skeleton is analogous to a bridge, with the limbs as the supports and the backbone, neck and tail as the spans of the bridge. Just as a suspension bridge has ties holding the parts together, the backbone has ligaments passing between the processes on the vertebrae to transmit tensile stresses. These are generally absent in fish skeletons and reflect the supporting function of the backbone in terrestrial vertebrates.

In animals the mechanisms for supporting the body are also related to those involved in locomotion. Again this is less of a problem for small terrestrial invertebrates than for the larger vertebrates. Most fish swim by rhythmic contractions of the blocks of muscles on either side of the body which produce sinuous undulations of the whole body. Fish are generally flattened from side to side so that the undulations react against the fairly viscous water to produce forward propulsion. The locomotion of the earliest tetrapods and that of newts and lizards at the present day is little modified from the basic fish undulations. The prime difference is that limbs project on either side (figure 76). We can imagine, by watching a newt, the slow and ponderous movements of the first amphibians dragging themselves over the mud as they emerged from pools. An immediate effect of the increased weight of the body on land is that it becomes compressed dorso-ventrally rather than from side to side as in fish. The earliest known fossil amphibians already have their bodies dorso-ventrally flattened, despite their other strong resemblances to their fish ancestors.

Apart from the main two effects of leaving water, the danger of desiccation and lack of support, several other problems arise in attempting the transition to land. Some forms of aquatic feeding, such as ciliary filter feeding, are impossible in air. It is true that birds like swallows (*Hirundo rustica*) and many bats filter feed from aerial plankton (insects) in the same way that true whales filter oceanic

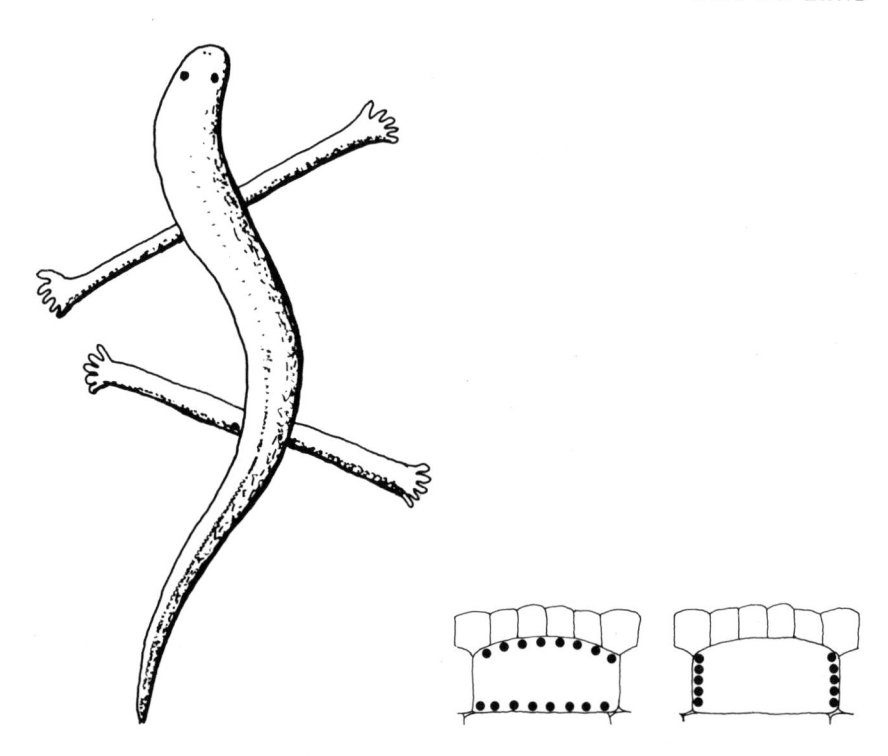

76. The gait of a newt or lizard; it involves basically the same undulations as occur in the body of a swimming fish, but with limbs protruding from the body. Real limbs are, of course, capable of more independent movement than shown.

77. The positions of chloroplasts in cells of the leaves of duckweed (*Lemna*) in A, weak light and B, strong light. (After C. L. Duddington, *Evolution in plant design*, fig. 20, p. 94, 1969.)

plankton, while web-spinning spiders are passive filter feeders analogous to sea pens or crinoids in the oceans. Nevertheless, these animals have developed their own means of filter feeding in the air, and no exclusively filter-feeding aquatic group, like bivalves, brachiopods or crinoids, has made the transition to land. The earliest terrestrial animals were vegetarians, carnivores or deposit feeders. Feeding on land presents no problem for green plants once an adequate supply of water is safeguarded.

Another problem concerns radiation and body temperature control. Water absorbs the sun's rays much more than air and, even in the clearest seas, light does not penetrate more than sixty metres or so. Exposed on land, animals and plants have to deal with much more intense radiation. For most plants there is little problem as they thrive on sunlight. Even so, leaves can overheat on a sunny day and the chloroplasts adopt different positions with the leaf cells of some plants in conditions of shade compared with their positions in intense light (figure 77). Animals are more sensitive to intense radiation, and develop protective pigments in their skins. Heat is associated with the light from the sun and this also poses problems in adapting to a subaerial existence. Apart from a few mammals like whales and seals, aquatic animals are cold-blooded – or more correctly poikilothermic. Their blood and bodies take up the temperature of their surroundings. In most aquatic environments short-term temperature changes are small. Even in a rock pool filled with cool sea water at high tide and exposed to the full heating effect of the sun during the day, the temperature range is unlikely to exceed 15°C, and most large bodies of water would not change by more than a tenth of this in a day. On land, daily temperature variations may exceed 25°C in deserts and in mid-latitudes will normally range over 15°C. The annual variation in continental climates may well exceed 50°C. Animals may avoid these extreme variations behaviourally, by burrowing underground in deserts or seeking out shade in other areas during the hottest part of the day. Structural and physiological modifications also occur and these are the only defences plants have, being unable to move. Pelycosaurs (figure 78), a peculiar group of Permian reptiles on the line leading to the mammals, had a remarkable sail-like dorsal fin. It has been suggested that it may have been used to help control the reptile's body temperature. With the fin broadside on to the sun, a pelycosaur would absorb heat quickly, while at noon it could turn to face the sun so that the fin was edge-on to the sun's rays and radiated heat from the body. The peculiar dorsal bones along the backbone of the dinosaur, *Stegosaurus*, are also interpreted as having served the same basic function. The most obvious physiological adaptation to body temperature control on land is warm-bloodedness or homiothermy. In warm-blooded animals the body remains at the same temperature irrespective of conditions outside the body. Warm-blooded animals are more active than cold ones, which is why snakes and lizards bask in the sun. Although it requires more energy and hence more food to maintain body temperature against the ambient temperature, homiotherms gain by controlling their body chemistry more efficiently. Many enzymes, the organic catalysts in our bodies, are particularly temperature-sensitive so that prolonged deviations of body temperature by only 5°C are usually fatal. Some vital reactions

78. (*left*) A pelycosaur to show the enormous dorsal sail. (After an original drawing by Dr T. Kemp in Rhoda H. Black, *The elements of palaeontology*, fig. 16od, p. 259, Cambridge University Press, 1972.

79. (*right*) *Rhynia*, one of the earliest emergent plants, from the Lower Devonian Rhynie Chert of Scotland. (A. Lee McAlester, *The history of life*, © 1968, Prentice-Hall Inc., New Jersey.)

virtually cease if the temperature falls below a certain level. Thus poikilotherms can only carry out certain processes in warm weather, while homiotherms can do so all the time. Insulating material like fur or feathers is developed to reduce heat loss in homiotherms, while sweat glands help to disperse surplus heat on hot days. The latter, of course, means a loss of some water and body salts. Some desert animals achieve a compromise between the needs of temperature control and water loss. The camel's body temperature may rise by 2–3 °C during very hot spells as a means of reducing water loss due to sweating.

Finally, the functioning of many sense organs differs in air and in water. Light, sound and tiny traces of compounds that can be smelt all travel at different rates and intensities in the two media. As we all know, light is bent, or refracted, when it enters or leaves water. Open your eyes under water and although you can see, everything is blurred and it is difficult to judge distances. Our eyes are adapted to see in air, a fish's to see in water. Furthermore, a delicate organ like an eye is kept moist in water, but not in air. Tear glands and ducts and protective eyelids are structures developed to cope with vision in air.

Sound is transmitted much more easily in water than in air and the 'ears' of aquatic animals tend to be relatively clumsy structures compared with the delicate structures in mammals, especially those with acute hearing like bats. Sound is important to some invertebrates; for example, stridulation of crickets and cicadas is a means of specific identification in courtship, but the mechanisms of sound reception are not well understood. Vertebrate ears are concerned with balance as well as sound. It seems likely that fish ears are primarily organs of balance and, as we shall see, fish have other means of detecting pressure changes in water. In terrestrial vertebrates a membrane is present, the tympanic membrane or eardrum, which receives the delicate vibrations travelling through the air. Amphibians and reptiles have a single bone which amplifies and transmits these vibrations to the inner ear where they are heard. Mammals have three bones, the *incus*, the *malleus* and the *stapes*, for the same purpose. The changes in the function of these bones from gill arches in jawless fish, through jaw structures in bony fish, to their final position in the middle ear of mammals, is one of the more remarkable stories of vertebrate evolution.

If the ears of fish are primarily for maintaining balance, the lateral line system contains abundant pressure receptors which probably detect sound waves as well. The lateral line system consists of a series of pits or canals along the side of the body and over the head, which carry organs sensitive to disturbances in the water. The basic sensory receptor is called a neuromast and very similar structures are found in the semi-circular canals of the ear, where they detect changes in orientation. Neuromasts consist of a blob of jelly connected to the skin of the fish by a bundle of fine hair-like threads and one special thread which strongly resembles a cilium. If a change in the water pressure moves the jelly, as for example when the fish begins to swim, the special thread increases or decreases the frequency of electrical impulses sent down the nerve which connects with the neuromast. Neuromasts may occur on the surface or within the canals of the lateral line system. The latter are more useful in detecting local disturbances of water such as are made by the approach of prey or predators. Blind fish can avoid objects without touching them, and may well do this using the concentration of lateral line canals over the head. When the bow wave of a swimming fish encounters a solid object it is reflected, causing a slight pressure change which the neuromasts on the head probably detect. At any rate for our purposes the lateral line system is a purely aquatic sensory system unknown in any terrestrial vertebrate. The well developed lateral line canals of some fossil and living amphibians are a good indication of their return to a permanently aquatic mode of life.

The sense of smell is not fully understood, perhaps because it is not very important to humans. There is no doubt that the antennae of moths, for instance, or the complexly folded mucous membranes in the nostrils of some terrestrial vertebrates, are closely related to smell. Detection of smell under water seems to be achieved by simple pits in the heads of fish. In terrestrial vertebrates, not surprisingly, smells are detected in the inhalant air stream. The modification of nostrils so that they open internally, allowing air flow without opening the mouth, is a case of what is called pre-adaptation. Many bony fish developed lungs and internal nostrils long before the first amphibians evolved. The ability to breathe air, and possibly a fully terrestrial sense of smell, were both developed long before amphibians required them to live permanently on land. Many freshwater fish and snails even today have lungs in addition to, or instead of, gills. They come to the surface and gulp air periodically, which enables them to survive in stagnant water where purely gill-breathing fish and snails cannot survive. In both groups the presence of air bubbles in a lung or gas gland is also associated with buoyancy, and it is not easy to be certain which function came first. In fish it is assumed respiration preceded buoyancy and this may well have been the case with some freshwater snails. Many freshwater snails are thought to be terrestrial forms which returned to an aquatic mode of life, although this need not necessarily be the case. The great ramshorn snail, *Planorbarius corneus*, seems to have gone full cycle, losing its original gills, developing a lung and then returning to water and evolving a secondary false gill. *P. corneus* lives in rather stagnant habitats and the possession of its false gill enables it to make less frequent trips to the surface to breathe than other pond snails with which it lives, like *Lymnaea peregra* or *L. palustris*.

The purpose of this fairly extensive review of the problems involved in the transition from an aquatic to a terrestrial mode of life is to emphasize that the change could not have taken place at one go. It is not just a matter of breathing through lungs rather than gills.

Secondly, these problems needed to be overcome by plants and invertebrates as well as by vertebrates. In most discussions of the transition to life on land only the latter are considered. The rewards of life on land are evident when one considers the groups that have made the adaptation successfully. The vertebrates, molluscs and arthropods are the principal animal groups on land, while the bryophytes and tracheophytes are the main plant groups. It is true that some algae and animal protistans, fungi, worms and so on occur on land, but most are confined almost entirely to very damp habitats. For example, I have found alive the minute freshwater bivalves *Pisidium obtusale* and *P. personatum* in damp ground under which moles had burrowed in Hayley Wood, Cambridgeshire. While this is hardly a freshwater habitat, I would not want to argue from these exceptional occurrences that bivalves were adapted to life on land. Accepting, then, that the vascular plants, molluscs, arthropods and vertebrates are the principal terrestrial phyla, it is significant that the arthropods and molluscs are the two largest animal phyla in terms of numbers of species and that this is largely due to the proliferation of the insects and land snails. Equally, vascular plants outnumber most other plant phyla. Those organisms that have made the change have proliferated spectacularly. However, organisms other than man cannot reason. The mere fact that once on land insects, for example, have radiated until they outnumber all other animals is, in itself, no reason why arthropods should have adapted to life on land in the first place. Joshua may have realized that if he captured Jericho it would be the vital first step to inheriting the Promised Land, but no arthropod, mollusc or plant could have realized what lay ahead when it made the first transitional steps towards life on land. So we come again to the 'when' and 'why' of the emergence of life on land. The 'when' is fairly certain, the 'why' less so, although I think a plausible sequence of events can be outlined. First the 'when'. What fossil evidence do we have on the evolution of life on land?

The fossil record of the groups most intimately involved in the transition – insects, land snails, non-woody plants, – is not normally considered to be good. However, we do have some evidence to date the first appearances. Some of the earliest undoubted vascular plants occur in freshwater cherts near Rhynie in Scotland. Because they are freshwater deposits it is difficult to correlate them accurately and they have been variously assigned to the Upper Silurian or Lower Devonian. Either way, at about this time, approximately four hundred million years ago, undoubted vascular plants and some

LIFE ON LAND

primitive insect-like arthropods had evolved. *Rhynia* (figure 79, page 263), a primitive psilopsid fern from the Rhynie Chert, had no leaves, but the stems branched dichotomously and bore spore-producing structures at their tips. The plants were up to thirty centimetres or so high and emerged from the water. *Rhynia* also reproduced vegetatively by means of a branching rhizome-like structure. In among the plants of the Rhynie Chert are found some of the first terrestrial arthropods. The first undoubted amphibians, the ichthyostegids (figure 80), occur in the Upper Devonian of Greenland, while the first undoubted land snails (figure 81) come from the Carboniferous of North America. These events seem to follow on in a fairly short period of time and, I suspect, are probably related. Incidentally, the first freshwater bivalve, *Archanodon*, occurs in the Devonian of Ireland. Finally, let us examine the problem of why life should have adapted to conditions on land.

The transition from fish to amphibian is the best documented of any emerging terrestrial group. We know that the predecessors of *Ichthyostega*, the first amphibian, were a group of bony fish called rhipidisteans, with functional lungs, internal openings to the nostrils and fleshy lobes at the bases of the fins like the modern coelacanth, *Latimeria*. We can even match up the limb bones of the ichthyostegans with those of the fleshy fin lobes in rhipidisteans. Now it is well known that lungfish are adapted to stagnant water. By breathing air some of them even survive temporary drying out of the

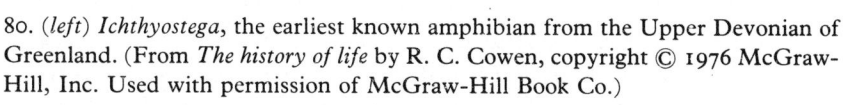

80. (*left*) *Ichthyostega*, the earliest known amphibian from the Upper Devonian of Greenland. (From *The history of life* by R. C. Cowen, copyright © 1976 McGraw-Hill, Inc. Used with permission of McGraw-Hill Book Co.)

81. (*right*) *Anthracopupa*, one of the first land snails from the Upper Carboniferous of Ohio, USA. (After G. A. Solem, *The shell makers. Introducing molluscs*, fig. 2, p. 175, John Wiley & Sons, 1974.)

pools in which they live. They form a cocoon-like structure in the bottom mud and await the onset of the next rains. This idea has been advanced as an explanation of the evolution of amphibians. It has been suggested that the ability to crawl using the fleshy fin lobes and to breathe air may have enabled the proto-amphibians to survive in near desert conditions by moving from a pool that was drying up to one that was more permanent. The trouble with this idea is that it is logical but animals are not. A prospector in the American West sitting by a water hole that was drying up would know that unless he moved or rain fell he would die. He could weigh up the chances of either event happening and act accordingly, but no animal can do this. Anyone who has watched any freshwater animals suffering desiccation knows that they literally cling for dear life to the last vestiges of water. Only the threat of imminent death would drive an animal away from a drying pool, and we have fossil evidence of mass deaths under precisely these circumstances. Certainly the ability to disperse from pool to pool during the wet seasons would have increased the chances of some proto-amphibian's finding a pool that was permanent through the dry season, but this still does not provide positive selection for better locomotion on land. To my mind there had to be some immediate benefit for the organisms that made even the slightest adaptation to emergence on land, especially when one considers all the problems that have to be overcome.

From our review of the problems of life on land it seems likely that the first plants to emerge had fewer difficulties than the first animals. They did not have to locate and eat food; they had no problems of locomotion, nor sense organs. Once a vascular system had developed with roots to absorb nutrients and water, the first steps to life on land were solved. Green plants have an immediate advantage in emerging from water–they are bathed directly in sunlight and can photosynthesize much more quickly. Thus I imagine that first devices were developed to float green tissues to the surface of pools just as modern water-lillies have floating leaves. These devices may well have included tubular spaces as in the stems of the water-lily, *Nymphaea*, or *Myriophyllum*, and could possibly have led to the development of the tracheids, the sap-conducting vascular bundles of the true vascular plants. Certainly, if there were small spaces in the stems, capillarity would tend to raise fluids within them. A combination of evaporation above and capillary replacement below could have initiated the first vascular system, provided that tubules existed in the stems. So I imagine the first emergent organisms were plants which were selected because of their improved photosynthesis. Once aquatic vascular plants evolved it would be a short step to terrestrial plants.

As to animals, small fish-fry swim in shallow water at the very edge of pools, rivers or the sea. Similarly, small frogs disturbed by a person walking along the edge of a lake which leap into the water often swim very vigorously back to land. The reason for both actions is to avoid large aquatic predators. Fish-fry or frogs which venture into deep water soon fall prey to a waiting pike. So once marsh plants had developed at the edges of pools they would have provided shelter for small arthropods, molluscs and the fry of larger animals – more so because at first there would have been no terrestrial or aerial predators, like modern birds, to attack them from the land side. Any snail or arthropod which could crawl out of the water onto or among the plants would have been safe from predators which at that time were all aquatic. If these organisms fed on vegetable matter or the algal bacterial slime that covers aquatic plants and is the main food of freshwater snails, they would not only have found protection, but a hitherto untapped source of nutrition as well. Furthermore, transpiration of water from the plants would have kept the humidity of the atmosphere high so that water conservation would not have been an immediate problem.

If you are a predator and your prey migrates, you migrate too. So almost as soon as invertebrates colonized marsh plants at the edge of pools, vertebrates and predatory insects would have followed them. Equally, if competition between aquatic vegetarians was severe, even vegetarians would have had an immediate advantage in feeding around the edge of the pool. So we can imagine that a combination of a stick, predation pressure, and a carrot, an untapped source of food, reinforced each other in 'urging' animals to follow plants out of the water. Even some of the plants may have been selected by escaping 'predators'. An emergent plant with aerial reproductive structures such as those of *Rhynia* would have gained some protection for the gonads by putting them out of the reach of aquatic vegetarians. So, to summarize, I suggest that the sequence of events was as follows: plants emerged because they could photosynthesize more effectively in direct sunlight; invertebrates and vertebrates followed the plants for food and protection; and the larger predators followed in their turn, as new food resources developed at the edges of bodies of water. Once the process was under way it would have been self-perpetuating, because competition would have continually driven some new pioneer species of plant to grow further and further away from water where no other plant could overshadow it. As soon as the pioneers were established, the second wave of colonists would soon have followed.

By whatever path, life did adapt to conditions on land; once the first pioneer species were established the whole range of terrestrial environments became open to colonization. An almost immediate radiation of amphibians took place, and they dominated life on land until they were eclipsed by the reptiles which, in turn, have been superseded by the mammals. Plants seem to have followed a similar pattern to terrestrial vertebrates, with each new adaptation being eclipsed by the next as pteridosperms were replaced by gymnosperms and finally angiosperms, the flowering plants which bring us so much pleasure. Once started, the process of colonization of land progressed steadily to the present-day world we know.

Epilogue

Inevitably in a book like this, which attempts to review what is known about fossils and to illustrate their uses in solving geological and other problems, the impression may be given that all there is to know about fossils is already known; that the great discoveries of palaeontology were all made in the last century; and that all we can do is to summarize them and, perhaps, to feel vaguely envious of those who were alive when the history of life was being unravelled for the first time. This impression can only be reinforced by my insistence that the fossil record is adequate for all our purposes and that already by 1900 a fairly good outline of the major features of evolution was known. In fact nothing could be further from the truth. As I have stressed repeatedly in discussing the uses of fossils, there is an immense amount we do not yet know (much of which I believe we will understand sooner or later), and new fossil discoveries are being made every day. Some will be routine, merely adding yet another species to a large, well-known genus; others may be as startling as the discovery of *Archaeopteryx*, the first bird, or of a new type of dinosaur. Some will cause us to change our ideas radically, others merely confirm what we already know. To be sure, there is unlikely to be another event as momentous as the publication of Darwin's *The Origin of Species*, but there is still enormous scope for research. Less than twenty years ago Precambrian fossils were not generally held to exist; now we have a considerable number from what must prove to be the most exciting part of the fossil record, where the earliest forms of life are preserved. However much the Precambrian fossil record has improved over the last two decades, it is still meagre compared with that of the succeeding Phanerozoic. There must be enormous numbers of Precambrian fossils still to be found, some of which will no doubt be judged by twenty-first-century scientists to be vital to a correct understanding of the history of life on earth. In the same way a new theory can place already known facts in a completely new and exciting light, as the ideas of continental drift and plate tectonics have for past distributions of fossils. We now have an immense task in sifting already accumulated data on fossil distributions to see how well they fit in with plate tectonic models of the earth at various times in the past. There is much still to be done and plenty of opportunities for all, from the enthusiastic amateur to the most venerable professional, to contribute to the process of unravelling the history of life.

As an example of the sort of thing that can, and should, be done, one may contrast the usual methods of collecting fossils with those of an archaeological excavation. In the past (and still largely at present) we have relied almost entirely on accidental exposures, cliffs and crags, quarries and roadcuts, which, whether they are natural or man-made, have not been opened up specifically to solve some geological problem. One wonders how much would be known about archaeology if no specific digs had ever been organized. Even when we do collect, we tend to be highly selective. We may remove all the brachiopods perhaps, or all the echinoderms, or possibly take samples from which we will extract all the microfossils. Often we are even less thorough, and very rarely is the whole fauna and flora collected. It is true that some workers have developed a system of collecting a substantial mass of rock, removing it to the laboratory or museum, breaking it up and attempting to identify everything, but they are still the exception rather than the rule. Imagine an archaeological excavation from which only metallic artifacts or only potsherds were removed and everything else discarded! In general we have yet to reach the stage in palaeontological excavation that archaeology reached in the 1920s. We would do well to copy the methods pioneered by the late Sir Mortimer Wheeler of removing all material carefully, collecting everything, recording its location and orientation and leaving only the walls of the pits to record the stratigraphy of the site. Rarely has this even been attempted in palaeontology, let alone adopted as a routine procedure.

Early this century the Swedish professional collector, Lilljeval, was employed to collect samples every ten centimetres through a Silurian section up a waterfall near Visby, the capital of the Baltic Island of Gotland. He did a magnificent job, but only in the last few years has his material been studied and some additional samples recovered. The Wattenfellet Project, as it has come to be known (*wattenfellet* is simply the Swedish for the waterfall) is unique; it involved nearly forty specialists to identify all the fossils, and produced some quite unexpected results. A few rare groups of fossils,

EPILOGUE

which even practising palaeontologists had scarcely heard of, turned out to be present in significant numbers when *all* the fossils were collected and identified. The publication of the results, due in 1979, should produce a wealth of very important data and set a standard for future work. More importantly, only when collecting is carried out in this way can we hope to test the completeness of the fossil record rigorously. How can we complain that the fossil record is 'notoriously incomplete' when we leave half the evidence behind in the rocks? Indeed, it might be suggested that most of the incompleteness of the fossil record is due to our own inadequacies, not those of the record.

It is true that a lot of exciting discoveries have been made already, but I doubt if we have found even half of the fossil species that have been preserved. In this case, at least as many exciting discoveries remain in the rocks waiting to be revealed. Palaeontology, despite its literal meaning and its popular image, is a young science. There is still an immense amount to do.

References and further reading

Introduction

1. G. Agricola, *De natura fossilium lib.* (Basiliae, 1546). For a modern translation see M. C. Bandy & J. A. Bandy, *Spec. Pap. geol. Soc. Am.*, **63** (1955).
2. C. Linnaeus, *Systema naturae, sive regna tria naturae systematice proposita per classes, ordines, genera et species*, 10th rev. edn. (Holmiae, 1758).
3. Chapters on death, disintegration and burial in W. Schäfer, *Ecology and palaeoecology of marine environments* (Edinburgh, 1972).
4. N. Stenonis, *De solido intra solidum naturaliter contento dissertationis prodromus* (Florentiae, 1669); translated into English by J. D. Garrett (New York, 1916); reprinted 1968.
5. W. A. Smith, *A delineation of the strata of England and Wales, with part of Scotland*, scale 5 miles to 1 inch; together with a memoir of the map (London, 1815).

Chapter 1

1. I. P. Tolmachoff, 'The carcasses of the mammoth and rhinoceros found in the frozen ground of Siberia', *Trans. Am. phil. Soc.*, new series, **29**, part 1, article 1 (1929).
2. R. F. Lundin, '"Baby mammoth Dima"; a new discovery', *J. Paleont.* **52** (1978), 941–2.
3. W. H. Fritz, 'Geological setting of the Burgess Shale', in 'Extraordinary fossils', *Symposium of the North American paleontological convention 1969* (1971), 1155–70.
4. R. G. Johnson and E. S. Richardson Jr, 'A remarkable Pennsylvanian fauna from the Mazon Creek area, Illinois', *J. Geol.* **74** (1966), 626–31.
5. R. G. Johnson and E. S. Richardson Jr, 'The morphology and affinities of *Tullimonstrum*', *Fieldiana: Geology*, **12** (1969), 119–49.
6. A. Seilacher, 'Fossil behaviour', *Scient. Am.*, **217** (1967), 72–80.

Further reading
A wide-ranging general account of preservation history will be found in

W. Schäfer, *Ecology and palaeoecology of marine environments*, while numerous articles on trace fossils have been published in the following:

T. P. Crimes and J. C. Harper (eds.), *Trace fossils. Proceedings of an international symposium held at Liverpool 6–8 January, 1970* (Liverpool, 1970).

T. P. Crimes and J. C. Harper (eds.), *Trace fossils 2. Proceedings of an international symposium held at Sydney, Australia 23–24 August, 1976* (Liverpool, 1977).

Chapter 2

1 C. K. Wentworth, 'A scale of grade class terms for clastic sediments', *J. Geol.*, **20** (1922), 377–92.
2 R. L. Folk, 'Spectral subdivision of limestone types', in W. E. Ham (ed.), 'Classification of carbonate rocks', *Mem. Am. Ass. petrol. Geol.*, **1** (1962), 62–84.
3 R. J. Dunham, 'Classification of carbonate rocks according to depositional texture', in W. E. Ham (ed.), 'Classification of carbonate rocks', *Mem. Am. Ass. petrol. Geol.*, **1** (1962), 108–21.
4 A. C. Neumann, J. W. Kofoed and G. H. Keller, 'Lithoherms in the Straits of Florida', *Geology*, **5** (1977), 4–10.

Further reading

Clastic sedimentology is covered very well in R. C. Selley, *An introduction to sedimentology* (London, 1976), while carbonate rocks are discussed very thoroughly in *Mem. Am. Ass. petrol. Geol.*, **1** (1962) and in R. G. C. Bathurst, *Carbonate sediments and their diagenesis. Developments in sedimentology*, **12**, 2nd edn., (Amsterdam 1975).

Chapter 3

1 C. R. C. Paul, 'Revision of the *Holocystites* fauna (Diploporita) of North America', *Fieldiana: Geology*, **24** (1971).
2 K. R. Walker and W. C. Parker, 'Population structure of a pioneer and a later stage species in an Ordovician ecological succession', *Paleobiology*, **2** (1976), 191–201.
3 E. N. K. Clarkson and R. Levi-Setti, 'Trilobite eyes and the optics of Des Cartes and Huygens', *Nature, Lond.*, **254** (1975), 663–7.
4 R. T. Jackson, 'Phylogeny of the echini with a revision of Palaeozoic species', *Mem. Boston Soc. nat. Hist.*, **7** (1912).
5 R. P. S. Jefferies, 'Photonegative young in the Triassic lamellibranch, *Lima lineata* (Schlotheim)', *Palaeontology*, **3** (1965), 362–9.
6 Paul, '*Holocystites* fauna of North America'.
7 R. F. Hecker, *Introduction to Palaeoecology;* translated from the Russian (New York, 1965).

8   A. M. Ziegler, 'Silurian marine communities and their environmental significance', *Nature, Lond.*, **207** (1965), 270–2.
9   See for example W. S. McKerrow (ed.), *The ecology of fossils: an illustrated guide* (London, 1978).
10 Ziegler, 'Silurian marine communities', 254.
11 H. G. Owen, 'Continental displacement and expansion of the earth during the Mesozoic and Tertiary', *Phil. Trans. Roy. Soc. Lond.*, series A, **281** (1976), 223–91.

Chapter 4

1   F. J. Vine and D. H. Matthews, 'Magnetic anomalies over oceanic ridges', *Nature, Lond.*, **199** (1963), 947–9.
2   Owen, 'Continental displacement . . . .
3   G. G. Simpson, 'Notes on the measurement of faunal resemblance', *Am. J. Sci.*, **258A** (1960), 300–11.
4   A. Williams, 'Distribution of brachiopod assemblages in relation to Ordovician palaeogeography', in N. F. Hughes (ed.), 'Organisms and continents through time', *Spec. Pap. Palaeont.*, **12** (1973), 241–69.
5   H. B. Whittington and C. P. Hughes, 'Ordovician trilobite distribution and geography', *Spec. Pap. Palaeont.*, **12** (1973), 235–40.
6   C. R. C. Paul, 'Palaeogeography of primitive echinoderms', in M. G. Bassett (ed.), *The Ordovician System. Proceedings of a Palaeontological Association symposium, Birmingham, September, 1974* (London, 1976), 553–74.
7   For example P. M. Sheehan, 'The relation of late Ordovician glaciation to the Ordovician–Silurian changeover in North American brachiopod faunas', *Lethaia*, **6** (1973), 147–54.
8   M. Lindström, 'Conodont palaeogeography of the Ordovician', in Bassett (ed.), *The Ordovician System*, 501–22.
9   D. Skevington, 'Ordovician graptolites', in A. Hallam (ed.), *Atlas of Palaeobiogeography* (Amsterdam, 1973), 27–35.
10 W. G. Chaloner and W. S. Lacey, 'The distribution of late Palaeozoic floras', *Spec. Pap. Paleont.*, **12** (1973), 271–89.
11 G. M. Philip and R. J. Foster, 'Marsupiate Tertiary echinoids from south eastern Australia and their zoogeographic significance', *Palaeontology*, **14** (1971), 666–99.
12 U. Asgaard, '*Cyclaster danicus*, a shallow burrowing non-marsupiate echinoid', *Lethaia*, **9** (1976), 363–75.
13 W. J. Rees, 'A review of breathing devices in land operculate snails', *Proc. malac. Soc. Lond.*, **36** (1964), 55–67.
14 F. G. Stehli, 'Permian zoogeography and its bearing on climate', in A. E. M. Nairn (ed.), *Problems of Palaeoclimatology* (London, 1964), 537–49.

15 L. Agassiz, *Études sur les glaciers* (Neuchatel, 1840). The subject of an address to the Helvetic Society in 1837.
16 F. C. Ton, J. D. Hudson and M. L. Keith, 'Jurassic (Callovian) palaeotemperatures from Scotland', *Earth planet. Sci. Letters*, **9** (1970), 421–6.
17 C. Emiliani, 'Pleistocene temperatures', *J. Geol.*, **63** (1955), 538–78.
18 C. Emiliani, 'Quaternary paleotemperatures and the duration of the high temperature intervals', *Science, N. Y.*, **178** (1972), 398–401.
19 S. J. Johnson, W. Dansgaard, H. B. Clausen and C. C. Longway, 'Oxygen isotope profiles through the Antarctic and Greenland Ice sheets', *Nature, Lond.*, **235** (1972), 429–34.
20 C. Spaeth, J. Hoefs and U. Vetter, 'Some aspects of isotopic composition of belemnites and related paleotemperatures', *Bull. geol. Soc. Am.*, **82** (1971), 3139–50.

Further reading
N. F. Hughes (ed.), 'Organisms and continents through time', *Spec. Pap. Palaeont.*, **12** (1973).
F. A. Middlemiss, P. F. Rawson and G. Newall (eds.), *Faunal provinces in space and time* (Liverpool, 1971).
G. Faure, *Principles of Isotope Geology* (New York, 1977). See chapter 17 for radiocarbon dating.

Chapter 5

1 F. W. Anderson, 'The law of ostracod growth', *Palaeontology*, **7** (1964), 85–104.
2 H. B. Whittington, 'The ontogeny of trilobites', *Biol. Rev.*, **32** (1957), 421–69.
3 R. A Fortey and S. F. Morris, 'Discovery of nauplius-like trilobite larvae', *Palaeontology*, **21** (1978), 823–33.
4 See Sir D'A. Thompson, *On growth and form*, (abridged edn.), (Cambridge, 1961), 238.
5 G. R. Clark II, 'Periodic growth and biological rhythms in experimentally grown bivalves', in G. D. Rosenberg and S. K. Runcorn (eds.), *Growth rhythms and the history of the earth's rotation* (London, 1973), 103–34.
6 C. L. MacKenzie Jr, 'Growth and reproduction of the oyster drill *Eupleura caudata* in the York River, Virginia', *Ecology* **42** (1961), 317–38.
7 T. E. Crowley, 'Age determination in *Anodonta*', *J. Conch., Lond.*, **24** (1957), 201–7.
8 Thompson, *On growth and form*, chapter 2.
9 S. J. Gould, 'Allometry in Pleistocene land snails from Bermuda: the influence of size upon shape', *J. Paleont.*, **40** (1966), 1131–41.

10 S. J. Gould, 'The shape of things to come', *Syst. Zool.*, **22** (1973), 401–4.
11 S. J. Gould, 'Muscular mechanics and the ontogeny of swimming in scallops', *Palaeontology*, **14** (1971), 61–94.
12 C. T. Scrutton, 'Periodicity in Devonian coral growth', *Palaeontology*, 7 (1965), 552–8.
13 L. V. Morrison, 'Changes in the earth's rotation from astronomical observations', in Rosenberg and Runcorn (eds.), *Growth rhythms*, 445–57.
14 P. M. Muller and F. R. Stephenson, 'The accelerations of the earth and moon from early astronomical observations', in Rosenberg and Runcorn (eds.), *Growth rhythms*, 459–534.
15 Clark, 'Periodic growth', in Rosenberg and Runcorn (eds.), *Growth rhythms* 103–34.
16 C. A. Hall, 'Latitudinal variation in shell growth patterns of bivalve molluscs: implications and problems', in Rosenberg and Runcorn (eds.), *Growth rhythms*, 163–74.
17 R. E. Mohr, 'Measured periodicities of the Biwabik (Precambrian) stromatolites and their geophysical significance', in Rosenberg and Runcorn (eds.), *Growth rhythms*, 43–56.
18 G. Faure, *Principles of isotope geology* (New York, 1977), 305–21.
19 C. W. Ferguson, 'Dendrochronology of bristlecone pine, *Pinus aristata*. Establishment of a 7,484-year chronology in the White Mountains of east-central California, USA', in I. U. Olsson (ed.), *Radiocarbon variations and absolute chronology. Proceedings of the 17th Nobel symposium held at the Institute of Physics at Uppsala University* (Stockholm, 1970), 237–59.
20 E. Fromm, 'An estimation of errors in the Swedish varve chronology', in Olsson (ed.), *Radiocarbon variations*, 163–72.
21 D. J. Schove, 'Tree-ring and varve scales combined, c.13,500 BC to AD 1977', *Palaeogeogr. Palaeoclimatol. Palaeoecol.*, **25** (1978), 209–33.

Further reading
G. D. Rosenberg and S. K. Runcorn (eds.), *Growth rhythms and the history of the earth's rotation* (London, 1973).
I. U. Olsson (ed.), *Radiocarbon variations and absolute chronology* (Stockholm, 1970).

Chapter 6

1 N. Stenonis, *De solido intra solidum naturaliter contento dissertationis prodromus*, (Florentiae, 1669).
2 W. A. Smith, *A delineation of the strata of England and Wales, with part of Scotland* (London, 1815).

3 G. Cuvier and A. Brogniart, 'Essai sur la géographie minéralogique des environs de Paris', *Journal des Mines*, **23** (1808), 421–58.
4 See J. M. Eyles, 'William Smith: some aspects of his life and work', in C. J. Schneer (ed.), *Towards a history of geology* (Cambridge, Mass. and London, 1969), 142–58.
5 Cuvier and Brogniart, 'Géographie Minéralogique',
6 Smith, *A delineation of the strata of England and Wales*.
7 A. Sedgwick and R. I. Murchison, 'On the Silurian and Cambrian systems, exhibiting the order in which the older sedimentary strata succeed each other in England and Wales', *Rep. Br. Ass. advmt Sci.* (for 1835), transactions of the sections 59–61 (1836).
8 Sir R. I. Murchison, 'On the Silurian system of rocks', *Lond. Edinb. Dubl. Phil. Mag.* **7** (1835), 46–52.
9 C. Lapworth, 'On the tripartite classification of the Lower Palaeozoic rocks', *Geol. Mag.*, decade 2, **6** (1879), 1–15.
10 American Commission on Stratigraphic Nomenclature, 'Code of stratigraphic nomenclature', *Bull. Am. Ass. petrol. Geol.*, **45** (1961), 645–65.
11 A. B. Shaw, *Time in stratigraphy* (New York, 1964).
12 C. Darwin, *The origin of species by means of natural selection or the preservation of favoured races in the struggle for life* (London, 1859).
13 C. Lyell, *Principles of Geology* (London, 1833).
14 W. Thompson, 'Secular cooling of the earth', *Trans. Roy. Soc. Edinb.*, **23** (1864), 157–69. (The ideas were first published in *McMillan's Magazine* for March 1862.)
15 Lord Kelvin, 'The age of the earth as an abode fitted for life', *Lond. Edinb. Dubl. Phil. Mag.*, 5th series, **47** (1899), 66–90.

Further reading
M. J. S. Rudwick, *The meaning of fossils. Episodes in the history of palaeontology* (London, 1972).
J. Challinor, *The history of British geology. A bibliographic study* (Newton Abbot, 1971).
G. Faure, *Principles of isotope geology* (New York, 1977). Chapters 3–17 cover principles and practice of all major radiometric dating methods.

Chapter 7

1 G. Mendel, 'Versuche über Pflanzen-Hybriden', *Verh. naturf. Ver. Brünn*, **4** (1865), 1–47.
2 G. Cuvier, 'Mémoire sur les espèces d'Elephans tant vivantes que fossiles', *Magasin encyclopédique*, 2ème Année, **3** (1796), 440–5.
3 J. B. Lamarck, *Système des animaux sans vertèbres* (Paris 1799–1801).
4 G. Saint-Hilaire, *Philosophie anatomique* (Paris, 1818–22).

5   G. Cuvier, *Essay on the theory of the earth, with geological illustrations by Professor Jamieson* (Edinburgh, 1813).
6   C. Darwin and A. R. Wallace, 'On the tendency of species to form varieties; and on the perpetuation of varieties and species by natural means of selection', *J. Linn. Soc. (Zool.)*, **3** (1858), 45–62.
7   T. R. Malthus, *An essay on the principle of population* ... (London, 1798).
8   Darwin, *The origin of species*, chapters 10 and 11.
9   Mendel, 'Versuche über Pflanzen-Hybriden'.
10 F. A. Bather, 'A phylogenetic classification of the Pelmatozoa', *Rep. Br. Ass. advmt Sci.*, **68** (1899), 916–23.
11 A. B. Shaw, *Time in stratigraphy* (New York, 1964), chapter 18.
12 Shaw, *Time in stratigraphy*, chapter 18.
13 F. A. Bather, 'Carodocian Cystidea from Girvan', *Trans. R. Soc. Edinb.*, **49** (1913), 359–530.
14 Shaw, *Time in stratigraphy*, chapter 18.
15 C. R. C. Paul, '*Thomacystis*, a unique new hemicosmitid cystoid from Wales', *Geol. Mag.*, **106** (1969), 190–6.
16 O. Jaekel, 'Phylogenie und System der Pelmatozoen', *Paläont. Z.*, **3** (1918), 1–128.
17 E. Haeckel, 'Amphorideen und Cystoideen Beitrage zur Morphologie und Phylogenie', *Festschrift zum Siebenzigsten geburtstage von Carl Gegenbaur am 21st August 1896*, 1 (1896), 1–180.
18 The best account of this idea is in M. J. S. Rudwick, 'The inference of function from structure in fossils', *Br. J. Phil. Sci.*, **15**: 57 (1964), 27–40.
19 P. H. A. Sneath and R. R. Sokal, *Numerical taxonomy. The principles and practice of numerical classification* (San Francisco, 1973).
20 W. Hennig, *Phylogenetic systematics* (Urbana, Ill., 1966); reissued 1979.
21 For an alternative viewpoint and incidentally the best account of Hennig's methods of which I know, see R. P. S. Jefferies, 'The origin of chordates – a methodological essay' in M. R. House (ed.), *The origin of the major invertebrate groups* (London, 1979), 443–77. I accept that Riedl's concept of burden enables distinction of primitive and advanced morphology (provided that secondary simplification has not occurred), but maintain that ancestor–descendant relationships between genera and species are best determined using the fossil record.
22 Shaw, *Time in stratigraphy*, chapter 24.
23 P. D. Gingerich, 'Paleontology and phylogeny: patterns of evolution at the species level in early Tertiary mammals', *Am. J. Sci.*, **276** (1976), 1–28.
24 N. Eldridge and S. J. Gould, 'Punctuated equilibria: an alternative to phyletic gradualism', in T. J. M. Schopf (ed.), *Models in Paleobiology* (San Francisco, 1972), 82–115.

25 P. D. Gingerich, 'Patterns of evolution in the mammalian fossil record in A. Hallam (ed.), *Patterns of evolution as illustrated by the fossil record*, (Amsterdam, 1977), 491. The original statement is in H. E. Wood, 'Patterns of evolution', *Trans. N. Y. Acad. Sci.*, **16** (1954), 324–36.
26 W. F. R. Weldon, 'A first study of natural selection in *Clausilia laminata* (Montagu)', *Biometrika*, **1** (1901), 109–24.
27 M. Sambol and R. M. Finks, 'Natural selection in a Cretaceous oyster', *Paleobiology*, **3** (1977), 1–16.
28 J. W. Valentine, *Evolutionary paleoecology of the marine biosphere* (Englewood Cliffs, N.J., 1973).
29 A. L. McAlester, 'Animal extinctions, oxygen consumption and atmospheric history', *J. Paleont.*, **44** (1970), 405–9.

Further reading
For an excellent account of the history of ideas on fossils and evolution see M. J. S. Rudwick, *The meaning of fossils. Episodes in the history of palaeontology* (London, 1972), chapter 5.

Chapter 8

1 S. L. Miller, 'A production of amino acids under possible primitive earth conditions', *Science, N. Y.*, **117** (1953), 528–9.
2 J. B. S. Haldane, *Science and human life* (New York, 1929).
3 I. A. Oparin, *The origin of life*, translated from the Russian (London, 1936).
4 See I. A. Oparin, *The chemical evolution of life*; translated from the Russian (Edinburgh, 1957), chapter 3.
5 W. W. Rubey, 'Development of the hydrosphere and atmosphere, with special reference to probable composition of the early atmosphere', in A. Poldevaart (ed.), *Crust of the earth – a symposium, Spec. Pap. geol. Soc. Am.*, **62** (1955), 631–50.
6 H. G. Owen, 'Continental displacement and expansion of the earth during the Mesozoic and Tertiary', *Phil. Trans. Roy. Soc. Lond.*, series A, **281** (1976), 223–91.
7 L. V. Berkner and L. C. Marshall, 'The history of oxygen concentration in the earth's atmosphere', *Proc. Faraday Soc. Disc.*, **37** (1964), 122–41.
8 K. M. Towe, 'Oxygen–collagen priority and the early metazoan fossil record', *Proc. nat. Acad. Sci.*, **65** (1970), 781–8.
9 A. L. McAlester, 'Animal extinctions, oxygen consumption, and atmospheric history', *J. Paleont.*, **44** (1970), 405–9.
10 J. H. Stitt, 'Late Cambrian and earliest Ordovician trilobites Wichita Mountains area, Oklahoma', *Bull. Okla. geol. Surv.*, **124** (1977).
11 R. B. Clark, *Dynamics of metazoan evolution.* (Oxford, 1964).

Chapter 9

1 Sir D'A. W. Thompson, *On growth and form*, 1st edn (Cambridge, 1917).

Further reading
Good general accounts of the history of life can be found in:
A. L. McAlester, *The history of life*, (Englewood Cliffs, N.J., 1968).
R. Cowen, *The history of life* (New York, 1976).
Perhaps the best recent account is D. Attenborough, *Life on earth* (London, 1979).

Index

Acanthothiris, 90
Acetabularia, 123
acorn worms, 36
Acropora palmata, 125
actualistic arguments, 6, 122, 125, 128, 193
adaptive peaks, 212–13
adaptive threshold, 243
adenosine phosphates, 222
Africa, 80, 113, 119, 130, 193
Agassiz, L., 128
Aglais urticae, 146
Agricola, G., 1
Alabastrina quinquefasciata, 145
Alaska, 12, 114
algae, 37, 40, 64, 69–71, 86, 97, 122–4, 134, 229, 233, 241, 266; blue-green, 228–30, 234, 236; coralline, 70, 122, 125; filamentous, 70; green, 229
allochems, 65, 67
allometric growth equation, 147, 149
allometry, 148–50
allopatric speciation model, 213
amber, 12
American Museum of Natural History, New York, 210
American West, 13, 268
amino acid, 221–4, 226
ammonites, 10, 20, 23, 41, 45, 82–3, 87–8, 91, 102–5, 116, 134, 137, 141, 146–7, 166, 170, 172–3, 198–9, 205, 216, 218–19, *138*, *148*; plates 4, 5, 6A–C
amnion, 258
amniotic egg, 215, 258
amphibians, 4, 199, 215, 249–51, 258–60, 264–5, 267–8, 270; fossil record of, 199
amphipods, 36
Amtjärn, Sweden, 97
Anderson, F. W., 89, 139
angiosperms, 215, 250, 270
Anglesey, 165, 169
Annelida, 239–40
Anodonta, 254; *anatina*, 147

Antarctica, 121, 123–4, 130, 134
Anthracopupa, 267
ants, 198–9
Appalachian Basin, 101; coalfields, 72; Mountains, 119
aragonite, 18, 20, 22, 23, 64–5, 67, 70, 123, 134, 240; mud, 67, 70, 123
Archaeocyatha, 240
archaeological excavation, 272; sites, 159
Archaeopteryx, 201, 271
Archaeospheroides, 228–9
Archanodon, 267
Arctostrea, plate 7C
Arenicola, 36
Arenicolites, 37
Arenig Series, 200
argon, 183–4
arthropods, 17, 36, 88–90, 122, 138–9, 141, 144–6, 239–40, 244, 249, 251–2, 266–7, 269
Asia, 112, 114, 119
associations, fossil, 94–6; brachiopod, 99, 100
astogeny, 137, 150, 152
Atlantic Ocean, 81, 109, 111–13, 134
atmosphere, primitive, 222–3, 231
atomic clocks, 153–4; number, 131; weight, 131, 156
atoms, 130–1
Atrypa, 11
Australasia, 118
Australia, 24, 71, 114, 121, 124, 126, 224, 232, 237

bacteria, 33, 227–30
Badister, 39
Balanoglossus, 36
Baltic region, 120–1
Baltic Sea, 12, 75, 125
banded ironstones, 233–4
barnacles, 40, 80
Bather, F. A., 196, 201–2, 206
bats, 260, 264

bauxite, 50
Beagle, HMS, 217
bedding, 31, 56; cross, 59, 62–3, 68, 74, 105, 123, 178, *60*, *179*; dune, 124; graded, 58, 62, 178, *59*, *179*; planes, 56, 214; surfaces, 31, 33, 56
bedding/cleavage relationships, *180*
bees, 258
Belemnitella americana, 132
belemnites, 23, 87, 104, 132, 134–5, 166; guards, 22, 26, 40; plates 3B–C
Bell, B. N., 93
Bering Straits, 114
Berkner, L. V., 234–5
Berkshire, 86
Betula, plate 16C
Biblical Flood, 7, 192
Big Pine Key, Florida, 71
bioherms, 21, 69, 70, 96–8, 101, 125, *21*
biological classification, 5
biomeres, 235, 244
biomicrite, 67
biostratigraphy, 168–70, 172–3
bioturbation, 31
biozone, 171
Biplex, 145
birch, plate 16C
birds, 29, 201, 215–16, 237, 242, 248, 251, 255, 257–8, 260, 269
Bitter Springs Chert, 229
bivalves, 11, 14, 16–17, 43, 64, 67, 69, 80, 83, 88, 90–1, 94, 100, 102, 104, 116, 126, 137, 145–6, 155–6, 205, 214, 218, 239–40, 255, 261, *84*; plates 7A–D, 9A; boring, 37–40; freshwater, 74, 79, 147, 266–7; infaunal, 16, 27, 42; non-marine, 101; tellinacean, 27; unionid, 79, 101, 256
Black, R. M., 11, 138, 263
blackbird, 116
blastoids, 98
Boda Limestone, 96

283

INDEX

body fossils, 11, 26, 30, 41, 238
Bombyx mori (larvae), 150
bone, fossil, 157, 159, 190; growth of, 142; preservation of, 6, 17–19; strength of, 259
borings, 26–7, 36–40, 43, 91; of parasitic gastropods, 85; of predatory gastropods, 39
boron, 232
Boston, Mass., 155
Brachypodella, 147
brachiopods, 6, 11, 14, 16–17, 20, 40, 44, 64, 82–3, 85–6, 90–3, 95–6, 98–101, 103, 117–20, 127, 137–8, 146, 149, 199, 201, 208, 217, 239–41, 244–5, 247, 255, 261, 272, *21, 84; plates 10A–B;* articulate, 245; atrypid, 150; inarticulate, 245; orthid, 245; rhynchonellid, *plate 10B;* spiriferid, *92;* terebratulid, *plates 10A–B*
bracken, 256
Bridport, Dorset, 96
Bridport Sands, 96
bristle cone pine, 160
Britain, 2, 29, 49, 57, 62, 72, 94, 116, 125, 163–5, 167, 169, 171, 187, 192, 198, 237; southern, 79, 170
British Columbia, 13, 244
British Museum, Natural History, 113, 192
Brittany, 48, 124, 130
brittlestars, *plate 14A*
Brogniart, A., 163–4
bryophytes, 250, 256, 266
bryozoans, 69, 80, 86, 96, 98, 103, 137, 146, 150, 152, 239, *plate 11B*
Buccinum, 29, 39
Buckinghamshire, 20, 147
Budleigh Salterton Pebble Bed, 48
Burgess Shale, 13–14, 17, 24, 244
burrows, 1, 26–7, 31, 33–9, 82, 96–7, 178, 241, *32; plate 9B;* U-shaped, 36, 236
butterflies, 87, 138, 141, 146, 198–9

caesium, 153
Cainozoic, 167, *8*
Cala Salada, Ibiza, 127
calcarenite, 65
calcilutite, 65
calcirudite, 65
calcisiltite, 65
calcite, 18–22, 25, 46, 62, 64–5, 132, 134, 144, 177, 240; ferroan, 65; high magnesian, 64, 65, 134; low magnesian, 64, 134
calcrete, 63
Caledonian Mountains, 119, 121
Callianassa, 37
callianassid crustaceans, 97, 103
Calymene, plate 10D
Camarotoechia, 100
Cambrian, 13, 17, 41, 117, 119, 165–6, 168, 181, 227, 234–8, 240–7, *8*
Cambridgeshire, 24, 266
Cambridge University, 165
camel, 263
Canadian border, 119, 217
Caradoc Series, 202–3
carapace, 89, 139, 141
carbohydrates, 222, 250
carbon, 72, 131, 156, 159, 161, 221; isotopes, 131, 156–7, 184, 228
Carboniferous, 14, 27, 39, 41, 97, 101–2, 117, 121, 165, 267, *8*
Carboniferous Limestone, 44, 70, 97, 169, 171
Caribbean, 80, 122, 127, 147
carnivores, 157, 261
Caryocrinites, 95
casts, artificial, 23; flute and groove, 58–9, 61–2; load, 60; natural, 29, 30
Central America, 217
cephalopods, 17, 42, 64, 101, 240
Cerastoderma edule, 155
Ceriantharia, 35–6
chaffinch, 5
chalk, 37, 41, 47, 55–6, 62, 72, 74, 92, 164, 166–7; rock, 56, 72
Challenger expedition, 193
Chapman's Pool, Dorset, 24
Chara, 101
Charmouth, Dorset, 20
Charnian, 237

Charnwood Forest, Leicestershire, 237
Chasmatopora, plate 11B
Cheirocrinus, 201
Chert, 228, 233
chitons, 64, 101
chlorophylls, 225–6, 229
chloroplasts, 226, 262, *261*
Chondrites, 34–5
Chonetes, 90
chromosomes, 230
chronostratigraphy, 168
cicadas, 264
Cidaris, plate 13A
Cincinnati, Ohio, 93–4; Arch, 127; region, 92
Cirencester, Gloucestershire, 47
Clark, D. L., 237
Clark, R. B., 241
cleavage (of rocks), 179, *180*
Cliona, 37, 40
Clwyd, 44
Clypeaster, plate 13B
Cnidaria, 5
coacervate drops, 226–7
coal, 72, 74, 159, *73;* balls, 72; cyclothem, 77–9, *73;* forests, 14, 72, 74, 77; measures, 14, 62, 77–8, 165; plants, 72; rank of, 72
Cochlodina laminata, 213–14
cockle, 155
coelacanth, 193, 268
coelenterates, 5, 238–40
coelom, 239, 241
collagen, 234–5, 240
colloids, 226
communities: brachiopod, 100, *99;* fossil, 81–2, 88, 94, 98; recent, 80
composites, 259
composite standard section, 209
concretions, 14, 19, 46, 60–2, 72
conodonts, 120–1
continental drift, 81, 106, 124, 128, 271
copepod crustaceans, 39
corallian, 86, 125
corals, 5, 39, 64, 70–1, 83, 95, 98, 101, 103–4, 122, 124, 126, 134, 144–5, 151–2, 154, 169, 236, 238, 240, 255; *plates 14B, 15A–C;* ahermatypic, 69; auloporoid, 91–2; colonial,

83, 137, 150, 176;
  hermatypic, 4, 69, 121;
  hexacorals, 69, 125,
  242–3; *plates 14B, 15C*;
  octocorals, 69; rugose, 69,
  125, 151, *plate 15B*;
  solitary, 95, 137; tabulate,
  69, 95, 125; *plate 15A*
Cornbrash, the, 169
cornflakes rock, 67
correlation, 7, 8, 43, 78,
  116, 130, 163, 167–73,
  189, 197, 199, 203, 209
crabs, 14, 30, 89, 138,
  140–1, 146; fiddler, 257;
  hermit, 15, 95
crawfish, 39
Cretaceous, 10, 47, 49, 79,
  105, 116, 132, 135, 147–8,
  164–7, 170, 173, 181–2,
  193, 198, 215–16, 242
crickets, 264
Crimes, T. P., 32–3
crinoids, 39, 40, 44–5, 82,
  95, 98, 246, 261; *plates
  12A–B*; articulate,
  242–3; attachment
  structures, 96, 98;
  camerate, 95; columns,
  44–5, 97, 143; flexibles,
  95; inadunate, 95
cross cutting relationships,
  174, 179, 186, 189
crustaceans, 139
Cruziana, 29, 30
crystal apples, 20; *plate 11C*
Culmann, 142–3
cutin, 18
cuttlefish, 87, 244; *plate 3A*
Cuvier, G., 163–4, 190–3,
  196, 213
Cyclonema, 95
cyclothems, 74, *73*
Cylindroteuthis, *plates 3B–C*
Cystoblastus, 201
cystoids, 20, 22, 39, 45,
  95–6, 199, 203, 235, *24*,
  85; *plate 11C*; diploporite,
  84, 86; fossil record of,
  199–202, 205–7, 219, *200*,
  207

Dactylioceras, *plate 6A*
Dalarna, Sweden, 97
Danian, 166–7
Dartmoor Granite, 48
Darwin, C., 8, 181–2, 190,
  192–6, 208, 210, 213, 217,
  247–8, 258, 271

Darwin's finches, 215
dating: absolute, 182;
  radiometric, 182–3;
  relative, 162, 173, 179
daytime, 152–4
Dead Sea, 46
dedolomitization, 22
Dee Estuary, 78
dendrochronology, 156, 160,
  185
Denmark, 12, 126, 166–7
Derbyshire, 97
derived fossils, 10
Devon, 48, 165, 167
Devonian, 57, 90, 95, 101–2,
  121, 124, 128, 154, 156,
  165, 167, 193, 263, 266–7,
  8
De Vreis effect, 159
diachronous boundaries,
  170–1
diagenesis: of coal, 72; of
  fossils, 17, 19–21, 23–4,
  43, 134, 136; of
  limestones, 63–4; of
  sandstones, 96; of
  sediments, 46–7, 56, 61,
  186; of shells, 159
Dickinsonia, 239
Didymograptus, *plate 11A*
dimorphism: sexual, 88
dinosaurs, 5, 13, 17, 41,
  195, 198, 216, 218, 260,
  262, 271; footprints, 29,
  30, 58; growth of, 142
diploblasts, 239
Diplocraterion, 37, 39
DNA, 228, 230
dogs, 6, 12, 216; Labrador,
  195–6
dolomite: mineral, 20, 22–3;
  rock, 22, 47, 237
dolomitization, 22–3
dolphins, 15
Donnetz basin, Russia, 78
Dorset, 20, 24, 74, 96
Dreissena, 256
Drybrook, Forest of Dean,
  97
Drybrook Sandstone, 97
Duddington, C. L., 261
Dunham, R. J., 65–6

earthworms, 35, 239
East Anglia, 10
Echinocardium, 35
echinoderms, 6, 17, 19, 39,
  45, 64, 91, 93, 101, 103,
  118–20, 122, 132, 134,

142–3, 196, 199, 208, 218,
  234–5, 239–41, 244–7,
  272, *24*, *85*; *plates 11C*,
  12A–B, *13A–C*, *14A*;
  plates, 19, 22, 65; tests,
  45
echinoids, 16; irregular, 215,
  242; regular, 215
Echiurus, 36
ectoderm, 238–9
Ediacara, South Australia,
  236; fauna, 24, 236–9, 241
edrioasteroids, 93, 98
eelgrass, 102
eels, 102, 254
Eglwyseg Mountain, North
  Wales, 169
Eldridge, N., 210, 212–13,
  215
elephants, 13, 149, 150, 191;
  African, 190–1; Indian,
  190–1; fossil, 164, 190
Elgin, Scotland, 29
Emiliani, C., 134
endoderm, 238–9
England, 74, 163, 236;
  southern, 10, 49, 242
enzymes, 223, 226, 262
Eobacterium, 228
Eocene, 113, 166, 181, *8*
Eocoelia, 100
epifauna, 43–4, 86, 90–4, 96,
  98
epiflora, 86
epiphragm, 127, 250
Epithyris, 11
epizoans, 24
Equator, 121, 124, 128, 135,
  156, 158, 217; magnetic,
  108
erosion, 15, 30, 36, 38,
  41–2, 46, 48, 50, 57, 65,
  75, 124, 188, 205
Essex fauna, 62
eukaryotes, 229, 230
Eupleura caudata, 145
Europe, 75, 106, 111–13,
  116, 119, 121, 128, 163–4,
  166, 168, 192, 217;
  northern, 10, 116, 191;
  southern, 116, 120–1;
  western, 56, 169
eustatic changes in sea level,
  78, 121
evaporites, 46, 63, 180
evolution: course of, 9, 189,
  196; inorganic, 220, 227,
  247; theory of, 9, 190, 192
exoskeleton, 138, 141

INDEX

expansion of the earth, 106, 113–14, 232

facies, 103–5, 170, *99*
Faringdon, Berkshire, 86
fats, 222
faults, 56, 61, 163, 174
faunal succession, principle of, 8, 163–5, 173
faunizone, 171
Favosites, 95, *151*
Felis, 4, 5; *domesticus*, 4; *sylvestris*, 4
felspars, 26, 50, 124
Fig Tree Chert, 228–9, 232
Filipendula ulmaria, 5
finch family, 117
fish, 6, 15, 30, 42, 102, 122, 193, 244, 249, 254–6, 260–1, 264–5, 267; *plate 1B*; rhipidistean, 4, 268
Fjäcka Shale, 97
flatworms, 239
flint, 47, 48, 62, 74
Florida, 125; Bay, 70, 123; Keys, 69, 71, 125; Straits of, 68
fluorine, 232
Folds, 56, 61, 176, *174*
Folk, R. L., 65–6
footprints, 26–7, 29–30, 58, *28*
Foraminifera, 20, 64, 101, 134, 173
Forest of Dean, 97
formation (stratigraphic), 164–5, 167–70, 172
Fortey, R. A., 139
fossils: assemblages, 81, 98, 104, 115; associations, 94–6; behaviour, 11; communities, 81–2, 88, 94, 98, 115; confederations, 81, 98–100, 105; impressions, 23, 237
fossil record: incompleteness of, 2–3, 10–11, 190, 193–200, 203, 213, 273; tests of, 199, 203, 206; gaps in, 199, 218, *200*
fossilization, 10–11
Foster, R. J., 126
France, 126, 163–4, 191
Fringilla coelebs, 4
Fringillidae, 117
frogs, 269
fungi, 37, 41, 227, 229, 266

Galapagos Islands, 215
galena, 184
Gametophyte, 256–7
garnet, 48
gastropods, 20, 39, 45, 64, 86, 95, 134, 145, 172, 205, 250; *plates 8A–C*; platyceratid, 82, 95
geological column, 8, 162, 164–6, 168, 173–4, 186, 189–90, 203
geopetal structures, 21, 68, 70, 177
Germany, 165
gills, 35, 238, 249, 252, 256, 265
Gingerich, P. D., 210–11, 213
Girvan, Scotland, 61
glacial deposits, 54, 123; drift, 10; epochs, 130; periods, 75, 129
glaciations: Hirnantian, 120–1, 128, 130, 219; Permo-Carboniferous, 78, 130, 218; Pleistocene, 49, 71, 130, 135; Varangian, 130, 236
glauconite, 20, 186
Glenobotrydium aenigmatis, 229
glochidium, 256
Glossopteris flora, 121
Glyptocystites, 201
gneiss, 48
gnomon, 147, *149*
goats, 216
Gomphoceras, *148*
Gondwanaland, 121
goniatite shales, 104
Gotland, 125, 272
Gould, S. J., 149–50, 210–13, 215
gradualist model of evolution, 210, 212
grainstone, 66–8
Grand Bahama Bank, 122–3
granite, 48, 187
graptolites, 82, 101, 104–5, 120–1, 137, 150, 172–3, *172*; *plate 11A*
graptolitic shales, 100, 104
Great Basin, 75, 77
Great Salt Lake, 75–7, *76*
Greenland, 123, 128, 134, 227, 267
groups (stratigraphic), 168
growth: accretionary, 137, 143–4, 149–50, 154; allometric, 146–50; continuous, 144–5; discrete, 144–6; gnomonic, 146–8; mode of, 137; moulting, 137, 143–4; style of, 144–7, *146*; with modification, 137, 141–4
growth history, 126
growth increments: daily, 144–5, 154–5; semi-daily, 144, 155–6
growth lines, 137, 145, 154
growth phenomena, 126
growth rates, 136, 145–6, 152
growth records, 154–6
growth rings, 133, 135, 142, 159
growth series, 139
growth stages, 137–9, 152
growth studies, 136, 152, 156, 161
Gryphaea, 10, 83, 92, *84*
Gualt Clay, 170, *170*
Gulf Coast (USA), 123
Gunflint Chert, 229
gymnosperms, 250, 270; *plate 16A*
gyroscope, 108

Haeckel, E., 208
Haldane, J. B. S., 223
half-life (of radio-isotope), 157–8, 183, 184, 185–6
Halimeda, 70
Halkyn Mountain, Clwyd, 44
Hallam, A., 148, 246
Halysites, *plate 15A*
Hampshire Basin, 79
hardgrounds, 56–7, 98
Harefield, Middlesex, 37, 41
Harvard University, 211
Hayley Wood, Cambridgeshire, 266
heavy minerals, 48, 105
Hecker, R. F., 97
Hennig, W., 209, 210
herbivores, 150, 195
Herculaneum, 17
Hexaplex, 145
Hicetes, 95
Hirnantian, 118, 124, 130
historical geology, 162
holaspis (stage), 140
Holocystites, 84–6, 96, 143
homiotherms, 262–3
homonym, 117

INDEX

Hope, Derbyshire, 97
Huxley, T. H., 258
Hydrobia ulvae, 102
hydrogen, 72, 131, 221, 231
hydrological cycle, 180
Hyopsodus: miticulus, 211; *simplex*, 211
hypsodonty, 150

Ibiza, 127
ice age, Pleistocene, 128, 133, 191
Iceland, 109
Ichthyostega, 267
ichthyosaurs, 14–15, 23; plate 2
ichthyostegids, 267–8
igneous rocks, 46, 48, 107, 111, 186–7, 224; intrusions, 48, 175–6, 187
Illinois, 14, 62; Basin, 72
Incus, 264
India, 121, 124
Indiana, 19, 57, 84, 86, 92, 94, 96–8, 169
infauna, 31, 38, 83
information losses (during preservation), 2, 11, 13–14, 18, 23–4, 26, 41
insects, 12, 41, 80, 101, 138, 141, 199, 209, 242–3, 248, 251–2
interglacial periods, 75, 129–30
interstitial organisms, 33
intraclasts, 65–7
invertebrates, 7, 250, 257, 265, 269–70; terrestrial, 258–60, 264; marine, 255
Iowa, 167
Ireland, 70, 118, 267
iron, 107, 124, 222, 232–3
Islamorada Nature Trail, Florida, 71
Isle of Arran, 61
isopods, 251
isostacy, 74, 77–8
isostatic adjustments, 75–8
isotopes, 130–1, 156, 183, 227; carbon, 131, 156–7, 184, 228; daughter, 156–7, 183, 185–6; oxygen, 131–4, 227–8; parent, 183, 185–6; radioactive, 131, 156–8, 183, 185–6, 188, *184*
isotopic fractionation, 132, 227
Isthmus of Panama, 119

Jackson, R. T., 91
Jaekel, O., 206
jellyfish, 5, 41, 199, 236, 238–9
Jura Mountains, 165
Jurassic, 10–11, 14, 20, 24, 38, 47, 86–7, 94, 96, 101–2, 113–14, 116, 125, 138, 165–6, 173, 182, 198, 215–16, 242, *8*

kangaroo rat, 149
kelp, giant, 258
Kelvin, Lord, 181–2
Kemp, T., 263
Kennedy, W. J., 148
Kent, 167, 170
Key Largo Limestone, 69, 125
Kimmeridge Clay, 24
kingdoms, animal, 5, 192
Kosmoceras, 137, *138*; plate 6B
Krakatoa, 169
Krumbein, W. C., 51–3
kyanite, 48

Labrador, Canada, 123
Lake Bonneville, 75–7, *76*
Lamarck, J. B., 192
Laminaria, 86
laminates, algal, 69–70, 103–4
Lanice, 30, 36
Lapworth, C., 166
lateral line system (of fish), 264–5
laterite, 50
Latimeria, 193, 267
Laurel Limestone, 98
lead, 183–4, 186
Lemna, 261
Lewisian Gneiss, 187
Liass, the, 23, 169; Lower, 20, 74
life crises, 210, 215–16, 218–19; Permo-Triassic, 218, 242–3
Lilljeval, 272
Lima, 94
Limacidae, 257
limestones, 19, 47, 63–8, 71, 73–4, 86, 94, 96, 103–4, 122–3, 125, 158, 228
limpets, 42, 80
Lingula, 16, 100
Linnaeus, C., 4, 20, 117
Linnean Society of London, 193

lipoprotein vesicles, 226
lithification of rocks, 46, 58, 60
lithoherms, 68, 70
Lithophaga, 38; plate 9A
lithostratigraphy, 168–9, 171
Lithostrotion, 151
Lithothamnion, 70
Liverpool, 29
lizards, 250, *261*
Llandovery, 99
lobsters, 146
London, 113, 192; basin, 79
lophophore, 150
Lower Greensand, 10, 169
lungfish, 267
lungs, 4, 249, 252, 265
Lyell, Sir Charles, 164, 181, 190, 192–3, 203, 206, 210
Lyme Regis, Dorset, 20
Lymnaea: palustris, 265; *peregra*, 265
Lynx, 5

Macrocystella, 45
Macrocystis, 258
Madison, Indiana, 92, 94
magma, 46, 186, 225
magnesium, 225
magnetic anomaly, 109–11, 114, *109*; field of earth, 108–9, 111, 161; inclination, 108, *109*; reversals, 108–10; reversal time scale, 111, *110*
magnetization: induced, 107–8; normal, 110; permanent, 107; remanent, 107–8, 110; reversed, 110
magnetometer, 107, 109
Maine, 155
Malleus, 264
Malthus, T. R., 194
mammals, 164, 191–3, 211, 216, 232, 237, 242, 248, 251–2, 257–8, 260, 262, 264, 270; marsupial, 119–20, 216–17, 232; placental, 119–20, 216–17; predatory, 42
mammoths, 11–13, 26, 164, 190–1; plate 1A; Beresovca, 12
Manchester Museum, 74
Manitoulin Dolomite, 95
Manitoulin Island, Ontario, 95
marker horizons, 169

287

INDEX

Marshall, L. C., 234–5
Matecumbe Key, Florida, 71
Matthews, D. H., 110–11
Mazon Creek, Illinois, 14, 24
McAlester, A. L., 217–18, 235, 263
meadowsweet, 5
Mediterranean: area, 116; Ocean, 134
Mellita, plate *13C*
Mendel, G., 190, 195
meraspis (stage), 140, *139*
mesoderm, 239
Mesozoic, 24, 37, 69, 87, 100–2, 104, 110, 125, 134–5, 167, 172, 192–3, 195, 197, 199, 216, 242, *8*
metamorphic rocks, 46, 48, 184, 186
metamorphism, 26, 186–8, 205
metazoans, 238, 240, 242–4, 247–8
meteorites, 185, 188, 224; Murchison, 224
Miami Oolite, 125
micas, 50
Michigan Basin, 70, 167
Micraster, 92
micrite, 65–8, 123, *66*; envelopes, 40
Micritic Limestones, 68, 70, 103–4, 123
microfossils, 26, 41, 172–3, 272
microspar, 68
Mid-Atlantic Ridge, 109, 111
Middlesex, 37, 41
midwest (USA), 20, 22
Miller, S., 222–4
Miocene, 12, *8*
moles, 266
molluscs, 64, 71, 101, 103, 122, 132, 134, 137, 145, 158, 181, 192, 199, 203, 206, 214, 239–41, 266, 269; bivalve, 11, 14, 139, 141, 144, 154; cephalopod, 101; monoplacophoran, 193; polyplacophoran, 101; scaphopod, 101
Monocraterion, 36
monoplacophorans, 193
Montastrea, 71, 125; *annularis*, 125

moon, 71, 154, 161, 188, 231
Morocco, 130
Morris, S. F., 139
mosasaur, 45
Moscow, 12
mosquitoes, 248
moths, 257, 265
moulds: internal, 23; natural, 11, 18, 23–4
moults (of arthropods), 88–90, 138–40, 144
Murchison, Sir R. I., 165
Muricanthus, 145, *146*
Muricidae, 39, 145
mussels: freshwater, 254, 256; marine, 205, 256
Myriophyllum, 268
Mytilus, 256

Naticidae, 39
natural selection, 190, 193–6, 208, 210, 212–13, 216, 227, 230–1, 235, 247
Nauplius larva, 139
nautiloids, 141, 147, 244; ascoceratid, 87, 90, *88*; brevicone, 148, *148*
Nautilus, 10, 146
Neanderthal man, 91
neontology, 7
Neopilina, 193
Nereites, 25
Neritina, plate *8A*
neuromasts, 264–5
New Creek, W. Virginia, 151
Newell, N. D., 243
Newfoundland, 80
New Red Sandstone, 61–3
newts, 260, *261*
New York City, 211
New York State, 167
nitrogen, 157, 221, 231
Norfolk, 62
North Africa, 120–1, 124, 128, 145
North America, 70, 72, 80–1, 98, 111–13, 118–21, 127–8, 163, 167–9, 217, 267
Northern Ireland, 113
North Germany, 128
North Sea, 6, 15, 101
Norway, 113, 122, 124, 127
Nottinghamshire, 147
nucleic acids, 221–4, 227
Nucleolites, 86

nucleotide bases, 221–4
Nucula, 100
numerical taxonomy, 209–10
Nuneaton, Warwickshire, 237
Nymphaea, 268
Nymphalis polychloros, 146

Ohio, 90, 94, 267
Öland, Sweden, 20
Old Red Sandstone, 165, 167
Oligocene, *8*
Ontario, 95, 229
ontogeny, 136–7
Onverwacht Group, 228
oobiomicrite, 102
ooids, 65, 67
oolites, 122–3, 125
ooliths, 86, 122–3, *66*
oosparite, 67
opal, 19
Oparin, I. A., 223, 226
operculum, 127, 250
Ophiomorpha, 37, 97
Opisthostoma, 147
opossum, 119, 217
optical activity, 225, 227
Ordovician, 20, 25, 39, 48, 61, 70, 86, 92–7, 100–1, 105, 117–21, 124, 127–8, 130, 166, 172, 187, 217, 219, 232, 235, 241, 244, 246–7, *8*
origin of life, 219–20, 226–7, 247–8
Origin of species, 182, 194, 271
Osgood Formation, 96
Osgood Limestone, 84
Osgood Shales, 86
Oslo Region, Norway, 127
osmoregulation, 252–5
osmosis, 252, 254, *253*
osmotic pressure, 254
osteoblasts, 142–3
osteoclasts, 142–3
ostracods, 101, 139, *89*
Ottawa-St Lawrence Lowland, 127
Owen, H. G., 113–14, 232
Owen, Sir R., 192, 196
Oxford Clay, 10, 20
oxygen, 13, 17, 36, 49, 72, 131–3, 152, 157, 221–2, 231, 233–5, 239, 241, 249, 254; levels in atmosphere, 216–18, 231–6, 240
oyster drill, 145

INDEX

oysters, 10, 24, 57, 67, 102, 103, 214; *plates 7C, 10A*
ozone, 234

Pacific Ocean, 82, 112–13; Triassic, 114
packstone, 67–8, *66*
palaeobotany, 7
Palaeocene, 37, 167–8, *8*
palaeoclimates, 128
palaeoclimatology, 7
palaeocurrents, 60
Palaeodictyon, 33–4, *32*
palaeoecology, 7
palaeogeography, 7, 79, 105, 127
palaeolatitudes, 127–8
palaeomagnetism, 69, 108, 128
palaeontology, 6, 7, 13–14, 136, 181, 194, 197, 219, 271–3
Palaeoporella, 97
palaeotemperature analysis, 132–6
palaeothermometry, 7, 136, 227
Palaeozoic, 39, 44, 69–70, 87, 93, 95, 100–4, 113, 115, 118, 121–2, 125, 166, 195, 197–200, 216, 218, 242–3, 245, 248, *8*
palaeozoology, 7
Palinurus vulgaris, 39
palynology, 173
pandas, 248
Panopea, plate 7D
panspermia, 220
Panthera, 5
paradigm method, 208
Paradoxides, plate 10C
Paramoudras, 62
Paraonis, 31, 33, *32*
parasites, 13, 85, 91, 143, 240
parasitism, 39
Paris Basin, 23, 78, 164; Museum, 164
Parkinsonia, plate 4
Pasteur point, 234–5
Pecten, 150
pectinids, 155
peloids, 65, *66*
Pelycosaurs, 262, *263*
Penicillus, 70, 123
Pennsylvanian, 14
Penrith Sandstone, 55

Pentacrinus, plate 12B
Pentraeth, Anglesey, 169
periwinkles, 42
Permian, 48, 95, 121, 127, 165, 216, 246, 262, *8*
Permo-Carboniferous, 124, 130
Permo-Triass, 55, 62
Perm Province, Russia, 165
Peru, 158
Petrocrania, 96
Phacops, 90
Phanerozoic, 189, 241, 243, 271, *8*
Phaselus larva, 139
Philip, G. M., 126
Phinney, R. A., 109
Pholas, 37–8
phosphorus, 221
photic zone, 40
photosynthesis, 69, 81, 124, 157, 222, 225–6, 228–9, 231–3, 235, 241, 247, 251, 268–9
Phylloceras, plate 5
phylogenetic systematics, 209
phylogenies, 196, 199, 207–9, 238
phytane, 229
Piedmont Province, 113
pike, 269
Pinus aristata, 160
Pisidium obtusale, 266; *personatum*, 266
pisoliths, 123
plaice, 15
Planorbarius corneus, 265
Planorbis zone, 173
plant compressions, 24
plate tectonics, 111, 113, 232, 271–2
Platyceras, 95
Platyhelminthes, 239
Platystrophia, 95
Pleistocene, 49, 75, 120, 125, 127–30, 134–5, 187, 191, *8*
Pleurocystites, 201, 206
Pleurocystitidae, 202, 206
Pleurodictyum problematicum, 95
Pliocene, 217, 232, *8*
poikilotherms, 262–3
polarized light, 225
polar wandering, 108–9
poles: geographic, 108, 114, 127, 158; magnetic, 108, 114

pollen, 255, 257–8; analysis, 129; arboreal, 129; fossil, 129–30, 173; grains, 173, 255; non-arboreal, 129; zones, 160
Polycosmitidae, 206
Polydora ciliata, 36–7
Pompeii, 17
Porifera, 238
Portland Island, 102; Series, 102–3
potassium, 183–4, 186
Precambrian, 24, 26, 70–1, 119, 124, 130, 156, 187, 220, 224, 228–30, 232–4, 236–8, 240–4, 247, 271, *8*
preservation history, 2, 3, 6, 10–11, 43, 134, 136; potential, 11, 41–2, 82, 205, 213, 237
pressure solution, 25, *24*
pristane, 229
Productus, 83, 92, *84*
prokaryotes, 228–9
Protaspis (stage), 140, *139*
proteinoid microspheres, 226
proteins, 221–4; synthesis, 223
Protista, 5
protistans, 238, 266
protozoans, 20, 238–9, 255
provenance: of sediments, 47, 55; of limestones, 63
province, Baltic, 118–20; Boreal, 116; faunal, 3, 81, 114–15, 117–18, 120–1, 172, 197–9; floral, 121, 197; North American, 118–20; South American–Australian, 118–19; South European–North African, 118–20; Tethyan, 116
pseudotrachea, 252
Psilopsid ferns, *263*
Pteridium aquilinum, 256
pteridosperms, 270
punctuated equilibria (model of evolution), 210, 213
Purbeck Series, 102–4
Pustulocystis, 96
pyrite, 10, 18, 20, 22

quadrupeds, 260
quartz, 48, 50
quartzite, 48, 237

289

INDEX

rabbits, 216, 248
radiations, 210, 215–16, 230, 242–3, 266, 270; late pre-Cambrian/Cambrian, 231, 234, 236, 240, 242–3, 248
radioactive decay, 157, 186
radioactivity, 182–3
radiocarbon ages, 158, 160; dating, 156–8, 183–5; time scale, 156, 161, *160*
radiometric dates, 133, 182, 186–7, 189–90; dating methods, 156, 158, 183, 185–6, 188–9
radon, 184
Rafinesquina, 92–4
razor shells, 83
red beds, 124, 233–4
Red Rocks, Cheshire, 63
Red Sea, 50
reefs, 97–8, 101, 104–5; coral/algal, 69, 122, 124–5; fossil, 4, 21; organic, 21, 69; *Sabellaria*, 36
regressions, 78
reptiles, 192, 201, 215–16, 248, 251, 258, 260, 264, 270, *15*, 263; plate 2
Reykjanes Ridge, *109*
Rhaetic Series, 166
rhinoceros, woolly, 12
Rhipocephalus, 123
Rhynia, 267, 269, *263*
Rhynie Chert, 102, 263, 267
Rhynie, Scotland, 266
Richardson, E. S. Jr, 14
River Colne, 147
River Thames, 47
rodents, 250, 252
Rubey, W. W., 231
rubidium, 184
Rudwick, M. J. S., 16, 92, 208
Rumina decollata, 127
Rusophycus, 30
Russia, 78, 116, 165
rutile, 48

Sabellaria, 36
St Hilaire, G., 192
salamander, European, 258
salmon, 102, 254
Salop, 45
saltation, 53
Salter, J. W., 90
salt pseudomorphs, 103–4
Saluda Formation, 169
sand dollars, 5; plate *13C*

Sao hirsuta, *139*
scallops, 150, 155
Scandinavia, 75, 121
Scaphites, 147, *148*
scaphopods, 64, 101
Schove, D. J., 160
scolecodonts, 41
Scotland, 29, 61, 102, 113, 118, 123–4, 128, 171, 187, 263, 266
Scourian (Gneiss), 187
Scrobicularia, 27
sea anemones, 5, 35, 95
sea: birds, 39, 82; cucumbers, 5; floor spreading, 111, 113, 232; lilies, 5, 19; plates *12A–B*; pens, 236, 239, 261; urchins, 5, 14–6, 19–20, 35, 39, 80, 86, 91–2, 126, 255; plates *13A–C*
seals, 262
seaweeds, 80, 86, 141, 258
Sedgwick, A., 165
Sédillot's puppies, 142
sedimentary rocks, 27, 46–8, 61, 65, 72, 101, 107–8, 174, 186, 227; chemical, 46; clastic, 63–4; composition of, 47; organic, 47, 63; textures of, 47, 50, 55
sedimentary structures, 47, 56–8, 94, 176, 178–9, 229; bedding plane, 56–7, 177; diagenetic, 56; internal, 56; primary, 56, 60; secondary, 56, 60
sediments: beach, 54; carbonate, 122; clastic, 46–7, 50, 68; composition of, 50; glacial, 128; grain supported, 66–7; marine, 186; matrix supported, 66–7: maturity of, 50, 105; mechanical analysis of, 46, 51, *53*; sorting of, 51, 53; terrigenous, 55
seeds, 242, 250, 256, 258
Seilacher, A., 25
septaria, 61–2
septarian nodules, 61–2
Sequioa gigantea, 159
sharks, 17
Shark's Bay, Australia, 71
Shaw, A. B., 169, 197–9, 203, 205, 209

Shineton, Salop, 45
Shineton Shales, 45
shrimp band, 103
Siberia, 11–12
Silica, 18–19, 22, 46, 55, 62, 228, 237, 240
Silica Shales, 90
silicon, 224
Siljan District, Sweden, 127
silkworm, 150
sillimanite, 48
Silurian, 11, 20, 22, 57, 69, 70, 84–5, 95, 97, 99–101, 118–19, 125, 151, 162, 165, 169, 172, 187, 201, 217, 219, 232, 235, 248, 266, 272, *8*
similitude, principle of, 148, 259
Simpson's index, 115
Skagerrak, 122
Skolithos, 36
Sloss, L. L., 51–3
slugs, 248, 251, 257–8
Smith, William A., 8, 163–5, 169, 192
snails, 15, 17, 20, 29, 86, 88, 90–1, 104, 137, 141, 147, 240, 249, 255, 269, *146*; plates *8A–C*; fossil, 24; freshwater, 2, 79, 252, 256, 265, 269; land, 39, 127, 145, 147, 213–14, 250–1, 266–7, muricid, 145, *146*; parasitic, 85; platyceratid, 39–40, 82, 95; predatory, 39; pulmonate, 251; pyramidellid, 39; terrestrial, 102, 252, 258; viviparid, 101
snakes, 262
Sohn, I. G., 89
solar system, 71, 188, 221
Solem, A. G., 267
Solen, 83
sole structures, 61
solute, 253
solution, 252–4
solvent, 253–4
South Africa, 121, 124, 228
South America, 113, 118–19, 121, 124, 193, 217
South Australia, 236
South-East Asia, 118–19, 127

INDEX

South Pole, 120–1, 126; Ordovician, 124
Spain, 124, 130, 165
Spanish Morocco, 251
spar, 67; granular, 65; neomorphic, 64
sparite, 67, 66
sparrows, American, 117; European, 117, 149
Special Creation, 220
Speciation, 211
Sphaeronites, plate 11C
Sphaeronitid cystoids, 200
spiders, 12, 259, *259*; web spinning, 261
spiracles (of insects), 252
Spitzberger, 124
sponges, 37, 40, 69, 96, 151, 236, 238–40, 244
spores (plant), 25, 173, 256–7
sporophyte, 256
sporopollenin, 18
Spriggina, 239
Squamodictyon, 33–4
squids, 22, 87
standard mean ocean water (SMOW), 132
Stapes, 264
starfish, 5, 19, 172, 255
staurolite, 48
Stegosaurus, 262
Stehli, F. G., 127
Steno (Nils Stensen), 7, 8, 162
Stitt, J. H., 235
stomata, 251–2
stratigraphic practice, code of, 168
stratigraphic occurrences: of cystoids, *200*; position of fossils, 164, 197; range (of fossils), 171, 203
stratigraphic relationships, 209, *210*; units, 169
stratigraphy, 165, 168, 170–1, 192, 272; event, 169; 'layer cake', 169
stratotype, 167
Stromatactis, 21, *21*
stromatolites, 69–71, 156, 229
strontium, 184
subduction zones, 111, 114
subzone, 172
succession of life, 9, 190, 192–4, 196, 207
Suess effect, 159
sugars, 222

sulphur, 221
sun, the, 152–4, 159, 181–2, 193, 261–2
superposition, principle of, 8, 162–3, 165, 176
survivorship analysis, 202–3
swallows, 260
Swansea, South Wales, 26
Sweden, 25, 96–7, 127
syenite, 237
Sylvania, Ohio, 90

tectonic structures, 56, 187
teilzone, 171
Tennessee, 86, 94, 96–7
Terebella harefieldensis, 41
Tertiary, 12, 23, 37, 47, 69, 78–9, 101–2, 115, 126, 130, 135, 164, 166–7, 181, 192, 197, 199, 203, 206, 242, *8*
Tetradium, 151
tetrapods, 260
Thalassia, 71, 102
Thalassinoides, 37, 97
Thames Estuary, 47
Theriosynoecum fittoni, 89
Thomacystidae, 206
Thomacystis, 206
Thompson, Sir d'A. W., 142–3, 148, 259
Thompson, Prof. W., *see* Lord Kelvin
thrushes, 39
thrush family, 117
tides, 154, 156
till, 123, 128–9
tillite, 123–4, 130
tilloid, 123–4
time, 152–3, 161, 182; absolute, 162; measurement of, 153, 183; relative, 162
Tivela stultorum, 155–6
tourmaline, 48
Towe, K. M., 234–5
trabeculae, 142
trabecular bone, 142, *143*
trace fossils, 11, 26, 30, 41, 56, 65, 82, 96–8, 237, *25, 28, 32, 33, 34*; plate 9B
traces, dwelling, 26, 30, 35, 39, 241, *32*; feeding, 26, 31, 34–5, 39, *25, 34*; internal, 27, 30–1, 34–5, 42, *32*; locomotory, 29, 35; parasitic, 39
traces, resting, 26, 30; spiral, 34; surface, 27, 30–1, 35, 42, 57, *32*

trachea, 150, 259, 252
tracheids, 268
tracheophytes, 266
tracks, 26–7, 29–30, 178
trails, 26–7, 29–30, 178, 236, *32*
transgressions, 78; Lower Silurian, 99–100
tree rings, 126, 135, 142, 156, 159–61
trees, 126, 137, 142, 248, 250, 258
Tremadoc Series, 45, 103, 166
Trematocystis, 86, 96
Triamara, 96
Triassic, 29, 48, 57, 94, 113–14, 165–6, 216, 218, *8*
Trigonia, 23; plates 7A–B
trilobites, 6, 25, 29–30, 90, 101, 117–20, 138–40, 171, 194, 197–9, 235–6, 240–1, 244; plates 10C–D; agnostid, 236, 244, *237* olenellid, 198; redlichiid, 198
triploblasts, 239
Tullimonstrum gregarium, *14*
Tully monster, *14*
Tungusk, Russia, 12
turbidites, 58–9, 99
turbidity currents, 58–9, 61, 78, 242
Turitella, *146*
type areas (for geological systems), 165
type section, 167

Uca, 257
Udotea, 123
unconformities, 57, 163, 176, 187, *175*
uniformitarian methods, 6, 122, 128
uniformity, 181
Unionidae, 79, 256
Universities: of California, Santa Barbara, 217; of Chicago, 222; of Michigan, 210; of Missouri, 236; of Newcastle-upon-Tyne, 241
uranium, 183, 186
United States of America, 92, 113, 123; Geological Survey, 234; western, 75, 105, 235

INDEX

Unskarsheden, Sweden, 97
Upper Greensand, 170

Valentine, J., 217
van Huygens, 90
Varangian, 124
varves, 160, 233
vascular plants, 101–2, 248, 250–1, 256, 266, 268
ventifacts, 55, 124
vertebrates, 15, 17, 24, 141, 144, 192, 239, 249–52, 258–60, 264–6, 269–70; fossil, 164
Vesuvius, 17
Vine, F. J., 109–11
Viola: odorata, 4; *palustris*, 4
Visby, Gotland, 272
Viviparidae, 79

wackestone, 67–8, 66
Waldron, Indiana, 98
Waldron Shale, 97
Wales, 99, 101, 163, 165; North, 169; South, 20, 26, 72, 78

Wallace, A. R., 193–4, 196
Washington D.C., 234
water lilies, 268
Wattenfellet project, 272
way-up criteria, 176, 178, 189; of rocks, 21, 59
Wealden Clays, 79
Wealden District, 10
Wealden Sandstone, 49
weathering, 46, 48, 65, 96, 232; chemical, 49, 50, 124; mechanical, 49–50
Weldon, W. F. R., 213–14
Welsh Borderlands, 98, 100–1
Wenlock Limestone, 125
Wentworth, C. K., 51
Wentworth's Scale, 53, 52
West Africa, 113
West Bay, Dorset, 96
West Virginia, 151
whales, 15, 149, 258, 260, 262
Wheeler, Sir Mortimer, 272
whelks, 29, 39
Whittington, H. B., 139
Wilhelmshaven, 6
Williamsonia, plate 16A
Wiltshire, 170

winter rings, 126–7, 137, 144
Wirral, Cheshire, 63
Wisconsin, 128
wood, 159, 185, 238, 259; fossil, 24, 62, 126, 157; plate 16B; preservation of, 18–19
woodlice, 251–2
worms, 2, 23, 28, 30–3, 35–7, 40–1, 69, 80, 82, 91–2, 95, 199, 234, 236, 244, 250, 266; myzostomid, 39; polychaete, 36; segmented, 239; terebelloid, 37, 41; tubes, 91, 95–6, 92

Xenophora, plate 8B

Yale University, 217
year, the, 152–4

Ziegler, A. M., 99, 100, 105
zircon, 48
Zirfaea, 37–8
zone fossil, 171, 173
zones, 170–3, 187
zooxanthellae, 69, 124–5